Revolutionary hope
vs
free-market fantasies

Both detailed and illuminating, this is a theoretically and historically grounded work from a veteran Marxist scholar on the major challenges facing the struggle for the genuine liberation of Africa. Of vast scope and deep analysis, it needs to be read and debated by all Africa-oriented activists.

> — **Karim F Hirji**, Tanzanian professor and scholar-activist, author of *Growing Up With Tanzania*, and chief author of *Cheche: Reminiscences of a Radical Magazine*

The second in John Saul's trilogy of books examining what he terms the Thirty Years War for liberation in southern Africa, Volume 2 shifts the focus from global solidarity movements to the five theatres of war in the region. Saul's unique lens reveals the interconnected nature of the struggles in the contiguous countries in the region. Eschewing nationalist accounts boundaried by colonial borders, Saul connects race, gender and environment to capital and class. A tour de force from a scholar who exemplifies the value of praxis, in this volume John Saul encourages us as always to face grim realities while inspiring us to hope. Also: a cracking good read!

> — **Shireen Hassim**, Canada Research Chair, Carleton University, Ottawa, Canada and formerly of the University of the Witwatersrand (Johannesburg), she is author of *Women's organizations and democracy in South Africa: Contesting authority*

In his careful re-historicizing of so many political personalities and movements, past and present, John Saul has again demonstrated the essence of his prodigious career: more than six decades of a deeply reflected life of public intellectual activism and committed and brilliant Africanist scholarship. *On Building a Social Movement* is essential reading for those who want to know about the histories of the various southern African liberation struggles and about the ways in which an ethical, theoretically pellucid Marxist political economy can positively embrace changing intersectionalities ...with race and environmental concerns, among other things. Equally, it is the important for those who want to understand the nature of generosity, comradeship, and of just what the principled embrace of social movement solidarity can achieve.

> — **Pablo Idahosa**, Professor of African Studies and International Development Studies, York University, Toronto, and author of *The Populist Dimension to African Political Thought: Frantz Fanon, Amilcar Cabral, Julius Nyerere*

John Saul's *Revolutionary Hope vs Free-Market Fantasies* is far more than a collection of observations and analyses. It represents a framework, or a set of eyeglasses, through which to look at the revolutionary and non-revolutionary experiences in Southern Africa in the struggle for freedom. The opening chapter, along with the collection of essays, offers a brilliant examination of the challenges in prosecuting a struggle for consistent democracy, liberation and transformation. This is not a book to rush through, but one to savor as one would a fine wine. The relevance of the analyses goes far beyond Southern Africa, and beyond Africa, but leads one to consider the dimensions and challenges faced by a 21st-century emancipatory project.

> — **Bill Fletcher, Jr.**, trade union activist and former president
> of TransAfrica Forum and co-editor of *Claim No Easy
> Victories: The Legacy of Amilcar Cabral*, among other books

In this long-awaited second volume of his Southern African Liberation Trilogy, veteran scholar and activist John Saul provides a fascinating account of the ideas that drove his life-long commitment to the Southern African struggle. Rich in insights drawn from his close engagement with the key actors and events during what he calls a "thirty-year war," he concludes reluctantly that Southern Africa has been recolonized by global capital. It's a sobering, nuanced and deeply worrying assessment but underlying the disappointment are signs of hope that a more expansive liberation is still possible.

> — **Eddie Webster**, Distinguished Research Professor,
> Southern Center for Inequality Studies (SCIS) University
> of the Witwatersrand, activist and co-author, most
> recently, of *Grounding Globalization: Labor in an
> Age of Insecurity*

This immensely erudite yet highly readable volume of John Saul's trilogy reflects a lifetime commitment to building a better world. A true internationalist with a deep knowledge of Southern Africa, he pulls no punches in analyzing what went wrong with the movements for liberation in Southern Africa, or in recognizing the malevolent power of global capital as it pursues its recolonization mission. And yet. Saul sees revolutionary hope in contemporary alliances between socialists and feminists, environmentalists, anti-racists, activists around issues of sexual orientation and bearers of a whole range of identities joining up, alongside workers and precarians, within a broader left community-in-the-making. This is a book for all who strive and hope for an egalitarian and democratic future.

> — **Katherine Salahi**, one of the ANC's 'London Recruits'
> in the anti-apartheid days (when she was also labeled a
> 'gun runner'!) plus writer, publisher and a founding editor
> of the *Review of African Political Economy/ROAPE*

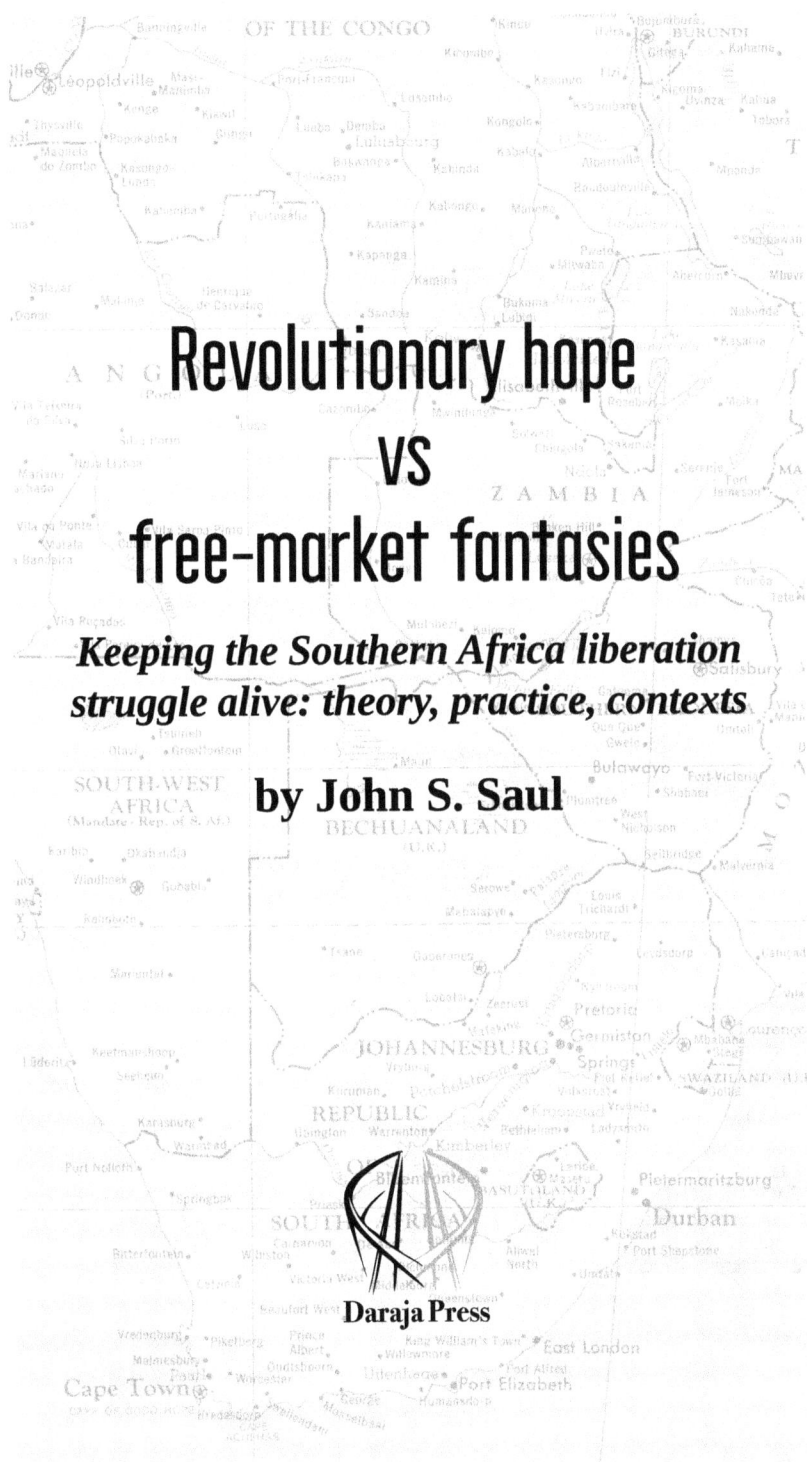

Revolutionary hope
vs
free-market fantasies

Keeping the Southern Africa liberation struggle alive: theory, practice, contexts

by John S. Saul

Daraja Press

Published by
Daraja Press
https://darajapress.com

Published in East Africa by
Zand Graphics Ltd
https://zandgraphics.com/

Revolutionary Hope vs Free Market Fantasies:
Keeping the Southern Africa Liberation Struggle Alive
Theory, Practice, Contexts

ISBN 978-1-988832-91-3

Cover design & typesetting: Kate McDonnell

Library and Archives Canada Cataloguing in Publication

Title: Revolutionary hope vs. free-market fantasies : keeping the southern African liberation
   struggle alive : theory, practice, contexts / John S Saul.
Names: Saul, John S., author.
Description: Includes bibliographical references and index.
Identifiers: Canadiana (print) 20210181508 | Canadiana (ebook) 20210181613 | ISBN 9781988832913
   (softcover) | ISBN 9781988832920 (PDF)
Subjects: LCSH: National liberation movements—Africa, Southern. | LCSH: Africa, Southern—Economic
   policy. | LCSH: Africa, Southern—Politics and government—1975-1994.
Classification: LCC DT1165 .S385 2021 | DDC 320.968—dc23

To the memory of Murray MacInness,
Mike Carr and Jim Kirkwood,
and
with love to Jo and Nick

Previous Books by the Author

Tanzania: The Silent Class Struggle, edited by Dick Urban Vestbro and
co-authored with Issa G. Shivji, Walter Rodney and Thomas Szentes
(Lund, Sweden: Zenit, 1971).

Socialism in Tanzania: Vol. 1, Politics, co-edited with Lionel Cliffe
(Nairobi, Kenya: East African Publishing House, 1972).

Socialism in Tanzania: Vol. 1, Policies, co-edited with Lionel Cliffe
(Nairobi, Kenya: East African Publishing House, 1973).

Essays on the Political Economy of Africa, co-authored with Giovanni
Arrighi (New York and London: Monthly Review Press, 1973).

Socialism and Participation: Tanzania's 1970 National Election,
co-edited as a member the Electoral Studies Committee, University
of Dar es Salaam (Dar es Salaam: Tanzania Publishing House, 1974).

Canada and Mozambique (Toronto: DEC/TCLPAC, 1974).

Rural Cooperation in Tanzania, co-edited with Lionel Cliffe and others
(Dar es Salaam: Tanzania Publishing House, 1975).

Words and Deeds: Canada, Portugal and Africa, co-authored with
the Toronto Committee for the Liberation of Southern Africa
(Toronto: TCLSAC, 1976).

The State and Revolution in Eastern Africa (London, Nairobi, Ibadan,
Lusaka: Monthly Review Press, New York and Heinemann Educational
Books, 1979).

The Crisis in South Africa, co-authored with Stephen Gelb (New York:
Monthly Review Press, 1981) and, in a second expanded edition
(New York and London: Monthly Review Press and Zed Press, 1986).

O Marxismo-Leninismo no Contexto Moçambicano
(Maputo: Universidade Eduardo Mondlane Press, 1983).

A Difficult Road: The Transition to Socialism in Mozambique, edited by
John S. Saul (New York: Monthly Review Press, 1985).

Socialist Ideology and the Struggle for Southern Africa (Trenton, N.J.:
Africa World Press, 1990).

Recolonization and Resistance: Southern Africa in the 1990s (Toronto and
Trenton, N.J.: Between The Lines and Africa World Press, 1994).

Namibia's Liberation Struggle: The Two-Edged Sword, co-authored/
co-edited with Colin Leys (London, Athens, Ohio and Cape Town, S.A.:
James Currey, Ohio University Press, and David Phillip, 1995).

Millennial Africa: Capitalism, Socialism, Democracy (2001)
(Lawrenceville, N. J./ Asmara: Africa World Press, 2001)

The Next Liberation Struggle: Capitalism, Socialism and Democracy in Southern Africa (Toronto, London, New York and Durban/ Pietermaritzburg: Between The Lines, Merlin Press, Monthly Review Press and University of Kwazulu/Natal Press, 2001).

Development after Globalization: Theory and Practice for the Embattled South in a New Imperial Age (Delhi, London & New York, Halifax and Durban/Pietermaritzburg: Three Essays Collective, Zed Press, Fernwood Press and University of KwaZulu-Natal Press, 2006).

Decolonization and Empire: Contesting the Rhetoric and Reality of Resubordination in Southern Africa and Beyond (Delhi, London & New York and Johannesburg: Three Essays Collective, Merlin Press and University of Witwatersrand Press, 2007).

Revolutionary Traveller: Freeze-Frames from a Life (Winnipeg, Canada: Arbeiter-Ring, 2009)

Liberation Lite: The Roots of Recolonization in Southern Africa (Delhi and Trenton, N. J.: Three Essays Collective and Africa World Press, 2011).

The Present as History – South Africa: From Mrs Ples to Marikana and Mandela, with Patrick Bond (Oxford and Johannesburg: James Currey and Jacana Press, 20110.

A Flawed Freedom: Rethinking Southern African Liberation (London, Toronto and Cape Town: Pluto Books, Between the Lines, and Juta/University of Cape Town Press, 2014).

The "Rethinking Southern African Liberation" Trilogy:

On Building a Social Movement: The North American Campaign for Southern African Liberation Revisited (Trenton, N. J./Cape Town and Halifax and Winnipeg: African World Press and Fernwood Publishing, 2017).

Revolutionary Hope vs Free-Market Fantasies – Keeping the Southern Africa Liberation Struggle Alive: Theory, Practice, Contexts (the present book).

The Thirty Years War for Southern African Liberation, 1960-1994: A History (Cambridge, UK: Cambridge University Press [in preparation for 2020/21])

[President Julius] Nyerere called on the people of Tanzania to have great confidence in themselves and to safeguard the nation's hard-won freedom. Mwalimu [Nyerere] warned that the people should not allow their freedom to be pawned as most of their leaders were purchasable. He warned further that in running the affairs of the nation the people should not look on their leaders as saints and prophets. The President stated that the attainment of freedom in many cases resulted merely in the change of colours, white faces to black faces without ending exploitation and injustices, and above all without the betterment of the life of the masses. He said that while struggling for freedom the objective was clear, but it was another thing to remove your own people from the position of exploiters.

– Julius Nyerere, cited in *The Nationalist,* Dar es Salaam, 1967

Study the historian before you begin to study the facts...It used to be said that the facts speak for themselves. This is, of course, untrue. The facts speak only when the historian calls on them: it is he who decides to which facts to give the floor, and in what order or context...By and large the historian will get the kind of facts he wants. History means interpretation.

– E.H. Carr, *What is History?*

[If the various analysts of particular social/historical events] all agreed to explain the same events and had made no mistakes of fact...it should still be clear that they would have continued to differ from each other. It should also be clear that their diverse purposes – to reform or conserve societies, to condemn or justify past policies, to reinforce theoretical structures – might well have been served by a stricter regard for truth, but could scarcely be replaced by it...However desirable as qualities of observation, "objectivity" and its last-ditch rearguard "intersubjectivity" still seem unable to organize an explanation or to bring men of different faith to agree about the parts or the shape, the length or breadth or depth or pattern, that an explanation should have.

– Hugh Stretton, *The Political Sciences*

There is something wrong with the simple interpretation of the national liberation movement as a revolutionary trend. The objective of the imperialist countries was to prevent the enlargement of the socialist countries, to liberate the reactionary forces in our country which were being stifled by colonialism, and to enable these forces to ally themselves with the international bourgeoisie.

– Amilcar Cabral

Table of contents

By Way of an Introduction

This book is the second volume of my Southern African Liberation Trilogy, which I have been writing for some sixty years, ever since I first took up residence in Tanzania in the 1960s (see chapter 2). The first volume, published in 2017 by Africa World Press in the North Atlantic zone and in South Africa and by Fernwood Books in Canada, was entitled On Building a Social Movement: The North American Campaign for Southern African Liberation Revisited. *A third volume,* The Thirty Years War for Southern African Liberation, 1960-1994: A History, *is to be published soon by Cambridge University Press. And you now have in your hands the second volume. This brief introduction will describe the overall set of three books and outline the contents of this particular book and the logic of its place within the trilogy.*

The "Rethinking Southern African Liberation" project and a situating of the present volume

This trilogy is intended to draw to an appropriate close my writing project on southern Africa and the region's complex attempts to realize liberation. The already published volume, *On Building a Social Movement*,[1] offers a close account of the North American campaign in support of the struggle for the liberation of southern Africa from racist, colonial, and white minority rule, a campaign in which I was deeply involved. But it also seeks to elucidate the worldwide nature of the global liberation support/anti-apartheid movement that, in its own right, provided an important and positive manifestation of progressive political action on a worldwide scale. And the forthcoming third volume, The Thirty Years War for the Liberation of Southern Africa, 1960-1994,[2] will make available a detailed account of the war on the ground in southern Africa, with full attention being paid to the war's five theatres of overt and militant contestation: Mozambique, Angola, Zimbabwe (formerly Rhodesia), Namibia (formerly South-West Africa) and South Africa.

How precisely can this present volume expect to complement the other two books of the trilogy, both of which focus directly on that war as it played out in the later years of the twentieth century? It is intended to do so in two ways. To begin with, this volume's first and second sections give a sense of the analytical and personal/experiential foundations that have helped frame and structure the writing of all the books in this trilogy. The third section seeks, through several recently written case studies of the countries that were the original theatres of war, to consider, despite their diverse histories, the all too similar – and all too disappointing – outcome their liberation has tended to produce.

Through such studies of the principal countries that comprise southern Africa we can begin to see what was won and lost in the course of the original liberation struggle. And we can also begin to assess what might yet be accomplished towards realizing a more substantive liberation than it has thus far proven possible to achieve.

In theory and in practice

Section A ("In Theory") seeks to clarify the emerging theoretical premises that have come to shape my overall approach. This represents my attempt, over sixty years, to develop a Marxist-rooted analysis of the workings of capitalism that could generate an accurate picture of, and support an expansive resistance to, capitalism's dictate of unjust and non-egalitarian economic and political outcomes (this not only in southern Africa but wherever capitalism has come to be a socially dominant force).[3] I begin in chapter 1 by identifying the epistemological premises that anchor my work, an approach that draws, in particular, on the work of Karl Marx and of many others writing from within the Marxist tradition. But it is an approach that draws equally fundamentally on the work of Hugh Stretton and others who see social and historical science as being necessarily, even inevitably, a moralizing science.

Such an approach also suggests a range of entry-points into fruitful analyses – these entry-points being linked not only to considerations regarding capital and of class but also to vital questions of gender, race (not to be underestimated in southern Africa), nation, religion, environment and democracy. In short, the chapter provides a theoretical registering of the inescapable complexity of the region's war, setting out an approach that has both served to guide my investigations of southern African matters and also helped to shape my understanding of the global political economy that has both undermined and underpinned prospects for social transformation more widely. Yet, as this first chapter also demonstrates, there is, generally speaking, much more happening in society than foci like capitalist accumulation and the attendant structures of exploitation can explain, even though a full understanding of such socioeconomic structures is of crucial importance.

I then proceed, while remaining a fundamentally Marxist-oriented commentator, to register a parallel awareness of the complex mix of factors that can serve to over-determine socioeconomic and political outcomes. As suggested, a full clarification of the precise interaction of these many variables is difficult to establish with absolute confidence. Nonetheless, this chapter concludes – in a sub-section entitled "The Science of Hope" – by drawing, in particular, on the work of Ernst Bloch and Neville Alexander in an attempt, after more than six decades of work both theoretical and applied, to set out the broader possibilities, prospects and potential shortfalls that challenge us all.

Recall, of course, that this first chapter of the present book began by highlighting the importance to my work of the likes of Marx and of Hugh Stretton. Nonetheless, I move here to also note again my equal debt to the two other mentors just mentioned, Ernst Bloch and the late Neville Alexander, the latter being, to my mind, the most distinguished of many outstanding South African writer-activists. Thus, I draw on Bloch's writings to bring very my first chapter to a suitable conclusion, very much as I return to my friend Neville's work several times in Part C. And, throughout, I will also evoke the writings of other such powerful African sages as Frantz Fanon (while from Martinique, Fanon became best known as a militant and a thinker about Africa), Amilcar Cabral, Steve Biko, Julius Nyerere and Samir Amin.

Let me underscore here, however, the emphasis I place on Bloch, on the substantial promise he attached to the principle of hope, and on the unique balance between a Marxist-based sense of possibility and an even more broadly based sense of hope necessary in order to realize utopias both concrete and progressive in the real world. It is this blend-ing of the possible and the utopian – the not yet realized, the to-be-real-ized – as his theoretical lodestone that has also served as a particularly powerful guidepost for me. Indeed, it is in deference to Bloch's brand of realistic and grounded hope that I have titled this book *Revolutionary Hope vs Free Trade Fantasies*. I also refer to the work of Lucio Colletti, Stephen Resnick, Richard Wolff and Gavin Kitching with an eye to extending the application of Stretton's model of social scientific work to encompass a range of what Resnick and Wolfe call "entry-points" (and Kitching calls "points of view"); I will use these to shape questions that can then, by following the procedures of scientific inquiry, provide us with tangible and useful knowledge. It is my hope that the reader will find the identification of such entry-points set out in the first chapter to be instructive and useful to their own attempts to structure theory and research relevant to their moral and scientific purposes.[4]

Nonetheless, if the present book makes some contribution to the realization of revolutionary possibility, it is not merely because I have increasingly been able to anchor my work in appropriate theory. No, it is also because that work has been the product of a self-defining (and scholarship-shaping) unity of theory and concrete practice, a unity that I have sought to develop throughout my career. Accordingly, the sec-ond part of the book (entitled *From Theory to Practice: In Person*) provides as chapter 2, "Rear-View Mirror: David McDonald Inter-views John Saul" – and, in question-and-answer format, a brief record of my practice[5] as rooted in active support for the cause of liberation in southern Africa over the years. For this was a struggle waged not only alongside determined southern Africans but also with comrades living throughout Canada and other countries – comrades who, like myself, became increasingly engaged in a battle against the states and corporations of numerous western-imperialist countries (like those of official Canada) that found themselves on the wrong side of the battle for the future of southern Africa.

I also see the struggle for a more genuine liberation in southern Africa as being one that continues in the region, in North America, and more widely. For I know too many people in southern Africa who are living their lives in such a way as to ensure that this struggle is ongoing, and I also know too many North Americans (to go no further afield) who are sustaining a fight against official tendencies (ongoing and designed to recolonize Africa) in Canada and the United States, tendencies that have defined so negatively our national practices in southern Africa and elsewhere.

After many years engaged in this struggle, I also know that it is not an easy struggle to win, the chief reason being that the other side – namely "the bad guys," both the state and in corporations – are determined to defend their own interests. But this simply means that sober understanding and clarity of purpose will be necessary if our side is ever to be victor in any campaign to realize a more expansive kind of liberation, in both southern Africa and in North America. My hope is that the interview makes some contribution to keeping alive a sense that what we did once can be done again, and more effectively, next time.

Towards the revival of the liberation struggle?

As for Part C *(In Practice: Towards the Revival of Liberation Struggle in Southern Africa)* that comprises the second half of this book, it seeks, in several recent essays, to further explore both the victories and defeats of the southern African liberation struggle. This is done in order to evaluate how the region is positioned now, well after its original liberation and two decades into the new century. To this purpose, recent essays on post-liberation southern African societies (Tanzania, Mozambique, Angola, Zimbabwe, and South Africa) explore, in some detail, these fronts of continuing struggle. These essays may help to underscore the complexities of achieving the genuine liberation that has, unfortunately, largely eluded the original generation of southern African liberation movements and to take note of the sobering and unsettling fact that these now exhausted, and all too corrupt movements still retain, several decades later, exclusive control of political power.

Nor is the situation much more encouraging in the metropoles of Empire; in North America, for example, both states and corporations still work diligently to reinforce the global prison of deep inequality and exploitation (with the added, and increasingly visible, reality that many of the global poor are now also resident within these countries). There is, in sum, much to worry about at both ends of the global spectrum. Still, such has been the nature of my political schizophrenia – with my political life and personal self-identity stretched out, as it were, between North America and southern Africa for decades – that I haven't been able to stop writing about the latter region, although I am more aware than ever of the global nightmare that capitalism has also created everywhere else.

This global nightmare can and must be confronted. We must find ways to awaken from it. After all, global capitalism was a crucial prop of centuries of unalloyed and repressive race-rule that scarred southern Africa. And yet, this global juggernaut has now become – even as it assertively markets the fact of its relatively unchallenged hegemony – expert at presenting, throughout the region, its system of class-defined material inequality and exploitation as being both a race-blind system and a benign one. Part of this current legitimacy of capitalism also rests on the presumption that "there just ain't no alternative." But it is also premised on what has been capitalism's most signal victory: its ability to establish, on the terrain of global culture, its superordinate legitimacy and commonsensical pre-eminent standing. For it seems to have been successful in persuading many/most of the globe's population that this is what freedom means: freedom of the market and, beyond that (and at best), the extremely individualized freedom of market man and woman.

In fact, in the phrase of my old teacher, C. B. Macpherson, it is not any kind of collective freedom that is at the center of things but instead possessive individualism pure and simple.[6] Recall, from the other end of the ideological spectrum, Margaret Thatcher's epigram: "There is no such thing as society; only individuals and their families." This, then, is what is at stake: the legitimate claims of the individual as best expressed through an enabling social environment of equality, decency, humane social order, and the expression of democratic voice, or instead as a self-centered bleat from within the rough-and-tumble of the marketplace. Fortunately, there are many in southern Africa who continue to aspire to the more humane of these two alternatives and are now taking significant collective steps towards a much more real liberation. For it is to realize such an outcome that the struggle continues.

What realistic and grounded hope is there that such an aspiration can be sustained successfully in southern Africa and that such a liberatory practice will prove possible? For it would certainly have to embody the pursuit of a far more expansive liberation than did the original liberation struggle, this latter having been heroic (even if, as I have chronicled in the present trilogy, only semi-successful). Even then, however, I cannot escape the hope – that word again! – that too much promise was generated by the thirty years' war for southern African liberation to expect its positive import and its promise to slip away without an echo – without, that is, some more tangible signs of revived theory and practice that could give a more resonant meaning to, precisely, liberation within the region.

We have seen signs of such a fight flaring dramatically if fitfully in Zimbabwe over the years, for example. And the practical expressions of comrades acting on some similar store of hope have demanded attention in South Africa in recent years. I have continued to poke at the smoldering embers of regional liberation and to write articles about ongoing struggles, their roots, and their resonance; in Part III of this volume, I draw several such recent writings together.

Of comrades in arms

Finally, there are many people to acknowledge and thank for their help in helping me to tie up the loose ends of my contribution to the history of the regional war for southern Africa. For the lonely grind of writing is not self-evidently (and unlike like other modes of political [and moralizing] practice) a brand of collective political work. And yet I have found it to be a genuinely collective practice, nonetheless. For I have been much assisted in my writing by the company I keep. I am always conscious of seeking to amplify the work I was involved in for so long as a member of the Toronto Committee for the Liberation of Portugal's African Colonies/Toronto Committee for the Liberation of Southern Africa (and on the editorial board of *Southern Africa Report/SAR* magazine). And I have also been inspired by my work as a writer/activist with the late Jim Kirkwood and his colleagues in their remarkable, albeit recently terminated, *Africafiles* initiative in which I also played some small part. And I have also been helpfully encouraged with my writing by several most-comradely editors over the years, notably Asad Zaidi of the Three Essays Collective in Delhi, India and Kassahun Checole, whose Africa World Press is based in Newark, New Jersey, in Eritrea and in South Africa. And should also record here my thanks to Firoze Manji whose new Daraja Press has agreed to take on publication of the present work. *Asante sana, rafiki yangu.*

My efforts have always been intended to contribute to other initiatives underway on many global fronts, initiatives that seek to recraft leftist theory and activist practice in more imaginative, impactful and less reductionist and predictable ways. I think here of those involved in the many publishing initiatives which I have been part of – from *Southern Africa Report* to *This Magazine* and *Studies in Political Economy in Canada*; to *Transformation, The Review of African Political Economy* and *The Socialist Register* (the latter begun by my old teacher at the UK's LSE, Ralph Miliband, and now edited by Greg Albo and, until recently, by Leo Panitch who, sadly, passed away in 2020), the latter two publications both long based in the UK; and *Transformation* in South Africa. Those of us who continue to be engaged in southern Africa-related work must, despite our earlier hopes, now work from a grim understanding that much has gone awry. Nonetheless, I find that reflecting on these failures (or, at best, mixed successes) has helped to broaden my critical understanding and to reenergize my writing. Can we – those of us who seek to keep alive a continuing commitment to a more expansive liberation for that region – not help to refuel the emergence of broader movements dedicated to further deepening and concretizing Marxist-based development theory and linking it more effectively to the struggle, in southern Africa and elsewhere? "Dare to struggle, dare to win," indeed.

But this leads me to a final thank-you to my cast of "usual suspects": my friend, my wife (and my helpful critic, careful reader, and designated copy editor) Pat; my longtime comrades in the old Toronto Committee for the Liberation of Portugal's African Colonies (TCLPAC) and the Toronto Committee for the Liberation of Southern Africa (TCLSAC), two of whom are amongst the dedicatees of this volume (the late Murray MacInness and the late Mike Carr), alongside the late Jim Kirkwood of *Africafiles* (and of so many additional committed endeavors); the many other comrades, friendships with whom were forged in shared solidarity work over the years both in southern Africa and elsewhere;[7] and also those with whom I have managed to establish close relationships through our joint involvement in the production of the journals and symposia as referenced in the previous paragraphs.

And, last but not least, thanks as well to my two adult children, Nick and Jo, themselves persons of considerable accomplishment to whom this book is also dedicated; they were kind enough to recently accompany Pat and me to South Africa where I received an honorary doctorate (my acceptance speech on that occasion is incorporated into Part II) and then go on for a wonderful visit to our old family haunts in both Mozambique and Tanzania, where, in the latter country, my kids were both born in the 1960s. A good time was had by all on this recent occasion.

In Theory: Towards a Moralizing Science and a Multivariate Marxism

Chapter 1

A Moralizing Science – and Diverse "Entry Points"

*What is the starting point in epistemological terms of my own theory and analysis? Speaking personally, there is no doubt a number of teachers were important in encouraging me to look beneath the surface of conventional wisdom in Political Science and other related disciplines and see the special role that class and power invariably play; I think here, especially, of C. B. Macpherson at the University of Toronto, and of friends and mentors like Hube Wilson at Princeton and Ralph Miliband at the LSE. Working with them and others I found a more radical approach both to the study of politics and its practice, one rooted in the work of Marx and his successors, taking shape. Equally crucial in validating my inclination to ask a more radical set of questions professionally – and to demonstrate the scientific legitimacy of doing so – was the analysis offered in an extremely important book by Hugh Stretton. For this book, **The Political Sciences**, has remained my chief methodological bible ever since I first read it many years ago.[1]*

Allow me then in this first chapter to pull together and synthesize some of the principal writings on the theoretical front that I have produced over the past several decades into an overall methodological statement.[2] In doing so, I will begin by first referring to the views of Stretton and others as they have helped to underpin one epistemological point that is central here: my commitment to the understanding of social science as being, necessarily, a "moralizing science."

A. On accepting the premise of a "moralizing science"

Why would anybody want to identify as a Marxist or a socialist in the first place? The simple answer is that we see capitalism as an inhuman and inegalitarian system of exploitation that needs to be overthrown. And what if we privilege this entry-point into social analysis in order

2

to place at the center of our concerns both the nature of the capitalist economic structure and the struggle of exploited classes to challenge that system? Need we apologize for the fact that this represents at least as much an arbitrary value judgment as a strictly scientific procedure? We don't need postmodernists to remind us that there are limits to the scientificity of the social science that we practice and apply. In fact, we don't need to dig very deep beneath the surface of common sense to realize that the most efficacious social science doesn't merely drive itself but is framed by the questions that social scientists choose to ask. In that primary text of hard-headed procedural common sense, E.H. Carr's *What is History?*, he writes: "Study the historian before you begin to study the facts." For

> ...the necessity to establish these basic facts rests not on any qual-
> ity of the facts themselves, but on an a priori decision of the histo-
> rian...It used to be said that the facts speak for themselves. This is,
> of course, untrue. The facts speak only when the historian calls on
> them: it is he who decides to which facts to give the floor, and in
> what order or context...By and large the historian will get the kind
> of facts he wants. History means interpretation.[3]

And where do such choices come from? Not primarily, I would suggest, from some evolving and shifting consensus as to what is pertinent to the best scientific explanations emerging within social science disciplines (even if that can have a certain weight). Thus, in his aforementioned book of clear-sighted common sense, the sagacious Hugh Stretton canvasses diverse approaches to the question of what caused late nineteenth century imperialism, concluding that even if his wide range of authors had

> ...all agreed to explain the same events and had made no mistakes
> of fact...it should still be clear that they would have continued to
> differ from each other. It should also be clear that their diverse pur-
> poses – to reform or conserve societies, to condemn or justify past
> policies, to reinforce theoretical structures – might well have been
> served by a stricter regard for truth, but could scarcely be replaced
> by it.... However desirable as qualities of observation, objectivity
> and its last-ditch rearguard intersubjectivity [these] still seem unable
> to organize an explanation or to bring men of different faith to agree

about the parts or the shape, the length or breadth or depth or pattern, that an explanation should have.[4]

Stretton concludes that neutral scientific rules cannot replace valuation as selectors and that the "scientistic" dream of developing an internally coherent, self-sustaining and [potentially] exhaustive model of society is not only misguided but dangerous in the sense of encouraging a blunting of debate about the political and moral valuations that necessarily help shape both the questions posed of society and the explanations that vie for our attention regarding social phenomena. Hence his argument for the self-conscious embrace of what he terms a (necessarily) "moralizing [social] science." We might wish to add that, once the questions themselves have been posed, the social scientist can still be judged by his or her peers in terms of the evidence discovered and adduced in the attempt to answer them, and in terms of the logic and coherence of the arguments presented. There are scientific canons of evidence and argument in terms of which explanations can, up to a point, be judged intersubjectively. But the questions themselves do not emerge from such concerns without other promptings.

Although not always acknowledged, this seems straightforward enough. But even if some social scientists are uncomfortable with this notion of an inevitably moralizing social science, the Marxist/socialist social scientist has no reason not to embrace it. After all, is this not what the unity of theory and practice is all about? This is the argument of Gavin Kitching, for example, who writes (affirmatively) that Marxism is much less a science than a point of view, and more specifically, a point of view "on or about the form of society that it calls capitalism."[5] For Kitching, the Marxist point of view (which Kitching adopts) turns out to be a "rationally motivated willingness to act to transform capitalism." It has been, Kitching argues, "the "objectively best" point of view to take on capitalism ... in order to change it into a better form of society"[6] – and hence also the basis for the kind of politics of persuasion and mobilization of interests that could alone make the struggle for socialism viable.

4

I find this convincing even though Kitching seems to take his argument much too far when he suggests that, whatever may be its positive moral-cum-political value, the Marxist point of view does not provide any privileged means of understanding the workings of capitalist society and its contradictions. The truth is that Marxists and socialists seek not only to change the world but also to interpret it, and their central concerns have indeed given them tools with which to do so. Still, it is appropriate to ask what, more broadly, is the kind of knowledge these concerns can produce. One well-known answer to this was articulated by Lucio Colletti in his widely-read essay "Marxism: Science or Revolution? "[7] Colletti focused on the wage relationship within capitalism and conceded that bourgeois social science (as viewed from "the point of view of the capitalist", as Colletti put it) offers an understanding of that relationship as a free exchange that is quite plausible (and, we might add, fits neatly into the scientific undertakings of neo-classical economics). But Colletti insisted that equally plausible (and even more pertinent to the cause of socialist revolution) is an understanding of this relationship – from the viewpoint of the working class – as one of exploitation, and this angle of vision can also offer a revealing (but very different) analysis of the workings of capitalism.[8]

The worker's point of view? It is tempting to put it like this (not least for purposes of political mobilization), but we can advance the case for the prioritizing of a class analysis grounded in Marxist/socialist premises somewhat more modestly, albeit with equal effect. Indeed, Resnick and Wolff have done so convincingly in their volume *Knowledge and Class*, rejecting both empiricist and rationalist epistemologies while announcing, unapologetically, that, as Marxists, they choose class analysis as their preferred entry point into social enquiry.[9] Interestingly, they make no claim that this is the only useful approach to society for purposes of theory or practice but assert merely that it is the one they find most illuminating to build upon, both analytically and politically: "Class then is [the] one process among the many different processes of life chosen by Marxists as their theoretical entry-point so as to make a particular sense of and a particular change in this life." But "why choose class as an entry-point rather than, say, racial or sexual oppression?":

Our answer may serve to clarify our relations both to Marx and to those people today (including friends) whose entry-points and hence theories differ more or less from ours. What Marx sought, and we continue to seek to contribute to struggles for social change, are not only our practical energies but also certain distinctive theoretical insights. The most important of these for us concerns class. Marx discovered, we think, a specific social process that his allies in social struggle had missed. The process in question is the production and distribution of surplus labor in society. Marx's contribution lay in defining, locating, and connecting the class process to all other processes comprising the social totality they all sought to change. Marx's presumption was that programs for social change had less chance of success to the degree that their grasp of social structure was deficient.[10]

In addition, Resnick and Wolff see this way of expressing things as avoiding reductionism and instead as defining a Marxism that is open to "the mutual overdetermination of both class and non-class" dimensions, and thus to "the complex interdependencies of class and non-class aspects of social life...that neither Marx nor we reduce to cause-effect or determining-determined essentialisms."[11] This latter point is crucial. But what, first, of the core argument I have presented regarding Marxism's scientific-cum-political standing – as moralizing science, as point-of-view, as entry-point – to our analytical understandings? No doubt there are theorists, Marxists and others, who may wish to carry this epistemological work further, but I'm not sure that the rest of us can't get on with our work while they're doing so. Isn't this approach, in any case, the best way to stake our claim to be heard, and to mobilize and expand the constituency for class analysis and class struggle, while also listening carefully to what others struggling alongside us, often employing different entry-points but for progressive ends, have to say?

As for the post-Marxist and post-modernist sages, can we not safely leave them to recycle such assertions as that of Ernesto Laclau to the effect that "class struggle is just one species of identity politics, and one which is becoming less and less important in the world in which we live." No doubt Laclau's attendant claim that class struggle is hopelessly old-fashioned will be good news to the transnational corporations and the IFIs and the U.S. State Department that drive the global economy, although they might be inclined to see this more as a whimper of defeat than a theoretical breakthrough. For Laclau's statement is linked in his text to a broader approach that characterizes anti-capitalism as "mere empty talk," the goal of socializing the means of production as a "rather peculiar aim," and the height of left aspirations as just enough reform of the economy so that "the worst effects of globalization are avoided."[12] As Slavoj Žižek then suggests (in critiquing Laclau), such a refusal to "even imagine a viable alternative to global capitalism" inevitably produces the conclusion that "the only option for the Left is ... palliative measures which, while resigning themselves to the course of events, restrict themselves to limiting the damaging effects of the inevitable."[13]

But let us be generous and also say to the "posties": go ahead, deconstruct our work to your heart's content, expose our premises (our Eurocentrisms, essentialisms and the like) . We're prepared to learn from you where we may have occluded things, thereby bettering both our science (our "moralizing science") and our politics. At the end of the day, however, Marxists and other socialists will also continue to insist that capitalism be taken seriously in its fundamentally oppressive reality – and to insist as well that, like all human constructs, it is not destined to last forever but can and must be replaced as soon as possible – and to assert that mobilizing people who are victims of that system around anti-capitalist themes and projects is essential to their liberation. In short, to ask of others why they would want, in all conscience, to blunt such a point of view, such an entry-point, both with respect to study and to political action.

B. Entry Points/Points of View: Capital and Exploitation, Global Recolonization and Class Struggle

My moral compass leads me to begin with the dialectic of class and capital as my initial entry-point. Indeed, it helps to focus in on what is, for me, the most disturbing feature of the current moment, albeit, paradoxically and simultaneously, the most promising. Thus, on the one hand, there is, as the epoch's central reality, the ever more naked capitalist exploitation and glaring inequality that capitalism's success has bred, a "success" so marked and blatant as to feed the preening power of capital in its ascendance. On the other hand, class polarization and, with it, the objective logic demanding struggle based on class and on related grounds for the transcendence of the capitalist mode of production, is still felt by many to be both necessary and possible. In fact, my entry-point #2 deepens this emphasis by bringing more recent aspects of the unfolding global capitalist system more firmly into the picture. And yet, nota bene, this is definitely not to say that any such theoretical starting-point, Marxist in essence, is far from giving us the whole picture of global constraints on freedom. In fact, there are other morally focused entry-points invoked in this chapter that are also of central importance, and that cannot be contrasted with factors rooted in class domination, exploitation, and class-struggle as being merely minor fronts or as being primarily class-determined in their most telling implications.

No, this second part of chapter 1 will then explore a further range of entry-points that can be considered to be particularly useful in advancing our understanding and focusing our practice. This leads me to advocate a multivariate analysis of social dynamics and social out-comes, a mode of analysis that sets off with a Marxist tilt but that then seeks, non-reductively, to link together other intellectual practices and other central variables that I identify as meaningful and reveal-ing entry-points, for these are other points of view that can be quite complementary to class analysis and to a Marxist take on the workings of the capitalist system, and of resistance to it. In short, it is important to eschew any temptation to not interpret a number of the dimensions then highlighted in this chapter as being somehow merely "dependent variables" or – in comparison with class factors – less important in their import and political significance.

In sum, this means that, in addition to dimensions of class and eco-nomic inequality, other factors can (and must) be permitted into our social equation: gender, sexual preference and sexual orientation; race (both expressed in narrow and oppressive racisms and in the more posi-tive assertions of racial identity); national, ethnic and diverse religious assertions; pressing environmental concerns; the acknowledgement of the complexity and implications of class/non-class identifications (as per the discussion of the claims to our attention of "proletariat" and "precariat" in chapter 2, for example); the honoring of democratic practice, processes and outcomes; and the moral texture of political practice (the importance of Ernst Bloch's "hope" as a component of successful movement-building as an example). There are certainly tensions and possible contradictions arising out of any lazy conflating of such diverse elements of social interaction and social struggle, but there are also potentially shared understandings, positive political links, and other complementary links between related brands of struggle to be assessed and collectively worked out. It is in this spirit that the several diverse entry-points will be discussed; it is also the exact place where we must seek to further specify the kind of self-assured development of a "multivariate Marxism" that I have signaled in the section title above. Indeed, I am confident that the radical logic of this manner, open and sharing, of proceeding in the crafting of both our theory and our practice will become clearer and more convincing as this chapter proceeds.

True, many will want, as Marxists (like myself), to begin with the fact of capitalism because we find that an understanding of its logic provides the crucial first step in our understanding of the world, and we find, as socialists, that it underwrites a struggle to modify, even overthrow, the logic of capitalism, this being seen as a necessary (if not a sufficient) condition for human emancipation. Here, however (and following the lead of Resnick and Wolf), I will in due course expand on the argument that there is simply no need, either theoretically or politically, for Marxists/socialists to downplay the importance of other forms of oppression or other kinds of meaningful resistance to such oppressions; despite all the huffing and puffing over the past several decades of post-Marxists, post-structuralists and post-modernists, Marxism has the resources to deal with a complete plateful of differences and to keep its honor bright. Once again, Kitching has effectively phrased the point:

> Marx simply was not an economic reductionist. He did not believe
> that all forms of politics, or culture, or social conflict were simply
> expressions of underlying economic or class interests, and it would
> be extremely difficult to find any evidence in his writing that he

did....Marx was often concerned with those aspects of politics, or culture, or social conflict that had class or economic dimensions. But he certainly would not have thought that, for example, all classical Greek culture (which he loved) or all the politics of the French Second Empire (by which he was fascinated) could be explained by or reduced to economic or class factors.[14]

Of course, there are tensions within Marx's work (and also within the tradition he spawned): he did want to say that the production process – and the capitalist production process in particular – was a (sometimes the) crucial variable for framing both social analysis and political practice. And there are those Marxists who will continue to argue, in quite subtle ways, the case for the primacy of the economic and of class struggle. Take, for example, the position asserted some years ago by Erik Olin Wright. He sought to sustain such a claim on the grounds that a tendency towards transformation of the class struggle is inherent in the very process of economic development (in the development of the productive forces), providing class relations with an "internal logic of development" denied to other forms of domination, asserting that:

> the apparent symmetry in the relationship between class and gender or class and race, therefore, is disrupted by the developmental tendencies of class relations. No such developmental trajectory has been persuasively argued for other forms of domination.[15]

This is suggestive, but even then much more reductionist and more confining with respect to thought and action than it needs to be. Not that suggestive is a bad thing: the pull towards economic-cum-class reductionism within Marxism can be illuminating, even if it is also dangerous.

And yet this can prove dangerous only if we fail to hold onto the expansive implications of the simultaneous pull towards agency within Marxism.[16] "Man [sic] makes his own history but he does not do so under conditions of his own choosing": a phrase from Marx that is often quoted but perhaps too easily forgotten. For if we take this (usefully contradictory) phrase seriously, we are acknowledging that there do exist tensions within our approach: tensions between structure and agency, tensions between the attractions of economic-cum-class reductionism (in both analysis and politics) on the one hand and the legitimate claims of a multivariate analysis and a politically inclusive approach to struggle on the other. What we are then claiming is that it is precisely on the cusp of these tensions that the Marxist chooses, as creatively and self-consciously as possible, to think and to act.

In fact, we need only build on the possibilities, and the tensions, inherent in one of Marx's most tantalizing formulations to see our way forward:

> It is always the direct relationship of the owners of the conditions of production to the direct producers – a relationship always naturally corresponding to the development of the methods of labor and thereby its social productivity – which reveals the innermost secret, the hidden basis of the entire social structure, and with it the political form of the relation of sovereignty and dependence, in short, the corresponding specific form of the state. This does not prevent the same economic basis – the same from the standpoint of its main conditions – due to innumerable different empirical circumstances, natural environment, race relations, external historical influences, etc., from showing infinite variations and gradations in appearance, which can be ascertained only by analysis of the empirically given circumstances.[17]

The absence of any mention of gender, of sexual orientation, religion or ethno-nationalism on Marx's list is its most troubling aspect. And there is also that word appearance to be dealt with. And yet, expand the content of that "etc." and of those phrases "empirical circumstances" and "external historical influences", and also interpret "appearance" in the strongest possible sense (as emanating from other structures of social relationships and also being capable of having pertinent effects in its own right). Then you have pretty much all that Marxists require: the ability to emphasize the production process as our chosen entry-point into social analysis and political practice while also taking seriously the concerns of those who wish to highlight, alternatively or simultaneously, the claims to our attention of other nodes of oppression and resistance (on this see the items included for discussion in Section C of this chapter). This done, all that Marxists need ask of those who speak out analytically and politically from the vantage-point of concern about these is that whatever else they do, they themselves take seriously the goal of substantially modifying, sooner or later (but preferably sooner rather than later), the capitalist system. But this will be discussed below; let us start by considering the entry-points that frame the importance of capital and exploitation, global recolonization and class struggle.

Entry point 1: Capital and Exploitation, Class Struggle and the Realities of Decolonization

From quite early on, both Marx and Stretton provided me with the components of a "methodological bible" in terms of which I could think through and validate my work in general terms. More concretely, I also determined, for purposes of writing a doctoral dissertation, to involve myself more specifically in Africa-related activities, both scholarly and political. And so, after graduate work at Princeton, I began to retool myself for that purpose in London (learning to speak Swahili at SOAS, for example), and then went to Tanzania for the next seven years, first undertaking my planned fieldwork and then taking a teaching job at the fledgling university in Dar es Salaam. I had chosen to focus on Tanzania deliberately since, under its then president, Julius Nyerere, it was a country seeking, in the name of African socialism, to build a better and more egalitarian future for all its citizenry. Indeed, the university where I now worked would soon become an important front of struggle for the future, being crafted in Tanzania in the name of the Arusha Declaration. In addition, Dar es Salaam had also become a crucial staging ground for most of the liberation movements contesting intransigent white rule further south. An important and stimulating site, in short, both for learning about progressive struggle, and helping it to triumph.

Radical transformation proved to be not quite as straightforward a task as many of us had hoped. We rejoiced in the Arusha Declaration and in the cumulative defeats of white rule further south. And, in the heat of battle – and, it must be said, in order to avoid giving aid and comfort to an implacable enemy (the minions of race rule and corporate profit in the southern African region) – we no doubt tended publicly to romanticize the forces of liberation throughout the region (or, at least, to say much less about their weaknesses and their risks of failure and compromise than an intellectual practice of full disclosure might have required). On the other hand, we conversed endlessly with members of the liberation movements, and it was difficult to escape the sense of positive adventure in liberation and reclamation of a future for their home countries. We may have tended to romanticize, but there was also a real enemy in view, and a scent of liberation in the air.

At the same time, it bears emphasis that those of us coming from outside who chose to support the cause of liberation tended not to be mere romantics and/or naïve enthusiasts (aka liberation movement junkies). We were far from naïve about either the nature of global capitalism nor about the strengths and weaknesses of either the liberation movements on the ground in southern Africa or our support work practices in Canada and elsewhere. And we spent many hours arguing amongst ourselves as to the liberatory potential of the struggles we supported, and of the likelihood of various liberation forces sustaining their struggles in such a way as to realize the kind of liberation that would change not just the fortunes of the leadership cadres but also those of their followers in the various pertinent territories.

In particular, from very early on we sought to avoid the claiming of any easy victories, even as success seemed to crown the liberation struggle in southern Africa. Indeed, as the essays in this book record and help explain, the long-term results were generally much less favorable than such regional victories seemed at first to indicate. In fact, it very soon became extremely difficult to avoid the conclusion that it was global capital (together with its indigenous partners, the new African elites that replaced the colonial officials as the new dominant governmental cadre) that had, through a process of false decolonization, southern African-style, actually won the day, both in southern Africa and in North America. Perhaps more careful study of global capitalism – however painful – could have prepared us better to anticipate or at least to understand such an outcome.

Nonetheless, as my thinking began to catch up with many of the grim realities underlying the southern African region's present and its future, I began to find the best texts to use as a basis for asking better questions about such matters to be available in African points of view offered by Frantz Fanon, Amilcar Cabral, Julius Nyerere, and Steve Biko. And a discussion of these seminal African activist-thinkers will be returned to throughout this book; I begin such a discussion in the section "Snatched from the Jaws of Victory: The Defeat of Southern Africa Liberation."[18]

Snatched from the Jaws of Victory: For there was undoubtedly a crucial catch (as regards the region's supposed liberation) in Africa's apparent victory: the fact that the impressive push from below seen in both Africa and more widely was to succeed only in part. Much of the success visible in southern Africa came, in part and quite paradoxically, because capital – finding itself under substantial political pressure (especially in South Africa but also in western countries) from anti-apartheid activism – came, finally, to an understanding that the profitable links that the global capitalist system had forged with racist and apartheid-defined structures in southern Africa were now making capitalism dangerously vulnerable to mass action. And this in turn moved capital to reconsider its options and to admit to itself that its links to race-defined rule were now best understood as having been merely a contingent, time-bound tactic in its quest, most centrally, for class privilege and power.[19] How much wiser, capitalists increasingly thought, to abandon apartheid, to co-opt the vanguard of the popular movement into capital's camp, and to thus pre-empt any more radical, even revolutionary, possibilities.

For this was prominent among the factors that would see "liberation" eventually to be conceded to movements for change throughout southern Africa – albeit in such a way as to produce a much more limited brand of liberation than had been anticipated by many activists of the time. Here the importance of the work of Frantz Fanon and Amilcar Cabral on the dispiriting outcome of an earlier round of victorious nationalism (in Africa north of the Zambezi) must be emphasized: "false decolonization," as they termed it.[20] Now, somewhat later in time, something of the same pattern came to be repeated in the name of liberation in southern Africa. Indeed, for all the success of our joint efforts, regionally and globally, and for all that the overthrow of formalized white power was genuinely liberating in many ways, the real winners in southern Africa were, again, global capital on the one hand and emergent local elites, most often those who had come to power with the ascendancy of the liberation movements in their respective territories, on the other.

Recall Fanon's succinct summary of the outcome of decolonization north of the Zambezi in his celebrated text of the time, *The Wretched of the Earth*. There he wrote acidly of the false decolonization that the movements against colonial rule had produced in the newly "liberated" territories of north, west and east Africa where he found that little had changed, the new African elites comfortably stepping into privileged positions as mere intermediaries, acting in their own class interests but also on behalf of capital.[21] Indeed, Fanon even underscored the fact that once the demand for freedom gathered momentum in their empires, the British and the French began to craft decolonizations of a kind that would serve primarily to safeguard their own continuing interests and those of global capitalism more generally. To accomplish this, they had to move quickly: as Fanon continued,

> That is why a veritable panic takes hold of the colonialist governments in turn. Their purpose is to capture the vanguard, to turn the movement of liberation to the right and disarm the people, quick, quick, let's decolonize. Decolonize the Congo before it turns into another Algeria. Vote the constitutional framework for all Africa, create the French Communauté, renovate that same Communauté, but for God's sake let's decolonize quick.[22]

Meanwhile, at more or less the same moment – in the 1950s and 1960s – a similar point was being made by a second distinguished theorist of Africa's push for liberation. Amilcar Cabral,[23] leader of Guinea-Bissau's liberation movement (the PAIGC), wondered aloud (as quoted in one of this book's epigraphs) as to the true nature of the national liberation struggle. Indeed, Cabral even went so far as to question whether, in the form it took, the "national liberation struggle [was] not [in fact] an imperialist initiative." As he continued,

> ...there is something wrong with the simple interpretation of the national liberation movement as a revolutionary trend. The objec-

tive of the imperialist countries was to prevent the enlargement of the socialist countries, to liberate the reactionary forces in our country which were being stifled by colonialism, and to enable these forces to ally themselves with the international bourgeoisie.[24]

Tough stuff, this. Cabral also asked whether the circumstances that demanded an armed liberation struggle – as in his Guinea-Bissau but also throughout southern Africa – might impose a different kind of internal logic upon such a struggle. Might it not push the African petty-bourgeoisie – elevated, almost inevitably, to positions of leadership of any such struggle by their formation and education – to be moved to "commit suicide" as a potentially privileged class? In fact, it was such thinking that would prompt many, in the southern African region and amongst supporters of the region's liberation elsewhere, to consider the possibility, even probability, that in that region a more genuinely radical movement (socialist in orientation and firmly based in self-aware popular action) would emerge. And yet more or less the exact same outcome as had transpired elsewhere on the continent – call it neo-colonialism, false decolonization or recolonization – was to occur in southern Africa.

Not surprisingly, the implications of such an anti-climactic denouement to struggle in southern Africa were also to prove chastening for many in the global anti-apartheid movement. Indeed, for all the "success" of our efforts, and for all that the overthrow of formalized white power was genuinely liberating, the real winners in southern Africa were, as already suggested, global capital on the one hand and emergent local elites, most often attached to the so-called liberation movements in their respective territories, on the other. A grim conclusion, albeit one that makes the writings of Frantz Fanon and Amilcar Cabral – in analyzing the dispiriting outcome of the earlier round of "victorious nationalisms" in Africa north of the Zambezi – particularly pertinent. But in now synthesizing the work of several professional historians we can see how others, via a route very different from that chosen by Fanon and Cabral, have produced a reading very similar to theirs as to the substance of Africa's apparent decolonization.

False Decolonization: From Fanon and Cabral to (some) Professional Historians: Nor was it merely militant and committed African intellectuals such as Fanon and Cabral who would begin cast such a sceptical eye on African decolonization. The very shallowness of decolonization was discerned by some of the best of professional historians too – although they tended to present these outcomes as being more normal and commonsensical than had Fanon and Cabral, who were more likely to consider them as being, quite simply, outrageous. Still, the main point stands: such historians, writers whose work focused directly on the complexities of imperialism and on processes of decolonization, took a very sceptical view indeed of the degree of actual change wrought by early rounds of decolonization on the continent. It is a point of view that is also worth reminding ourselves of here.

Particularly noteworthy in this respect were the Oxbridge scholars John Gallagher and Ronald Robinson, whose pertinent texts have become central within the scholarly literature on such matters. For Robinson and Gallagher effectively underscored the case that Northern and Western imperialism had already, well before decolonization, run far beyond the conventional definitional boundaries of formal colonialism. Hence the title of their most widely cited article, "The Imperialism of Free Trade."[25] As they then wrote:

> Are these [the overseas initiatives taken by the British government that Gallagher and Robinson itemize in the text] the actions of ministers anxious to preside over the liquidation of their British Empire? Do they look like "indifference" to an empire rendered superfluous by free trade? On the contrary, there is a continuity of policy which the conventional interpretation misses because it takes account only of formal methods of control...Refusals to annex are no proof of reluctance to control...The common assumption that British governments in the free-trade era considered empire superfluous arises from over-estimating the significance of changes in legalistic forms.

Indeed, as Gallagher and Robinson further argue (pp. 4-5), "responsible government, far from being a separatist device, was simply a change from direct to indirect methods of retaining British interests. By slackening the formal political bond at the appropriate time, it was possible to rely on economic dependence and mutual good-feeling [the reference here is, in the first instance, to the "White Dominions" in particular!] to keep the colonies bound to Britain while still using them as agents for further British expansion."

Another case in point for Gallagher and Robinson was in Latin America where (much as the Americans would eventually do with respect to the British and French empires after the Second World War) "the British governments sought to exploit the colonial revolutions to shatter the Spanish trade monopoly, and to gain informal supremacy and the good will that would all favor British commercial penetration." Thus, too, they cited in support of their argument, Canning's gleeful statement "in 1824, when he had clinched the policy or recognition, [that] 'Spanish America is free and, if we do not mismanage our affairs sadly, she is English'" (p. 9-10). In sum, for Gallagher and Robinson, imperialism is... whatever is sufficient politically to the "integrating [of] new regions into the expanding [capitalist] economy."

> It is only when the polities of [some] regions fail to provide satisfactory conditions for commercial or strategic integration and when their relative weakness allows, that power is used imperialistically to adjust those conditions...[Thus] the old, legalistic, narrow idea of empire is unsatisfactory, but so too is the old idea of informal empire as a separate, non-political category of expansion. A concept of informal empire which fails to bring out the underlying unity between it and...formal empire is sterile. Only within the total framework of expansion is nineteenth century empire intelligible.[26]

In short, "Britain followed the principle of extending control informally if possible and formally if necessary. To label the one method 'anti-imperialist' and the other 'imperialist' is to ignore the fact that whatever the method British interests were steadily safeguarded and extended. The usual summing up of the policy of the free trade empire as 'trade not rule' should read 'trade with informal control if possible; trade with rule when necessary.'"[27]

When we now return to consider the question of decolonization quite specifically, both the logic of this argument and the apparent evidence of subsequent developments would seem to lead ineluctably to a pattern of analysis not too dissimilar from that arrived at by Fanon – that the informal empire of the economy (now, as we will argue, spearheaded by the U.S., its capital and government) merely displaced the outgoing remnants of formal empire. In the period after World War II, formal colonialism was certainly on the defensive, under attack by nationalist forces in the colonies; it was also, increasingly, too expensive for war-torn economies in Europe to maintain their empires in that form. Finally, it came under very sharp questioning from Western Europe's major ally, the United States, as well – with the U.S. now marching to the head of the global Empire of Capital. For the United States looked negatively at the barriers that formal colonialism set in the way of free trade – and upon the free movement of capital and of finance. Indeed, the U.S. now sought, on the whole, to encourage the movement towards decolonization that was afoot, thereby seeking to establish, it seems clear, a post-colonial order within which it would become – as befitted its burgeoning economic power – increasingly pre-eminent.

Was this not, again, free trade imperialism, albeit with the center of imperial gravity now shifted to the United States? For the moment, and rather surprisingly, Robinson (now writing with his American colleague, W. Roger Louis) did not further push this argument, professing to see the American role as being primarily driven by Cold-War preoccupations,[28] with any American suspicion of conventional colonialism springing primarily, they claimed, from its own supposed anti-colonial history.[29] In fact, for a time, the only sounding of the familiar suspicion of their being an empire of free trade in the offing – although one now to be orchestrated principally by the United States – comes not from the lips of Robinson and Louis themselves but, rather, from those of a senior British official, one Christopher Eastwood, head of the General Department of the Colonial Office whom, more or less *en passant*, they do quote. Thus Eastwood, after reading the U.S. State Department's 1942 Declaration on National Dependence for Colonies, wrote in 1943 that "the word independence occurred in the document nineteen times altogether." But his conclusion from this was that the "Americans were [themselves] now tempted to establish a sort of informal empire" of their own. As he argued:

> Independence is a political catchword which has no real meaning apart from economic. The Americans are quite ready to make their

dependencies politically "independent" while bound hand and foot to them [the U.S.] and see no inconsistency in this.

As for Robinson and Louis, it was not until a decade later (in 1994) that Robinson, still writing with Louis, would again make the concept of an "empire of free trade" central – though now the British system was seen as having been neo-colonized even more intensively "as part of the Anglo-American coalition."[30] As for the states of the global South: "far from being decolonized, in this view the British [imperial] system [and other imperial systems like it] were neo-colonized more intensively under new management" (p. 49). Note the phrase "under new management" as they engagingly put it, referring to the new management of the United States. In sum,

> The formal empire contracted in the post-war years, as it had once expanded, as a variable function of integrating countries into the international capitalist economy. Under Anglo-American auspices, the remains of the system were progressively nationalized and... informalized. Only now the American economy would drive the economic development of the system. Such was the imperialism of decolonization [p. 73].[31]

Not too surprisingly, their concluding sentence also serves as the title of the article: "The Imperialism of Decolonization." Their conclusion: "Visible empires may be abolished; the thraldom of international economy remains" [p. 74]. But: think Fanon and Cabral. You heard it there first![32]

Of course, others in Africa glimpsed this prospect as well. Indeed, I was to hear Tanzania's president, Julius Nyerere, make a closely related point at a public meeting in Dar es Salaam at about the same time; as a Dar newspaper of the time epitomized the President's speech:

> Nyerere called on the people of Tanzania to have great confidence in themselves and to safeguard the nation's hard-won freedom. Mwalimu [Nyerere] warned that the people should not allow their freedom to be pawned as most of their leaders were purchasable. He warned further that in running the affairs of the nation the people should not look on their leaders as saints and prophets.

> The President stated that the attainment of freedom in many cases resulted merely in the change of colours, white faces to black faces without ending exploitation and injustices, and above all without the betterment of the life of the masses. He said that while struggling for freedom the objective was clear, but it was another thing to remove your own people from the position of exploiters.[33]

Moreover, there was the somewhat conflicted case of Steve Biko, the brilliant South African activist of the 1960s and 70s, who, in the name of a politics of Black Consciousness (a politics concept well beyond the chosen remit of the ANC), was an important force in driving South Africa's youth rebellion in the 1970s; in fact, his philosophy was also an important element of the many that fed into the broader mass resistances (as focused through the United Democratic Front and the Mass Democratic Movement) of the 1980s. Nonetheless, he was also student enough of Fanon (and knowledgeable enough about South Africa) to sense clearly the possibilities of a singularly false decolonization there. True, he remained right up to the time of his murder by the South African state, sufficiently convinced of the overdetermining strength of race-thinking and race rule amongst South Africa's white population and polity, as to think such a decolonization impossible. But he gave – as we shall see – an uncannily accurate picture of what it might in theory have come to look like if it were possible. And thanks to the ultimate meeting of minds between global capital and the ANC leadership, it was! Voila: false decolonization, Southern African-style.

Entry point 2: The New Empire of Capital and Global Recolonization

But what was the broader context for the more positive results that we have seen, albeit somewhat intermittently, in southern Africa? I would argue[34] that the region's liberation was part of a worldwide anti-colonial movement and a global process of decolonization that was, overall, the single "most significant event of the entire 20th century."[35] In sum, southern Africa saw the culmination of something noteworthy – and yet all too easy, it would seem, for orthodox historians to overlook or to underestimate.[36]

Thus, in 1939, 13 million square miles and almost 500 million people lay under the domination of the West's economic and political power thanks to the centuries-old frenzy for conquest and enforced colonization indulged in by Western Europe.[37] Moreover, the overweening racism and cultural hubris of the white inhabitants of that same West were both entangled with and further amplified by the process of global conquest. And yet by the end of the century the authoritarian structures of the once overpowering colonial overlordship spawned by "the Great White West" – structures that served almost exclusively to further the latter's interests – had, quite simply, been effaced. One is forced to recall W. E. B. DuBois' ringing 1903 prophecy: "The problem of the twentieth century is the problem of the colour-line – the relation of the darker to the lighter races of men in Asia and Africa, in America and the islands of the sea."[38] And the upshot of that problem? DuBois' "darker races" – "the darker nations" as Vijay Prashad has more recently also termed them[39] – had fought back against their oppressors in the latter half of the twentieth century and, no longer as part of the problem but as part of the solution, had won.

And won? Well, not quite. For there was more to western global power than racism, however important that dimension was in its own right. Thus, if western imperialism was motivated in its rise to global prominence not only by white arrogance, Christian hubris and profound cultural insensitivity, it also manifested at its core firm economic motives spawned by the capitalist socioeconomic system that had found its feet in Western Europe but then, slowly but surely, reached out its multiple tentacles to embrace the entire world. It was on this stage that the epic drama of successful anti-colonialism was also to play itself out. Yet it is equally the case that, even as racist structures (as exemplified by direct colonial domination) were, by the end of the decolonization process, peeled back, it was clear that much of the economic basis of the West's predominance was still in place, framing a system that many were soon to term "neo-colonialism."

In this format of domination, the United States – itself the artifact of remorseless capitalist territorial expansion at an earlier stage of its history[40] – increasingly stood at the center of the global system of continued capitalist domination and expansion. But the U.S. had much less interest in territorial conquest than it had in economic control of the now ostensibly autonomous countries beyond the North Atlantic core. Realizing its global reach through its powerful corporations and financial organizations – and its willingness to employ, when necessary, the brute power of its fearsome military machine – it was the U.S. and not the former European centers of formal colonization that became the hub of the neo-colonialism which came to hold the Third World in its grip. Indeed the U.S. proved to be the major beneficiary of the very demise of formal colonialism, a demise that now opened the world's borders even more widely to the unchecked expansion of American capitalism's control.[41]

And yet the process of capitalist evolution and the transformation of the parameters of global domination did not stop there. For the imperialism of neo-colonialism was being slowly but surely superseded in its turn. Thus, if the key to American imperialism in the early post-colonial era was market power articulated on an ostensibly open economic terrain (open primarily, it bears emphasizing, to the ever freer run of capital), the fundamental logic at work has continued to roll out to a next stage. To be sure, the combination of U.S. capital and the U.S. state retains a powerful role within the world of capital and its ongoing expansion – not least, as noted, because of the importance of American military weight as the global cop of last resort. Moreover, the American empire, as some see fit to term the global capitalist system even now, is policed economically in considerable part by such international organizations as the International Monetary Fund, the World Bank and the G8/G20, in which the United States continues to have preponderant power.

At the same time, however, new contenders for economic primacy were now to emerge – including runaway American corporations for whom the new semi-borderless world was to become a major attraction, promising new markets but also cheaper labor at other sites of production around the world than at home.[42] Equally importantly, newly aggressive staging grounds for capital beyond the familiar North Atlantic centers also began to emerge, and these too increasingly provided new countries and corporations to help spearhead the global capitalist game. Japanese interest had already presented itself as just such a global (capitalist) player. And now China also began to step ever more assertively into the world's capitalist arena.[43] And so did the capital of Korean, Indian, Brazilian and other provenances.

Thus a newspaper headline of 11 December 2012 reports baldly that "Asian economies to outstrip Western nations by 2030: 'Spectacular rise' of Asia redoing U.S. power, trends report says." And the "trends report" that it is drawing on? It is the "Global Trends 2030" released by the National Intelligence Council/NIC and, as the article says, "timed for the start of the new presidential administration ...aimed at helping U.S. policymakers plan for the future." The report's chief thrust: "The United States could see its standing as a superpower eroded and Asian economies will outstrip those of North America and Europe combined by 2030, according to the best guess of the U.S. intelligence community. 'The spectacular rise of Asian economies is dramatically altering U.S. influence,' said Christopher Newton" (Newton being the chair of the NIC).[44] Indeed, a second journalistic account of this report is headlined: "U.S. Intelligence Analysts: American Power is in Terminal Decline."[45]

In short, it is a whole new world of capitalist power that is dawning with, increasingly, the diverse nodes of capital themselves coming to collectively define the several protagonists of a new imperial project. Such nodes of capital are still dependent, in many ways, on their states to help discover how to both police the overall system and keep it running smoothly. But – and this is the crucial point – they have also increasingly found a distinctive global weight and substance in their own right. No longer primarily American capital, Canadian capital, Chinese capital, German capital or Indian capital, but ever more united by common (if also divided) interest as a force – the world's predominant force! – in and of itself. Capital: fractured, competitive, and in unresolved tension with differing state structures ("can't live with them and can't live without them!") but bent, nonetheless, on a joint project of further crafting the world in their own image. As something new: an "Empire of Capital."[46]

But one further conceptual foray is necessary here in order to clear the ground for concrete analysis. Begin with colonialism and then decolonization. For decolonization into a new world of unadorned western capitalist global supremacy was no longer to be premised on the structures of formal colonialism virtually anywhere. As we have seen, independence for the global South originally had been sited within a powerful global capitalist economy defined, in the first instance, by American market-based hegemony with the stage thus set for neo-colonialism. At the same time, this brave new world of free-market imperialism was, at least in principle, by no means simply nation-based, this in turn suggesting that this world was now ever more open, theoretically, to a fresh array of capitalist undertakings. True, in much of the global South (not least in Africa) the theoretical possibility of finding effective traction for an assertive domestic (and globally expansive) capitalism was not always readily available in practice: global capital based in the strongest of economies was certainly omnipresent and ready to cream off attractive natural resources, attractive investment opportunities, and the like from the so-called Third World. But the fact remains that the world, at least at its apex, was a much more competitive place and also one more open to the emergence of multiple rivals within a dawning Empire of Capital. This too must be encompassed in our analysis.

For there is certainly a lot of Empire now going on, including most notably the ever less apologetic subordination of the global South to the rule of capital. But it bears emphasizing that this is happening on two levels. One level is defined by the unalloyed workings of capitalism, the manufacture and exacerbation of a global hierarchy, reinforced by the supposedly free workings of the market but in fact creating ever more unequal opportunities and material outcomes for the world's inhabitants. Indeed, the gap between rich and poor continues to grow and not exclusively along geographical lines: there are, after all, many poor in the global North and some rich players and some assertive corporations from territories in the global South – Japan, China, India, Korea, and Brazil for starters. In short, the "free" workings of capital, all euphemisms and long-term prognostications aside, merely reinforce an ever grimmer polarization of rich and poor.

Moreover, this hierarchy is only in part self-created and self-sustaining, this by logic of forward momentum and capitalist expansion if you like. But, as noted, it has also been crafted and willed into place by the aforementioned imperial states themselves, by their governments in power, and by their quasi-international panoply of institutions (the IMF, the World Bank, the WTO, the G7 and the like). This had certainly been true of the empires against which people in the colonies revolted in the post-Second World War period – the classic empires of the British, the French, the Dutch and the Portuguese, principally: these had been clearly and cruelly imperialisms both of markets and of guns. But the same is true now too: there is an imperialism and it also has political clout. Not least, it has guns – many of them, as noted, in the hands of what is still the global system's principal agent and beneficiary, the United States.

Nor can the actions of those holding the guns be determined solely as manifestations of some logic of capital per se. Agents have agendas, and these are defined at least in part on the terrain of the global system of political power and calculation. Differences of opinion about what is of special importance exist between those with, primarily, economic power (who themselves do not always agree on what is in their own best interests, either severally or together) and those with, primarily, political power.[47] Do the George Bushes and Donald Trumps of the world speak exclusively for capital? If so, what fractions of it? And what else do they speak for – bizarre religious imaginings or global visions of something they choose to call democracy or populism? In the end, though, the elective affinity between capital and power is real enough to justify using the phrase "Empire of Capital" (despite the pertinent contradictions and tensions within the term and within the reality it invokes).

Thus, as the myth and practice of capitalist globalization became ascendant, as the logic of the global marketplace and the march of unfettered capital has become the operative motif of the United States and its allies in the worldwide imperial project, and as the international institutions dominated by capital have consolidated themselves, the imperial game has come to have a different flavour. Of course, as the Empire of Capital has taken on global and imperial dimensions, this has meant merely more of the same for those, especially in the global South and not least in Africa, that find themselves at the bottom of the global hierarchy. For the latter have more difficulty than ever in defending themselves against the "free global market" as now projected upon them by the U.S., by the IMF, the WTO, and by an ever wider range of capitalist actors of multinational provenance: what else could this be, then, if not recolonization, and by a new empire, the Empire of Capital.

In short, I use the term *recolonization* (rather than false decolonization) to signify what is happening to the losers in the global race to the bottom, and not least throughout Africa. True, all the words and phrases that signify the modification of the conventional notion of colonization present us with difficult challenges, both conceptual and practical. We would not want to see the thrust of the term *decolonization* blunted, deflected from its signifying, as it did throughout the global South, the impressive challenge offered to the arrogant racism and crude power of Europe's project of worldwide colonial empire; what this challenge underwrote was an historical accomplishment of an especially notable and heroic order. At the same time, the fact that the continuing, post-independence, reality of economic subordination to the advanced capitalist centers was soon well enough known to earn the term the critical qualifier "false" (as in "false decolonization") is, at the very least, significant.

But "recolonization"? The fact is that even the degree of relative freedom from western and capitalist dictate that existed in the global South in the immediate postwar period as a result of the worldwide decolonization revolution has been clawed back by capital. The Soviet bloc which, given its Stalinist definitions of what socialism might mean, had proven a misleading, even costly, model and point of reference for revolutionaries of the 1950s, '60s and '70s.[48] Nonetheless, as a potential arsenal of opposition and real if quite opportunist ally it had guaranteed space for some quasi-left experimentation. Now even that was gone and capitalist spokespersons and practitioners in power have, in such a context, merely become more assertive, no longer paying even semi-tolerant lip service to the kind of "developmental" objectives and "progressive state activities" that once they had done.

Entry point 3: Gender Inequality and Feminist (and Other Gendered) Assertions

But I must now return to the issue raised, at the outset of this chapter's part 2: how best to blend a class-alert Marxist understanding of current challenges to the status quo with other potential vectors of resistance that can offer, on other fronts, similar promise of hope and progressive struggle: In doing so I will start with a consideration of factors linked to gender and to diverse sexual assertions and identities.[49] But it also bears emphasizing that it has been those engaged in gender-sensitive analysis and feminist struggles who have had most to contribute to the development of Marxist analysis along these expansive lines. This can be seen first with reference to the very notion of class. Himani Bannerji has underscored the absurdity of attempting to see "identity and difference as historical forms of consciousness unconnected to class formation, development of capital and class politics." But in doing so she also emphasizes the impossibility of considering class outside the gendering (and "race-ing") that so often significantly characterize it in the concrete.[50] Not that there need be anything so very startling in this. Katha Pollitt makes the relevant point about the United States (but the point is true more generally) in answering her question: "Are race and gender and sexual orientation distractions from basic issues of economic inequality and social class?"

> All you have to do is look squarely at the world you live in and it is perfectly obvious that ... race and gender are crucial means through which class is structured. These are not side issues that can be resolved by raising the minimum wage (although that is important) or even by unionizing more workplaces (although that is important too). Inequality in America is too solidly based on racism and sexism for it be altered without acknowledging race, and sex, and sexuality.[51]

But this point can also be turned around, underscoring the extent to which gender oppression is also classed and the extent to which feminist assertions must interpenetrate with socialist ones in order to be pertinent to the life-conditions of most women. As Lynn Segal argued some years ago, "at a time when the advances made by some women are so clearly overshadowed by the increasing poverty experienced so acutely by others (alongside the unemployment of men of their class and group) it seems perverse to pose women's specific interests against rather than alongside more traditional socialist goals."[52] Consider, too, Nancy Fraser's twin framing of the conditions of women's oppression (and a number of other oppressions as well) within the spheres of both distribution and difference:

> Demands for "recognition of difference" fuel struggles of groups mobilized under the banners of nationality, ethnicity, "race," gender, and sexuality. In these "post-socialist" conflicts, group identity supplants class interest as the chief medium of political mobilization. And cultural recognition displaces socioeconomic redistribution as the remedy for injustice and the goal of political struggle.[53]

And yet, she then observed, it seems extremely unlikely that tensions rooted in struggles for recognition can be resolved, in the long term and in any very effective and healing manner unless tensions rooted in struggles for redistribution (broadly defined) are also being addressed. Her aim, she suggests, is "to connect two political problematics that are currently dissociated from one another."

True, Fraser casts her concerns about the economic realm in fairly narrow redistributional terms rather than, more radically, in terms of overcoming capitalism's class oppressions more fundamentally. Nonetheless, her refusal to let feminist scholarship and practice merely disappear into the morass of "difference" and discourse theory is a bracing one. Moreover, other, more Marxist feminists have been prepared to take the point much further in viewing feminist struggle as being in essence "a class war over resources, knowledge and power" and in seeking to "reclaim [an] anticapitalist feminism." Thus, Hennessy and Ingraham have bemoaned the fact that "debate among first-world socialist and marxist feminists has drifted so far into theorizing women's oppression in terms of culture, consciousness and ideology that concerns over how to explain the connection between patriarchy and capitalism, or the links between women's domestic labor and ideology, have been all but abandoned."[54] In contrast, as they and their co-authors have demonstrated in their work, a preoccupation with the mode of production and with the realities of wage labor, commodity production and consumption is crucial both to "the scientific understanding of sexual inequality" and to feminists gaining "a sound basis for the evaluation of short- and long-term political and economic objectives."[55]

Such a position is not seen as pre-empting the claims of anti-patriarchal struggle as carried out in its own right. It is a commonplace, albeit a crucial one, that a mere overthrow of capitalism will not, in and of itself, resolve the issues of oppressive sexism and gender emancipation (issues that have haunted all previous experiments in socialist construction). As Hennessy and Ingraham are quick to acknowledge, "violations of women's needs and rights as human beings by patriarchal practices like rape, battering, clitoridectomy and other forms of sexual violence, as well as the neglect and infanticide of girls, are not exclusively bound by or peculiar to capitalism." But they do assert that "the historical forms these practices take and their use against many women in the world are not independent of capitalism either," concluding that "because marxist feminists see the continuous historical connections between women's oppression and capitalism, theirs is a politics of social transformation that ultimately looks to the elimination of class."[56]

Indeed as Hennessy – in articulating her commitment, as socialist, feminist and lesbian activist, to Marxist analysis and politics – concludes another of her studies: "Full democracy [deemed by her to be essential to, amongst many other things, sexual emancipation of all kinds] cannot be achieved within capitalism."[57] In short, there are inextricable links between capitalism and patriarchy, between class and feminist struggles, that Hennessy and others identify: we must learn from this model of left-feminism (and also from certain recent writings on ecological politics)[58] as we turn to an examination of other forms of identity politics.

There is one final preliminary point to be made, however. This concerns the complexity of morally grounding the resistance to oppression that might link feminist and other movements for equality and justice closely to socialist ones. What are we moralizing about in our science, after all? Those on the Left have sometimes shown unease with any such question, preferring instead the assumption what is at best a tacitly shared hunch as to what positive values might ultimately find expression if the workers of the world really were to unite to build a new society. The challenge offered by postmodernist deconstruction and feminist theory has made it more difficult to let the matter rest there, however.

Fortunately, many feminist thinkers – Sabina Lovibond, writing against the grain of post-modernist feminism, for example – have confronted the issue head on. Advocating the global agenda of an "abolition of the sex class system, and the forms of inner life that belong to it," she has defined this program as being global "not just in the sense that it addresses itself to every corner of the planet, but also in the sense that it aims eventually to converge with those of all other egalitarian or liberationist movements." And the basis of such convergence? "The movement should persist in seeing itself as a component or offshoot of Enlightenment modernism, rather than one more 'exciting' feature (or cluster of features) in a post-modern social landscape."[59]

Not that the problem will even then simply disappear, insists Lovibond. And this is even more true if we want to expand beyond gender and feminism per se and consider, under the broader rubric of sexual identity, the panoply of issues raised by the LGBTQ acronym: Lesbian, Gay, Bisexual, Transgender (LGBT), with the final "Q" (in LGBTQ) standing for "Queer" or "Questioning"; we may find it easier to know what we are against (capitalism and its multiple alienations and oppressions, for example) than to clearly state what it is that we are for on each of these fronts and what "spaces of hope" we seek to divine here – although concepts like emancipation from oppression and the freedom for self-expression and self-realization, of community and equality, can be expected to help us define our counter-hegemonic universalism more specifically as we proceed. Perhaps, too, we can affirm that any such universalism as we embrace in this regard will have to be global in its referent and democratic in the modalities of its emergence.

Entry point 4: Other Contested Fronts –
Race, *Ethnie*/Nation and Religion

It is also imperative to examine several additional thorny issues that spring from the political and social reality of identities (and from the social structures that underpin them). We find ourselves confronted by variables at least as difficult to pin down as are those of class and gender, although they are variables with a wide and undeniable range of pertinent effects. Nor can any of them be reduced to mere reflexes of the economic, the material or the class-determined, either for purposes of analyzing oppression or for mobilizing resistance. Indeed, Marxists and non-Marxist socialists have every reason to argue that these variables cannot be treated, either in their cause or their effect, as being any less real (too often to be treated as "mere identities") in their cause or in their effect than are class-based or gender identities. But I would argue that such variables are best interpreted as defining entry-points whose full meaning and import can most effectively be rooted in links to a self-conscious analysis (and politics) of anti-capitalist class struggle. As I will seek to argue in this sub-section.

Race: To begin with it is absurd, as we have seen Bannerji to argue, to ignore the intersection of class not only with gender hierarchies but also with racial discrimination in advanced capitalist settings. But it would be even more foolish to do so when we focus on capitalism as a global system. As Oliver Cox and others have demonstrated, many of the central features we think of as constituting modern racism in the cultural sphere were, in the first instance, shaped in close interaction with the expansion of global capitalism.[60] In fact, this "cultural variable" served both as rationale and booster rocket for "the European consumption of tribal society" which "when viewed as a single process...could be said to represent the greatest, most persistent act of human destructiveness ever recorded."[61] Such a meshing of race and class had numerous faces: in driving American imperialism, for example, the vigorous seed of racism planted by the slave trade was complemented fatefully by what Drinnon has called the ideology of "Indian-hating." This, he continues,

...reduced native peoples to the level of the rest of the fauna and flora to be "rooted out." It reduced all the diverse Native American peoples to a single despised "non-white" group and, where they did survive, into an hereditary caste. In its more inclusive form, Western racism is another name for native-hating – in North America, of "niggers", "Chinks", "Japs", "greasers", 'dagoes", etc.; in the Philippines of "goo-goos"; and in Indochina of "gooks," ... Racism defined natives as non-persons within the settlement culture and was in a real sense the enabling experience of the rising American empire."[62]

Drinnon goes so far as to suggest that "in the [American] experience race has always been of greater importance than class, the cornerstone of European property-based politics." We may think the dialectic of class and race is rather more complicated and central than that, but of the impact of race per se we can have no doubt. Thus, even when the most overtly racist canons of imperial ideology have been self-consciously modified by the Western powers (in order to rationalize the decolonization process of the post-war years, for example), that ideology's central premise of (racial) superiority has tended to be only lightly recast in moral terms for both elite and popular consumption. As Frank Furedi notes:

Increasingly the vocabulary that is applied to the South is morally different from that which is used in relation to the North. Many societies in the South, especially those in Africa, are treated in pathological terms. Africans are routinely represented as devoid of moral qualities...The new moral equation between a superior North and an inferior South helps legitimize a two-tiered international system... Race no longer has a formal role to play since the new global hierarchy is represented through a two-tier moral system. Gradually, the old silent race war has been replaced by moral crusades and by "clashes of civilization."[63]

The latter is the netherworld of right-wing ideology-making inhabited by the Samuel Huntingtons, the Bernard Lewises and the Robert Kaplans of the academy and the Donald Trumps of the political realm.

Moreover, the sordid reality of global inequality has certainly reshaped the advanced capitalist centers themselves, the impoverished empire having struck back (through migration to the metropole) to produce general populations of diverse ethnic and racial composition.[64] Writers like Bonacich and others more recently have explored the split labor markets that this process has produced, and their implications for divided working-class responses to capital.[65] And Stuart Hall and his colleagues presented, in rich detail, an understanding of some of the cultural/ideological and political effects of racial diversity, and the complexity of developing counter-hegemonic strategies in advanced capitalist countries that acknowledge this diversity while seeking to encompass and transcend it.[66]

My work, both scholarly and political, on South Africa has also schooled me here. The semi-autonomous but always tightly linked (and shifting) imperatives of class exploitation and racial oppression that for so long drove both apartheid and a distinctive form of racial capitalism there have proved to be challenging to disentangle analytically. And consciousness of nation, race and citizenship has often been even more crucial than class consciousness in driving resistance in southern Africa. Perhaps the fact that, ultimately, the pull towards (somewhat) color-blind class relations has produced a grim post-apartheid false decolonization along neoliberal lines may seem like a retrospective vindication of class analysis. But the situation has never been that simple, nor has the politics it demands.[67] In fact, once taken seriously, the irreducible simultaneity of class and race can be seen everywhere to warrant "the forging of alliances between the democratic movement and the labor and socialist movements for multi-racial organization and solidarity rather than sectarianism and chauvinism...(thus producing) a strategy that links the struggle for reforms within capitalism with the struggle for that system's transformation."[68]

However, for present purposes, let us focus our aim further by returning to the wider world and the intersection of class and race in the relationship between the capitalist center and its periphery. As Biel has argued, "Dependency theory uncovered part of this relationship, essentially the racial capitalism that exists between the North and the South."[69] Of course, we know that the geography of global exploitation has become more complicated, the Third World now to be found within the First and the First within the Third, such that Hoogevelt can even suggest that "the familiar pyramid of the core-periphery hierarchy is no longer a geographical but a social division of the world economy."[70] But do we not also gain considerable ground by not only underscoring both the gendered and quasi-racial structuring of the present global system (and of resistance to it) but also by inferring a broader range of global cultural diversity than that? For we thus develop a greater sensitivity to the realities of difference within the global system that can be linked creatively with a class-defined analysis of the capitalist workings of that system.[71]

But note too that the likes of Bob Sutcliffe – who sees value in an analytical turn towards acknowledging the substantive import of culture and diversity[72] – can, nonetheless, find some danger in a criticism of the standard development model that seems at times too total, this because the old destination [of "progress"], which in the West we [see the contradictions of] every day, seems so unsatisfactory, that all aspects of it are often rejected [out of hand and] as a whole. Along with consumerism out goes science. technology, urbanization, modern medicine and so on. And in sometimes comes a nostalgic, conservative post-developmentalism."

> In all projects, there is a danger of losing the baby when we throw out the old bathwater. In this case the baby is the material, economic, productive basis of whatever satisfactory utopia can be, to echo Vincent Tucker's suggestive words, imagined and democratically negotiated among the inhabitants of earth. One way of rephrasing all these concerns would be to say that development and globalization are experienced in practice in conditions of profound inequality of wealth and power between nations (imperialism) as well as between classes and sexes (capitalist class exploitation and patriarchy). It is necessary to distinguish which of the rejected aspects of development and globalization are inherent in these concepts and which come about because of the unequal circumstances in which we experience them. If we reject them completely because of the form in which they arrive we will always be struggling against the wrong enemy.[73]

One world then, or two, three or four? Most certainly and at minimum our attention is at least drawn back to the real and grim world – the universalism – of capitalist globalization. Yet can there be any doubt that the "race-ing" of the existing world (like its gendering) presents one reality autonomous enough in its workings (if also one rooted in material realities) to be a focus of political work in its own right? From this point of view, anti-racist consciousness-raising must surely complement anti-capitalist mobilization. But, beyond that, what more can be said with regard to the contribution of a heightened consciousness of race as part and parcel of a progressive movement?[74]

This is clearly delicate ground, and it is to the credit of black writers like Paul Gilroy that they have sought to negotiate it. Gilroy is well aware of the liberatory potential of some degree of racial self-identification in helping overcome the psychological and material scars inflicted upon people of color by the malignant workings of racism.[75] And he is also a fierce critic of any too easy evocation of universalism – as his crisp exposé of the racist stereotypes underlying Kant's enlightenment values eloquently demonstrates. And yet, at the same time, Gilroy identifies the dangers of a black "raciology" that, in the name of identity and "the disabling assumption of automatic solidarity based on either blood or land," risks merely being a narrow inversion of white and racist definitions of difference made by black "victims" and that liberate no one. Instead, he urges, in the name of a "resolutely non-racial humanism", a "fundamental change of mood upon what used to be called 'anti-racism'" by asking it "in an explicitly utopian spirit to terminate its ambivalent relationship to the idea of 'race' in the interest of a hetero-cultural, post-anthropological and cosmopolitan 'yet-to-come.' "[76]

Not all militants, black or white, will agree with this Blochian manner (see below) of posing things, of course. Many Marxists, for example, will wish to ground their pursuit of utopian goals more firmly in terms of class struggle than Gilroy's brand of humanistic voluntarism seems to promise.[77] Following Sutcliffe's distinctions, they may also want to qualify Gilroy's premise that, for victims of capitalism, "corrective or compensatory inclusion in modernity should no longer supply the dominant theme."[78] And yet, at the same time, race does matter: Marxists must seek to avoid all traces of smugness as we accept the assistance of Gilroy and others in crossing the racial divide.

For Gilroy's attempt to imagine political culture beyond the color line does help stake out terrain where the continuing effort to synthesize diverse resistances to oppression can occur.

Ethnicity and Nationalism: Attempts to define the attributes, both shared and distinctive, of nation/nationalism, ethnic group/ethnicity, tribe/tribalism, and other related terms have filled hundreds of combative volumes. For present analytical purposes, the term ethnie may help us to link all these notions: as defined by Anthony Smith, ethnie refers to a community "which unites an emphasis upon cultural difference with the sense of an historical community. It is this sense of history and the perception of cultural uniqueness and individuality which differentiates populations from each other and which endows a given population with a definite identity, both in their eyes and in those of outsiders."[79] It has become a commonplace to recognize that such "communities" are imagined, and even willed into active existence by class-defined protagonists and political actors, but that does not make the often long-lived histories and cultural attributes thus evoked entirely arbitrary. Nor does it make irrelevant the variable circumstances under which a sense of difference cast in such terms can become politicized. Or make less real the effects of actions taken by people (often in large numbers) in terms of such identities, as the last several centuries of history have made perfectly apparent. Marxists have been understandably troubled by this phenomenon, as ethno-national claims have cut across class identities and consciousnesses in wildly varying ways, so much so that Tom Nairn once famously argued that "the theory of nationalism represents Marxism's great historical failure."[80]

Not that Marxists need apologize for their profound suspicions of ethno-nationalism: an emphasis on "inter-nationalism as the expression of a revolutionary humanist viewpoint" and on "socialist, democratic and emancipatory alternatives to national exclusivism, chauvinism and xenophobia" is at the core of their perspective.[81] We have supped full of the United States' Great Power chauvinism and Israel's brutally self-righteous project (both being defined at the grisly intersection of racism, nationalism and religious pomposity, as these things so often are); and we have scarcely recovered from the ethnic cleansings of ex-Yugoslavia and Rwanda (to cite only two of the grimmest recent cases). But, as Ronaldo Munck has asked, is this pull towards the tribe always and everywhere to be interpreted by Marxists as mere problem, or should it not instead be treated as "an integral element of the human condition"[82] – as being, quintessentially, one of those "different empirical circumstances/historical influences" referred to by Marx that affect "the economic basis" in ways that can be "ascertained only by analysis of the empirically given circumstances"? Thus, even Lowy, citing the range of manifestations of nationalism, from Nazism to the Vietnamese revolution, is prepared to emphasize "the contradictory role of nationalism"; to define it as being "one of the great paradoxes in the history of the twentieth century."[83]

Religion: Something similar can also be said of religious identities. Perhaps most Marxists may be atheists, comfortable enough with a materialist perspective on the transcendental and the "last things"; this is certainly true of the present writer. They may even edge towards what Bryan Turner has termed reductionist approaches to understanding the realm of the religious – tending to see religion "as an epiphenomenon, a reflection or expression of more basic and permanent features of human behavior and society," with the further implication that "religious beliefs are false by reference to certain scientific or positivistic criteria and that the holding of religious beliefs is irrational by reference to criteria of rational thought."[84] But is there any need for Marxists to be so reductionist? Our very silences regarding issues of death, evil and enchantment risk appearing one-dimensional. Surely people can be encouraged to find their own workable truths, spiritual or otherwise, regarding such issues. In sum, there seems no reason for Marxists to feel they must advocate existential materialism to others, and, quite apart from the unlikelihood of succeeding in persuading them,[85] there are many reasons not to even attempt it.[86]

Once again, then, it is not religious belief *per se*, but the way in which religion is institutionalized, politicized or classed, that should concern Marxists. And here there are good reasons to be suspicious.

Once again, Michael Lowy asks the most pertinent of questions: "Is religion still, as Marx and Engels saw it in the nineteenth century, a bulwark of reaction, obscurantism and conservatism? Is it a sort of narcotic, intoxicating the masses and preventing them from clear-sighted thought and action in their own interests?" To which he replies: "To a large extent, the answer is yes."[87] And yet Lowy, in the very book in which he writes these words, is primarily concerned to evoke the reality of liberation theology (which he terms "liberationist Christianity") and the positive ways in which it has come to frame certain contestations for radical space in Latin America. This reality, too, suggests that there is work to be done by Marxists and socialists in better comprehending and acting upon the world's complexities.

Lowy then proceeds to document the extent to which a significant tradition within Marxist theory has been alert to such issues. Both Marx and Engels, he argues, acknowledged the role that religion could play both in defining political hegemony and in inspiring political protest.[88] And Lowy also praises the efforts of Rosa Luxemburg "to rescue the social dimension of the Christian tradition for the labor movement ... [i]nstead of waging a philosophical battle in the name of materialism." True, "Luxemburg's insight, that one could fight for socialism in the name of the true values of original Christianity, was lost in [the] rather crude and somewhat intolerant 'materialist' perspective"[89] prevalent in the Marxist circles of the time. But he can also cite Gramsci, Bloch and Goldmann as Marxist writers who countenanced the possibility of a creative (if contested) interface between the utopianism and faith principles in both Marxism and religious belief.[90] For Lowy, the Peruvian Marxist José Carlos Mariategui is particularly central in this respect[91] – not least in influencing directly the work of his fellow Peruvian, the founder of liberation theology, Gustavo Gutiérrez. For, as noted, it is in the emergence of liberation theology that Lowy identifies most clearly "the appearance of religious thinking using Marxist concepts and inspiring struggles for social liberation [and] the creation of a new religious culture, expressing the specific conditions of Latin America: dependent capitalism, massive poverty, institutionalized violence, popular religiosity."[92]

Lowy is well aware that this is contested terrain in Latin America as elsewhere; his analysis of the virulent reaction against liberation theology by the established Catholic church in Latin America (and in Rome) and the interests clustered behind it, as well as the American-sponsored offensive of evangelical Protestant missionaries on that continent, is usefully sobering, as is his discussion of tensions within the camp of the liberationists themselves (with some, not surprisingly, being much more romantic and/or populist than Marxist). Still, it is the possibility of a progressive articulation between religion and popular-cum-class struggle that bears primary emphasis here. As Dwight Hopkins also concludes: "Religions embodied in disparate human cultures have served as the foundations for national differences, racial conflicts, class exploitation, and gender discrimination, on the one hand, as well as for the resolution of hostility and the achievement of full humanity for those at the bottom of all societies, on the other."[93]

Did we not conclude something similar for both religious sectarianism and ethnic and national assertions? Certainly, the positive promise for the left of such identities is not always readily apparent. For such perspectives easily lend themselves to the purposes of great power chauvinism, for example, and to the rationalization, for popular consumption, of bourgeois interests in wealthy countries. Moreover, "the pitfalls of national consciousness" (in Fanon's phrase[94]) are familiar in poorer countries where they often mask petty-bourgeois infighting over power and serve to divide and rule popular forces in the interests of elites, warlords and their sponsors. But even as we move to re-pose the next obvious question – why do large numbers of ordinary people, especially in impoverished circumstances, become available for the narrowest, most combative kind of mobilization in such terms? – we must pause. In fact, as Munck writes,

> The critique of nationalist discourse should not blind us to the popular struggles it has [also] fostered and animated. ... The struggles of the subaltern may take many forms – nationalist, ethnic, regional and religious amongst others – and a Marxism that seeks to have global influence needs to understand these and not just struggle to "demystify" them and reassert a "true" class struggle.[95]

For the Marxist there will be two key foci here, the claims of universalism/internationalism on the one hand and the diverse modalities of articulation between ethnie and class (just as between religion and class) on the other. Once again, the Marxist tradition does have helpful contributions to draw on, an internationalism that has been open to a diversity of struggles (including those cast in national terms) while also emphasizing their "indivisible interdependence" (in Trotsky's phrase).[96] Both Lowy and Munck cite Otto Bauer as advancing "a concept of the nation as historical process of rich and subtle historical analysis," and acknowledge the contributions of Gramsci as well in this regard.[97]

In my work I have found the early formulations of Laclau – written before his post-Marxist turn – to be particularly helpful.[98] For here one finds a non-reductionist model that rejects the notion that nationalism belongs to any class and insists instead (through the deployment of case studies of 1930s Germany and Peron's Argentina) that it can be articulated with quite diverse class projects. More work certainly needs to be done along these lines – not least in the light of the argument of Ahmad, Panitch and others that, despite globalization, the nation-state will remain crucial to the struggle for radical outcomes. For if the latter point is true, the challenge of imagining, on the left, a nationalism that is at once inclusive (with reference to difference), expansive (with reference to internationalism) and progressive (with reference to class) will persist.

It should be apparent from our earlier argument that a similar approach can also illuminate the political economy of religion. As noted, some Marxists may wish merely to challenge religion's irrational claims root and branch (as the Frelimo leadership chose to do in Mozambique) or, faced with religion's often negative articulation with class and power, merely to urge an assertive commitment to secularism and to tolerance as being the Left's optimal program. And yet even this latter approach, if pushed too smugly, can easily overlook the kind of potentially positive articulations between religion and class that many situations may demand and that liberation theology exemplifies.[99] Certainly, making links with those who are moved by the universally humane themes in the world's religious traditions must often be the correct approach by the Left to such a powerful, virtually inevitable, form of identity. In short, religion must not be abandoned to the Right.

Here, perhaps, we can take our lead from Dusserl's sense that liberation theology "will be practiced in other parts of the Christian world, such as Africa and Asia [beyond Latin America], and by theologians of other world religions...This theological perspective emerges from a commitment to the poor of the South, that is, those who have been excluded from the present globalization modernizing process."[100] It is in this spirit, too, that Radhika Coomaraswamy, writing on recent developments in Sri Lanka, refuses to elide the distinction between Buddhist humanism and Buddhist chauvinism and then argues more generally (she comments on Hinduism, Islam and Christianity in addition to Buddhism) that "all religions have this contradiction between orthodox doctrine and the humane heterodox traditions." Herself a secularist, she nonetheless suggests that "to collapse humanism and orthodoxy at this historical juncture would be a major setback."[101]

And yet we must also face the fact that it will be uphill work to claim the high ground here. Recent studies have recognized not merely the vested interests that can benefit from stoking the fires of fundamentalisms (cf. Islam in the political economy of contemporary Iran, Pakistan, Bangladesh and elsewhere, for example; Buddhist radicalism and its links to Sinhala chauvinism in Sri Lanka; or the tight mesh in India [and Nepal] of the Hindu right with reactionary modernism as epitomized by U.S. imperial hegemony and by repressive Hindu nationalism. And this is not to begin to mention the resonance of the Christian right in the United States which helps fuel all of the horrors perpetrated by Bush, Trump, and company from there). But they have also emphasized the morbid global conditions that can encourage ordinary people to see such identities, both for better and for worse, as weapons in their own hands. In this sense, Dusserl's use of the phrase "globalization modernizing process" as a touchstone for progress suggests problems of its own. For many students of the religious right have found the latter's main roots to lie not so much in exclusion from modernity as in resistance to it.

Karen Armstrong, a particularly subtle and sensitive writer on world religions, has underscored the extent to which the fundamentalist version of religious activism is an unsurprising effect of the disruptions that modernity brings, and of the fact that "in the developing world...modern Western culture [is experienced as being] invasive, imperialistic and alien."[102] Similarly, Mark Jurgensmeyer writes that "in many cases, especially in the areas of the world where modernization is a synonym for Westernization, movements of religious nationalism have served as liberation struggles against what their supporters perceive to be alien ideologies and foreign powers."[103] Faith and fundamentalism, humanism and secularism, universalism and modernity: self-evidently, the complexities evoked by engaging such expansive terms outrun the limits of these pages. What can be insisted upon here, however, is that modernity must not be identified as readily with capitalism as Armstrong and Jurgensmeyer (however tacitly) both seem prone to do. Contemporary socialists must insist (once again, with Sutcliffe) that the promise of the modern can be blended with the integrity of the local and the sacred in much more meaningful and efficacious ways than the "universalism" of capitalist modernity (Benjamin Barber's "McWorld"[104])can ever hope to allow.[105]

Universalism? But is not socialism a key piece of the puzzle of building a different, more positive kind of universalism? I would suggest that this is the way the issue should now be framed, with Marxists forced to see the fever so often attendant upon rabid ethno-nationalisms and religions-turned-fundamentalist as a reflection not merely of the victory of capitalism but also the failure, at least for the moment, of "progressive nationalism and revolutionary socialism throughout the globe." Panitch elaborates the latter point: "Opposition to capitalism and imperialism is inevitable, but the atavistic form it took on 11 September can only be understood in terms of what, on that day, tragically filled the vacuum of the 20th century Left's historic defeat."[106] And what, in addition, can be said of the nature of capitalism's victory? As Arrighi reminds us, it has primarily been a victory for the continuing hegemony of capitalism's vicious irrationality – a victory scarred by inequality and the dramatic failure to realize the developmentalism that that system has so often promised.

Indeed, it is the latter failure that has sown so many of the seeds of contemporary decay, producing "a crisis which is most clearly visible in the rise of Islamic fundamentalism in the Middle East and North Africa but is apparent in one form or another throughout the South."[107] For capitalism's grossly uneven development across the world has produced, as Ralph Miliband once put it, "extremely fertile terrain" for the kind of "pathological deformations" – predatory authoritarianisms and those "demagogues and charlatans peddling their poisonous wares of ethnic and religious exclusion and hatred" – that now scar the global landscape.[108] Losing confidence in socialist and other humanely modern, humanly cooperative, projects, people turn for social meaning to more ready-to-hand identities, often with fundamentalist fervor.[109]

And where, despite this, is meaningful hope to come from? Progressives committed to class struggle must continue to view the identities we have been exploring as contingent in their sociopolitical implications and, in many cases, as not being in contradiction with socialist purposes. And we should continue, when possible, to invite the bearers of such identities to be partners – alongside feminists, environmentalists, anti-racists, activists around issues of diverse sexual orientation, opponents of the high-handed abuse of political power, and the like – within a broader community-in-the-making and within a universalizing democratic project of global, anti-capitalist transformation. This remains the bottom line. We will return to the matter of hope later in the present chapter.

Meanwhile, it is true that, yes, Marxists and other socialists are themselves ensnared in discourse; but it is a discourse – a moralizing science, a point of view, an entry-point – of class analysis and class struggle that is user-friendly, meaningful and important to us, and one that, politically, can be rendered important to many others. And not, I would suggest, as folded into the melting pot of diverse oppressions, diverse resistances and diverse movements, under such rubrics as radical democracy, but as articulated – non-reductively, non-economistically, non-Eurocentrically, but centrally – with them. For Marxist and other socialist discourses imply a crucial demand to transcend the structural and cultural limits of capitalism that is too easily lost to view, not only by postmodernists but also within the commonsensical hegemonies and glib universalisms that currently haunt us. It is a discourse that is both central to human emancipation and essentially non-cooptable either by liberalism or reformism. Of course, the demands Marxist/socialist discourse encompasses are corruptible, as history has demonstrated, but that is another, if by no means irrelevant, story. Let us merely affirm that, at bottom, class-based politics and anti-capitalism are too central to the cause of human emancipation to be drowned in difference, however sensitive we must be to the latter's claims. Struggle along such lines – at once methodological and practical – must continue.

Entry point 5: The Environment: What Environmentalists Are Fighting For

The "environmental fact" is perhaps the dimension of our larger social reality and of the political challenges that confront us that I have been slowest to think through. Indeed, the title of this section is not my own but one drawn from a challenging paper recently presented in Toronto by my nephew, Graham Saul, and it is from Graham and his activist comrades who focus on such issues that I am seeking to learn.[110] But other writings had already made it clear to me that the human species is, quite literally, fouling its own nest to a remarkable degree and that the feckless mantra of sheer unfettered growth and consumerism as chanted by a capitalist system that has so ensnared humankind merely goads the system down a dangerous path. True, there are some counter-tendencies (carbon taxes, anti-pollution sanctions, certain attempted environmental protections, and the like) but the outcomes of these have been, to say the least, mixed and inadequate. As Graham Saul writes,

> Humanity is extracting resources and converting forests, grasslands, and wetlands in farms and urban areas at an alarming rate. We are undermining our rivers, lakes and oceans by diverting freshwater for human use and dumping massive amount of chemicals like nitrogen and phosphorus into our waterways. We are also releasing a cocktail of toxic contaminants into the environment on a daily basis without fully understanding the impact they have on the health of humans and ecosystems.

To make matters worse, climate change is no longer a distant threat. It is happening today, with more severe droughts, increasing pressure on groundwater supplies and longer and more damaging wildfire seasons. Plant and animal ranges are shifting, coral reefs are dying, hurricanes are becoming more severe, oceans are acidifying, and heat waves and other extreme weather events are more frequent and intense.

Climate change is already killing people, destroying and displacing communities, undermining food security, sparking conflict and human migration, and spreading disease. But the sad truth is that we have barely begun to witness the scale of catastrophe that we will be facing if we continue on the trajectory we are on today.

In 2009, the prestigious health journal The Lancet argued "climate change is the biggest global health threat of the twenty-first century." Unless action is taken to reverse the trends, climate change will "put the lives and wellbeing of billions of people at increased risk," especially the poorest people in the world.[111]

How, then, to give such concerns the resonance they require in order to focus the political will and commitment that they demand? Not surprisingly, one of the collective preoccupations of the Toronto meeting was the search for a word or phrase to focus, galvanize and link the many fronts such a broad movement seeks to waken. After all, other parallel movements, those focused on confronting a variety of oppressions (class inequality, imperialist domination and racial and gender high-handedness) had found their battle-cries in stirring claims to entitlement: socialism, national liberation, black power and the vote, the various articulations of feminist concern (from the suffragettes to the "me too" movement). What should environmentalists be articulating as they sought to rally a broader constituency? But isn't their constituency, ultimately, all of humankind? Survival, then? But isn't that too bald, too daunting, too sobering, too much of a downer, to serve the purpose? And yet, isn't it an entirely apt rallying cry? Listen up, people, for in the not so long run we may all, quite prematurely, be dead!

True, the editors (Leo Panitch and Colin Leys) of another exemplary work that trained its sights on the environment as a major issue of human (and especially left) concern in its annual volume in 2007 (entitled *Coming to Terms with Nature*[112]) have argued, in resisting any such sloganeering, "that is important to avoid an anxiety-driven economic catastrophism that announces the inevitable demise of capitalism. A more complex understanding of the role of crisis and contradictions and required." It should be pointed out here that is not just capitalism but human existence that is in danger and that this risks being a final catastrophe. Still, Panitch and Leys emphasized that the fate of the environment "may well be the most important issue facing socialist in our lifetime,"[113] and they assembled, as contributors to their volume, a strong team of writers to consider the indifference of most capitalist governments and enterprises to such outcomes and the rising tide of "commodification of more and more areas of nature and life": in sum, the "growth-based consumerism" that define their policy choices, as well as the mushrooming rise of resistance on many fronts to what has largely been a case of official non-response. It is also true that they include in their volume a particularly strong essay by Michael Lowy entitled "Eco-Socialism and Democratic Planning,"[114] that merits further consideration here.

Lowy begins his essay with a quote from Richard Smith to the effect that

> If capitalism can't be reformed to subordinate profit to human survival, what alternative is there but to move to some sort of nationally and globally planned economy? Problems like climate change require the 'visible hand' of direct planning... Our capitalist corporate leaders can't help themselves, have no choice but to systematically make wrong, irrational and ultimately – given the technology they command – globally suicidal decisions about the economy and the environment. So then, what other choice do we have than to consider a true eco-socialist alternative?[115]

As Lowy then continues, "Ecosocialism is an attempt to provide a radical civilizational alternative to what Marx called capitalism's 'destructive progress.' It advances an economic policy founded on the non-monetary and extra-economic criteria of social needs and ecological equilibrium. Grounded on the basic arguments of the ecological movement and of the Marxist critique of political economy, the ecological synthesis – attempted by a broad spectrum of authors, from André Gorz (in his early writings) to Elmer Altvater, James O'Connor,

Joel Kovel and John Bellamy Foster – is at the same time a critique of 'market ecology' that does not challenge the capitalism system, and of 'productivist socialism' which ignores the issue of natural limits."[116]

It is a useful, even inspiring, essay but it does not end on an upbeat note. Lowy elaborates effectively on the overall problem and even finds rays of hope in how some attempts to "meet eco-socialist demands [that, as he highlights,] can lead to a process of radicalization if such demands are not adapted so as to fit in with the requirements of 'competitiveness.'" For then "partial victories being not only welcome in themselves but...contribute to [the raising of] ecological and socialist consciousness and...promote activity and self-organization from below." And both of these ingredients, Lowy argues, "would be necessary and indeed decisive pre-conditions for radical, i.e., revolutionary, transformation of the world." How then to frame such "partial victories" within a broader critique and a broader politics that could hope to win? Unfortunately, it is here, in his final paragraph, that Lowy feels compelled to sound that sobering note I hinted at above:

> There will be no radical transformation unless the forces committed to a radical socialist and ecological program become hegemonic, in the Gramscian sense of the word. In one sense, time is on our side, because the global situation of the environment is becoming worse and worse, and the threat are coming closer and closer. But on the other hand, time is running out, because in some years – no one can say how many – the damage may be irreversible. There is no reason for optimism: the entrenched ruling elites of the system are incredibly powerful, and the forces of radical opposition are small. But they are the only hope that capitalism's 'destructive progress' will be halted. Walter Benjamin defined revolutions as being not the locomotives of history, but humanity reaching for the train's emergency brakes before it falls into the abyss.[117]

Sobering indeed, and yet environmentalism must be a central component of the kind of resistances that we are alluding to here – I continue to learn from the likes of Graham Saul, Panitch and Leys and Michael Lowy – but I am also listening to those voicing related concerns in southern Africa, not least the eminent scholar-activist, Jacklyn Cock[118] in Johannesburg. Cock takes a lead from Leys and Panitch by echoing their view that "we must fight for new relation of humankind to nature," while writing that "an ecological transformation is required as part of a 'new liberation struggle' in South Africa." She urges the necessary "comprehensive and transformative change," one that could promise the "embryo of post-capitalist eco-socialist society." This in turn could help to underwrite new struggles against "the present fossil-fuel regime that is leading us towards ecological collapse and catastrophe," the move towards "socially owned renewable energy," the "collective, democratic control of production for social needs, rather than profit," and the "localization of food production [which would mark] a shift from carbon-intensive industrial agriculture to food sovereignty." All of which would imply a growing recognition that "the fundamental cause of deepening climate crisis" and other environmental challenges is "the expansionist logic of capital." She marshals considerable evidence that such a crisis does indeed face South Africa and she also gives a fine-grained account of a growing environmental movement in the country where, in her view, "new social forms...embody fragments of a vision of an alternative post-capitalist future." Here too, then, the struggle continues.

Entry point 6: The Class Struggle Plus
On Proletarian Messianism and the Precariat

Everywhere the logic of an ever more globalized capitalist economy has shifted the goalposts as regards both ongoing capitalist exploitation and also the resistance to it. We must begin by facing the fact that global capitalism, while still profoundly controlling of the world economy, no longer has the promise to transform the world in a positive manner. Nor is it vastly simplifying global social contradictions as it once was said to promise/threaten to do, and as Marx and Engels once thought it would:

> Our epoch, the epoch of the bourgeoisie, possesses... its distinctive feature: it has simplified the class antagonisms. Society as a whole is more and more splitting into two great hostile camps, into two great classes directly facing each other: Bourgeoisie and Proletariat...The bourgeoisie has stripped of its halo every occupation hitherto honored and looked at with reverent awe. It has converted the physician, the

lawyer, the priest, the poet, the man of science, into its paid wage-laborers...The other classes decay and finally disappear in the face of Modern Industry; the proletariat is its special and essential product.[119]

Instead, in much of the global South (and perhaps particularly in Africa) any such transformation has proven to have been, at best, incomplete. Global capitalism has certainly become a dominant reality, capable of imposing upon Africa, for example, a grid of continuing inequality, exploitation and the recolonization of ostensibly liberated and independent peoples in the interests of corporate profit. But the outcome is complicated in class terms, a matter that I explore in the essay "The New Terms of Resistance: Proletariat, Precariat and the Present African Prospect," which is, in part, reproduced here.[120]

For the socioeconomic system now in place in Africa (to go no further afield) is quite incapable of producing anything like the relatively straightforward, and theoretically bipolar and proto-revolutionary, society of bourgeoisie and proletariat that Marx and Engels anticipated, either now or in any foreseeable future. In fact, much of the global South is, quite simply, trapped between history's ostensible phases in ways that we shall have to examine. Undoubtedly a key feature of this shift is the ever-increasing saliency of what has come to be termed *precarious* work. We will have to explore this reality. But we will also have to examine the even more basic and more general reality of precarious populations existing throughout the global South – not least those who embody in their persons the phenomenal growth of the urban areas in Africa. What implications must this have for our time-honored sense of the working class as epitomized in its most organized and its most generic essentials – and also of our attendant sense of the revolutionary agency that the working class has, on the left, typically been thought uniquely to exemplify? How best now – in the world of both proletariat and "precariat" – to articulate the possible terms of any effective challenge from below to the inhuman, inequitable and exploitative capitalist system that continues to dominate Africa and to produce as many unsavory outcomes as it has? If not a proletarian revolution, what then?

Precarious Work in Africa and Beyond: The Ambiguities of the Working Class: Here we will let Wikipedia – because in its relevant entry it draws so heavily on the estimable scholarly work of Fudge, Owens and Vosko – give us a first lead on our topic with regard to "precarious work":

> Precarious work is a term used to describe non-standard employ-ment that is poorly paid, insecure, unprotected and cannot support a household. In recent decades there has been a dramatic increase in precarious work due to such factors as: globalization, the shift from the manufacturing sector to the service sector, and the spread of information technology. These changes have created a new econ-omy which demands flexibility in the workplace and, as a result, caused the decline of the standard employment relationship and a dramatic increase in precarious work. An important aspect of pre-carious work is its gendered nature, as women are continuously over-represented in this type of work. Precarious work is frequently associated with the following types of employment: "part-time employment, self-employment, fixed-term work, temporary work, on-call work, homeworkers and telecommuting." All these forms of employment are related in that they depart from the standard employment relationship (full-time, continuous employment with one employer). Each form of precarious work may offer challenges, but they all share the same disadvantages: low wages, few benefits, lack of collective representation, and little to no job security.[121]

Moreover, in Africa such a definition/description begins to describe the vast bulk of the urban population, so great in their numbers that, as many more flock into the urban areas, they are hard pressed to find any formal work at all, even of the kind most readily defined as being precarious – not so much precarious workers, then, as they are precari-ous populations. And it is here that the most orthodox Marxist may be tempted to give up in despair, faced with the reality of an emer-gent capitalist society very different from the kind – one much more straightforward, at least in theory, in terms of revolutionary potential – that Marx and Engels had foreseen (as quoted above) to be slowly but surely simplifying and clarifying social contradictions. Should we be surprised that some Marxists are tempted to view with such alarm the kind of society that a powerful but nonetheless non-transformative (or, at the very least, not as yet transformative) capitalism produces in Africa and elsewhere in the global South? For, to repeat, such inter-mediate (and not necessarily transitional) societies seem – in Africa certainly – very unlikely to produce some entirely straightforward and conventionally "bourgeoisie-proletariat" pattern of polarization in the foreseeable future.

Of course, Marx and Engels themselves spoke nervously of the social realities they saw to be scarring the transitional period to a full-bodied capitalism, noting, in particular, the possible resonance of a resultant (in their term) "dangerous class," one defined by them as

> the social scum, that passively rotting mass thrown up by the lowest layers of the old society, [which] may, here and there, be swept into the movement by a proletarian revolution; its conditions of life, however, prepare it far more for the part of a bribed tool of reactionary intrigue.[122]

As Marx writes elsewhere, "Alongside decayed roués with dubi-ous means of subsistence and dubious origins, alongside ruined and reckless casts of the bourgeoisie, were vagabonds, discharged sol-diers, discharged jailbirds, escaped galley-slaves, swindlers, mounte-banks, *lazzaroni* [lay-about/hobo], pickpockets, tricksters, gamblers, *maquereaux* [pimps], brothel-keepers, porters, literati [literary hacks] organ-grinders, rag-pickers, knife-grinders, tinkers, beggars – in short the whole indefinite, disintegrated mass, thrown hither and thither, which the French term *la bohème*."[123] In addition, in a second and related text, he speaks critically of the Mobile Guards, the most asser-tive strike force mobilized on behalf of France's reactionary Provi-sional Government, suggesting that

> they belonged for the most part to the *lumpenproletariat*, which, in all the big towns, form a mass strictly differentiated from the industrial proletariat, a recruiting grounds for thieves and criminals of all kinds, living on the crumbs of society, people without a defi-nite trade, vagabonds, *gens sans feu* and *sans aveu*, with differences according to the degree of civilization of the nation to which they belong, but never renouncing their *lazzaroni* character.[124]

This litany of not easily "classed" elements does not quite directly evoke African social conditions, though it points at a somewhat similar urban social milieu. To begin with, a much more gender-sensitive and diverse listing of urban dwellers would now be expected; women, for example, are crucial players in Africa both amongst the semi-proletarianized and within the cadre of urban sociopolitical actors than Marx and Engels' itemization would suggest. But the term lumpenproletariat cannot – and certainly should not – be so dismissively employed, not least with reference to the South African case. Not that the more settled and more organized working class need ever be displaced as a particularly central vector of possible progressive promise. Marx was the key thinker in emphasizing – and for good reason – the extent to which the concentration and centralization of this working class were central to its potential socialist aspirations and endeavors – and, indeed, in Africa and elsewhere the consciousness and organizational presence of the working class has often been central and crucial both to anti-colonial struggles and to resistances to contemporary recolonization. Yet, as we shall see, the sheer population living in the congested urban settings of Africa can also produce vital expressions of political energy in their own right – breaking the conceptual boundaries of conventional working-class action and finding voice in particularly dramatic ways, as we have seen most recently in Cairo and in Tunis. We will return to this.

It is also true that there is stratification within this vast mass[125] – shades of difference that can have pertinent sociopolitical effects amongst those below the elite and affluent. Such divisions within this lower tier of society can be diverse in provenance, and can have, for both good and ill, a wide range of expressions: contestations between criminals and their victims for example, or between those differentially defined in terms of gender, or diverse ethnic, national (think of the recent xenophobic excesses that have scarred South Africa, for example), and religious affiliation. Nonetheless, where full-time employment is a relative luxury and the availability of working-class organizations of self-defense a rarity, divisions within the urban mass along socioeconomic lines can also be important: not least between the fully employed who are generally more effectively organized at the worksite than are those who are more marginalized, precarious and often less well organized for worker and popular self-defense. Many decades ago Giovanni Arrighi and I employed, albeit somewhat controversially, the term "labor aristocracy" (for want of a better phrase) to distinguish these upper echelons of the poor (those relatively stabilized in employment) from those much more marginalized from capital's activities than themselves.[126] So controversial was this application of the term that I soon after (1975) felt myself forced to clarify and to qualify its use – though I first reestablished our earlier point:

> The "more privileged" and better organized workers have been encouraged to identify upward – to become partners (albeit the most junior of partners) in the jostling for surpluses among the internationally and domestically powerful (including more prominently in the latter category the elites and sub-elites themselves) – rather than to identify downward with the even more "wretched of the earth": the urban marginals and the average inhabitant of the...rural areas.[127]

But, I also added, in a capitalism in crisis the "classic strengths of the urban working class" could become "more evident," with "the upper stratum of the workers [then] most likely to identify downward [and become] a leading force within a revolutionary alliance of exploited elements in the society." And I also conceded that, in any case, the concept "labor aristocracy" – whether its usage had once been sanctioned (in his *Imperialism: The Highest Stage of Capitalism*) by Lenin or not – seemed a harsh one to apply to workers in Africa who remain, to this day, exploited and even more relatively disempowered and impoverished vis-a-vis the dominant circles of their societies than they are relatively empowered and privileged vis-a-vis their fellow denizens of society's lower orders. True, as Eddie Webster (one of my best-informed South African correspondents) notes,[128] there may be "more evidence for the concept's appropriateness now," but at the same time he also speaks strongly to this same point, thinking, to repeat, that its use is "misleading because neoliberal globalization is eroding the core of the labor market, making this 'elite' itself very precarious." Moreover and "secondly, even these core jobs are often below R2000 per month; and, thirdly, almost all workers share their income with a household with an average of five members." And yet, as we also know, such differences as distinguish these lower orders (as Webster adds: "to have a job at all in these times may be seen as a privilege rather than a curse") can also make for differences in terms of divergent class practices.

As a result, if we carefully frame any such divergences of interests and actions with reference to their social basis and to such matters as differential remuneration and job security and differing degrees of effective self-organization, they can be understood to likely to have tangible political weight in their implications. And this is true not merely within the working class, between the settled proletariat and the more precariously employed. But it is even more the case as between those of both these categories of proletariat and those of the urban precariat even more broadly defined – as further examination of the South African case will demonstrate. For the politics of urban dwellers per se as distinct from those of the urban proletariat (there is some obvious overlap between categories, nor should their preoccupations be seen as being contradictory) can have a dynamic and thrust of its own.

The realm of the precariat is that of street-level politics – as named and focused upon so effectively by Jonathan Barker, among others. A debate has arisen as to the import of such street-level politics[129] – not so much *workers take to the streets* as *street-dwellers take to the streets*. But we can say that in such circumstances we find people ready for sociopolitical upsurge (in both township and rural settings) – although their actions will perhaps be directed most forcefully against the state and the polity, their programs and their minions, rather than, directly, against employers and capital.

Perhaps, too, this latter kind of action is not quite as likely to readily expand into socialist challenge as are the workplace-centered confrontations of more formally "proletarian" provenance. And yet even translating workplace confrontation into socialist-style scepticism about, and hostility towards, capitalism per se takes creative political and ideological work to help it happen. More work is necessary to blend the two worlds of working-class/workplace protest and of urban-rooted protest into resistance at the highest level of clarity and consciousness, even if the varied resistances do implicitly set themselves against the same broader reality of capitalist control over, and definition of, the logic of the particular social milieu that provides the context of struggle. If we were to expand our definition of potentially revolutionary resistance to include both working-class and township fronts of struggle, is something in danger of being lost – namely, the kind of systemic, more formally proletarian, struggle, most often brought into confrontation at the workplace level? But were Marx and Engels correct in seeing "precarious politics" as being primarily dangerous[130] rather than as often being proto-revolutionary? Or is it not entirely possible to see these two worlds of resistance and protest as having the potential to relate to and to reinforce each other? If so, we might then ask of contemporary South Africa how we might hope to see the mix of clearly defined proletarian and precarian resistances being blended into a coherent and cumulatively counter-hegemonic project of genuinely socialist and democratic impact.

This circle can and must be squared. For there are certainly proletarians and even semi-proletarians in the global South generally (and in South Africa more specifically) who can come to develop a working-class consciousness that permits them to understand that their grievances with their specific employers should, even more fundamentally, be directed against the capitalist system. And there is also "a people" – poor people, marginalized in both urban and rural settings – who are as capable of sociopolitical upsurge as those engaged in confrontation at the workplace; these can perhaps be called an under-class/precariat (or even, in a far more metaphorical and much less scientific way, seen as members of the working class). In short, a politics that seeks to engage in a broad-based mobilization of both proletariat and precariat could indeed, if mounted deftly, have cumulative and positive revolutionary potential – even if a movement so defined is as much a left-populist movement as it is one that is working-class based. In fact, however, it must be something of both.

Lagos and Beyond: The Politics of Precarious Settings: What, in such terms, of Africa more specifically? Africa presents an increasingly urban setting, cities growing exponentially throughout the continent, with the population of places like Lagos or Cairo already reaching quite staggering proportions. Of course, this is a global phenomenon, as George Packer writes in an article on Lagos entitled "The Megacity," of the global South more generally:

> Around a billion people – almost half of the developing world's urban population – live in slums. The United Nations Human Settlements Program, in a 2003 report titled "The Challenge of the Slums," declared, "The urban poor are trapped in an informal and 'illegal' world – in slums that are not reflected on maps, where waste is not collected, where taxes are not paid, and where public services are not provided. Officially, they do not exist." According to the report, "Over the course of the next two decades, the global urban population will double, from 2.5 to 5 billion. Almost all of this increase will be in developing countries.[131]

But Packer's main focus is Africa and what is, for him, a megacity *par excellence*: Lagos in Nigeria. In that city, as he argues, "in 1950, fewer than three hundred thousand people lived." However, he continues, "in the second half of the twentieth century, the city grew at a rate of more than six per cent annually. It is currently the sixth-largest city in the world, and it is growing faster than any of the world's other megacities (the term used by the United Nations Center for Human Settlements for "urban agglomerations" with more than ten million people)." Indeed Lagos could, within the foreseeable future , have as many as twenty-three million inhabitants." And it is in such cities that urban dwellers can become socioeconomic actors in ways that may far transcend the proletarian and semi-proletarian descriptors that in past was applied to them. And this can be expected to have radical implications!

The working class? Yes and no. Thus, as Freund once wrote of Africa:

> While it might seem at first sight that urbanization and direct subjection to market production would have brought about a class of workers that could be relatively easily understood and subsumed under

the categories of capitalist industrial society familiar to Westerners there are problems...in comprehending labor...in the African city... Only a small section of African workers actually are wage workers operating in the sphere of mass commodity production. Nor is this section growing very significantly.[132]

Indeed, says Freund, "a conservative...estimate of the working population of the Nigerian metropolis of Lagos in the 1970s suggested that only a minority is to be found registered as wage workers." True, Freund's argument here antedates emergence of the massive Lagos evoked above. But the same point still holds. What is one to make of this mass, sometimes epitomized as the informal sector? As Freund continues,

The state in colonial times and often thereafter has taken an ambiguous stance at best towards the "informal" sector of the economy and those who work within it. Classic development theories focused on industrialization and its consequences in an urban context or the development of a prosperous peasantry in a rural one. The world of shanty towns, of corner stalls and makeshift sweatshops, of women selling little packets of flavoring for stew, individual cigarettes and bars of soap do not belong to the structures that it proposed and planned. It is supposed to be a mark of backwardness and a temporary phenomenon only. In reality, though, it is precisely the "informal sector" that has flourished most in post-colonial Africa and any serious assessment of the African workers has to give it a serious share of attention.[133]

Peter Gutkind had anticipated this point in an earlier analysis. Under colonialism, he stated, urbanization could only "produce a 'marginal' urban population who live in precarious conditions, exploited in one form or another by the dominant colonial group and relegated ecologically to the peripheries of towns and economically to the peripheries of a producing and consuming society." Indeed, he continued, the African city is best seen as being "made up of three basic population groups, a plebeian urban mob, workers and artisans."[134] True, Gutkind saw fit to characterize this heterogeneous urban population as having a broad-gauged proletarian consciousness. Again, "yes and no" must be the most accurate response, proletarian consciousness becoming, in such a formulation and as noted earlier, as much a metaphor as a scientific description. For what does such proletarian consciousness amount to since post-colonial urban Africa has not been so fundamentally altered structurally from its earlier colonial profile? No wonder that many have felt forced to understand in fresh ways the complexities of an unfinished transition to a cleanly and clearly defined (and polarized) capitalist-based society that might otherwise be thought to merely stymie revolutionary aspiration in present-day Africa.

Thus, observers like Ken Post and Phil Wright have persisted in taking a high road in their understanding of those social elements set adrift by a failed capitalist transformation. They take a first step in allowing our sense of class contradictions – and of class belonging – to be expanded, especially with respect to Africa and the rest of the global South. For there, in societies profoundly altered but not transformed by the impact of capitalism, the roster of those exploited (and potentially available for apparently class-based action) is far wider than narrow classist categories can hope to elucidate – and this is not just to speak of peasants/rural dwellers either. Hence their key formulation:

> The working out of capitalism in parts of the periphery prepares not only the minority working class but peasants and other working people and minorities for a socialist solution, even though the political manifestation of this may not initially take the form of a socialist movement. In the case of those who are not wage laborers (the classical class associated with that new order) capitalism has still so permeated the social relations which determine their existences, even though it may not have followed the western European pattern of "freeing" their labor power, that to be liberated from it is their only salvation. The objective need for socialism of these elements can be no less than that of the worker imprisoned in the factory and disciplined by the whip of unemployment. The price [of capitalism] is paid in even the most 'successful' of the underdeveloped countries, and others additionally experience mass destitution. Finding another path has...become a desperate necessity if the alternative of continuing, if not increasing, barbarism is to be escaped.[135]

Yet even this may not quite go far enough. Such forces do indeed struggle for equality, but not necessarily and primarily for socialism. This is the maelstrom of struggles that we have seen Jonathan Barker, above, epitomize in his writing[136] as constituting a world of protest and resistance that stretches beyond the workplace and often elaborates its politics in terms that are not readily recognized as progressive in the most conventional Marxist terms. Yet should we not recognize systemic contradictions where we find them? Barker, for example, sees the phenomenon he refers to as a "social response to the expansion of market logic into social relationships that have more than economic meaning to people." And elsewhere he speaks of the existence, in Africa and beyond, of "thousands of activist groups addressing the issues of housing, functioning of local markets, availability of local social services, provision and standard of education and abusive and damaging working conditions."[137]

As suggested, this does not mean that it will be easy to get the poor, both urban and rural, to see their negative situations in effectively proletarian and anti-capitalist terms. After all, the vector of oppression these poor often feel most tangibly is that of the state, the state that has been designated to police a semi-transformed society, and often to refuse, on behalf of capital and the locally powerful, legitimate popular claims for social services and social redress. Hence the tendency for the poor and the "untransformed" to give at least as much importance to street-level politics as to workplace contestation in defining the overall texture of their political aspirations and actions.

Indeed it is under such conditions that the left must be motivated, more imaginatively than ever (in terms of clear principle and by means of compromise and assiduous political work), to seek to draw the best of various claims and assertions (both street-corner and work-site) as arise from diverse but closely related contradictions into effectively counter-hegemonic projects.[138] These must become the claims and assertions that represent the highest common factor of their protagonists' social locations. These will include workers' specific shop-floor demands, but the poor more generally can be mobilized across a broader front and behind a revolutionary and eminently progressive left-populism that brings them to defy not only oppression per se but also the rule of capital. For we cannot stop at a more expansive class definition of agency. Instead, we must also make a positive force in our struggle for liberation of other tensions in society that can be wed to claims and assertions advanced in the name of class-defined redress if we are imaginative enough to do so.

Moreover, as Ralph Miliband has noted, capitalism's grossly uneven development around the world has produced "extremely fertile terrain" for the kind of "pathological deformations" – predatory authoritarianisms and those "demagogues and charlatans peddling their poisonous wares...of ethnic and religious exclusion and hatred"[139] – that, as with the spectacular success of such a right-wing populist as Donald Trump, now scar the global landscape. I would add: losing confidence in socialist and other humanely modern, humanely cooperative, projects, people turn for social meaning to more ready-to-hand identities, often with fundamentalist fervor. And yet, despite this, progressives committed to class struggle can and should continue to view such identities as contingent in their sociopolitical implications and as not necessarily being in contradiction with socialist purposes. And we should, when possible, invite the bearers of such identities – alongside feminists, environmentalists, anti-racists, activists around issues of sexual orientation and the like – to join us within a broader community-in-the-making and within a universalizing democratic project of global, anti-capitalist transformation. In fact, as Miliband continues,

> ...everywhere there are common goals and aspirations -- for democratic forms where they are denied and for more democratic forms where these are no more than a screen for oligarchic rule; for the achievement of a social order in which improvements in the condition of the most deprived – often a majority of the population – is the prime concern of governments; for the subordination of the economy to meeting social needs. In all countries, there are people, in numbers large and small, who are moved by the vision of a new social order in which democracy, egalitarianism and cooperation – the essential values of socialism – would be prevailing principles of social organization. It is in the growth of their numbers and in the success of their struggles that lies the best hope for humankind.[140]

And a corollary of this position is equally compelling: we on the left had better learn to operate in the complex world of diverse faiths, races and ethnic kinships, to unite such belongings to our cause of class liberation, or they will continue to return to haunt us – as merely divisive identifiers and claims that can, at their worst, turn rancid and dangerous to humane purpose. So, too, must gender-defined and environmental projects be ever more assertively articulated as being, not reducible to, but coequal with and potentially enlarged by an assertion of class considerations.

In short, one of our key goals must be, as argued above, to think of agency not merely in terms of abstractly defined working class interest. For such an apparently simple slogan of "workerism" – correct but excessively schematic – has presented far too open an invitation to arrogance and high-handedness (in the interest of the working class, don't you know) to left-wing vanguards, steeped in essentialist world views and ever quick to assert arrogantly what "the class" must and should do. Instead, we need to reach towards the range of shades of identity within and beyond strict class boundaries that can be won to revolutionary praxis. Not that tensions between diverse goals and purposes will then simply disappear. Yet seeking to realize such an enlarged project of "class struggle" also underlines the requirement of much more democratic methods of negotiation of both the means and the ends of revolutionary work than has characterized most past socialist undertakings – in mobilizing the forces both to launch revolutionary change and to sustain the process of socialist construction in the long run.[141]

There was a third sub-section to the original essay from which the emphases linked to this entry-point have been drawn; it is entitled "South Africa: Proletariat and Precariat." In it I acknowledge that South Africa is the country in Africa that has experienced a more modern and conventionally capitalist transformation than the rest of the continent – and it has had a greater degree of a recognizable proletarianization, due, in particular, to its dramatic (and ongoing) "mineral revolution" of the past 150 years. But it is also a society marked by the perpetuation and further growth of Marx's "dangerous class" of which we have spoken (those mired, especially in the vast urban townships, in the swamp of precarious work and less). It is certainly true, for example, that the organized working class has been a key player in the country's politics – a major actor, for example, at the intersection of class struggle and anti-apartheid assertion.[142] It was the crucial role played by COSATU as it emerged as the key center of organized black labor in the 1980s that gave observers, who were sceptical from quite early on as to the revolutionary credentials of the ANC/SACP, the sense that something much more radical was afoot in South Africa than could be easily imagined by the ANC and the SACP. Moreover, the promise was even wider than that epitomized by COSATU, for it also lay in the broader movement of township-based self-assertion on the part of many Africans of different genders and diverse social locations. Although this kind of popular assertion was not facilitated by the ANC's reassertion of its vanguardist mindset during its ascension to power,[143] it was to revive in opposition to the policies of state and ruling party in the 1990s and, especially, in the first decade of the new century.

Now some have begun to see the possibility of the dawning of a new kind of self-conscious joining of workplace and street-level assertions of the kind that had – thanks to the saliency and universality of apartheid as shared enemy – underpinned broad-based struggles in the 1980s. But I have written of this possibility elsewhere[144] and will not repeat that argument here, except to draw strength from Gillian Hart's related arguments. For there are two main schools of thought as to how to conceive the class belonging of those involved in the array of protests that has been occurring in contemporary South Africa. One view of this moment, as clearly exemplified by David Harvey and Patrick Bond, sees in the energies evidenced by these and other assertions of civil society the manifestation of a genuinely proletarian reality of struggle directly linked to other tangibly workplace-centered actions by those of more familiar working-class belonging. For such writers of the left, Hart continues, "the central task is to rip away the mask that obfuscates neoliberal class power [confident that] such an exposé will help pave the way for a coherent resurgence of mass movements ...[moving] beyond race, ethnicity, gender, and other dimensions of difference in order to achieve class-based solidarity in an increasingly dangerous world."[145]

But this is not quite good enough, Hart asserts. For Hart's position, she asserts, is ("*pace* David Harvey") that

> the task confronting the left in South Africa and elsewhere is considerably more complex than that of exposing neoliberal class power. Nor is it adequate to posit a shift from race to class apartheid. Most immediately, the ANC government's embrace of GEAR constitutes a re-articulation of race and class that is also part of an activist project of rule.[146]

Note too this last sentence: "class," "race," "rule" (and, in another context, she would no doubt add "gender"); small wonder that, for her, "the challenges facing the left are far more complex" than Harvey seems readily to countenance. Thus,

> The drama that exploded at Polokwane [site of Zuma's challenging of Mbeki] was as much about contesting the meaning of nation and liberation as it was about the fallout from a neoliberal class project and socioeconomic structure, and we ignore these sentiments and struggles at our peril.[147]

In sum, she is saying, the claims of a left-populism[148] that self-consciously takes the liberatory claims centered on considerations of gender, race and the exercise of democratic voice with great seriousness, must not be obscured by any too exclusive a preoccupation with the simultaneous reality of class determination.

To repeat: how best to square this particular circle: "class politics" vs. "a more broadly liberatory politics"? The short answer: both. For the Bonds and the Harts are equally correct, as far as they go. However, it is in making the two pieces of the puzzle – the puzzle as to what can and will drive the lower orders in their pursuit of equity – fit together for revolutionary purposes that the challenge lies. It is easy to see how they might not fit: the most organized of workers going deeper and deeper into the (minimally) gilded ghetto of privilege; township dwellers more and more seduced down the blind-alleys of the most dangerous of consciousnesses: criminality, xenophobia, ethnic rivalry and the like.[149] But, on both sides of the equation, such postures remain so far from being the whole story of workplace and township life that many South African activists reach for a different narrative, a different possibility.

Add to this the fact that, on both sides of the equation, claims are, at their best, being driven by a demand for equity and fairness, disturbingly liberal-sounding substantives in their vague and potentially windy abstraction, but words with meaning nonetheless. And one thing more: the varied terrains of struggle need each other. For class preoccupations pursued without full attention to the terrains of struggle for gender and racial equality and environmental security and for a guarantee of access to a democratic voice are as unlikely to make a meaningful revolution as are movements based on gender, race, voice and environment that don't take demands based on class considerations sufficiently seriously.[150] Genuine liberation, genuine socialism, genuine liberatory socialism, demand all four of these multiple components – and others besides, notably (as suggested) those evoked by environmental concerns.

Entry point 7: Democracy:
Beyond "Passive Empowerment"

So, there you have it: a multivariate left analysis certainly but one built, firmly, on the foundation of Marxist political economy. For I have continued to take up similar general issues even as I have brought my southern African preoccupations ever more front and center (see my 2012 essay "Race, Class, Gender and Voice: Four Terrains of Liberation."[151]) There I emphasized, alongside class, race and gender, the issue of "voice," with this latter concept seeking to underscore the necessity both to empower and to effectively institutionalize the expression of voice from below – this ensuring the primacy of a democratic practice and the assertion of the kind of control from below that is necessary within all political parties and within every conceivable state in order to preempt any and all temptations to unbridled vanguardism. For aren't the evils of vanguardism, whether it be of left or right provenance, one lesson we should all have learned from the grim story of twentieth-century politics?

Not that such eminently political considerations regarding the realities of political power have ever been absent from my work. I may have despaired of "political science" (the discipline within which I originally trained) from time to time and come to style myself a "political economist" or a "social scientist" in order to give full resonance, within a more unified approach, to the realities of class and the dynamics of economic realities as they helped define the concrete workings of power and influence. But I never lost my sense of "the political" per se, as linked with (but not subordinated to) my growing awareness of the realities of exploitation and the saliency of selfish interests as rooted in the economy at play. True, one of my very first books, co-authored with my friend (economist and later sociologist) Giovanni Arrighi, was indeed entitled *Essays on the Political Economy of Africa* (1973). I also included in that book a chapter entitled "Populism in Africa" which had been one of my very first publications when it was first included in their book on populism by Ghita Ionescu and Ernest Gellner only a few years earlier.[152] And my book with Arrighi was to be followed by my *The State and Revolution in Eastern Africa* (1979) that contained such chapters as "The State in Post-colonial Societies: Tanzania" and "The Unsteady State: Uganda, Obote and General Amin."[153]

Moreover, as time went by, my studies demonstrated to me that the apartheid state, for example, was as important to the workings of apartheid's oppressive system in South Africa as was the logic of capital. And was certainly not reducible to it. It was also true that each of the freshly liberated states of southern Africa that I knew so well (even the Mozambican state as directed by Frelimo) soon became, in one way or another, authoritarian ones that allowed chiefly for the political expression of the interests of global capital and those of the newly "liberated" black elites in immediate political control. In short, I was becoming, from this and other experiences, ever more suspicious of vanguardism, this in spite of understanding that leadership was a crucial variable in virtually every political setting. No, mine was a critique of self-righteous and/or self-seeking authoritarian political structures (however benignly they might occasionally have been intended).

Not that I have felt any inclination to switch over to faith in sheer voluntarism. For there certainly is a necessary role for political leader-

ship, albeit leadership in tandem with genuine democratic empowerment, from the bottom up, of the entire mass of the population. True,
this suggests a particularly complex dialectic. For the potential contradiction between leadership and mass action cannot be wished away:
with luck and honest effort it has to be resolved again and again over
time through concrete political practices. And yet, if there is one thing
the left could have learned from the twentieth century it is that vanguardism – while it may often sound like a good idea at the time – has
never produced a sociopolitical outcome that justifies its exorbitant
costs in terms of malignant authoritarianism and human suffering. Not
that this is an easy circle to square: leadership needs to lead, to suggest
and argue for a plausible way forward politically, socially and economically. But also needs to be checked by democratic pressure from
its followers if it is not to become dangerously arrogant and high-
handed in effecting its purposes.

And the fact is that this is a tension that cannot easily be resolved,
even in theory, reflecting as it does a contradiction and a challenge
that must be worked on self-consciously by all those who would seek
to effect progressive social change. Hence one must be drawn ever
more urgently to consider, carefully, the issue of voice. Of course, this
may not be entirely surprising given that I first trained as a political
scientist with issues like modalities of democracy and the nature of the
state being central. Nonetheless, I had to "come back" to politics for,
without ever quite abandoning a preoccupation with it, I realized that I
had never properly theorized such preoccupations; This was, perhaps,
because over the years I had seen enough of global capitalism in action
to become ever more acutely aware that the chief weakness of "political science" *per se* – as embedded in the intellectual work of most of
its practitioners – is its relative deafness to the crucial determinations
that production relations (both local and global), economic exploitation and economically grounded inequality impose upon the polity. It
was therefore easier to gravitate towards becoming a political economist than to be, narrowly, a political scientist. At the same time, it was
difficult in the long run not to recognize both the liberatory potential of
assertions framed in political terms (the demand for democratic voice,

for example) on the one hand and, on the other hand, the weight of the oppressive reality of corrupted political institutions – of party, military might and state – in their own right. Difficult to not find oneself posing some pretty basic questions: what, in sum, is liberation, after all, if not egalitarian in intent and democratic in practice?

In what ways and to what extent had southern Africa actually been liberated? How necessary was a second liberation struggle? It would clearly be foolish to downgrade or underestimate the scope of what has been accomplished, both in South Africa and throughout the region, through the overthrow of racial dictatorship. Nor should we underestimate the cruel constraints imposed by the fact that global capitalist hegemony is at its strongest in Africa and that western/global capital is reinforced in its power by working with and through the complex domestic structures of class and other divisions that the continent has to offer. After all, imperialism is determined to defend its own interests and it would be sheer voluntarism to ignore the severe constraints that have been placed upon the leaderships of the liberation movements come fresh to power in that region, not least upon those among them who had envisaged other, more progressive, possibilities. We must not, in short, fall into a voluntarist cul-de-sac by ignoring the diverse structures of cooptation that have too often pressed the southern Africa liberation-elites into becoming mere junior partners in the new Empire of Capital.

Yet one must also sense the danger that the loss of faith in principled voluntarism can give way to a far too comfortable acceptance of some supposed structural determinism. For this is what has allowed failed liberation movement elites to rationalize their passage into privileged positions as beneficiaries of a process of post-liberation domestic class formation with the self-serving excuse that "Imperialism made me do it"! No, questionable choices have been made in southern Africa, and they have not, by and large, been choices favorable to the life chances of the poorest of the poor or to their empowerment: to their liberation, in sum. For the facts are there, including the unsettling reality that even if in South Africa the income gap between black and white has narrowed somewhat, the gap between rich and poor has widened; that related gaps along similar lines could be readily documented in the spheres of health, education, food and the like; that democracy has stalled, even in South Africa, at the level of a relatively passive act of voting rather than an active engagement of people in the transformation of their own lives; and that the pace of a genuine levelling up of the role and status of women has slowed to a relative standstill. So, in the end, the question is not merely "what is liberation?" but, to repeat, whether the glass of liberation is best considered as being half empty or half full. And if, as I suspect to be the case, it is at best merely half full, we must seek to identify and to encourage such social forces (and their organizations) as we can reasonably expect to engage in a next liberation struggle. For the undertaking of such a struggle that will be necessary in order to further advance the cause of African liberation in its fullest, most multi-faceted and most meaningful sense.

Entry point 8: The Struggle for Socialism: The Possible Dream

What, then, can be said about any parallel struggle for socialism – for this is what there would have to be.[154] Africa is comprised of nations very different from Canada and other bastions of the G8 and the Global North and East. Of course, national sites throughout the world – north, south, east and west – are subject to the pressures of the global capitalist production marketplace and the workings of the Empire of Capital), although in markedly different ways. For example, I am confident, for reasons explained above, that some form of socialism (alongside the fruits of other attendant struggles: for greater racial and gender equality, for more firmly democratic political practices, and for a deeper concern for the environment, for example) is necessary to restore the social health of the currently dominant Northern and Eastern locations in the world. How much more important to the global South, so deeply scarred by capitalism and imperialism, is the kind of healing that only the realization of social justice and of self-consciously collective activity can promise it? So, I will concentrate on Africa, the continent I know best, in what follows, although the implications will be seen, I trust, to be more generally relevant in import.

There are those on the left who argue that such is the economic strength, selfishness and deeply ingrained ruthlessness of the Global North and East that the future of the global South – including the very availability of room within which it can begin to breathe socially and economically – can only occur if progressive changes first occur in the present centers of the global economy, thereby lifting the weight of Northern/Eastern economic and military power from the backs of their counterparts in the global South. Just the other day, for example, a letter comes from a friend, a comrade of vast African experience, replying, in private correspondence (and hence unnamed here), to my cry for help in the framing of a related argument:

> I am no clearer than you about how to move forward. I don't see how the South can ever liberate itself in the absence of a new social-ist project becoming powerful in the North and I don't see that hap-pening until people are hurting and see no prospect of meeting their personal needs under globalized neoliberalism, and until a new left movement with a serious attitude to organization and democracy (to both, that is) emerges to displace the social democratic collabo-rators with capital. And the trouble with that is that the right are more effective in the present situation, having resources, including the state's security apparatus, that the left will not have without a dramatic revival of militant trade unionism and a new left party. The rapidly deteriorating environmental situation will aggravate the problem, not help. All of which means that very much against my will and my nature I feel very pessimistic.[155]

Well, yes, and no. How indeed can one hope to confront such pes-simism of the intelligence (about Africa and about the world more generally) with an optimism of the will – which I take to characterize my own response to the grim realities of global inequality and exploi-tation – that goes beyond mere romanticism to ground itself in genuine possibilities of liberation? True, for socialists of the global South the task ahead will be a daunting one. Yet, as I have argued for decades, it is not an impossible one – even if, as is also true, any attempted socialist transformation in the South would be much reinforced by any serious effort here at home to transform the North too. Yet the truth is that residents of the global South cannot afford to wait.

Let's be clear about the limited claims of the present entry-point, however. Even if the South must find its own way forward, I have neither the wish nor the wisdom to elaborate detailed suggestions as to how socialists in the global South (and elsewhere) can realize their aspirations. Let me merely offer a few conceptual windows, synthesizing ideas from my earlier writings, that offer a less bleak prospect than may seem possible along these lines. And also give some clues as to how those engaged in socialist practice, particularly in Africa, might expect to navigate their way forward. What is to be done – and how? Even if mildly repetitive of some points made earlier in this chapter, I have chosen to include here my take on three main areas of necessary creativity in (as I originally proposed in the Canadian periodical *Studies in Political Economy* (#88, 2010) in an article entitled "Is Socialism Still an Alternative?") in responding to this challenge. These areas of inquiry concern the questions of revolutionary agency, socialist accumulation, and revolutionary/structural reform each of which might be of some help in ensuring a more effective range of future socialist practice including, not least, its essential democratization

(i) Beyond the working class and towards radical agency more broadly defined: expanding the constituency

Marx had good reason to emphasize the role of the working class in divining potentially revolutionary contradictions within an emerging capitalist mode of production: they were the most exploited (at least in the technical sense in which he deployed the word) and were also brought together as a potentially self-conscious class by the very capitalist dynamic of concentration and centralization that also defined its exploitation. It is not surprising that this formulation has served as the staple of left understanding and action since the nineteenth century.

As described above, within the working class there are also fissures and hierarchies and divisions (along lines of race, ethnicity, and gender, to go no further afield) that impede its self-consciousness and its praxis. As Leo Panitch affirms (albeit almost apologetically): "To speak of strategy for labor needs some justification today... Class, we have been reminded so often, is not everything." Still, he feels moved to add immediately, "But nor is class nothing."[156] Fair enough, yet I sense that Marxists must make even more of a virtue than this of the necessity to think outside the box of rigid class identities, especially in analyzing the realities of the global South. For there are, indeed, other things out there that are also "not nothing" (as we have ourselves argued above) and they are things entirely germane to our revolutionary aspirations.

For starters, our sense of class contradictions – and of class belonging – has to be markedly expanded, especially with respect to a global South that has been profoundly altered by the impact of capitalism but not totally transformed by it. For such societies, transforming but not transformed, provide a far wider roster of those who are exploited than the narrower classist categories of left discourse about Western capitalisms can hope to elucidate. I grounded this point in my original version of this article by synthesizing some of the points that I have touched upon earlier in this chapter and also by citing work (as quoted above) of such authors as Post and Wright, Jonathan Barker and Ralph Miliband in doing so. And I reiterated my sense that we can and must, in terms of clear principle and by means of compromise and assiduous political work, learn to draw the best of such claims and assertions as arise from socioeconomic contradictions into effectively counter-hegemonic projects that represent the highest common factor of their social locations and their most pressing demands, demands that add up collectively to defying the rule of capital. In short, we must invite feminists, environmentalists, anti-racists, activists around issues of sexual orientation and bearers of a whole range of identities to join up, alongside workers and precarians, within a broader left community-in-the-making to promote a universalizing democratic project of global, anti-capitalist transformation.

The alternative: if we on the left do not learn to operate in our complex world of diverse faiths, races and ethnic affiliations and to unite with such forces in pursuing our cause of class liberation, they will continue to return to haunt us – some of them becoming divisive identifiers that, at their worst, can turn rancid and dangerous to humane purpose. So, too, must projects concerned with gender and environment be articulated as coequal with, and illuminated by, class considerations.[157] In sum, we must seek to define agency not merely in terms of some rather abstractly conceived working-class interest. For any such simple slogan – correct but excessively schematic – presents far too open an invitation to arrogance and high-handedness (ostensibly in the interest of the working class) and to essentialist vanguards of all kinds, ever quick to assert arrogantly what the class must and should do. Instead, we need to reach towards embrace of the range of shades of identity within and beyond strict class boundaries that can be won to revolutionary praxis. Not that tensions between diverse goals and purposes will then simply disappear. Yet seeking to realize such an enlarged project of class struggle also underlines the requirement of much more democratic methods of negotiation of both the means and the ends of revolutionary work than has characterized most past socialist undertakings – with new method of work promising to better mobilize the full range of forces needed to launch revolutionary change and, in the longer run, to better sustain the process of socialist construction.

(ii) Grounding the delinking imperative:
globalization and the socialism of expanded reproduction

It would be naive to think that the increased globalization of the capitalist economy can somehow be ignored by advocates of a socialist alternative. Not only is the free global market a major point of reference for efforts by global capital (including those of its enforcers like the World Bank and the IMF) to enforce its writ, by force and/or by the seduction of Southern elites. The overbearing weight and allure of the global marketplace has its seductions, as a smorgasbord of sparkling goods are on offer and as an apparent source of quick and relatively easy profits and of the inflow of foreign capital. But the fact is that such capital is most often pegged to the production and overseas sale of mineral and other resources and to such limited additional production as meets the consumer needs of resident elites. How, then, to balance – on some kind of national developmental balance-sheet of left provenance – costs and benefits? And how to factor in new and essential kinds of democratic control over such linkages as are being established?

For only some such control can expect to make countries of the global South the beneficiaries rather than the victims of global embrace. Without this, there is no intrinsic magic of the market, no equal exchange between rich and poor; there is only, with the market left unchecked, the upward redistribution of resources from poor to rich.

Samir Amin points a way forward only through an ever more radical decolonization from central capitalist control. In his dramatic formulation, this would demand an actual delinking of the economies of the global South from the Empire of Capital that otherwise holds the South in its sway.[158] But I have highlighted Amin's delinking formulation earlier in this chapter and will return to in the final paragraphs of this book. What it does minimally demand, however, is the substitution of the present political economy of recolonization with an alternative that tilts effectively towards delinking as a notional goal, one founded on a new project of genuine socialist planning – established on a national or regional scale – that seeks to smash the crippling (il)logic of present market limitations upon development.

This, in turn, suggests the need for a program that, following the formulations of Guyanese economist Clive Thomas which I will also mention in Chapter 6 in the discussion of Tanzania (where Thomas, from Guyana, taught in the 1970s). For Thomas' model insisted upon "the progressive convergence of the demand structure of the community and the needs of the population"[159] – this being the very reverse of the market fundamentalist's global orthodoxy. On this basis one could then ground, he proposes, a "socialism of expanded reproduction" – one that refuses the dilemma that has heretofore undermined the promise of the many socialisms that have proven prone to falling into the Stalinist trap of violently repressing mass consumption in the name of the supposed requirements of accumulation. For, far from accumulation and mass consumption being warring opposites, the premise would now be that accumulation could be driven forward by finding outlets for production in meeting the growing requirements, the needs, of the mass of the population.

Such an industrialization strategy would thus base its expanded reproduction on ever increasing exchanges between city and country, between industry and agriculture, with food and raw materials moving to the cities and with consumer goods and producer goods (with the latter defined to include centrally such modest items as scythes, iron ploughs, hoes, axes, fertilizers and the like) moving to the countryside. Collective saving geared to investment could then be seen as being drawn essentially, if not exclusively, from an expanding economic pool. Note that such a socialism of expanded reproduction makes the betterment of the people's lot a short-term rather than a long-term project and thus promises a much sounder basis for an effective (rather than merely rhetorical) alliance of workers, peasants and others and for a democratic road to revolutionary socialism.

This emphasis is not intended to underestimate the potential importance of South-South relations or of those linkages, as foreshadowed in the World Social Forum, that seek, multinationally, to sponsor a redefinition of the workings of the global economy. Nor, on another level, is it a call for the extirpation, within the national economy, of any and all market relations – dangerous though these undoubtedly can be in terms of the possible generation of class differentiation that they imply. For if the predominant importance of the kind of planning (democratic and needs-focused) that we have suggested is maintained this will ensure that the center of gravity of the economy remains egalitarian, collectively premised and popularly centered; we may in this way also counter-balance the costs of any judicious deployment of the market and thus also avoid unduly risking the overburdening of public enterprise and the planning mechanism. Yet the bottom line is this: a self-consciousness about societal transition away from market power and entrepreneurial class interest is absolutely crucial. For the bourgeoisie, foreign or domestic, will play no role that could justify any claim it might seek to make in order to claim for itself inordinate wealth or superordinate power.

(iii) Democratizing the struggle: revolution by "structural reform" and popular empowerment

One final term we need to interrogate here is the word "revolution." It is a tempting word since we know how big and aggressive is the capitalist enemy that must be overcome if we are to realize anything even proximate to a socialist alternative. But perhaps, despite this, it's just a bit too tempting – and somewhat too romantic – a notion. For what we have seen so far suggests that the "socialist revolution" will not spring easily from some sudden social paroxysm nor be consolidated quickly or well, even (or perhaps especially) under the leadership of some unusually beneficent and wise vanguard.

It is in rethinking along such lines, particularly about southern Africa but also more broadly, that I've been drawn, over the years, to the writing on "structural reform" of such authors as Andre Gorz and Boris Kagarlitsky.[160] The point of their argument is relevant both to the phase of building a successful movement of revolutionary intent and to building socialism once such a movement is in power. Gorz makes a key distinction right from the outset between a "genuinely socialist policy of reforms on the one hand [and] reformism of a neo-capitalist or 'social-democratic' type" on the other. Thus, he writes, "If [most often] immediate socialism is not possible, neither is the achievement of reforms directly destructive of capitalism. [Yet] those who reject all lesser reforms on the grounds that they are merely reformist are in fact rejecting the whole possibility of a transitional strategy and of a process of transition to socialism."

Yet what, within such a transition, is to distinguish "structural reform" from "mere reformism"? There are two chief attributes of the former kind of reform. One lies in the insistence that any reform, to be structural, must not be comfortably self-contained (a mere improvement) but must, instead, be allowed self-consciously to implicate other necessary reforms that flow from it as part of an emerging and ongoing project of structural transformation in a coherently left-ward direction. Secondly, a structural reform cannot come from on high: instead it must root itself in popular initiatives in such a way as to leave a residue of further empowerment – in terms of growing enlightenment/self-consciousness and in terms of organizational capacity – for the vast mass of the population who thus strengthen themselves for further struggles, further victories: "The emancipation of the working class [and its allies] can become a total objective only if in the course of the struggle they have learned something about self-management, initiative and collective decision – in a word, if they have had a foretaste of what emancipation means."[161]

My initial proposal (presented some years ago in the *New Left Review*, but still apposite) on this approach to transformative/revolutionary/socialist endeavor elicited some favorable response but also sharp criticism from the likes of Alex Callinicos (a noted "big bang" theorist of socialist revolution) in a subsequent issue of *NLR*.[162] The latter chose to see my advocacy of structural reform as "a detour on, rather than an abandonment of, the road to revolution" – but also as representing a serious mistake on my part. And yet my claim was even bolder than Callinicos suggests, and I would stand by it as an appropriate amendment to much conventional language.

I argued that there is good reason to insist that a strategy of structural reforms not be seen as being, at best, some mere detour but rather, under most circumstances, as being the essence of revolution – and that that's a good thing too. For it suggests a model of socialist activity that can force the most unromantic reading of the odds against any immediate transformation of existing capitalist circumstances and yet permit a definition of sites, modes of struggle, tactics and strategies that open up the possibility of moving towards a transformation. Moreover, it promises to underscore the saliency of substantive issues (rather than vague revolutionary nostrums) in terms of which leaderships can most effectively be held to democratic account by their constituencies and these very constituencies can become ever more conscious of their very classness – not as some theoretical given but as the practical content of their own lives and public activities.

In the real world there are many temptations to abandon the lessons articulated above and also to abandon reasoned strategy in favor of militant rhetoric: in short, to choose vanguardist self-righteousness over processes of dialogue and negotiation between and among comrades. For the slow, negotiated accretion of a culture of socialist common sense within which conflicting claims on the left – as to specific issues or as to overall direction – can be democratically debated and resolved is key. As distinct from a liberal consensus as ground for political contestation, we need to work towards the establishment of an emerging socialist consensus, not at the expense of politics and difference but as the ground for their fullest expression and debate: for real debate and struggle, in short, but on the increasingly agreed grounds of shared socialist and democratic premises and not capitalist and liberal ones.[163]

Callinicos, for his part, flags many dangers in such an approach. Certainly, one mustn't be naive: the side of resistance to revolutionary change – the dominant class, its military and its external backers (as in many of the struggles against white power during the initial years of liberation struggle in southern Africa) – will often play pretty violent hardball.[164] Then the escalation of confrontation may sometimes, of necessity, pass beyond the boundaries of anything like structural reform – though with long-term costs to socialist and democratic outcomes that can be severe. After all, the cost, human and political, of such necessary escalation is one of the main reasons why many of us continue to fight so hard against the current imperatives of class and profit within our western societies that so often put our governments on the wrong side of struggles for freedom in the global South.

Yet to simultaneously caricature the claims (and virtues), under many conditions of revolutionary endeavor, of structural reform and of the creative tensions that it can promise, seems to mean, by definition, no opposing leaders, no conflicting political organizations or popular initiatives, no differences of opinion about strategy and tactics – in effect no politics – within the broader movement that claims to be seeking a transition to socialism. Indeed, when a thinker like Callinicos comes up against the complexities that real politics can reveal, he tends to back away and merely invoke that magic talisman, mass struggle, to outrank competing arguments. For if we have learned nothing else from the history of socialism it is that substituting the pure flame of revolutionism for the hard calculation and subtle politics of structural reform is a recipe for disaster.

As Boris Kagarlitsky concludes, in a text that emphasizes the crucial potential importance of structural reform to the struggle for socialism, Marx "was convinced that reforms prepare not only for revolution but also for socialism. In other words, for Marx the value of reforms was not in that they undermined the old system – sometimes they even strengthen it – but in their creation of elements of the new system within the framework of the old society. This theme in Marx's theory has been completely ignored by revolutionaries and reformist social democracy alike."[165] But such a silence cannot be allowed to continue if success in a long, wearing struggle for socialism is to become a possibility.

It would be naive to think that – even if we asked better questions and acted more clear-sightedly to answer them – all would then be clear sailing. After all, those on the side of global capitalism are also active on the side of their own cause. Indeed, it is no accident that, as I have quoted elsewhere and do so again here, Adam Przeworski could dourly conclude of the present global conjuncture: "Capitalism is irrational, socialism is unfeasible, in the real-world people starve: the conclusions we have reached are not encouraging ones."[166] Yet a genuinely liberatory socialism is not as unfeasible as writers like Gabriel Kolko, John Gray and Adam Przeworski may think.[167] Difficult to realize, certainly. Risky for those who try to do so, definitely. But it will be well worth the candle when, in its full and expansive meaning, we may ultimately see it come to pass.

C: The Science and Practice of Hope

But is it impossible to strike the kind of balance between democracy and socialism that can underpin a more humane outcome than any we have known? That will be difficult to accomplish, certainly, and risky too, if/when those on the other side become especially determined to actively defend their own "interests." And we are no angels either, for the pervasive lure of consumerism and the pull towards lazy social indifference bred by the capitalist dreamworld of possessive individualism are extremely strong, even amongst the dispossessed. In sum, there are many contradictions to be resolved. And yet a left response to them does continue to surface: the buildup to Marikana in South Africa, for example, and some of its subsequent reverberations, the Occupy Wall Street movement in North America, and the antagonism felt towards the one percent worldwide. But these same grievances can too often be channelled into the most narrow of essentialist and ultra-right political channels: from Trumpism to right-wing racism to religious essentialism and the like. How do we keep the hope for something better and more positively transformative alive?

The objective conditions of deprivation and disempowerment play a role here, of course. But how do they translate into clarity and confidence of purpose in seeking to reshuffle a stacked deck? And here, one of the chief tasks of the ideological and organizational efforts is, precisely, to build a base of committed people with leftist attitudes and the sense that change is both necessary and, even more, that it is possible. Too often Marxists have fallen back on the "objective conditions" provided by exploitative realities to assume that radical politics will follow. But what is missing here is the consolidation of intention, something Marxist – but not too many ordinary folks, it seems – have been too inclined merely to read off the supposed logic of pre-existing class-defined conditions rather than to probe more carefully the complexities of self-willed and self-conscious intentionality.

And yet there are Marxist resources to be drawn upon to help deal with this issue, notably the thinking of Antonio Gramsci and of Ernst Bloch, for example. Thus, John Merrington sees Gramsci (like György Lukács, whom Merrington also mentions in this respect) "moving beyond the terms of the earlier 'revisionist debate' – both 'revolutionaries' and 'reformists' had remained locked within the same basic problematic – carrying out a new diagnosis and prognosis from their experience of the postwar defeat, placing a renewed emphasis on the active, voluntary component of social change, on the problem of agency in the making of revolution." For "the recurring tendency of Marxism to become petrified into a schematic system of fixed categories, eternally valid, invoking concepts rather than rediscovering them in relation to each new conjuncture, has made the work of Gramsci particularly relevant." What, then, were the general features of Gramsci's renewal of Marxism, Merrington asks.

A precondition for such a renewal was for Gramsci, as for Lenin and Lukács, the rejection of "economism" in all its forms, the tendency to reduce the levels of the superstructure to the status of "appearance" or "phenomenon." In the hands of the "professorial" Marxists of the Second International, this tendency had produced an evolutionary-determinist conception of history, governed by objective laws whose unfolding lay beyond the scope of human intervention. The practical result was a catastrophic fatalism in the face of events, sustained by a blind belief in the "forces of history," in the inevitable collapse of capitalism due to its internal contradictions...[In short] a widening of focus requires a new emphasis on the roles of consciousness and ideas in the transformation of society.[168]

What was necessary, in sum, for such a "transition from the purely economic struggle" to occur was a "new conception of the role of ideology, of the 'intellectuals' (in a broad sense, of all those who have an organizing and educative role), [and] an emphasis on the voluntary character of the revolutionary organization as an agency bringing about the transformation of consciousness and cultural renewal at all levels of society."[169]

Ideology and organization: much work remains to be done certainly, both then and now, to create a new future, but its necessary parameters begin to become somewhat clearer, and all the more so if we add the insights of Ernst Bloch into the equation.[170] For Bloch took his Marxism in a rather different, if equally stimulating, direction, not merely reinvestigating the past and the present to define new revolutionary possibilities but, most centrally, blasting on into the future: the world of the not yet conscious, of the complementarity of Utopian imagination and real possibility, of the concrete Utopia and the liberation of the Utopian function, of the reclaiming of the terrain of fantasy, of "remembering" the future, and of the principle of hope.[171] For Bloch knew that, given the odds (and the raw power of capital and other complementary forces) stacked against radical transformation, those who had most to gain from transformation would have to learn how best and most clearly to hope, to learn how to embed such hope within the real world of existing possibilities, and learn how to act most effectively in terms of such hope.

Thus, even while taking strength from Marx's analysis of the objective conditions of revolutionary possibility being created by capitalism's evolution, Bloch nonetheless argued that this merely defined an opportunity that could only be seized upon if enough people began to have a realistic hope for the realization of a different kind of future. And possibility is just that, the reference being to a range of possibility but not to inevitability or even to probability. Bloch's deployment of Marxism allows him to mark out a frame of reality that indicates the parameters, not of rootless, speculative utopian daydreaming, but of a much more grounded kind of utopian thinking and acting. For Bloch, the tension is manifest. The range of the not-yet-conscious is real enough to set genuine goalposts for the art, science and practice of the possible but it does not seek to determine outcomes. Humankind must act to push at the outer limits of the parameters of possibility, but as to the nature of the new we are, with respect to many of its particulars, not-yet-conscious. "Man makes his own history but (s)he does not make it just as (s)he chooses"; this defines the centrality of Marx's "Theses on Feuerbach" to Bloch's intellectual project. But it also delineates the assistance Bloch is prepared (over three volumes) to give us in beginning to think our way towards the grasping the "not-yet-conscious" and to be further empowered to act in terms of it.

So, how are we to become more conscious about the "not-yet-conscious"? Bloch in his voluminous writing – and especially in the three-volume *The Principle of Hope* – is intent upon alerting us to some of the resources necessary to thinking and imagining such futures and acting upon their possibility. For such possibility must both be situated within the material reality of the context within which we find ourselves and have the parameters that reality defines ever subject to challenge by the creativity and imagination of the human mind. A dialectic of change, indeed, but don't take my word for it: search out the three volumes for yourselves. For in them (and in his other books) Bloch takes us on a masterful tour of the (primarily Western) cultural resources for consolidating a new sensitivity towards possibility, a new openness to hope, a new, more efficacious and more humane aspiration for the social home that human beings could yet build, one rooted in reality but subsuming that reality in both aspiration and achievement. A socialist revolution in new clothes, both philosophically and in actuality, as it were.

Bloch was a Marxist, of course; indeed, at times and at one level he could even be a fairly rigid one, his theoretical work perhaps occasionally bordering on an unpromisingly absolute class reductionism. And yet, simultaneously and even when he took class determinations quite seriously, he stopped short of a rigid class determinism. For he saw no inevitability based in class positioning as necessarily producing either a particular form of class consciousness or a particular modality of class action; indeed, Bloch argued quite to the contrary, and therein lay what was his most important intellectual contribution. For radical class consciousness, Bloch asserted, could only be expected to catch fire when linked to a firm and solidly based sense of class possibility, and to the emergence and consolidation of the hope (again, his key concept) that circumstances were such that something better could and must be realized. In short, what was needed was a sense that only acting on hope grounded in the possible could make the creation of a human utopia practical and, through committed and conscious political effort, fully realizable.

Interestingly, *The Principle of Hope* was largely written in the (somewhat) liberal confines of the United States in the years after Bloch's effective exile from Nazi Germany (this to be followed by an unhappy postwar sojourn in East Germany before the final phase of his academic life spent in West Germany). True, Bloch was so opposed to what he found to be the soul-numbing socioeconomic world of western capitalism that he retained too strong a loyalty to Stalinism's brutal politics to provide us with fully reliable counsel. Most important, however, was his sustained sense in his work that somewhere in the tension between "the actual" (as defined and analyzed most clearly by Marx, in his view) and "the possible" (a possibility often felt by people to be so, even though "not yet" ever fully realized by human beings) – was a way home to the better life that we all can and must discover. Indeed, this is the point where science and hope meet: we push, aided by scientific understanding, at the very edge of possibility even as our utopian sensibility begins to learn from the parameters of the new social world that we hope, even expect, to build.

SECTION II

In Person:
From Theory to Practice

Chapter 2

Rear-View Mirror: David McDonald Interviews John S. Saul

This interview was conducted several years ago by my friend David McDonald for a festschrift being prepared in my honor by two of my ex-students, Carolyn Bassett and Marlea Clarke, eventually published in two issues of the South Africa-based *Journal of Contemporary African Studies*,[1] which include an edited version of this interview in the second of its two issues. The original interview as here restored traces my evolving pattern of political work as well as a record of my writing and research over decades. Primarily, the focus is on my southern Africa-linked practical and scholarly activity and was intended to add to our collective understanding of that region's achievements and continuing travails. But it also seeks to understand the shifting patterns of change and "development" in Canada and in the wider world that have helped to define southern Africa's emergent situation. My moves across different sites of activity and different foci of intellectual emphasis are recounted and the dynamics of my overall enterprise of support for and involvement in the struggle for a free southern Africa, a struggle carried out both in the region and in North America where our governments and corporations have continued to be on the wrong side of various relevant struggles, are discussed.[2] Several years have passed since the interview was carried out, however, and while I have included it here in pretty much its original unabridged form I have updated some publication details and added a brief postscript to bring the account forward.

John S(hannon) Saul has come a long way from a North Toronto childhood – at John Ross Robertson Public School and Lawrence Park Collegiate – to an ongoing political and intellectual practice well to the left on the Canadian and international political spectrums. Africa has been key here, with periods spent teaching, writing about, and participating in attempts to realize profound social, political and economic change – genuine liberation and effective socialism – in Tanzania, Mozambique and South Africa.

These were also years of active engagement on the left in Canada, working, in particular, as an activist in the southern African/anti-apartheid solidarity movement: seeking to raise committed consciousness amongst Canadians as to the human importance of ongoing struggle there. Such a commitment has also involved challenging the social and economic structures – capitalist and imperialist – that so often moved official Canada to support the wrong side in southern Africa during the years of white dictatorship. Moreover, such structures, Saul has argued, have led Canada to participate to the more recent recolonization (by capital) of that region.

An author of note (some 26 volumes over the years and a vast number of academic and popular articles), an editor (*This Magazine, Southern Africa Report*), and an activist (notably with the Toronto Committee for Southern Africa (TCLSAC)), Saul remains committed to anti-imperialist/anti-capitalist work in Canada, Africa and elsewhere.

David McDonald: *You've been involved in liberation struggles in Southern Africa for a long time. When and why did you first get involved?*

John S Saul: I first went to Africa to teach in Tanzania from 1965 to 1972. Those were exciting times, the years of the Arusha Declaration and of the heyday of Tanzanian socialism. I became involved, as did many others, in the struggles for change that then took place throughout the society – principally, in my case, in efforts to move the university too in a more socialist-relevant (in terms of pedagogy and academic practice) direction. True, as things transpired, I was soon to be fired for such activities by Canada's External Aid, my original employer, but I was then strongly encouraged by my colleagues to take up a local contract. This I did quite happily for a number of years (although, as the contradictions inside Tanzania deepened, I was eventually to find that contract terminated as well). But I had learned a great deal and written a lot (especially with Giovanni Arrighi and Lionel Cliffe) during my years in Dar and had made many close friends, both Tanzanians and expatriates.

In addition, Dar es Salaam during those years was the key center for various liberation movements engaged in struggle in the white-ruled territories further south – and I got to know them all. This was especially true with respect to Mozambique's Frelimo, for I was soon working with them on their English-language publications while learning a great deal more, as I went along, about what was happening in southern Africa more generally. Then, in 1972, and as I prepared to leave Dar, Samora Machel, Frelimo's president, came to see me and invited me to travel with a group of Mozambican guerrillas deep into their country to see the liberated areas there and to gauge the meaning of Frelimo's struggle. When I got back to Tanzania from this "long march" Machel then asked me to speak out, when I returned to Canada, about Frelimo's efforts and about what I had learned. Looking back, I can see that my lifelong involvement in the struggle for liberation in southern Africa, and in encouraging Canadians to also take it seriously, was grounded both in this direct experience and in Samora's request.

DM: *In retrospect, the late 1960s and early 70s were particularly fertile years for progressive scholarship and activism in Africa. Were you aware, at the time, of how momentous this period was, and how did it shape the way you saw yourself as a scholar-activist?*

JSS: You're right, it was a fertile moment indeed. In Tanzania, in Mozambique, in southern Africa more generally, you felt that you were swimming with the tide of history for a change, and not merely against it. There were people – I think in particular of Cabral, Eduardo Mondlane, Samora Machel – and movements (Frelimo certainly) in which you could ground both your hopes and your writing as a comrade in revolutionary change as well as a careful scholar: a "scholar activist," as you say.

We were well aware of countertrends: Frantz Fanon's *Wretched of the Earth* became a particularly resonant point of reference in both my teaching and writing during these years, especially his powerful Chapter 3, "The Pitfalls of National Consciousness." We also knew – as I would discover at closer hand when I returned to Canada in 1972 – that western countries and global capitalism did not wish such revolutionary aspirations in southern Africa well: indeed Frelimo was to invite me, of all unlikely people, rather than the Canadian government, to come to Maputo on behalf of our now active Toronto Committee for the Liberation of Southern Africa (TCLPAC) in order to represent the Canadian people at Mozambique's independence day celebration in 1975 – because Canada had been on the wrong side, the side of Portuguese colonialism, during their struggle.

In short, in a whole host of ways we did know that something momentous was afoot, part of a promising global shift towards socialism and genuine independence that was even more clearly exemplified by Vietnam's historic victory. And we basked in it and took inspiration from it – even though, momentous as it was, the "moment" of triumph also proved to be transitory. To be honest, we didn't quite grasp how fleeting such victories would prove to be, or how strong the forces pulling southern Africa back into the orbit of recolonization actually were.

Despite this, there's no doubting that these instances of genuine accomplishment – like the ongoing struggles for freedom that, beyond 1975 and well into the 1990s, continued in Zimbabwe, in Namibia and in South Africa – shaped many of us profoundly. Cumulatively, living this history helped lock me firmly into the role of "scholar-activist" – ever more committed to anti-capitalist/anti-imperialist politics, to a closely-linked intellectual practice as both teacher and writer, and to the genuine liberation of Africa. As I still am.

DM: *Can you expand a bit on the ups and downs of the past 50 years of struggle in the region: What would say have been the biggest successes (sustained or otherwise) and what have been the biggest disappointments?*

JSS: The past 50 years have seen both successes and disappointments, the biggest success being, without question, the removal, by armed liberation movements and by dramatic popular mobilization, of the parasitic – "evil" seems not too dramatic a word for it – grip of racist rule as defined by the dominance of whites in firmly institutionalized positions of power (riding apartheid and other such malevolent ideological vehicles). Of course, the long-term results have not as yet turned out quite as we hoped they would: in terms of the attendant realization of class and gender equality and the establishment of genuine democratic control by the poorest of the poor in the region. Yet this, in political and cultural terms, was a great triumph – and one that, due to heroic efforts by the people of southern Africa, occurred rather against the odds.

One must hope that some memory of the accomplishments of the thirty years war for southern African liberation (1960-1990) survives, however, for it could be one resource useful to any attempt to spawn a next liberation struggle. And make no mistake: this is what is desperately needed presently in southern Africa. Indeed, to return to the question asked, the failure of the region's liberation struggles, once their leaders had come to power, to make any very dramatic difference, economically and in many other ways, to the lives of the vast mass of the population there constitutes the greatest single disappointment of recent years, both for residents of the region as well as for any committed outsider who would wish the peoples of southern Africa well. Put simply, the region has been recolonized by global capital in the wake of its ostensible liberation and the grim results – in terms both of continuing poverty and exploitation by capital, both global and local, and of an absence of any meaningful popular empowerment – are all too evident.

DM: *The neoliberal turn of the African National Congress (ANC) in South Africa has been one of these disappointments. Mainstream analysts tell us that the ANC had no choice but to become market-friendly – given the collapse of the Soviet Union and the potential for white, reactionary revolt – and yet there seemed to be a period in the early 1990s where a more transformative politics seemed possible. What, if anything, do you think could have shifted the balance at that time?*

JSS: The simplest answer would be that the ANC leadership had come, primarily, to represent aspirant black middle-class elements (a tendency never, from the outset, far from the surface of the movement in any case) who saw little advantage to themselves in the pursuit of more egalitarian and socialist policies. The Soviet Union argument is a bit of a canard here because, although that country had been close to many in the ANC leadership, it exemplified no real socialist alternative anyway, entirely hostile to the kind of democratic empowerment of the mass of the South African population that could alone have dissuaded the ANC leadership from taking the line of least resistance towards global capitalism.

That said, it is also true that great pressure from the global capitalist system was also crucial. As were both "white" mining, financial and commercial capital players within the country and the full range of additional black aspirants, from within the state and private sectors (the Black Economic Empowerment set), to personal economic advancement. To deflect these pressures would have required a great deal more commitment to popular mobilization and continuing struggle to realize a broad-scale liberation than the ANC (including, I'm sorry to say, Mandela) was interested in.

For starters there was probably more room for active popular empowerment, egalitarian policies, and defiance of imperial dictate – in the honeymoon period of possibility that existed after first overcoming apartheid at any rate – than the ANC ever conceived of availing itself of. The questions then multiply: Did the ANC elite become too comfortable in their novel power and privilege? Were they simply tired of struggle? Or perhaps too nervous about the risks involved in defying a generally hostile world? Or what?

For the fact is (as longtime ANC and SACP cadre Rusty Bernstein has emphasized in a private [but since published] letter he wrote to me) that, either due to mere class opportunism or to failure of nerve, they turned their backs on genuine mass politics (running down rather than further enabling any independent and ongoing UDF [United Democratic Front] initiative, for example) – and on real popular liberation. They thus settled comfortably for SA's becoming, in Neville

Alexander's chilling characterization of the country's post-apartheid landscape, "just another country," one marked by the acceptance, on the part of the ANC, of extreme inequality and of a very soft landing indeed for both global capital and the new African elite.

DM: *And what of the other members of the Alliance – COSATU and the SACP? What is your take on their acquiescence at that time?*

JSS: On the COSATU side, with liberation the union made a fateful miscalculation – a failure, encouraged by the ANC, to cast its lot with grassroots organizations still struggling within civil society but instead to link itself ever more closely to the party in power. But this absorption – oh, so tempting, even for a movement that had been so crucial to the resistance to apartheid inside South Africa – into a (not terribly effective) proximity to power was also being reinforced by sociological and organizational trends. An increasingly high percentage of workers in South Africa were marginalized, semi-employed and/or informally employed and certainly not organized (within COSATU or any other union body). Increasingly, COSATU (and its leaders) has found itself the organization of a kind of labor aristocracy, incapable of reaching out to the vast mass of the unorganized and the marginalized in both the urban and rural areas in order to build the left force that the ANC has refused to become.

The SACP, for its part, was, historically, a pretty Stalinist outfit, important though its links to the Soviet Union had been in getting the ANC favored status as a movement to be armed and otherwise assisted. Neither the Soviet Union nor the SACP directed the ANC, but the SACP did have an important role in shaping the ANC's form of radicalism, albeit one of a Stalinist, vanguardist and not particularly left character: much more rhetorical than real, as events would soon show. At the same time, the SACP was also imprisoning itself within a nationalist movement problematic, where it still finds itself. It has a certain radical base, and some of its members are now mildly left-wing ministers. But the party is chiefly to be thought of as just one more agent of ANC power, wielded from above.

In short, both COSATU and the SACP remain players within post-apartheid South Africa, but players who have been primarily defined by their short-sighted opportunism: definitely, at the moment, part of the country's problem rather than part of its solution.

DM: *Where does this leave the struggle for more radical liberation in South Africa today? What are the potential rupture points, who can pry them open, and how might things be done?*

JSS: Living now far from the frontline, I'll refrain from offering too precise a recipe as to the most effective and appropriate form of ongoing struggle. Nonetheless, some facts are clear. There are vast numbers of people who are dissatisfied in South Africa and with good reason. This discontent can all too easily curdle, as we have seen, into crime, xenophobia, violence against women and the like in the absence of a convincing and resonant counter-hegemonic socioeconomic imaginary and a movement that can give such an imaginary full expression. In other words, the challenge for the aggrieved is to craft increasingly effective long-term vehicles that give clearer and more sustained political voice to their grievances and through which they could press them ever more forcefully and appositely.

We have already seen many such positive expressions of protest, the apparent building blocks of a counter-hegemony, so to speak. I felt, for example, that I saw something of this as early as 2002 when I had the opportunity to join many thousands (20,000-plus) of demonstrators, representing the Anti-Privatization Forum, the Landless People's Movement and the like, as we marched from impoverished Alexandra township to affluent Sandton to protest against the ANC (it was then hosting in Johannesburg a World Summit on Social Development) – although, unfortunately, at the time, such protest could not long sustain itself at that high level. But I also felt the same kind of oppositional energy to be close at hand when I was invited to speak, in Cape Town and under the banner of the Municipal Services Project, to a large and impressive workshop of activists from the townships and rural settlements in 2007. It was difficult not to sense that the initiatives those comrades represented were the seeds of something much broader in the making.

Even more striking are the statistics of fledgling resistance to the present system's severe defaults – as expressed in shortfalls in housing, electricity supply, water and sanitation, in the lack of availability of meaningful skill training and of jobs, and in the massive inequality that is now twinned so dramatically to widespread corruption. "Service delivery protests," as they are termed, are rampant, and said to be at a rate that is among the very highest in the world, and the level of anger is marked. True, such anger has still not found its voice as a firm, coordinated and proto-hegemonic political force. Nonetheless it is around such issues, and with the further release of these palpable popular energies, that the dispiriting stalemate and profound sense of anticlimax that has come to define post-apartheid South Africa might really be beginning to be pried open.

DM: *As you note, much of this new resistance is being led by social movements and community groups, often in conflict with unions that are seen to be too cozy with the ANC. Some commentators see this as a healthy move away from restrictive class politics that open up of a broader potential for counter-hegemonic action and dialogue, while others are concerned that it runs the risk of losing coherent analytical punch and practical force. What are your thoughts on this?*

JSS: I think that, despite some small risk of a possible loss of focus and clout in the formula you first suggest, it is indeed time to get away from any too rigid a preoccupation with exclusively class-derived concepts of revolutionary agency – not least with regard to southern Africa. Of course, Marx had good reason to emphasize the role of the working class in divining potentially revolutionary contradictions within a capitalist mode of production: it was the most exploited (at least in the technical sense in which he deployed the word) and is also brought together as a potentially self-conscious class by the very capitalist dynamic of concentration and centralization that has also defined its exploitation. It is not surprising that Marx's formulation has served as the staple of left thinking and action for generations.

Yet there is a vast multitude [what I have termed earlier in the present book to be the precariat] beyond the ranks of the organized working class (and outside their workplaces) who also live, in southern Africa, in teeming urban and peri-urban settings where social inequality is at its most extreme. There is a whole range of legitimate urban grievances – service delivery failure (in terms of health, housing, electricity, water, education and so much more) and unemployment, for starters – that are on the agenda and that people are seeking to deal with directly at the grassroots and on their home ground. And this is not even to begin to speak about the more desperate situation in many of the rural areas from where people are teeming to the cities.

But recall here an apposite formulation from Ken Post and Phil Wright [a formulation I quoted in an earlier chapter of the present book]. They declared the objective need for a socialist solution to service the needs of the many on the global periphery who, although not wage laborers, are so socially located as "peasants and other working people, women, youth and minorities" that they find themselves in situations where "capitalism has so permeated the social relations which determine their existences...that to be liberated from it is their only salvation." Indeed, "finding another path has...become a desperate necessity if the alternative of continuing, if not increasing, barbarism is to be escaped."

In short, the label "working class" must never be so overbearingly and all-inclusively defined as to cut indifferently across fissures and hierarchies and divisions (along lines of race, ethnicity and gender, to go no further afield), even if such fissures do make the crystallization of self-conscious and collective practice by the under-classes more complex and difficult. For, self-evidently, such diverse identities also speak to grievances and demands that are entirely real in their own right and must not be glibly reduced and subordinated to the rigid terms of some sloganized "class struggle."

It is clear that such identities and the grievances they give rise to cannot stand alone. For they are best understood as taking on any negative and divisive forms only within the selfish, unequal and individualistic ethos of a capitalist society. In fact, it is safe to say that the bearers of such inherently positive identities – "precarians" and workers, feminists, environmentalists, anti-racists, activists around issues of sexual orientation, and others – can and must join into a broader community-in-the-making and within a universalizing project of anti-capitalist transformation. Moreover, that's what the best of militants in South Africa and beyond are beginning to do even as we speak.

Note, too, one other corollary of this kind of approach to movement building. For the inevitable tensions and differences of emphasis between the bearers of such diverse goals and purposes will not then simply disappear, even under the umbrella of a broadly shared socialist purpose. In short, no vanguardist edict can cancel out the necessity that such a project be a firmly democratic one. This enlarged definition of class struggle underscores the pressing need for more open methods of negotiation of both the means and the ends of revolutionary work than has characterized most past socialist undertakings. This will be true both in the mobilizing the forces to launch revolutionary change and in the sustaining of the process of socialist construction in the long run. Hard political work plus genuine democracy then: but South Africans (and others elsewhere) have a future to win along such lines.

DM: *But how does one operationalize this democratic process/practice in South Africa, where there is a dominant party that claims left-wing credentials yet marginalizes any radical thought and action, a union movement and communist party that show few signs of progressive resistance, and a fragmented and under-resourced set of social movements, particularly in rural areas? When compared to Latin America, South Africa seems a long way from any sustained anti-capitalist realization. What is your practical advice to people working on the ground?*

JSS: A very tough question. You can see why I've chosen to become an historian in my old age, primarily seeking to trace the evolution of the "thirty years war" (1960-1990) for southern African liberation both in the region and, as a worldwide liberation support/anti-apartheid movement, more globally. In fact, I feel myself (as I said previously) to be too far from the nitty-gritty of struggles on the ground in southern Africa now to have a right to speak on such pressing contemporary matters.

That said, I do feel the way you summarize the current situation is accurate, albeit quite bleakly phrased. But at the same time, it's a bit like the futility and disempowerment many of us, both in the region and beyond, felt some fifty years ago – after Sharpeville and the like. To argue that the Portuguese, the Rhodies and the Nats could all be defeated: now that really seemed fanciful. But, of course, it wasn't. Moreover, it ain't over yet – that's what I would want to say to people on the ground (who don't need me to tell them this, in any case). True, some would argue that there are too many on the left in South Africa who merely wallow in a sellout narrative regarding the ANC and what has happened in the past 20 years in the country. But I'm not convinced that this is the truth. In fact, most of the skeptics (skeptical, to be clear, regarding the actual liberatory content of liberation) whom I know well are largely correct in their negative evaluations of what has occurred in South Africa.

More importantly, most such skeptics are also actively involved, and simultaneously so, in painstaking work within civil society and the interstices of the system (from the Treatment Action Campaign to the Anti-Privatisation Forum to the Rhodes Must Fall/Fees Must Fall assertions) that gives promise of real human betterment and substantive change. At minimum, such work is immensely helpful and healing – on many fronts – to ordinary people in the present difficult moment. But one senses that it is also sowing the seeds of the kind of more general challenge to the status quo – radical reform, in the militant sense of that concept forged by Gorz and Kagarlitzky – that promises, cumulatively, to be substantively revolutionary. Here, in short, is the basis for the necessary next liberation struggle in South/southern Africa the substantial promise of which I have often invoked.

True, it is certainly the case that such instances of resistance as continue to manifest themselves in southern Africa haven't yet begun to add up into a forceful counter-hegemonic movement. The ANC still lives, for popular consumption, off its liberation history and its struggle credentials. And, as I said earlier, COSATU and the SACP are far too comfortable with their insider status to help in overcoming the fragmentation of the left and in facilitating any efforts by others to wage, publicly and entirely confidently, full-fledged anti-capitalist struggle. And this is a problem, to put it mildly.

But this is simply to say, trite but true, that the struggle continues. Perhaps I'm just too Irish to quit. More generally, though, we must take hope from the fact that the numbers (made up of the vast and swelling ranks of the exploited and the marginalized) are, potentially, on our side, the revolutionary side, in southern Africa – and more globally as well. Here's the basis for what I once called, in South Africa, a possible small-a alliance of popular forces (as distinct from the big-A alliance of the ANC, the SACP and COSATU): a genuine and increasingly effective movement in the making, what the late Fatima Meer found often to be both separate from and opposed to the wielders of established power. Of course, the other side (imperialism and its local henchmen) are determined to defend their own interests, but the stakes – in terms of human decency, equity and equality – are simply too high for us, here or there, to merely walk away from the table.

DM: *And what of other countries in the region, where social and class forces are very different and where many nations remain under the (sub)imperial thumb of a re-energized South Africa? Do you see similar potential for 'small-a' alliances? If so, where, and what is the potential for a broader regional (or even pan-African) anti-capitalist movement in the next 10-20 years?*

JSS: For the moment South Africa seems the most promising site for the genesis of a counter-hegemonic political project – and we've already discussed how difficult it is to see anything transformative happening anytime soon even there. Elsewhere in the region the prospect for a renewed challenge to the debilitating stranglehold of global capital and its local puppets (a term I don't feel comfortable in using but, under the circumstances, it's difficult to think of an alternative) is even less immediately promising.

For example, I've recently felt forced to write extremely pessimistically of Mozambique in whose national left experiment I had once invested many of my hopes. And Zimbabwe, so bedeviled by the horrors perpetrated by Mugabe and his cruel coterie of ZANU followers (and by the support this gang receives from countries like South Africa, present-day Mozambique and China), has seen the high hopes once placed in the more promising kind of opposition originally offered by the Movement for Democratic Change (MDC) there forced to wither. Angola, Namibia: not pretty pictures either, as agreed by many other observers.

I also wrote articles a year or two ago on what I called "the strange death of liberated southern Africa" and another on the far too narrow notion of liberation that we have been content to settle for – national and racial liberation (up to a point), but not also a parallel liberation in class, gender and other terms. In evaluating the liberation struggle in southern Africa in these broader terms, the results of the liberation struggle must thus be seen as having been very mixed – and I speak as one who devoted a great many years to liberation support and anti-apartheid work both in the region and also here in Canada.

But as I've already told you, I've now become a card-carrying historian and consequently have felt constrained to hand in my crystal ball and to return my prognosticator-of-the-future badge. That doesn't mean I no longer care about future outcomes. The next 10-20 years that you mention does seem like a long time, with the situation – in terms of inequality and sheer penury, of disease (AIDS, for starters) and malnutrition, of environmental despoliation – too drastic for us to easily imagine that people, especially in the global South, will passively accept their fate.

Dare to struggle, dare to win: I quite simply don't feel I/we have got any other choice, as trite as that cliché sounds and as bleak as things look right now. But I'll keep any of the dark thoughts about the future that occasionally assail me to myself, if you don't mind. Instead, I'll hope to continue to hear more hopeful thoughts from engaged activists on the ground, those who are seeking to assist more positive things to happen in South Africa and in North America more actively than I am now able to do and who continue to take the pulse of the practice of the moment.

DM: *Let's return, then, to the 1970s, and your role in creating aware-ness about, and activism against, repression in southern Africa from your home base in Canada. You were instrumental in the establish-ment and continuation of the Toronto Committee for the Liberation of Portugal's African Colonies (TCLPAC) (later the Toronto Commit-tee for the Liberation of Southern Africa (TCLSAC)), and an editor of Southern Africa Report (from 1985-2000). What impact did these organizations and publications have on the anti-apartheid struggle in Canada and on Canada's official (or unofficial) policies towards oppressive regimes in the region?*

JSS: I've written quite a bit on this (as have others), including in my memoir *Revolutionary Traveller,* and also in a book that I've recently published that reflects on the North American front of the worldwide movement to support the original southern African liberation struggle.[3] Of course, looking back, it is very difficult to tell the actual extent of the impact we had on western policy. What we can say at a minimum, perhaps, is that our efforts and those of other like-minded militants across Canada communicated to and reinforced the confidence of the liberation movements in the region by demonstrating that they were not without friends and supporters in Canada (as was also true in other imperial centers where the elites otherwise tended, for commercial and investment reasons, to back white power).

That said, we also ruffled the feathers of the right people, cor-porate and governmental, here in Canada, with our campaigns that targeted government complicity with racial rule and corporate invest-ment in oppression. We hosted representatives of the region's libera-tion movements in Canada, we wrote and publicized the situation in southern Africa in the media, we held endless meetings (including our popular Cinema of Solidarity series), and we mounted what we felt to be imaginative assaults upon such things as government support for Portugal through NATO, Canadian banks and their unconsciona-ble loans to apartheid, Gulf Oil Canada's exploitative involvement in Angola, the Hudson's Bay Company and its pursuit of karakul pelts in Namibia, and Canadian mining companies like Falconbridge in a variety of regional settings. We know, for example, that, in retaliation, Gulf Oil infiltrated a corporate spy into our TCLPAC ranks during our public campaigns against the company in the 1970s, and though we caught and expelled him pretty quickly, who knows how many others may have sought to follow in his wake? We were extremely open and transparent (and penetrable) in our activities after all. Just last year, for example, when I finally managed to extract the CSIS file on TCLPAC/TCLSAC from the National Archives, it was, quite legally but entirely immorally, stripped by the government of well over 50 percent of its contents – for security reasons, it was said, even though it was 30 or 40 years after the fact. What remains does admit, furtively, to moments of governmental infiltration by individuals (names not revealed) into our ranks, but who knows what else was on those blacked-out pages?

In any case, it was, above all, the successes of the movements in the region that made the main difference. Soon the Mulroney government – fixated on terrorists and reds, it remained extremely reluctant to give any aid and comfort to the liberation movements themselves, including the ANC – was faced with the reality of the latter's success, the parallel success of widespread popular resistance in the townships and beyond, as well as some continuing embarrassment at home arising from the resistances perpetrated by ourselves and others across Canada (we liked to think). At that point, official Canada began to distance itself from apartheid (well before Reagan, before Thatcher, who were both more racist than Mulroney could ever be), becoming a prominent cheerleader for liberation as recolonization. Our government now readied itself, in short, to egg on Canadian corporations to join in on the suffocating embrace of the New South Africa by the global Empire of Capital: business and exploitation as usual, hold the racism please.

So, by the end of the thirty years' war for southern African liberation, it was clear that we, in the region and beyond, had won a significant victory. And yet it was also a pyrrhic one: difficult, in short, to know whether to cheer or to cry, especially as the modesty of the ANC's intentions once in power became apparent. In Toronto we kept our magazine *Southern Africa Report/SAR* going until 2000 hoping to take an active part in any struggle in southern Africa that might be forthcoming. But, to most Canadians, the initial high of apparent liberation was more tangible than were the sober realities that followed. Though many militants from the anti-apartheid days did move on to other fronts of the global justice struggle, the movement in Canada for equity and equality in southern Africa had, like apartheid, simply melted away.

DM: *What does this say about the Canadian political psyche? Although blatant racism mobilizes anger and resistance, more complex debates over the nature of capitalism seem increasingly difficult to sustain in a popularized way. What can we do in Canada today to generate better and more widespread understandings of ongoing inequities in South(ern) Africa?*

JSS: National political psyches: I'm not sure I know how to think about those. But the problem you allude to is a real one, nonetheless – and I'm afraid it's not just germane to understanding our responses to southern Africa. For starters the situation in most of the global South is the real issue here. And yet the truth is that for many – most? – Canadians the gross inequalities that define the gap between the world's rich and the world's poor seems to be fielded as being, at best, the unavoidable "common sense" of the marketplace and, at worst, a matter of mere indifference. The fact is that we're very far from being self-conscious members of a real global community, one built on empathy and mutual caring and respect, and the results of this you can see quite clearly – if you care to look.

Mind you, the same is true even closer to home. Canada is a pretty unequal society and becoming all the more so all the time as our local chapter of the architects and beneficiaries of the system of global greed distinguishes itself ever more sharply in terms of income and lifestyle from the creatures set below it in the social hierarchy. My son is the executive director of a community food center in West Toronto and he lives such contradictions every day. His organization is doing good work and helping make some difference, but he would love to make the accessibility of good healthy food for all a matter of right, not of market-defined privilege – and not a matter of mere charity either. He finds it difficult enough work to make such points here; how much more difficult it is at the global level.

Of course, this global picture is the subject of much hand-wringing amongst those who care – but even lefties can sometimes get discouraged. Thus a friend with a shared commitment to Africa writes to me recently that (if I may quote) "I don't see how the South can ever liberate itself in the absence of a new socialist project becoming powerful in the North and I don't see that happening until people are hurting and see no prospect of meeting their personal needs under globalized neoliberalism, and until a new left movement with a serious attitude to organization and democracy (to both, that is) emerges to displace the social democratic collaborators with capital." His conclusion: "All of which means that very much against my will and my nature I feel very pessimistic."

As noted, I'm not inclined towards pessimism, although I can understand this kind of response. And my correspondent may also understate the will and the scope for local action, at once radical and transformative, in the global South. But at least this letter has the virtue of bringing the issue back here to our own doorsteps. We must continue to support southern Africans in their efforts to help themselves by all means; many of us spent a lot of time over the years doing that and we need make no apologies for having done so. But we must also continue to work to challenge and to change the global system from the center, beginning here in Canada too: work, in short, for equity and for the continuing viability of the global environment.

Unfortunately, our national government [in Canada] refuses to hear the terrible tidings about injustice and ecological vulnerability and about the inability of the market to magically deliver fair and mutually beneficial social outcomes. What we need, I continue to think, is a more self-conscious and self-confident challenge to the workings of the market – a real not rhetorical project of socialism – mounted by popular majorities committed to social and economic justice. I sense that many Canadians, old and young, are beginning to wake up to the pressing environmental challenges that face us, and perhaps they are also becoming more aware of the many other weaknesses and dangers of our market and dominant-class driven system. So much depends on many more people doing so, both here in Canada and elsewhere.

DM: *I note the phrase "I continue to think," when you talk about the need to resist the logic of the market. Your commitment to this goal has been noteworthy in an era of trendy shifts in academia. What has changed for you intellectually since the 1960s and what remains the same?*

JSS: I sense a whole other interview coming on, since this is a very big question. But fortunately, it's also something I've written about elsewhere [most recently in text entitled "Is Socialism a Real Alternative?" that has been incorporated into chapter 1 of this present book] so I'll only ad-lib the main points briefly here. To begin with, my understanding of the logic of global capitalism that I first began to articulate with Giovanni Arrighi and others in my Tanzania days has remained, to the present, pretty much the same in broad outline. I simply see no reason to think of global capitalism as being developmental in any expansive and egalitarian sense of the word, but rather as having been and remaining primarily parasitical and hurtful, especially to Africa. In short, as Samir Amin emphasizes, delinking the central dynamic of the economy of Third World countries from the global marketplace is crucial.

This is not some simple-minded plea for autarky. There are useful and societally beneficial external links that an economy in the global South can and must avail itself of. But such links will not automatically make developmental sense in any sound and democratically meaningful way unless these links are subordinated to a new internal logic for the economy concerned. And this must mean the primacy of conscious collective intervention that overrides any apparent market logic (a false, if seductive, quasi-logic that favors the strong in the world economy over the weak). This in turn would allow for crafting an internally focused, not externally focused, economy for the country concerned, one that links the city's productive activities and consumer needs to the productive activities and consumer needs of the countryside in an ever expanding set of exchanges – thus providing the basis for a "socialism of expanded reproduction," as Clive Thomas has effectively characterized it. Am I just being stubborn by sticking to my last on this and other economic and social fronts? Well, the fact is that capitalism hasn't worked for the vast majority of the world's citizens and shows no signs of doing so. The socialist goal and vision therefore remains, for me, in this and other particulars, the preferred option.

Of course, the socialist vision has taken a ferocious pounding, especially in the later years of the twentieth century. And this has been not only the work of imperialism. For there have certainly been severe weaknesses in the so-called socialist camp. Here I feel that, in my negative take on the Soviet Union and its progeny, I was pretty consistent. But I was much too soft on vanguardism – as exercised, for example, in Mozambique (a country I thought I knew well). For there is no evidence that vanguards can be trusted for long anywhere, however benign their original intentions may have been. Leaders (for they have a role) simply have to be controlled democratically – from below and by the very populations in whose names they claim to speak. In short, socialism has to be profoundly democratic (although, at the same time, it must also be genuinely socialist, something that social democrats have forgotten time and time again, to our cost).

In short, I'm no less a socialist but ever more of an unqualified democrat than once I was. But I've adjusted my thinking on other fronts too. For example, I'm more open to expanding the definition of potential revolutionary agents along the lines I've suggested in quoting Post and Wright: to include peasants, yes, but, especially to embrace, in Africa, the full range of urban dwellers, well beyond the organized working class. And I'm even less inclined to reduce resistances based on gender, race, religion, ethnic and anti-authoritarian political demands to their presumed class belongings but to see them as making rightful claims to expression and to redress in their own terms. They can give rise to political expressions of both right and left provenance. So how they can be encouraged to intersect with class/socialist projects is a matter of creative political work, and negotiation and democratic interchange as well.

This also underscores the need to move away from mere revolutionary rhetoric and incantation as well – though not away from the cause of genuinely radical and structural change. Here I've found the thinking of Gorz and Kagarlitzky on structural reform especially suggestive and I've tried to expand on it elsewhere. Two points here, however. Firstly, any reform, to be structural in the sense I mean, must be understood by those who press for and achieve it not as a single, self-contained event, but as a step taken, self-consciously, as part of a longer term struggle for genuinely radical transformation. Secondly, the organization and empowerment of the popular elements that prove necessary to realize any such short-term campaigns of would-be structural reform can also be seen as contributing to the broader and more general self-organization that will prove necessary to the undertaking of even broader struggles for transformation in future.

Moreover, such an emphasis of popular engagement and genuine empowerment once again implies a democratic process of revolution-making – a process that, as I have argued, is essential in order to realize any long-term positive effects. At the same time, one mustn't be naïve: the side of resistance to revolutionary change – the dominant class, its military and its external backers (as in many of the struggles against white power during the initial years of liberation struggle in southern Africa) – will often play violent hardball indeed. Then the escalation of confrontation may sometimes, of necessity, pass beyond the boundaries of anything like structural reform – with, unfortunately, long-term costs to socialist and democratic outcomes that, even if the good guys win, can be very severe.

The cost, human and political, of any such escalation is one of the main reasons we in Canada and elsewhere in the West fought so hard (as we did during the stormiest days of the war for southern African liberation) against the state and corporate structures and class interests prevalent here that have so often put our governments on the wrong side of struggles for freedom in the global South – and continue to do just that. But this all evokes issues that demand continuing reflection on my part; and perhaps, should I live so long, I'll have a lot more to say about such questions in due course.

I shall not include here my original, more ruminative, answer to David McDonald's last question of this interview, which was: "And finally, what is next for John S. Saul? Your works in progress suggest no quiet retirement." I will repeat, however, that I have now, in that "retirement, all but finished my final trilogy, The Southern African Liberation Trilogy, of which the present book forms the second volume. And I will also add a final note here to round off this interview and to further foreshadow my exit stage left. Thus, among the handful of honors that I've received in my life, I particularly value the Honorary Doctorate granted me by my old alma mater, Victoria University within the University of Toronto, in 2010. And I was equally pleased to be awarded another by South Africa's University of Johannesburg in 2016. Indeed, on the latter occasion I was accompanied to Africa by my wife Pat and my two now grown children Nick and Jo to attend the event *en famille*. And we also managed to make a family nostalgia trip out of it, returning to Toronto by way of a visit to Maputo in Mozambique where we had all lived, played and worked together as a family in the 1980s. In addition, we stopped over in Dar es Salaam, Tanzania too, this being where both Nick and Jo were born in the 1960s (we even visited the hospital where they were both born and also our old house on the University of Dar es Salaam campus).

But, as I mentioned, part of that trip was the receiving of an honorary degree, its granting by the University of Johannesburg in South Africa being an especially rewarding moment for me, marking as it did a symbolic bringing together of my bifurcated life, stretched as it had been throughout my adult years between southern Africa and Canada. I therefore conclude by including here the acceptance speech, self-explanatory in both tone and substance and I hope of interest to the reader, that I gave in Johannesburg on the occasion (13 April 2016) of the granting of the latter degree:

I'm pleased to be back at UJ only one year after I was last here. Much has happened on this campus in the interim, but I think I saw some of the sparks that would set things alight when I was here last time. I gave a paper, some of you may recall, entitled "The Struggle for South Africa's Liberation: Success and Failure" [see chapter 7, below] and I was honored to have two veterans of the liberation struggle, Judge Albie Sachs and the ANC's Ben Turok, as commentators. The political atmosphere at the event was quite hot, however, and I thought, in retrospect, that it was a bit of a prefiguring of this past year's events.

My comments, critical of the ANC and what I took to be that party's exaggerated deference to the apparent neoliberal logic that has come, since liberation, to impose itself upon South Africa, seemed to arouse no negative response – indeed just the opposite. On the other hand, a large number of the students in attendance, while clearly respectful of the struggle credentials of my two commentators, were very far from being deferential to them. Quite the contrary, and I thought at the time that both Albie and Ben were surprised at and perhaps even a little shaken by the aggressive, questioning, atmosphere of the seminar.

Of course, you all know what happened in the months that followed, not in any way in response to the seminar, but in response to the deep contradictions that the state and the ANC find themselves to be facing vis-à-vis South Africa's university students. But this is also true with respect to other social sectors (e.g., as demonstrated by Marikana and by the protests of the urban poor within SA's civil society more generally). So, I'm glad to back here in SA to take some further soundings for myself of the political atmosphere and want to thank UJ for making that possible

I also want to thank this University for granting me the honorary degree, not least because, many years ago and in a quite different academic atmosphere thousands of miles from here (at Princeton University in the U.S.) I was NOT granted the doctoral degree, the Ph.D, that I had actually earned. And thereby hangs an instructive story that, in the few minutes I have, I will share with you.

I first came to Africa from Canada, my home and native land via the U.S. more than fifty years ago – to Tanzania – to do research for my doctoral thesis at Princeton on Tanzania's burgeoning rural marketing cooperatives. But this was a period in Tanzania full of promise, the years when Julius Nyerere was President there and socialist possibilities were in the air. It was too exciting a place and time for my wife (who is also here today with me) and I to think to leave very quickly. So, I signed on as a lecturer at the University of Dar es Salaam and we were there for the next seven years, and both our children, who also have come here from Canada for this UJ event, were born there as well.

But a distinctive brand of African socialism was also born at that time too, with the Arusha Declaration in Tanzania. And for seven years we lived the dream of a new kind of society in Africa that was being born there.

The demise of that dream makes for a long and complicated story, one that I've been worrying over ever since, but the personal implications are also of interest and bring us back to the current moment. For I did return to North America, and I did write my doctoral dissertation for Princeton on the prospects for socialism in Tanzania. But this was not the kind of topic that was popular within the world of American political science, and I had been in Tanzania too long and lived with its dream too intensely to conform to the models of modernization theory and other fetishes of American political science to comfortably write the kind of dissertation my professors wanted from me. So, of course, they flunked me.

My mother, rest her soul, was disappointed, and I was a bit flummoxed too – what was I going to do now? – although I was lucky enough to find a home at Toronto's York University despite not having a doctorate (until now!) and to have a fulfilling teaching career there. And I also continued to struggle politically in Canada in support of southern African liberation and also to write quite a few books, mainly on southern Africa. Enough books, apparently, to qualify for the degree UJ is today granting me.

But from this experience I also learned one big lesson that I would especially like to share with you today. It is that in the pursuit of a university degree you will have acquired skills important to making your opinion known as clearly, as carefully, and as eloquently as you possibly can – as I did during my time at both the University of Toronto and at Princeton; you will, in short, have learned how to think more clearly. But one thing you will not learn and that is: what to think. That you will have to figure out for yourself, while also letting the consequences be what they may.

At the same time, not having been granted, for my pains, a degree by Princeton, was a setback, albeit one that I managed to survive. Still, from this story, you can get some sense of why this degree from UJ that I'm receiving from you is doubly important to me, both as a doctoral degree and a degree that I've earned in Africa, in my home away from home.

But let me hasten to add that my degree is not any more important to me than your degrees, also granted today, are to you. For you are all aware of how much time and energy you have spent in order to obtain your degree and how much time, energy and resources your families have also devoted to making it happen. My congratulations to you and to your parents on your joint achievement.

And there is another point I would like to make as well. Again, I reflect back to my years in Dar es Salaam and to a discussion we used to have amongst ourselves as teachers and with our students as fellow participants in the relatively privileged life offered at the University of Dar es Salaam – a life of learning and training and empowerment. For we sometimes asked ourselves: what are we doing – helping merely to create new educated recruits to the country's elite of the privileged, or helping to create a new cadre of committed intellectuals who can, in turn, help to make Tanzanians – all Tanzanians (or, in your case, all South Africans) – stronger agents of positive change?

I will leave it to you to decide which side of the growing divide in SA – between rich and poor, between the educated elite and the popular movement – you are to be on. Because for today, at least, I feel especially honored to be standing with you as a fellow degree holder of the University of Johannesburg! My thanks and best wishes to each of you on this special day for us all.

In Context:
The Paradox of Liberation
in Southern Africa

Preface to Section III

On Failed Liberation...
and its Alternatives

As noted in the introduction to this volume section III that follows is intended to serve as an instructive contemporary complement to my book *Race, Class and The Thirty Years War for Southern African Liberation, 1960-1994: A History.* Here, as the present book's title indicates, a link is made to certain key dimensions of the past history of southern Africa, dimensions that cast a special light on the continuity between that history and the current situation in several countries of the region. It does so by pulling together materials that I have written in recent years and published, in significant part, only in southern Africa and can thus represent some of my farewell thoughts on the region, while also serving as an appropriate third section to this second volume of my Southern African Liberation Trilogy.

It may be useful to begin by restating several points from the two earlier sections of this book that can serve to anchor the argument presented here in Section C. First the concept of globalization, a concept that must be demystified and then used circumspectly. It evokes all the ways in which the world has become, to put it simply, smaller in recent decades through, at one level, the most dramatic of technological changes: from Skype to Smart Phones and the like. But most fundamentally the word speaks to the overbearing nature of our novel global economic relations (and, related to that, our global political relations). Increasingly, what we have – to an important degree and in place of the nationally premised, western-sited empires that Africa came to know all too well – is something new: an Empire of Capital that, through its supranational agencies (like the World Bank and the International Monetary Fund) and its intermediaries (the state elites of both capitalist countries at the center of the system and of states elsewhere, such as in South Africa), works to guarantee the (relative) stability of the overall system.[1]

This is a different empire from those produced by the nationally premised western imperialisms that preceded it. Consider the ambiguities of the liberation that has come to define the essence of southern African aspiration in recent decades. There has been a crippling narrowing of the definition of liberation – from one that, in the 1960s and 1970s, promised advances on the fronts of race, class and gender equality and the freeing of the full release of a genuine democratic voice from below; instead liberation has come to be to be defined in terms of racial and national advance only.[2] Compare this outcome with the critique advanced by Frantz Fanon, as he enunciated it in 1950s and 1960s and as I anticipated it in chapter 1. For he stated clearly that what had come to pass for liberation in the African territories then achieving independence was not so much decolonization as a false decolonization, the launching of what was little more than neo-colonialism:

> The national middle class discovers its historic mission: that of intermediary. Seen through its eyes, its mission has nothing to do with transforming the nation; it consists, prosaically, of being the transmission lines between the nation and a capitalism, rampant though camouflaged, which today puts on the masque of neo-colonialism. The national bourgeoisie will be quite content with the role of the Western bourgeoisie's business agent, and it will play its part without any complexes in a most dignified manner. but the same lucrative role, this cheap-jack's function, this meanness of outlook and this absence of all ambition symbolize the incapability of the national middle class to fulfil its historic role of bourgeoisie.[3]

But isn't this the fate of all the territories more recently liberated in southern Africa? Applying Fanon's words to what has transpired more recently in southern Africa is absolutely not to trivialize the importance of the defeat of racist colonialism and of apartheid in that region: this represented an important advance in ensuring a genuine measure of racial equality. Nonetheless, what an updated brand of Fanonist analysis also does is to take us right back to the general point made much earlier in these pages regarding the merits of the concept of recolonization. For the substitution of the word recolonization for the neo-colonialism and false decolonization of Fanon's time is a more accurate description of the present situation, capturing the logic of capitalist imperialism as freshly enacted principally by a global and multi-centric capitalism rather than by any specifically national (and western) centers of empire.

I won't elaborate again on Fanon's argument that the new African elites came to wield local power in a manner virtually unchecked domestically except to say that this has all occurred with little or no positive socioeconomic effect for the African populaces concerned. The elites (principally, for Fanon, state-based elites) merely brandished the single-party state and effective class dictatorship (even when there was more than one party) to supervise the pacification of the people, feeding the latter a diet of ethnic division and cruel overlordship rather than encouraging them to have any sense of their own possible empowerment. In fact, Fanon's litany of the pitfalls evidenced by post-colonial African history was formidable and grounded in a grim interrogation of the neocolonial aftermath of African decolonization and independence that has been virtually unmatched by any analyst since. And, unfortunately, it is this sobering analysis (as suggested above) that must now continue to guide any adequate conceptualization of the nature of the "liberation" that has occurred in southern Africa.

True, any overall imperial logic is now much more volatile and unpredictable – as the trajectories of capitalisms (successful if also formidably unequal in their internal social implications) in, say, China, Korea and even India have demonstrated in recent decades. But what of southern/South Africa in this turbulent world of 21st-century capitalist imperialism? Given the nature of its dependency and its still very subordinate economic position within the overall global system, Africa faces a dimmer prospect of realizing even the distorted benefits of a capitalist revolution than do many other parts of the global South. For if the immediate future of southern Africa is to be capitalist it will be a capitalism largely driven by global interests and worldwide capitalist priorities. And, to reinforce the point here, such a capitalism can foster only a very limited brand of development, one offering some wealth and power to the fortunate few and very much less to the vast majority of the region's impoverished populations. It is such a recolonization that seems set, in the absence of real resistance to it, to define the region's reality for the foreseeable future.

(i) Failed Liberation: The Region

We need to survey the ways in which imperial logic has come home to roost in Southern Africa. Those of us who were politically active and alert in the 1960s and 1970s had (with some reason we thought) hoped that southern Africa might be different, in genuinely progressive ways, from the broader African pattern so clearly identified and criticized by Fanon. Why? For starters, the liberation movements seemed unlikely to be readily offered even a false decolonization. This was because the white colonizers (in particular the white settler minorities in Rhodesia, Namibia and South Africa) were – unlike the British and the French further north in Africa – not prepared to concede any compromise that would not be readily controlled in the interests of continuing white skin privilege. Moreover, the Portuguese imperialist mission in Mozambique and Angola was, for reasons of its own, equally intractable with regard to prospective changes in the terms of its overrule. In addition, and throughout the region, capital – especially mining and related capital, both domestic and foreign-owned – was, for a considerable period, comfortable with the overall framework of racial rule and willing to compromise over any relatively minor contradictions that might exist in the meshing and re-tuning of racist and capitalist logics. This was in deference to its more crucial interest in ensuring the supply of labor, cheap and pacified, that southern Africa's settler/ apartheid rule guaranteed.[4]

There was also a counter-logic from which many who were concerned with progressive outcomes in southern Africa could draw inspiration: the intransigence of white-minority rule tended to radicalize popular opposition from the 1960s on. This meant, for example, armed struggle of some kind, especially in South Africa, which in turn suggested that a higher level of popular mobilization and action on the ground would be needed in order to focus an effective movement for change. True, the positive implications of this need imposed upon the nationalist-cum-liberation movements was (in and of itself and *pace* Fanon and his chapter 1: "Concerning Violence") not straightforward and self-evident. For the apparent imperatives of armed struggle also reinforced, negatively, various hierarchical and undemocratic pressures upon the political realm. And such pressures were further strengthened by another source of the *realpolitik* of tough, no-nonsense vanguardism – the politics that the liberation movements (and the governments they would eventually create) were also learning from both their autocratic hosts in the front-line African states bordering on the conflict zone and from their Stalinist allies in the East.

At the same time, such struggle did imply the need to mobilize people to a more sustained – albeit more dangerous (to the holders of capital at least) – level of commitment than any other outcome that the nationalist leadership could more easily leverage to take over power from the departing colonialists. Certainly, in South Africa, the actual motor of effective confrontation was less that of force of arms than it was the rising tide of assertion in workplaces and township, in Durban and Soweto in the 1970s, and ever more generally as the wave of resistance crested in the 1980s. And this, in turn, gave hope that even if (as many of us feared at the time) the ANC refused to sustain its struggle towards ensuring a more expansive outcome, its feet would be held to the fire of revolutionary purpose and democratic practice by the popular energies unleashed into a post-apartheid milieu by the nature of the anti-apartheid struggle. In so arguing, I don't think those of us who glimpsed such a possibility were merely – or even mainly – being naive. Instead, we were being hopeful.

But unrealistic, nonetheless, as events were to prove.[5] For the sober fact remains that the leadership of the southern African liberation movements proved, to an alarming degree, to be comfortable with the general pattern marked out by previous continental decolonization – and prepared to defend its own stake in it. After all, as elsewhere, such leaderships were comprised primarily of a would-be "national middle class" (Fanon again) – aspirant men on the make, prepared to face up to the somewhat harder path to power that intransigent white hierarchies forced upon them but in the end quite willing to conform (in pursuit of their nascent class interests) to the global status quo.

This logic was pressed on them by the many seductions and pressures of the global capitalist power wielders from state and corporations alike. And there was the temptation of subservience to the local status quo too, especially to white entrepreneurs in South Africa – at least when that local status quo was suitably modified to remove race as the major barrier to this new black elite's advancement.

There were complexities too, even beyond those imposed by white settler intransigence: complexities worth specifying on a case-by-case basis. Namibia's South West African People's Organisation (SWAPO), for example, was quite easily deflected from the task of internal mobilization. In the first place, its attention was divided, seduced by a tempting preoccupation with high diplomacy and the international cross-pressures that arose at the United Nations around the contested issue of South West Africa's status with regard to South Africa's illegal occupation. Closer to home, however, there was the crippling weight of the heavy-handed leadership of Sam Nujoma and of his complacent Swapo leadership more generally. When Swapo's leaders were challenged, in Zambia in the 1970s, by a majority within his movement, Nujoma was rescued by the shockingly ruthless support given him by both Kenneth Kaunda of Zambia and Julius Nyerere of Tanzania. Then, in Angola in the 1980s, only unspeakable terror (to which its Angolan host, the Mouvement Populaire de Libération de l'Angola/MPLA government, turned a blind eye) sustained the SWAPO leadership, a leadership that was then to reap the harvest of Namibian independence in 1990.[6]

In Angola the MPLA was, if anything, even more Stalinist, both in principle and in predisposition right from start than was the Swapo leadership, and, as its original leftist ideological cover (such as it was) fell away, quickly became an ever more ruthless and self-serving lot; the violence then unleashed within the movement is discussed carefully and at greater length in chapter 5. In addition, the movement and the country were never given much chance to grow beyond this sad state. In part this was a product of the external encirclement (by South Africa and the United States) and the linked internal war (waged by the União Nacional para a Independência Total de Angola – UNITA) forced upon

the country, to a significant degree from outside. But there also soon surfaced – as UNITA faded – the powerful invitations to the elite's greed and
to that elite's resistance to any kind of real accountability that were prof-
fered by the cornucopia of easy and readily available (to them) oil money.

Zimbabwe has had its own distinct wrinkles. Ibbo Mandaza captured the general pattern decades ago in a very strong early critique
of the newly ascendant African petty bourgeoisie as it took up formal
positions of power – in its narrow class interests and those of international capital (the flawed process that permitted the consolidation
of such a Zimbabwean government as led by ZANU and by Robert
Mugabe is traced in chapter 6). Thus, for Mandaza, while the new
state quickly became "an apparent mediator between capital and labor,
between the aspirations of mass of the people for the 'future of independence' and the role of international capital in its quest for more
profit" it also became "weighted in favor of the latter, inclined towards
controlling these popular demands, if only to appease capital in the
name of 'stability,' peace and security.'"[7] Indeed,

> change in the economic sphere meant essentially the gradual embour-
> geoisement of the African petit bourgeoisie as the latter found their
> class aspirations fulfilled... [For] there was more than a symbolic
> commitment to the capitalist order as the members of the African
> petit bourgeoisie variously bought houses, farms, businesses, etc.;
> political principles and ideological commitment appeared mort-
> gaged on the altar of private property.[8]

In sum,

> as the African petit bourgeoisie began gradually to find access to
> the same economic and social status as their white counterparts, so,
> too, did it become increasingly unable to respond effectively to the
> aspirations of the workers and peasants. [Meanwhile] the leader-
> ship would find it [even more] difficult to confront the leadership
> would find it increasingly difficult to confront former white settlers,
> let alone international capital.[9]

Zimbabwe would change, as I will explain, but Mandaza's early account
of the false decolonization of Zimbabwe is chilling, not least in its foreshadowing of what eventually was to come to pass in South Africa.

The situation in Zimbabwe was to become much worse. The new black elite first fastened on the opportunities provided by a more or less self-inflicted structural adjustment in the 1980s and early 1990s to further feather its own nest. Then came a dramatic negative popular response to this and other related trends, a response exemplified not least in the assertions of the trade union movement and the rise of a strong opposition, the Movement for Democratic Change. At this point, Mugabe and his gang felt compelled to turn, startlingly and in some desperation, to both a vocal anti-imperialist rhetoric and to long overdue land reform – this latter being quite visibly manipulated in favor of the elite's interests, however – in order to shore up the regime's fading political credibility. Yet such opportunist populism did not work to silence growing dissent, and Mugabe and company chose to reinforce the intensity and impact of its most basic tactic: sheer brute force. They thereby produced a country that was not only in worse social and economic shape than any of its other liberated neighbors, but also one that was no different from them – if even more brittle – in the basic logic of its neo-colonial structure.[10]

As for Mozambique (about which I have written at length else-where) it was different from the emergent sub-continental pattern, if only momentarily. For the Frente de Libertaçao de Moçambique (Fre-limo) possessed a leadership (Eduardo Mondlane, Samora Machel and others) that sought to push against false decolonization and towards more genuine liberation: beyond colonial and racist rule, beyond capi-talist exploitation and peripheralization and beyond male arrogance and domination. Briefly it showed promise: Norrie McQueen wrote of the Lusophone African liberation struggles (and especially Frelimo's actions in Mozambique) that they originally offered "a clear alterna-tive to the cynical manipulation of ethnicity and the neocolonial com-plaisance of the kleptocratic elites who increasingly defined African governance in the 1970s and 1980s." In sum:

> Whatever their fate, the projects of the post-independence regimes
> of Lusophone Africa were probably the most principled and decent
> ever proposed for the continent. They have not been superseded in
> this regard and seem unlikely to be.[11]

Yet the Frelimo leadership was, as discussed in chapter 4 below, also (at least from the time of Mondlane's assassination by the Portuguese) unapologetically high-handed and vanguardist however much its authoritarianism may have been, at least at first, in a good cause. Then Machel's death and the wasting effects of Rhodesian and South African (via the Resistência Nacional Moçambicana/Renamo) destabilization paved the way for a degeneration in Frelimo's own momentarily high purpose and Mozambique, too, stumbled into the snares of false decolonization, external dictates and elite aggrandizement.[12]

And what, finally, of South Africa – no exception, as we now know all too well, to Fanon's warning? Despite the enormous importance of the overthrow of one of the cruelest instances of institutionalized racist rule imaginable, it is impossible to avoid the conclusion that, on the ANC's watch, this country has not been genuinely liberated – except in the most limited (albeit still meaningful) sense of that term. Instead, as elaborated upon in chapters 3 and 7, it has been recolonized – recolonized by capital, with the ANC quite content, it would seem, and content also to hail the rise of a new African national middle class – a class only different from the newly ascendant stratum that Fanon had once excoriated (with respect to its role in the then newly liberated "rest of Africa"[13]) in having rather more assertive hopes for its own rise within the private sector. Thus, as seen in South Africa – as elsewhere in the region – the victors in the liberation struggle have been, (a) global capitalism, (b) this capitalism's principal protagonists in the private and public sectors (including their white indigenous-class counterparts, especially in South Africa), and (c) the new class of black businessmen, prominent politicians and professionals who have now consolidated themselves in positions of intermediary power and privilege.[14]

How, then, are we to interpret such an outcome?[15] One option would be merely to celebrate capitalism, its present and its ostensibly promising future – although this is a difficult position for an African to take, one might think, unless (s)he is one of the privileged few, or an employee of one or other of the international financial institutions. But in elevated circles in South Africa, it is simply common sense.

Nelson Mandela, for one – and despite his apparently having possessed a more radical and very different vision immediately upon his release from prison, came to accept the Growth Equity and Redistribution (GEAR) policy in just such a "commonsensical" manner, one not open for any real discussion.[16] And Finance Minister Trevor Manuel, Reserve Bank Governor Tito Mboweni and then President Thabo Mbeki (who had already played an important role in crafting such a future in the 1980s when meeting with South African businessmen in exile) and others joined right in (with many erstwhile ANC activists also moving briskly into the private sector).[17] Indeed, they now designed the firmly neoliberal GEAR strategy – said, by Manuel, to be "non-negotiable" – to replace the mildly more radical Reconstruction and Development Programme (RDP).[18] Yet it is hard to believe – it goes against almost all the evidence – that this was really the way to open a genuinely liberated future for the vast mass of South Africans.

True, one could argue that South Africa (or at least the South African elite, black and white) has fared marginally better than have its neighbors, in part because of its capital's neocolonial expansion into the continent. But there remains the nagging fact, alluded to above, that globally this is not terribly significant. There are two reasons for this: firstly, South Africa has not, after all, been markedly successful as a national economy in overall terms. And, secondly, domestically there has been a dramatic and widening gap between rich and poor – the gap between black and white having narrowed somewhat but the gap between rich and poor having widened significantly.

Consider, for example, the fact that – as recently publicized by the Congress of South African Trade Unions (Cosatu) – 24 million South Africans, 48 per cent of the population, live below the poverty level of R322 a month. Meanwhile, the Sunday Times has shown that the 20 wealthiest people in the country (these collectively worth R112.2 billion) have seen their wealth jump by 58.96 per cent in the past two years, while the wealthiest 100 people have seen their wealth shoot up by 62.19 per cent. Surely it is far from mere demagogy to contrast the less than R322 a month received by the 48 per cent of the population mentioned above with the income of one Whitey Basson,

CEO of retail giant Shoprite, who last year took home a cool R627.53 million in salary, perks and share options. After almost 20 years of South African "freedom" isn't it time to ask: what kind of liberation is this anyway?[19]

Of course, there is every reason to think that such outcomes were fully predictable under the capitalism the ANC chose to opt for with its victory – and bear in mind Trevor Manuel's proud boast that it was choice not fate that defined the post-apartheid trajectory.[20] For, truth to tell, widening inequality is the overt logic of capitalism, global or otherwise. The rationale of those who benefit from such a system is never that it will produce immediate equality. It is the well-publicized first principle of capitalist faith that those who profit most from the system can be counted on to reinvest the best part of their profits and that, as a result, the economy will expand, with all of us then benefiting, even unto the last generation. Yet that is not how capitalism actually works, especially in those parts of the world, shaped by centuries of colonialism and by contemporary global discipline, that are not able to compete on an even playing field with the big international players and corporations. Them as has gets (though even they are having difficulty in keeping the irrationalities of their global system from springing a leak, as those of us who live in North America are just beginning to understand) and those who don't have don't get.

The result is, as my countrywoman Naomi Klein has, in her brilliant book *The Shock Doctrine: The Rise of Disaster Capitalism* epitomized South Africa's situation in a chapter title in that book, *viz.*, "Democracy Born in Chains: South Africa's Constricted Freedom." And how did the ANC manage to miss, as she puts it, its "unique opportunity to reject the free-market orthodoxy of the day" and to come, instead, to stand, in her words, "as living testament to what happens when economic reform is severed from political transformation." For politically [she writes] "its people have the right to vote, civil liberties and majority rule. Yet economically, South Africa has surpassed Brazil as the most unequal society in the world."[21]

But how does she interpret why this had been allowed to happen in a South Africa where the national liberation movement had not merely defied for so long the racist state's sustained intransigence but had also previously articulated a refusal to bend by that apartheid state's capitalist allies? Klein's opinion: the ANC merely forgot, she suggests, to look to the economy, so preoccupied were they with the political challenges of transition. In her view, the plan for recolonization

> was executed under the noses of ANC leaders, who were naturally preoccupied with winning the battle to control Parliament. In the process the ANC failed to protect itself against a far more insidious strategy – in essence, an elaborate insurance plan against the economic causes of the Freedom Charter ever becoming law in South Africa. The slogan "the people shall govern!" would soon become a reality, but the sphere over which they would govern was shrinking fast.

But despite Klein's reliance on usually quite credible South African observers to testify to her version of events, this is not good enough. For example, she strongly associates herself with Vishnu Padayachee's opinion that, as she paraphrases it,

> none of this happened because of some grand betrayal on the part of the ANC leaders but simply because they were outmaneuvered on a series of issues that seemed less than crucial at the time – but turned out to hold South Africa's lasting liberation in the balance.

The same, apparently, goes for William Gumede's view (which she quotes directly) that

> "if people felt [the political negotiations] weren't going well there would be mass protests, but when the economic negotiators would report back, people thought it was technical." This perception was encouraged by Mbeki, who portrayed the talks as "administrative" and of no popular concern. As a result he [Gumede] told me, with great exasperation, "We missed it! We missed the real story."

True, Klein suggests, Gumede "came to understand that it was at those 'technical' meetings that the true future of his country was being decided – though few understood it at the time." But this is not a convincing argument, and I would argue, as suggested, that Klein is incorrect here. For ANC negotiators, not least Mbeki, did fully "understand it at the time." After all, Mbeki had already stated firmly in the mid-1980s that "the ANC is not a socialist party. It has never pre-tended to be, it has not said it was and it is not trying to be. It will not become one by decree or for the purpose of pleasing its 'left' critics." Indeed, a mere decade later, Mbeki (in announcing, with Gear, the ANC's turn further to the right) would quip: "Just call me a Thatcher-ite." Nelson Mandela's almost total reversal of his position from the radical assertions he made as he emerged from his Cape Town prison is also staggering in retrospect. In fact, the country's future was not merely accidentally stumbled into by the ANC leadership in a moment of inattention but had, in Manuel's words, been decided by its own choice – and not by inattention or by fate.

The fact is that Fanon's original hypothesis is far more credible than those of Gumede or Padayachee, or, indeed, of Klein. What had happened was that the ANC elite had simply changed the rules of the liberation game in South Africa, and stolen the chips.[22] Shortly before his death in 2001, Rusty Bernstein, veteran South African Communist Party (SACP) and ANC militant, posed this urgent question: "What is going wrong, and why?"[23] For he felt an answer to that question was "the essential precondition for any rectification, and thus for any return to optimism about South Africa's democratic future." Note, too, that the answer he gave to the question is not merely about economic choices made but about political ones as well:

> The drive towards power has corrupted the political equation in vari-ous ways. In the late 1980s, when popular resistance revived again inside the country led by the UDF, it led the ANC to see the UDF as an undesirable factor in the struggle for power, and to fatally under-mine it as a rival focus for mass mobilisation. It has undermined the ANC's adherence to the path of mass resistance as a way to libera-tion, and substituted instead a reliance on manipulation of the levers of administrative power. It has paved the way to a steady decline of a mass-membership ANC as an organiser of the people, and turned it into a career opening to public sector employment and the adminis-trative "gravy train." It has reduced the tripartite ANC-COSATU-CP alliance from the centrifugal center of national political mobilisation to an electoral pact between parties who are constantly constrained to subordinate their constituents' fundamental interests to the overriding purpose of holding on to administrative power. It has impoverished

the soil in which ideas leaning towards socialist solutions once nour-
ished and allowed the weed of "free market" ideology to take hold.

Indeed, even so loyal an ANC comrade as Ben Turok now feels constrained to say much the same thing, wondering in one of his recent
books why the ANC's "liberated" state has not "given equal attention
to empowering the masses as to [the empowering of] the elite? And
why has the insistence of parliament on broad-based empowerment
brought so little success?"[24] In fact, Turok feels forced to come to what
he calls the "irresistible conclusion that the ANC government has lost
a great deal of its earlier focus on the fundamental transformation of
the inherited social system." Which is to put the relevant point rather
mildly, I would suggest.

(ii) Alternatives

Alternatives? A next liberation struggle? Take, as one example of mild
distemper, Moeletsi Mbeki. Certainly he is no socialist and generally
seems quite content merely to deride the lack of any real attempt, by
his brother or by anyone else, to empower a kind of black national
bourgeoisie – here he quite specifically does not mean merely the predictable beneficiaries of the black economic empowerment initiative
he scorns – that, in his view, would alone have had a chance to slip the
leash of global capital's control and build a vibrant national capitalism
on South Africa. Failing that, however, Moeletsi Mbeki can see only a
kind of Tunisian/Egyptian denouement in the making:

> I can predict when SA's "Tunisia Day" will arrive. Tunisia Day
> is when the masses rise against the powers that be, as happened
> recently in Tunisia ...The ANC inherited a flawed, complex soci-
> ety it barely understood; its tinkerings with it are turning it into an
> explosive cocktail. The ANC leaders are like a group of children
> playing with a hand grenade. One day one of them will figure out
> how to pull out the pin and everyone will be killed.[25]

Small wonder that many in the union movement and in the township
organizations are far more restive (and, it would seem, far more leftist)
in inclination than is Moeletsi – this in spite of the apparent pattern of
their actual voting in elections. For, as Peter Alexander has recently
summarized the current situation:

> Since 2004 South Africa has experienced a movement of local pro-
> tests amounting to a rebellion of the poor. This has been widespread
> and intense, reaching insurrectionary proportions in some cases.
> On the surface, the protests have been about service delivery and
> against uncaring, self-serving and corrupt leaders of the munici-
> palities. A key feature has been mass participation by a new gen-
> eration of fighters, especially unemployed youth but also school
> students. Many issues that underpinned the [initial] ascendency of
> Jacob Zuma also fuel the present action, including a sense of injus-
> tice arising from the realities of persistent inequality ... [Moreover,]
> while the inter-connections between the local protest, and between
> the local protests and militant action involving other elements of
> civil society, are limited, it is suggested that this is likely to change.[26]

True, such societal distemper can produce some very unsavory results,
ranging from crime (including high rates of violence against women)
to the kind of xenophobic mob violence against Africans from elsewhere on the continent that recently scarred South Africa. For if the
mass of the populace is denied (and even actively discouraged from
seeking) the kind of liberation that the articulation of a sense of genuinely expansive social purpose might deliver – like socialism, tangible
communal endeavor and genuine democratic self-assertion – it can
become a very sour mass indeed. Thus, if Zuma temporarily fed off
such distemper (along with many other quite genuine grievances concerning the Mbeki leadership) in surging past Mbeki in 2008, ANC
Youth League leader Julius Malema momentarily promised/threat-
ened to play much the same card even more fiercely and intemper-
ately. Such at least was the apparent thrust – crudely nationalistic,
even racist – of his recent, apparently popular and potentially quite
explosive bombast. Thus, in June 2011, the Economist headlined its
account of the continuing rise of the outspoken Malema – a rise most
recently visible in his unopposed re-election as leader of the Youth
League – with the comment that "the black man who is rude about
whites is doing rather well." The article continued:

> Mr. Malema is no fool. He has proved himself a master at politics
> and at tapping into the anger of his young black audiences. More
> than half of black youths under 25 are officially unemployed; the
> real figure is much higher. Two-thirds leave school without any

qualifications. Most live in poor black townships or shanty towns, ineligible for state welfare. Seventeen years after the ANC came to power promising a better life for all, many can look forward only to a career of crime and drugs or to early death through AIDS. How good, then, to be told by Mr. Malema that they are in no way to blame for their plight. Scapegoats are at hand: the new greedy black elite with their hands in the public till, lazy self-seeking politicians, but most of all selfish whites – the 9% of the population who, thanks to the imperialist racist exploitation of blacks over the past 350 years, still have most of the country's land, wealth and top jobs.[27]

But, if not a fool, Malema was to prove too much of a loose cannon even for the ANC and he was expelled from the party for a variety of other reasons in 2012. Yet much of his analysis, as revealed in the above quotation, is – despite the heavy sarcasm of the Economist's tone in reporting it – uncomfortably close to the truth. And, indeed, similar points have been presented much more soberly and thoughtfully by others to whom we now turn.

Take, for example, the striking outreach towards a possible new format of politics by Cosatu president Zwelinzima Vavi. In October 2010 he and Cosatu met, independently (and in the face of sharp criticism from their ostensible ally, the ANC, for doing so), with representatives from a wide range of active civil society organizations, where he argued forcefully that

Inspired by the African proverb that says "if you want to go quickly, go alone. If you want to go far, go together" we gather here – as the progressive trade unions, social movements, NGOs, progressive academics, small business and street vendor associations, taxi associations, religious bodies, youth organisations, environmental groups, indigenous peoples' groups and other progressive formations – to say to ourselves that we have the capacity to make a decisive contribution in changing our current situation for the better.

Internationally, globalisation and neoliberalism have launched assaults on the working class, which include, but are not limited to: informalization, flexibilization, regionalization of states, deregulation, marketization, financialization, and securitization. The global governance, commercial and trade system is supported by political and ideological institutions, rules and enforcement mechanisms that only broad civil society coalitions have historically been able to challenge successfully.

In South Africa, the GEAR strategy epitomized the dominance of the neoliberal ideology within the leading sections of the government. The neoliberal logic still continues to be dominant, in spite of some talk about a developmental state. Increasingly though it has taken a more crude political expression and there are some emerging elements that tend to perceive the working class and active elements of civil society as merely being a nuisance that must be crushed with the might of the state apparatus. [However] today, as we gather here, there is panic in the ranks of the predatory elite, which is a new coalition of the tenderpreneurs. Paranoia elsewhere is deepening with the political elite, convincing itself that any gathering of independent civil society formations to confront our challenges is a threat to them.[28]

Vavi spoke equally sharply in February 2011, addressing the Southern African Bishops' Conference Justice and Peace AGM and asserting that "clearly we do not live in a society where everyone is happily living in peace. And the underlying reason is the continuation of poverty and inequality. Which brings me to my topic tonight – the poor." He continued:

We have a constitution which grants people certain rights. Yet in practice millions are denied those rights, especially socioeconomic rights, in what has become the most unequal nation in the world. The rich elite earns millions by exploiting the labor of the working class. A minority, including some of our former comrades in public office, make their millions by corruptly manipulating opportunities to win tenders, bribing officials or using political connections. Meanwhile the mainly black poor majority suffer from deep and widespread poverty, huge levels of unemployment, pathetic levels of service delivery in healthcare and education, housing and transport, and little hope of escaping from a life of struggling to survive from day to day. We are one of the most unequal countries in the world, and, unless we mobilise for changes, the levels of inequality will become entrenched.[29]

Another kind of response to the marked social distemper of the current moment is the attempt to transform unrest into a much more potent, organized and explicit challenge to ANC rule. There have been a number of such assertions. Indeed, I recall one promising, but ultimately somewhat illusory, herald of novel left prospects in the counter-demonstration to the ANC-hosted World Summit on Sustainable Development in Johannesburg and the march of thousands of protesters from Alexandra township to the conference center in salubrious Sandton. I was there and have recounted it elsewhere.[30]

More recently, however, other indications of similar purpose have been seen – still in a modest vein but with real long-term seriousness – such as, briefly, the activities of the now defunct Democratic Left Front (DLF), for example. Initial statements from the latter movement-in-the-making were to be found in the impressive documentation that followed the DLF's founding conference in early 2011,[31] with two of the chief organizers of this conference writing of this initiative as follows:

> Our conference is merely a milestone in a long journey that has to do with trying to reimagine a left politics through ethical practice. Our ethical compass is about living and inventing democracy inside this process (definitely through heated debates, differences and new ways of thinking about consensus), plurality as strength, collective intellectual practice, self-education and building transformative power through struggles. This is a process without preconceived outcomes and thus is unique in South Africa. Such a process means abandoning the illusions of a vanguardist while committed to a violent overthrow of capitalism or a reformist left seeking to make capitalism more humane. More importantly, we are about strengthening and advancing grassroots struggles through opposition but, at the same time, advancing transformative alternatives from below. This is illustrated by the ideas, proposals and campaigns that were adopted as part of our common platform of action dealing with ecological resources, unemployment, food sovereignty, education and public services.[32]

Other fledgling initiatives seemed to hold related promise. Thus, the great significance attached, however fleetingly, to the decision of NUMSA, the biggest trade union in South Africa, to abandon its longstanding COSATU and ANC ties and to seek (however unsuccessfully) to "throw in its lot with a growing movement in opposition to the neoliberal order in South Africa, and thus to the left of the ANC, rather than line up to the right."[33]

This new initiative – designed to stand as a new united front – foundered in its turn on both the difficulties of the task NUMSA had set itself and on the rocks of the overbearing vanguardism exemplified by the NUMSA leadership and notably by its executive secretary Irvin Jim. But the new mood of the times was becoming more tangible, some hoped, with related voices being heard even from within the ANC. For there were signs that "fuelled by a dangerous mixture of high unemployment, slow growth, weak leadership and fierce feuding within the governing party" some "influential factions" in the ANC are "pushing to transform the courts, the media, the economy and ... the much-praised constitution."[34] In sum, in all these varied voices is to be found the promise of a next liberation struggle.[35]

❀   ❀   ❀

Liberation, as defined in the first liberation struggle, has led ineluctably, throughout the region, to recolonization by the Empire of Capital. This has been borne out by many critical observers of the southern African scene, both in South Africa and beyond. Writing in much the same spirit elsewhere I was moved to entitle one of my recent books *The Next Liberation Struggle*. There I discussed the possible need in each of the southern African countries to realize just such a renewed struggle. But this is not the place to speculate on the possible particulars of any such next or ongoing liberation struggle, nor am I competent, as a practitioner/observer much more deeply implicated in the first liberation struggle than the present one, to do so. I would merely suggest that any such renewed struggle will seek to liberate the meaning and practice of liberation in order to embrace, in its name, a far wider range of achieved freedoms than those inherent in overcoming the institutionalized racism of the apartheid and other crude colonial variations of it (important as this was). For, unfortunately, the latter only realized a minimal kind of national liberation.

No, any such ongoing struggle would, this time, be seeking to deal more effectively with issues of class, gender and democratic empowerment,[36] even if we assume, for the moment, that the first liberation struggle managed, to some extent, to subdue racial and national oppression. Is a next liberation struggle plausible, even necessary? This is a sobering question and stating it a sobering note upon which to end an essay that was originally written for a conference about southern Africa's first liberation struggle. But it is not, I fear, an inappropriate question to pose, either at the conference at which this paper was originally presented or in the present book. For we must hope that the struggle does indeed continue, as we used – albeit rather more confidently – to declare.

Chapter 3

Socialism and Southern Africa: From Tanzania to South Africa[1]

The African continent has been marked by remarkably diverse flare-ups of apparent socialist and quasi-socialist intention – from Algeria in the north to Ghana in the west to Ethiopia in the east. But it is as one moves ever closer to South Africa that the intention becomes most marked, not only in rhetoric but even in practice – albeit in a practice not yet very concretely focused and realized. So, the question remains: what are we to learn from this southern African regional experience that can provide serviceable lessons for the ongoing struggle to realize equity, social justice and meaningful development in South Africa – and elsewhere, both within the region and on the continent as a whole?

(i) Tropes of Socialist Defeat

One of the stocks in trade of ANC-think since South Africa's formal democratization in 1994 has been to present a very negative version of African socialist endeavor elsewhere and, particularly, within the region. For this is intended, however crudely depicted, to warn against any feckless dream of a socialist outcome in South Africa – however often such an outcome may have been promised by the ANC/SACP during the years of struggle against white dictatorship that it shared with other liberation movements across the region.

Thus, one of the favored ANC tropes – albeit one more often offered in private conversation and intra-elite banter than in public statement – is to underscore the lack of realism of the aspiration in general and, in particular, under African conditions and circumstances. This is also seen in more scholarly offerings. Many decades ago, for example, Roger Murray queried whether, in Nkrumah's Ghana, the "historically necessary" (some form of socialism) was in fact the "historically possible."[2] More recently, Giovanni Arrighi suggests that even in the heyday of liberation movement enthusiasm (the 1960s and the 1970s) and despite his direct involvement in Zimbabwe he had been appropriately skeptical about the likelihood/possibility of socialist outcomes in a liberated southern Africa.[3] But the ANC variant of this argument, as offered in the musings of its leaders (it is difficult to find a paper trail of such utterances), is much more dismissive. And such a reading of recent history serves, in turn, to underpin an assumption as to the impossibility of the ANC's following any other course than the option of neoliberal accommodation with global capitalism that it has chosen.

The apparent common sense of this latter choice, evoking, in essence, the explanatory mantra "globalization made me do it." And yet acceptance, overwhelmingly, of the dictates of the so-called free market, both locally and globally, has been much more a choice than a necessity: a choice made very consciously in favor of capitalism and against socialism. Perhaps it is enough to recall Thabo Mbeki's statement from the 1980s (and quoted earlier) that the ANC is not a socialist party.[4] And this is the Mbeki who could also note during the South African transition that the National Party positions were "not very different from the position the movement has been advancing", and who, when speaking not long after the moment of liberation about his (and the ANC's) chosen economic policies, could even cavalierly assert "Just call me a Thatcherite."[5]

So, it comes as no great surprise that during South Africa's transition from apartheid, Mbeki was also comfortable (as comfortable in taking such a course as was Nelson Mandela, be it noted[6]) in encouraging the ANC to turn its back on any lingering skepticism it might have had as to the virtues of the global capitalist system. Of course, Mbeki also had qualified the argument in his 1984 text suggestively: "The ANC is convinced that within the alliance of democratic forces... the working class must play the leading role, not as an appendage of the petty bourgeoisie but as a conscious vanguard class, capable of advancing and defending its own democratic interests."[7] Here, indeed, was the apparent promise of some continuing commitment to radical class politics. Yet, in retrospect, the latter sentence seems only to have existed as a perfunctory footnote to his, and the ANC's, continuing rightward turn. Once in power he would prove entirely unwilling to work in any way whatsoever to help pull the ANC back onto a leftward track. Quite the contrary.

At the same time his formulation is suggestive. The kind of broader class understanding Mbeki purports to acknowledge may help explain the logic of his view from several years later (although such a statement may now come as a bit of a surprise to those who have lost track of Mbeki's startling ideological peregrinations over the years). Thus, as early as the late 1980s, he could be found (according to William Gumede) "privately telling friends that he believed the ANC alliance with the Communist Party would have to be broken at some point, especially if the ANC gained power in a post-apartheid South Africa."[8] In Mbeki's scenario, continues Gumede, "the ANC would govern as a center-left party, keeping some remnants of trade union and SACP support, while the bulk of the alliance would form a left-wing workers' party."

"A left-wing workers' party" in opposition to the ANC? A possible outcome devoutly to be wished for in the next round of South African history. But what of the choices that actually were made in post-apartheid South Africa? So careful an analyst as Mbeki's much-cited biographer Mark Gevisser, for example, affirms that as early as 1985 Mbeki had concluded that "a negotiated settlement [required] a far more liberal approach to economic policy" than had been the ANC position up to that time. Furthermore, by 1994 "[Mbeki] and his government [felt] forced to acquiesce to the Washington Consensus on macro-economic policy when they implemented their controversial GEAR program in 1996."[8] Felt forced? This is a choice of words for explaining the ANC's trajectory that bears further discussion. Yet the truth is we can also find veteran ANC/SACP activist Ben Turok suggesting something similar in explicitly agreeing with Gevisser as to the necessary nature of the deviation to the right that the ANC had been compelled to take.

Yet Turok also knows something more: the particularly grim outcomes likely to follow from a choice so made. In fact, more recently we can find Turok substantially qualifying his earlier view, now querying why the ANC government had not "given equal attention to empowering the masses as to the elite? And why has the insistence of parliament on broad-based empowerment brought so little success?"[10] Turok already knows the answer to this question – and, in consequence, is even willing (in later chapters of the book from which the preceding passages are quoted) to back away uneasily from the new ANC's hard-line capitalist position, and to come, in his words, to "the irresistible conclusion...that the ANC government has lost a great deal of its earlier focus on the fundamental transformation of the inherited social system."[11] Inevitable? Lost focus? Obviously, a core question remains unanswered here: why was there this ever firmer and untroubled preference for a conservative economic program on the part of the ANC elite in the first place?

Fanon had one explanation. What, he might have argued, we have in South Africa is merely the familiar trajectory of virtually all post-liberation movements-in-power in Africa: a new middle class that now chooses, in its own class interests, to opt for a junior partnership with capital, quasi-colonial and global. Though now updated to embrace the realities of the ever more globalized workings of capital, the same sad tale could easily be offered as one convincing explanation of the South African case as well. For here, in essence, we see the self-interested embrace by the ANC and its business-oriented cronies of the globalizing logic of capital; here, in short, is a submission to the recolonization of South Africa by diverse capitalists and as facilitated by a new South African elite eager to embrace just such an outcome.[12] True, this would make for a dour reading of what has happened in South Africa – but it is a reading that is quite difficult to dismiss.

Not that this is the way the ANC tells the story. Let us look at the tropes the ANC draws on in explaining its choices. One explanation favored by the ANC in rationalizing these choices is the global collapse of any genuine socialist alternative – the reference here being primarily to the fading away of the Soviet Union and its Eastern European wards. This, it is inferred, left ANC socialists and their aspirations stranded in a sea of capitalist globalization. And the latter system's stringent global imperatives had therefore, and of necessity, to be taken not merely seriously but as being prescriptive of policy in

ways they had not been in the past. Also consider the skewed definition of socialism with which this argument begins, one associated narrowly with the Soviet style of socialism. Yet that had been a limited,
mechanistic, undemocratic – in short, non-socialist – model if ever
there was one – and certainly not one that needed to be followed (or
relied upon) if a more open and imaginative socialist path were to
have been chosen. Instead, even as ruling elites in such countries as
China and the new South Africa casually abandoned socialist aspirations, they nonetheless managed to hold to many of the Soviet model's
most questionable attributes, notably its formidably arrogant and elite-
serving vanguardist mode of politics.

In this chapter, however, it is another trope, crucial to the ANC's
retreat from socialism, that will be emphasized. This refers, so it is
argued by the ANC, to the failure in practice of any operative socialism elsewhere in Africa. In particular, the reference is to those countries in southern Africa where ANC personnel in exile are said to have
witnessed at first hand such failures of socialism, notably in Tanzania
and Mozambique. These were where African socialist endeavor had
been taken least rhetorically and, for a period, most seriously. True,
these two countries have been reduced to impoverished supplication
vis-à-vis global capital, not so differently from other less militant African countries. Yet, as we will see, their strengths and of their weaknesses repay discussion. Through such discussion we can discover
many keys to the meaning of socialist practice in Africa and to the
lessons to be learned from it – lessons not at all illuminated by mere
caricature. For in the cases of Tanzania and Mozambique we see both
the nobility of the aspiration for a socialist Africa but also the weaknesses of the socialism actually practiced – weaknesses that tell us
more about what might need to be done to make socialism real than
they do about the irrelevance of the intention.

We will take as read the ANC's allusions to the failures of regional
socialism. Instead, I will seek in this and the following chapters to
query these regional projects, surveying their practice in order to discover what light their failures might cast on the choice of socioeconomic system being made in South Africa.

(ii) The Front-line States: The Tanzania Case[13]

To have experienced, some fifty years ago and at first hand, the drama of the Arusha Declaration years in Tanzania was to see the promise, if not yet the fully realized practice, of socialism in Africa etched in a particularly vivid light. For there, by the late 1960s, Julius Nyerere, the country's president and the man most closely identified with the dramatic moment of the Arusha Declaration and the announcement of the country's Ujamaa project, had announced on behalf of his people the launching of just such a socialist project. Then, briefly but dramatically – and far more so than any other country along the already liberated front line of the dawning southern African struggle – Nyerere and his political party, TANU, held out the prospect of founding a distinctive brand of socialism in Africa. This was to be a African socialism that could serve as a touchstone for something beyond the kind of neocolonialism and false decolonization that thinkers like Frantz Fanon had begun to identify as the sobering stigmata of the overall African decolonization process.

The moment was indeed one of promise, and even some promise in the most strictly Fanonist terms. After all, Fanon had seen the postcolonial African political leadership as being virtually a cadre of usurpers now seen to be working in their own class interests (and those of global capital) and against the earlier assurances of a sustained betterment in political and economic conditions that they had once promised as the obvious accompaniment to the attainment of freedom from direct colonial overlordship. And yet here, in Tanzania, there were, in addition to the Arusha Declaration, two easily overlooked but particularly striking portents that a more positive outcome might actually occur there.

One of these moments of promise occurred in Nyerere's speech at a large 1967 rally in Dar es Salaam around the time of the pronouncement of the Arusha Declaration and in the very first days of Ujamaa-inspired euphoria. I was present on that occasion, but it was also reported upon in detail by the *Nationalist* newspaper. I have quoted an extract from this speech in both my epigraphs at the front of this volume and Introduction, to which I would refer the reader. For here was practical Fanonism in full voice. Yet there was more.

For what of the danger of the successor black elite now elevated to power being merely in league with global capital? On this there was a second illuminating statement by Nyerere to consider, one in which he self-consciously expanded the import of the anti-colonial nationalist project beyond the merely political realm and onto the terrain of what he termed economic nationalism and of socialism:

> The real ideological choice is between controlling the economy though domestic private enterprise or doing so though the state or some other collective institution.

> But although this is an ideological choice, it is extremely doubt-ful whether this is a practical choice for an African nationalist. The pragmatist in Africa...will find that the real choice is a different one. He will find that the real choice is between foreign private owner-ship on the one hand and local collective ownership on the other, For I do not think there is any free state in Africa where there is sufficient capital, or a sufficient number of local entrepreneurs, for local capital to dominate the economy. Private investment in Africa means overwhelmingly foreign private investment. A capitalist economy means a foreign dominated economy. These are the facts of Africa's situation. The only way in which national control of the economy can be achieved is through the economic institutions of socialism.

> To Tanzania this inevitable choice is not unwelcome. We are social-ists as well as nationalists. We are committed to the creation of a classless society in which every able-bodied person is contribut-ing to the economy through work and we believe this can only be obtained when the major means of production are publicly owned and controlled. But the fact remains that our recent socialist mea-sures were not taken out of a blind adherence to dogma. They are intended to serve our society.[14]

Not, in other words, some Black economic empowerment along entre-preneurial lines, but collective action by the overall populace (helped to find focus through the exercise of a measure of leadership, to be sure, but this not initially intended to be of an overbearing, all-know-ing, unchecked kind). Meanwhile, linked to such general propositions (genuine popular power, both political and economic) there was a host of more specific initiatives that then attracted wide attention:

- a leadership code that sought to encourage leaders not to follow the path of private self-interest into any compromising entanglements with the private sector;
- a one-party electoral scheme that sought (albeit within severe limits) to open up the dominant party to public scrutiny;
- a program of rural transformation *("Ujamaa Vivijini")* designed to draw peasants together in more organized, cooperative and productive new villages;
- an expanded and transformed education system ("Education for Self-Reliance") to meet national needs but also to seek to steer students toward more selfless and responsible citizenship;
- the *Mwongozo* (Tanu Guidelines) of 1971 that stated an intention to facilitate the attack from below on bureaucratic and politically high-handed actions in the country, stating, in its Clause 15, that "there must be a deliberate effort to build equality between leaders and those they lead."[15] It was Mwongozo that Walter Rodney once described as an "even harder hitting document than the Arusha Declaration,"[16] momentarily seeming to herald, as it did, genuine popular empowerment from below.

As it happens, this latter suggestion presented one of the most difficult challenges to the creation of a politics at once progressive in import and democratic in substance. There is a case to be made for the necessity of enlightened leadership – sheer romantic and populist spontaneism is no answer. But, at the same time, no leadership can long go unchecked from below – not if it is to avoid a fall into high-handedness and self-indulgent elitism. Moreover, the resultant contradiction is not one that can merely be resolved easily and once and for all – either in principle or practice. Instead, it is a tension that must be lived and self-consciously struggled with within a process of ongoing and challenging democratic politics – leadership winning its case through convincing and responsive argument and practice, on the one hand, and an increasingly enlightened and self-conscious mass base exerting its democratic voice on the other.

And yet, in truth, the pursuit of democracy in Tanzania was already compromised by the adherence of Nyerere and TANU to the (ultimately contradictory) creation of a political system that institutionalized a "one-party democracy." But now the failure to work to realize the promise of Mwongozo – a late addition to the Arusha Declaration package and one that seemed to take the tensions alluded to here with the seriousness they demanded – would soon prove to have been one of the key failings of the Tanzanian experiment.

The dramatic thrust of the ujamaa project was stymied in a number of ways, these reflecting additional failures that can be briefly elucidated here. One of these was the failure – for all the talk about socialism and self-reliance – to move with any imagination towards an industrial strategy that could have serviced such a goal and permitted, in Samir Amin's term (cited with respect to this subject in chapter 1), a genuine delinking of Tanzania from the overbearing "il/logic" of the world of (global) capital. Not that the notion of delinking could ever be interpreted, in Amin's work, as signaling any unrealistic push towards autarky. But – as sympathetic but heterodox economists who had worked in Tanzania such as Clive Thomas and Bill Luttrell argued at the time[17] – what was needed was the forceful assertion of an alternative *internal* focus for the economy, one that any external economic links would be expected, first and foremost, to service.

Thomas' policy emphases (touched on in Chapter I alongside a further discussion in this book's conclusion of Samir Amin's delinking strategy) should be revisited here, pointing as those paragraphs do towards a possible set of actions that could, in principle and as the very reverse of the market fundamentalist's global orthodoxy, underwrite a socialism of expanded reproduction. As proved to be the case, this was an emphasis that Nyerere and company consistently turned their backs on. Thus Bill Luttrell,[18] writing explicitly within the analytical framework established by Thomas, demonstrates the almost complete failure of Tanzania's bureaucratic class to act in any such way, their continued subservience to the logic of global capitalism and to their class interest dictating a long-term failure to develop the country. He then spells out an alternative track that might have been taken had the elite really wanted to pursue transformation. Moreover, while Luttrell says little about Nyerere, another crucial missing link – industrial strategy (to be added to silences about democracy and failures of imagination in the rural sector) – in Nyerere's presumed socialist strategy here stands starkly exposed.

But what of that rural sector just alluded to? Here, unfortunately, an active skepticism towards the radical potential of peasants – alongside the resistance to any genuinely democratic empowerment of the mass of the population from below, be it expressed by workers, peasants, women or students[19] – ran deep amongst the Tanzanian leadership (as would also subsequently prove true of the Frelimo leadership in Mozambique). Thus, in spite of their many statements as to the crucial class belonging (as workers and peasants) of "the people," such class descriptors were all too readily collapsed into merely populist categories in Tanzania instead of their facilitating a view of such classes as being potentially empowerable in radical terms. Any commitment to an active democracy seems to have been the rub here. As Leander Schneider – one of the most careful and incisive of all scholars of the *Ujamaa Vijijini* initiative – suggests, in this central rural policy,

> several of the most inspiring strands of Nyerere's politics flow together – in particular, an exemplary commitment to improving the condition of the poor, as well as his theorizing about the nexus of development, freedom, empowerment, and participation. However, it is also in the field of rural development that problematic dimensions of Nyerere's leadership become, perhaps, most starkly apparent. Not only did the policy of enforced ujamaa/villagization fail to improve the material conditions of Tanzania's rural population, but the adoption of coercive means to further it also points to the authoritarian side of Nyerere's rule.[20]

Nor is the word "authoritarian" chosen lightly by Schneider with reference to the draconian effacing of the Ruvuma Development Association's experiment in revolutionary rural democracy from below and the conversion of rural socialism into an order to villagize coming from on high. For his use of that word lies at the very center of Schneider's argument. Small wonder that he then concludes his analysis of what he calls the "statist bent (and the related overtly coercive character observed in 1970s Tanzania)" with the observation that "Tanzanian history shows, above all, that turning a blind eye to the tensions of participatory development will neither make them go away nor allow one to avoid the serious costs implied by swiftly reducing participation to near meaninglessness."[21] Here then is yet another lesson – but there are similar lessons available from the treatment of workers and of students in Tanzania as well[22] – to be learned by anyone of progressive bent who would care to hear such tidings, depressing but also, potentially, instructive.

And what of women, whose liberation is perhaps as urgently needed as is those included in any other social category in Tanzania (and in the rest of southern Africa). The entire sphere of struggle for gender emancipation and gender equality was a front of freedom little discussed at the time in Tanzania, and, indeed, the record was not an encouraging one. For example, Bibi Titi Mohammed, admittedly no great socialist but a prominent TANU leader in the early days, underscored some years ago the starkness of the male sense of entitlement that marked TANU in those years, the vital role of women militants in the liberation struggle soon being more or less passed over.

> When power was transferred to the nationalist government...the story changed. Women's experience was no longer relevant to the postcolonial struggles against neo-colonialism, imperialism and the management of the state apparatus. In [our] discussion Bibi Titi ironically said, "I started smelling fish" when the first cabinet was named.[23]

Indeed, so incensed by this was Bibi Titi that, by her account, she refused Nyerere's offer to co-author with him a joint history of Tanzania's nationalist liberation struggle. Meanwhile, the prevailing silences of that time have continued to scar present-day reality in Tanzania, despite the best efforts of many women activists then and now to keep the struggle for gender emancipation alive. But, as we have also seen, the struggle for overall emancipation continues to confront all Tanzanians, male and female with many of them the poorest of the continent's (and of the world's) poor, as well. But this latter struggle is, of course, a struggle – for genuine democracy, for nationally focused and people-centric development, and much else – that also confronts the vast majority of similarly deprived – even if freshly liberated – South Africans.

[In the original text from which this chapter is derived, a third section looked briefly at the strengths and weaknesses of Mozambique's attempts to carve out for itself something like a socialist path forward in the country's post-liberation period. It seems to me clear that while there were severe weaknesses to Frelimo's efforts in this regard, these were not the themes that the ANC/SACP thinkers focused on in caricaturing regional attempts to commit to a socialism...the better to cover the rightward turn of its tracks during their post-apartheid period. For example, one of the main foci of criticism might have better been on the inordinate (and very costly) degree of swaggering vanguardism that characterized Frelimo's political style and political methods. But this style also marked the ANC, with the undemocratic premises of Frelimo's practices being little noted or critiqued by ANC leaders and members with whom I conversed. But I soon saw this theme as too big for inclusion as a mere section of the present chapter and I have therefore saved certain aspects of the Mozambican case for discussion in the following chapter.]

(iii) Socialism in Southern Africa and the South African Case

The logic of genuine economic nationalism, of the refusal of any abject, unqualified surrender to the forces of global capital, and of the necessary link of socialism to any such successful refusal were quickly lost on the ANC, that movement/party being only able (willfully or otherwise) to see the negative dimensions of Tanzania and Mozambique's failed attempts to realize a more humane and progressively transformative political economy. But the imperatives of genuine and empowered democracy, of a progressive (non-vanguardist) resolution of the tension between leadership and popular control, and of a non-dogmatic economic self-reliance were even more quickly lost sight of by the ANC than they had been, in the long run, by TANU and Frelimo. As was soon clear, the ANC's momentary toying with the modest measure of transformation that the Reconstruction and Development Programme/RDP represented soon slipped into its Growth, Employment and Redistribution/GEAR initiative,[24] and the movement's extremely brief flirtation with the promise of some sustained popular purpose and a real popular takeover of the process of transformation was lost.

Indeed, as Michelle Williams helps make clear, the latter outcome was never really on offer even from the SACP, much less from the ANC. Thus, in carefully contrasting the South African instance with that of Kerala, she suggests that in the latter case the Indian state's Communist Party premised its activities on what she calls a "counter-hegemonic generative politics" and "a reliance on participatory organizing" – a politics that has sought to genuinely empower people. In South Africa, on the other hand, the preference of the ANC/SACP grouping has been for "a hegemonic generative politics" and a reliance on mere "mass mobilizing" – to, in effect, the drawing a crowd to popularly hail its ascendancy.[25] Small wonder that, as quoted at greater length in the previous chapter, a saddened older ANC/SACP cadre like Rusty Bernstein could, shortly before his death, bemoan the fact that, by the 1980s/1990s, various new commitments by the ANC had undermined its "adherence to the path [of] mass resistance as the way to liberation, and substituted instead a reliance on manipulation of administrative power...[in this way] impoverishing the soil in which ideas leaning towards socialist solutions once flourished, [and allowing] the weed of 'free market' ideology to take hold."[26]

A grim balance sheet, in short, albeit not one so very different from that of the recolonized (by the world of capital) residues of colonial empires that its neighbors have also become. Indeed, despite its rather higher starting point, thanks to its mineral riches, on the world economic table, the South African populace is firmly lodged well down the world poverty table. For South Africa, in the absence of the imaginative planning that might have sought both an effectively self-centered (but, to repeat, not autarkic) economic model and a possibly transformative developmental future, remains primarily a "taker" of economic signals from the global corporate world. Its record in terms of provision of opportunities for urban employment and rural renewal, in terms of housing, electricity and water supplies, in terms of education and health services, in terms of a progressive package of environmentally sensitive measures – its record in terms of facilitating growing social inequality more generally – is not markedly better than the records of its neighbors in southern Africa.

In fact, the principal lesson to be learned from recent southern African history, including that of South Africa, is not so much what not to do as it is the high cost to be paid for choosing not to dare – not to dare to be self-reliant and economically imaginative and not to dare to be genuinely democratic and practically committed to the social and political empowerment of the people. For not to so dare is, in our contemporary world, merely to wallow in a stagnant pond of self-serving vanguardism and in a post-Fanonist pattern of elite aggrandizement – even if such attitudes are, in South Africa, sustained within what is now a formally democratic process. And it is to accept passively something else, that something else being most readily epitomized in one harsh, hard and unyielding word: recolonization. All that struggle, carried out so nobly, against apartheid – and, throughout the region, against a full panoply of arrogant colonialisms – to have come to this: a callous recolonization, by global capital and aided domestically by southern Africa's ostensible liberators. Sad, sad, sad.

Not that South Africa has escaped the grim politics of polarization that the ANC's choice of direction has willed for it. In fact, the concluding paragraphs of the previous chapter and some of the same doleful quotations could well be repeated here. After all, even though the ANC continues to win power (with a roughly similar high percentage of what is nonetheless an increasingly smaller turnout of eligible voters), it has to deal with an increasingly discontented population. The result, as Peter Alexander underscored in that chapter, was the surfacing of a virtual rebellion of the poor and, with it, a sharpened prospect of change.[27] Moreover, also cited in that chapter was Moeletsi Mbeki's speculation as to the possibility of a genuine Tunisia-like spring of discontent erupting ever more forcefully from below and now stalking South Africa (he sets the likely date as 2020).[28] And we cited there too Zwelinma Vavi, then head of the trade union central (COSATU), observing dramatically that "we have a constitution which grants people certain rights. Yet in practice millions are denied those rights, especially socioeconomic rights, in what has become the most unequal nation in the world."[29]

❋   ❋   ❋

In short, many of the ingredients for the emergence in South Africa of an effectively counter-hegemonic politics – possibly a politics of active, participatory mass empowerment – seem to be in place. It may well be that South Africa offers, with its impressive popular base-in-waiting, a more promising picture than did its fellow anti-socialist false decolonizers elsewhere in the region: Tanzania and Mozambique. For in South Africa's movements there are signs – "Fees Must Fall," the post-Marikana moment, the anti-Zuma backlash – that the country might eventually make good some of the hopes of Fanon (and of Williams). As Fanon put the relevant point:

> The Third World [including the countries of southern Africa] today faces Europe like a colossal mass whose project should be to try to resolve the problems to which Europe has not been able to find the answers.[30]

Fanon is still waiting. At the moment, the answers – capitalism, growing inequality and straitened structures of democratic aspiration and active participation – of Europe and North America are the structures southern Africa has taken as its own. Nonetheless, as Fanon also tells us,

> For Europe, for ourselves, and for humanity, comrades, we must turn over a new leaf, we must work out new concepts, and try to set afoot a new man [sic].[31]

The struggle to realize such an outcome continues.

Chapter 4

The African Hero in Mozambican History: On Assassinations and Executions[1]

"Politics in a literary work are a pistol shot in the middle of a concert, a crude affair though one impossible to ignore," writes Stendhal, the greatest of political novelists.[2] The same is true of death – especially death by assassination or execution – in the political analysis of Africa. Such intrusions of planned and orchestrated deaths have provided key moments in African politics (and, not least, in Mozambican politics) but moments that have too seldom been allotted the attention they warrant or the seriousness they deserve.

Here, in part one, different ways of approaching this matter are discussed and exemplified with reference to two of the most pertinent assassinations – those of Eduardo Mondlane and Samora Machel – that have scarred Mozambique. To what extent can we speculate as to what difference such assassinations have made to longer term outcomes? What can we learn from a closer examination of the "what ifs" of history?

The second section, also focused on the history of Mozambique, seeks to examine the broader meaning of "execution as a mode of governance": there it re-examines Frelimo's secret executions, in the first decade of Mozambican independence, of Uria Simango, his wife and a number of his colleagues who had been the movement's internal opposition in exile in Tanzania in the 1960s. Seeing these executions as exemplifying the negative outcome of the self-righteous vanguardism that has continued to haunt Frelimo in power up to the present, the second section of this two-part article concludes by examining the wave of mafia-style killings that has followed, in this century, the assassination of crusading journalist Carlos Cardoso in 2000 in what has come to be called Mozambique's quiet assassination epidemic. How can we interpret such unsavory recent phenomena?

147

In an essay written a number of years ago for ROAPE #127 – and entitled "Mozambique, Not Then But Now" – I explored that country's tension between would-be socialism and elite betrayal, and I draw on that text in the initial paragraphs here in order to set the stage for what follows.[3] Thus, in the ROAPE article, I quoted favorably Norrie McQueen's strong assertion that the initial plans of Portugal's guerrilla enemies offered "a clear alternative to the cynical manipulation of ethnicity and the neocolonial complaisance of the kleptocratic elites who increasingly defined African governance in the 1970s and 1980s." In sum,

> Whatever their fate, the projects of the post-independence regimes of lusophone Africa were probably the most principled and decent ever proposed for the continent. They have not been superseded in this regard and seem unlikely to be.[4]

This seemed to me, as I argued there, to have been especially true of the new Mozambique during its first heroic decade of independence. Equally dramatic, however, has been the reversal of direction that has taken place in the country since that time. For what has happened since, in Alice Dinerman's words,[5] was nothing less than a "rapid unraveling of the Mozambican revolution," with the result that Mozambique,

> once considered a virtually peerless pioneer in forging a socialist pathway in Africa, ... now enjoys an equally exceptional, if dialectically opposed, status: today the country is, in the eyes of the IMF and the World Bank, a flagship of neoliberal principles.

It is difficult now to avoid Dinerman's conclusion that, "predictably, many of the leading government and party officials rank among the primary beneficiaries of the new political and economic dispensation. Those who enthusiastically promised that Mozambique would turn into a graveyard of capitalism are now the leading advocates of, and avid accumulators in, capitalism's recent, full-blown resurrection."

Moreover, the outcome of such a shift has been bleak for the vast majority of Mozambicans. For what occurred, Bauer and Taylor suggest,[6] was the extremely rapid growth and dramatic spread of corruption (more or less unknown in the initial days of independence) in Mozambique, as well as a fevered "pursuit of individual profit [that has undermined] much of the legitimacy of Frelimo party leaders, who [have taken] advantage of market-based opportunities, like privatization, to enrich themselves." In short, as these authors then observe,

> the election of Guebuza [as the new President in 2004, and for a second term thereafter], holder of an expansive business network and one of the richest men in Mozambique, hardly signals that Frelimo will attempt to run on anything but a globalist, neoliberal agenda – regardless of the abject poverty suffered by most of its electorate.

Unfortunately, such a somber conclusion has seemed to many observers to be an all too accurate snapshot of Frelimo's power elite and its questionable national project. And, equally unfortunately, it remains so. Indeed, the present essay reflects my perplexity faced with the dramatic collapse (as pinpointed by Dinerman) of Frelimo's socialist ideals and by the movement's attendant curtailing of any very substantial democratic empowerment of popular forces in the country. As I have reviewed this record, I have been shaken once again by the role that assassinations – notably the brutal removal of such friends and personal heroes as Eduardo Mondlane and Samora Machel from the flow of history – have had in shaping these outcomes; hence my attempt to give such assassinations a more central focus here.

I have also been deeply disturbed by a fresh reminder from my recent research of the key role that execution of its critics by Frelimo has been seen by its leaders to be warranted as a means of consolidating its power. In addition to executions, a deep veil of secrecy is deployed to mask Frelimo's high-handed practices. This aspect was at least equally unsettling, and a further proof of the self-righteous vanguardism that came to swallow the movement. I regret that I have not given this matter sufficient attention in my previous writings on Mozambique; it is a silence that I attempt to correct here.[7] In consequence, this essay also constitutes a reflection on the weight and significance, within the broader turmoil of political change, of both assassinations and executions as events on which too little concern has been focused and concerning which too little scholarly debate has taken place.[8] Thus this essay is also an attempt to help rectify the weakness in our collective work in this respect.

❀   ❀   ❀

It is not hard to explain, structurally, the social realities that have over-determined and negated any more positive outcomes in Mozambique, realities that permit of a Marxist analysis of the demise of Mozambican socialism. Certainly, the country's inheritance from colonial domination was weak, reflected in the paucity of trained indigenous personnel and in an economic dependence that pulled the country strongly towards subordination to global dictate despite some efforts to resist it. There was also, in this first period, the ongoing regional war that weakened Mozambique and defined it as a principal target of destructive incursions by white-dominated Rhodesia and South Africa and also of the long-drawn-out campaign of terror waged so callously and destructively by those countries' then-sponsored ward, the RENAMO counter-revolutionary movement. Finally, and despite Frelimo's often benign intentions, there were the movement's sins once in power, sins of vanguardist high-handedness and impatience, and of the over-simplification of societal complexities and challenges. Underlying all this, and in the longer run, there grew a Fanonist-style crystallization of privileged class formation around the largely undemocratic successor state and economic structures that Frelimo cadres now came to inhabit. These latter weaknesses created enormous additional obstacles of their own – as they did elsewhere – to any further leftward progress.

Indeed, this has proven to be the case wherever in the world the myth of a necessary vanguardism has been confused (often quite willfully, it would seem) with a correctly perceived and essential need for leadership; for the truth is that, as a global phenomenon, vanguardism has almost inevitably degenerated (virtually everywhere it has been exemplified) into the spectacle of the political elite then nominating itself for such a role in perpetuity. And it is this, in turn, that has reinforced precisely the high-handedness, impatience, and oversimplification as to societal complexities and challenges referred to above. The fact is that the only cure for such proto-authoritarianism – even if it has been adopted in the name of some supposed higher cause of mass liberation and/or of some claimed socialist goal – are effective democratic structures that are crafted to hold leaders to popular account.

The difficult dialectic of socialist politics thus stands revealed. Leadership is necessary (good leadership can certainly problem-solve, educate and enlighten). But it must be linked to a simultaneous process, namely the creation of unequivocally democratic institutions, designed to empower the masses further to understand and to act upon their own class interests. For only in that way might they hope to defend themselves against such leadership if and when the latter begins to present itself as some absolutely necessary vanguard, and to then privilege itself overbearingly within the political equation, as it has almost invariably been tempted to do. The paradoxical outcome, one that truly deserves the label of democratic leadership, is always a work in progress, an ongoing effort to keep the terms "democratic" and "leadership" both in play; neither naïve spontaneism and shallow populism on the one hand nor some smug vanguardism on the other will meet the need for sustained political creativity.

(i) On Heroes and their Removal from History

Where does a more honest and responsible set of leaders fit into this complex equation? This is another important theme in recent African history, a theme that must complement our focus on the persistence of neocolonial economic structures and their cultural resonance and on the foundations of global economic control upon which imperialism has been able to build its continuing shaping of southern African economies in the post-liberation period. Thus, a significant variable shaping the direction of change has been the realm of willed intentionality, the shaping of both intention and hope in such a positive and grounded manner as to make the objective *possibilities* of change *actual*...as individuals and classes choose to avail themselves of the structural opportunities offered them by history – a theme also explored in my discussion of the politics of hope.[9] But note as well the flip side of this historical coin. For equally possible can be the *removal of hope*, including, not least, the physical removal – by the tactic of assassination as deployed by enemies of progressive purpose – of the tangible human stimuli of hope: the very leadership cadres who might seek to build and exemplify radical hope and encourage others to do the same.

In Africa, assassination has shaped the continent's recent history in ways that are impossible to measure, although even the strictest of those who emphasize structural determinations over other explanations must surely pause to give some autonomous weight to this factor. Consider:

- the killing of Amilcar Cabral by the Portuguese (on 20 January 1973 in Conakry) at a crucial stage of his movement's (the PAIGC) development of a struggle against Portuguese rule in Guinea-Bissau;
- the disappearance in October 1965 (explained, much later, by the revelation that his murder was carried out by Moroccan agents and French police[10]) of Morocco's Mehdi Ben Barka, head of his country's left-wing National Union of Popular Forces (UNPF) and secretary of the Tricontinental Conference;
- the horrific slaying of the Congo's elected progressive prime minister Patrice Lumumba on 17 January 1961;[11]
- the assassinations of leftist figure Pio Pinto in Kenya on 24 February 1965 and of such exemplary and left-leaning South African activists as Steve Biko (12 September 1977), Ruth First in Maputo (1982), and Chris Hani (10 April 1993);
- the still unsolved slayings of such important Rhodesian/ Zimbabwean militants as Herbert Chitepo[12] and Tichafa Parirenyatwa;[13]
- the execution of Ken Saro-Wiwa, environmental activist and firm non-violent critic of General Sani Abacha's military dictatorship, judged by a special military tribunal and hanged, quasi-judicially, by Abacha's government;
- the elimination of Thomas Sankara whose notably progressive presidency in Burkina Faso was ended on 15 October 1987 when he was assassinated in the course of a coup organized by his former colleague Blaise Compaoré.

Had they lived, who can say where the insight of these and other such cadres – and of the movements that they had inspired and could have helped to sustain – would have taken their respective countries and the continent as a whole? Meanwhile Mozambique was also to suffer particularly grievously, the loss of the movement's first two presidents, Eduardo Mondlane and Samora Machel, who fell to assassins – so the best evidence would suggest – who sought to deflect the process of both FRELIMO's and Mozambique's revolutionary consolidation. In short, posing questions as to the what-ifs of history is a tempting pastime for the historian of Mozambique.

But is it a worthwhile preoccupation? Obviously, this sort of daydreaming can open up endless speculations. Nonetheless, it can also suggest unrealized possibilities that have inspired important theoretical discussions, and haunted Marxist historians. After all, those assassinations occurred because their perpetrators assumed that the removal of those individuals would make a difference to the outcome of a situation in play. In the literature on such matters this has often been seen as linked to the question of the role played by the hero in history or, less dramatically, as the role of the individual in history. Such a discussion has been most clearly associated with, among others, the works of Thomas Carlyle in the 19th century, G. I Plekhanov at the very dawn of the 20th, Sidney Hook in the mid-20th and Leonid Grinin in the first years of the 21st.[14] I was also intrigued to hear of an Australian workshop – held in March 2019 at that country's National Center of Biography – featuring, centrally, a paper prepared by Rhys Williams entitled "From Carlyle to Plekhanov: The Role of the Individual in History." The workshop's announcement explains,

> The role of the individual in history has always been a concern for historians and biographers. [But] do individuals shape events or do events shape individuals? This workshop examines this old problem through the ideas of Thomas Carlyle and Georgi Plekhanov, the two historians who probably have most influenced our understanding of the individual in history. Carlyle developed, effectively, the best modern example of the Great Man theory of history – in *Heroes and Hero Worship* (1840). And Plekhanov developed the best Marxist thinking on the role of the individual in history in his *On the Role of the Individual in History* (1898). These two thinkers, in their opposing stances, continue to shape the way historians understand and deal with the issue. Key questions to be explored in this workshop include: What is the relationship between the individual and history? What is the relationship between the individual and society? Can the individual change the course of history? Can the individual break from history? Is history really the "biography of Great Men?"[15]

In short, such questions are still very much alive.

Carlyle, an eloquent Scottish writer of the 19th century, saw history as being made by "Great Men" – in particular by kings and noblemen. But society was already in considerable flux even as Carlyle wrote, driven by the development of capitalism on the one hand and by more urgent demands from below on the other. The notion of an expanded universe of potential sociopolitical agency had, therefore, to be much more carefully considered. By the end of the century, Marxism emerged as a serious contender in the historiography sweepstakes. By then Carlyle's position was still so visible and so contradictory to Marxism's emphasis on the importance of larger structural determinants that Georgi Plekhanov challenged Carlyle quite specifically while also spelling out the case for a history much more deeply grounded in social-structural concerns and by such broad realities as those linked to the mode and relations of production, to the telling impact of capitalism's emergence and to the class determinations of social struggles. Plekhanov acknowledged the role of the individual within the social equation, but found the individual to be a frail reed indeed within the context of overdetermination by socioeconomic structure and the realities of class.[16]

Sidney Hook in turn took dead aim at Plekhanov's approach half century later – finding room for the hero's role in history (his most referenced title being *The Hero in History*). But Hook was also aware of the tension he evoked in the subtitle *A Study in Limitation and Possibility*. As he wrote in chapter 6, "The Framework of Heroic Action,"

> Whenever we are in position to assert that an event-making man [sic] had had a decisive influence on a historical period, we are not abandoning the belief in causal connection or embracing the belief in absolute contingency. What we are asserting is that in such situations the great man is a relatively independent historical influence – *independent of the conditions that determine the alternatives – and that on these occasions* the influence of all other relevant factors is of subordinate weight in enabling us to understand or predict which one of the possible alternatives will be actualized. In such situations we also should be able to say, and to present the grounds for saying, that if the great man had not existed, the course of events in essential respects would in all likelihood have taken a *different* turn... [Indeed,] the fact that [we] can offer grounds for believing what the

154

historical record would be like, if some person had not existed, or if some event had not transpired, indicates that in the realm of history, as in the realm of nature, pure contingency does not hold sway. Contingent events in history are of tremendous importance, but the evidence of their importance is possible only because not all events are contingent. [In fact] the whole answer to our inquiry depends upon the legitimacy of our asking and answering – as indeed every competent historian does ask and answer – what would have happened *if* this event had not happened or that man had not lived, or this alternative had not been taken.

Hook had a checkered intellectual/political career, of course.[17] But he took seriously the implied tension between limitation and possibility. As Grinin summarizes the point:

Hook's book was a noticeable step forward in the solution of Great Man influence on historical development and [is] by far the most profound work on the issue in question. Hook convincingly and at times rather figuratively states a number of important propositions that allow [one] to avoid extremes to a certain extent. In particular, in Chapter 6, he notes that, on the one hand, an individual's activity is limited by the environmental circumstances and the society's character, and, on the other hand, where there appear alternatives in the society's development [wherein] the role of the individual increases dramatically up to the point when it becomes an independent force.[18]

Hook was seeking to identify the space wherein principled leadership, at once heroic and progressive, could operate creatively and expect to *make a difference* (see for example his account of Lenin's role in Russia in his chapter 10, "The Russian Revolution: A Test-Case"). Chapter 7, entitled "'If' in History," is especially interesting.[19] Here he points to moments when individuals have had a significant role to play, although he acknowledges that any such argument is to be embarked upon cautiously and circumspectly. In addition, in his strong and exhaustive paper, Grinin also investigates a number of theoretical tensions that hover around such a juxtaposition of the individual and history, including, not least, the "what if" question.

(ii) Assassinations: Mozambique, Mondlane and Machel

We must take similar care as we approach the "what ifs" of Mozambican history. For few countries have paid such a high price for the tactic of assassination, deployed as a scorched-earth means of its enemies' resistance to change, as has Mozambique. Two highly regarded presidents, Eduardo Mondlane and Samora Machel, were both, it seems clear, assassinated by the enemies of their country's freedom: Mondlane by the Portuguese defense apparatus and Machel by South Africa's apartheid state. The impact upon the future of Mozambique of the disappearance of such "heroes in history" is impossible to determine. We have already alluded to the structural and historical factors that played a role in over-determining outcomes in Mozambique. Precisely what weight we can allot to the presence or absence of particular "heroes" within such a tangle of determinations goes beyond the scope of any singlemindedly structural explanation, however. Marxists feel the pull of our preferred emphasis on structures that are formidably determinant but we must be wary of methodological overkill.

Eduardo Mondlane: Such "heroes" have often made a difference in defining the nature and (relative) success of the liberation struggle as led by Frelimo; moreover, their deaths certainly weakened the forward thrust of the radical project. Mondlane, for example, was a towering figure, a Mozambican who had escaped the socioeconomic prison of colonial Mozambique, had done undergraduate studies in South Africa[20] (from which country he was expelled by the apartheid government in 1949) and in Portugal and, with the help of American missionaries, had then proceeded to the United States and Oberlin College for his B.A.; subsequently he took up graduate work at Northwestern where he earned a doctorate in anthropology. He then worked for the United Nations' Trusteeship Commission (including assignments in several parts of Africa) and even visited Mozambique towards the end of his UN days. He concluded his American stay (by then seeking the freedom to undertake the kind of Mozambique-related political work barred by his UN appointment) by accepting an appointment at Syracuse University. And it was from there that he returned to Africa to participate in the founding and consolidation of Frelimo.[21]

Mondlane was the one figure who could command the attention of the three pre-existing exile nationalist movements (UDENEMO, MANU and UNAMO) scattered around the region, as well as other young activists (he had been a founding funding organizer of National Union of Mozambican Students/UNEMO, which had on one occasion led to his arrest by the Portuguese authorities). Slowly but surely, he and others began to bring members of these diverse groups together under a shared banner. Not easy work, as George Roberts had reminded us in identifying the maze of cross-currents (global, intra-Tanzanian and intra-Mozambican, ethnic, racial and ideological) that tore across Dar es Salaam in the 1960s.[22] And yet, as Herb Shore also adds in noting that Frelimo's unity was crucial, Mondlane and his immediate colleagues "avoided the imposition of rigid dogma and hierarchy, and constantly allowed for the interplay of conflicting views and positions."[23] Was this an anticipation of what politics under Mondlane's leadership might have looked like had the latter lived to see Mozambique through to independence?

It is also possible that such tensions played a role in Mondlane's assassination. Nonetheless, by the time of his death he had succeeded in overseeing the building of a movement that was strong and united enough to mount an effective military challenge to the Portuguese. In addition, and in large part because of Mondlane's credibility, Frelimo found support for itself from within the OAU and, in particular, from Julius Nyerere (who had become a close friend of Mondlane's); indeed, it was Nyerere who granted Frelimo guerrillas a just-across-the-border rear base from which to enter Mozambique in order to engage their colonial enemy. And this latter in-country guerrilla presence then played a crucial role not only in rallying Mozambique's African population but also in undermining the self-confidence and commitment of large numbers in the Portuguese army. Small wonder, then, that Mondlane was a particularly important target of those Portuguese army ultras who preferred to fight to the end.

There are some complications to the story of Mondlane's murder, even if, importantly, the Tanzanian police were able to trace the assembly of the bomb that killed him to Lourenço Marques and to the Portuguese; the latter is a credible attribution that most observers now accept. How the package containing the bomb – the package that Mondlane opened – found its way through the Frelimo internal mail system is less clear, however, with this suggesting that other hands were also at work within Frelimo. Here, as one of my correspondents noted, "Silverio Nungu was blamed, but nobody else was ever named, or brought to justice in independent Mozambique, although I think some people had a pretty good idea of who they were. I think the silence was for internal political reasons. So such loose ends as there are, are now deeply buried."[24]

What did Mondlane have to offer that made him such a marked man for the Portuguese? Certainly, his organizational capacity and political savvy warranted Lisbon's special attention in its war to shore up its imperial presence in Mozambique. In addition, his political line had come to crystallize around an ever more radical economic approach. As he put the point:

> I am now convinced that FRELIMO has a clearer political line than ever before...The common basis that we had when we formed FRE-LIMO was hatred of colonialism and the belief in the necessity to destroy the colonial structure and to establish a new social structure. But what type of social structure, what type of organization we would have, no one knew. No, some did know, some did have ideas, but they had rather theoretical notions that were themselves transformed in the struggle.

> Now, however, there is a qualitative transformation in thinking that has emerged during the past six years which permit me to conclude that at present FRELIMO is much more socialist, revolutionary and progressive than ever and that the line, the tendency, is now more and more in the direction of socialism of the Marxist Leninist variety. Why? Because the conditions of life in Mozambique, the type of enemy which we have, does not give us any other alternative. I do think, without compromising FRELIMO which still has not made an official announcement declaring itself Marxist Leninist, I can say that FRELIMO is inclining itself more and more in this direction because the conditions is which we struggle, and work demand it.

Indeed, as Mondlane argued in the same interview, it would be "impossible to create a capitalist Mozambique" because "it would be ridiculous for the people to struggle to destroy the economic structure of the enemy and then reconstitute it in such a way as to serve the enemy."[25]

But what about another question of contemporary resonance: "Mondlane the democrat"? The implications for the future of such a question is no less speculative than the question "Mondlane: the socialist?" perhaps, but both questions provoke thoughts about the possible future of a post-independence Mozambique under Mondlane's leadership. Would Mondlane not also have said that "It would be impossible to create an undemocratic Mozambique"? In retrospect it might be argued that, insofar as Mozambique's future lay in Frelimo's hands at the moment of independence, the most fundamental flaw in its project was its broader weaknesses in the sphere of democratic theory and practice.

Frelimo, in the post-Mondlane years, did not ignore this issue altogether. Indeed, the Frelimo leadership reveled in the fact that a great deal of its military success had come from listening to and working with the people on the ground as the movement advanced its armed struggle. Moreover, one of its most dramatic policy initiatives in its very first days of holding power was the attempt to deepen the populace's sense of fundamental empowerment through the establishment of the *grupos dinamizadores* in urban neighborhoods, rural villages and workplaces. However, the messiness of such democratic processes-in-the-making did not greatly appeal to those used to the military orderliness of Nachingwea camp. It proved all too easy for Frelimo leaders, in their arrogance of power (albeit often, at least in the early days of power, with the very best of intentions and with full commitment to the popular cause) to convince themselves that they knew best, and knew, absolutely, what was required. Moreover, this was an organizational trajectory that, very soon, the adoption of official Marxism-Leninism – with its stern Stalinist rationale for vanguardism and its firm sense of the Party's historical certainty – could only reinforce.

Thus, opposition was sometimes merely crushed (as we will see) and mass organizations (the women's organization and the trade unions and the like) created ostensibly as mechanisms of popular empowerment all too quickly became more like transmission belts for delivery of the party line. Critical debate that should have been the lifeblood of a revolutionary process all but dried up within a stale and predictable media milieu (there were signal exceptions). Tradition (seen to have its most negative impact in spheres like gender relations and an exaggerated deference to old-style authority), religious conservatism, and ethnic and regional sensitivities became, as examples of *obscurantismo*, as, that is, merely negative constraints to be overridden from on high rather than being viewed as the deep-seated social realities they were: realities that needed to be worked upon politically, while balancing, in this respect, both leadership on the one hand and mass initiative on the other in much more nuanced and open-ended ways. At its most grotesque the more high-handed of these possible practices was revealed in the solution – a way to relieve problems of urban overcrowding, it was said – that became *Operação Produção*. Here – this forced removal of "excess" and unemployed populations out of the cities and to more rural sites, in 1983 – was a prime example of the kind of raw tactics of intended transformation that, in their negative impact, would ultimately provide hostages to RENAMO and also help to rot out much of the high moral purpose that had originally inspired Frelimo.

This is not to be wise after the event. In a foreword I wrote for the second edition of Mondlane's book *The Struggle for Mozambique* in 1983, I had already evoked such thoughts, seeing them as being as relevant to the still somewhat open future of Mozambican socialism as they may now be to writing an epitaph for Frelimo's entire left experiment. I noted the danger signs that threatened the vigor of the emancipatory process that Frelimo professed to value, including considerable "inertia in facilitating mass action and self-organization by the workers and peasants"; in the "over-valuing of top-down interventions and administrative solutions"; and in the adoption of an official Marxism whose sterile definitions could only serve to deaden Marx's emancipatory message. Such tendencies worked against the profoundly democratic thrust both of Mondlane's book and of his political proclivities more generally. As I then wrote, Mondlane's socialist, even Marxist-Leninist premises (as expressed in an interview given to Aquino de Bragança and previously cited), remain framed in his book, by an insistence that Frelimo's political project cannot exist outside of or above the Mozambican people; indeed, as I added,[26] "as long as the [democratic] sensibility that had informed Mondlane's book remains at the center of Frelimo's practice, there is a strong likelihood that the country's goals will be achieved."

Once again, we cannot say for a certainty what would have become of Mondlane's democratic sensibility.[27] It is true that the pressures that sprang from the regional conflagrations, institutional disorder and economic difficulties faced by his successors augmented the temptations of power and privilege that ensnared so many of them. What is sure is that his successors in the Frelimo leadership did not manifest enough democratic sensibility, as a number of the old militants from that period have confessed to me. It is difficult to isolate out this one factor, the lack of democratic sensibility, from all the other relevant and at least equally determining variables. Nonetheless, the costs of the absence of such a sensibility were high. What if Mondlane had lived? As suggested above, he might have made a difference in facilitating the consolidation of a genuinely democratic Mozambique, one to build a more open future on.

Samora Machel: What of that other fallen comrade, Samora Machel – who, after a bitter battle both within Frelimo and within the Tanzanian government, became the first and most credible of Mondlane's successors as party president?[28] Unlike Mondlane, Machel lived long enough to become, after the 1974 army coup in Portugal, the first president of a free and independent Mozambique. But his heroic stature had already been established, during the liberation war, by the role he played in consolidating a viable and successful Frelimo armed wing. Others were involved, but Machel's energy and personal charisma were a magnet. Thus, he moved from his job as a male nurse in southern Mozambique to, in exile, a role within Frelimo's fledgling military where, by the sheer force of his will and charisma, he made things happen, emerging as that army's commander and its inspiration. In doing so he had to step past Uria Simango[29] politically, the man who initially, after Mondlane's death, formed, with Marcelino dos Santos and Machel, a short-lived leadership triumvirate. But this leadership format was most unlikely to last and, with Nyerere's blessing and against the views of some other prominent Tanzanian politicians, Machel's elevation to the leadership of Frelimo was confirmed and sanctioned by Tanzania.

As president of Mozambique, Machel and his team faced a new set of challenges in the post-liberation world. In fact, much was accomplished in the early years, although even then Frelimo's overall system of governance, set within a framework of one-party rule but also as the product of many cross-cutting forces, remained a firmly top-down one. And this in turn framed a comfortable environment for Machel's own larger-than-life personality and vanguardist bent. Perhaps it is not surprising that, by the time of Machel's death on 19 October 1986, the Frelimo system as a whole (as carried over from the war experience) was fraying, with many of the cadres – not least within the military – becoming merely older and more comfortable. Many corrupt practices and a stale and rather slipshod bureaucratization also became more pervasive, with such distemper particularly evident within the country's military leadership (which was by then also under considerable pressure from apartheid South Africa and its then ward, Renamo). Indeed, it was much anticipated that, on his return from Lusaka, Machel – as he confided to several colleagues – planned to move to clean up the Mozambican military, beginning with the sacking of its commandant, Sebastião Mobate. This had once been the sphere of command in which Machel had exemplified his most heroic character, but it was now increasingly a focus of his most scathing criticisms. Could he have helped turn things around? No time for that in any case, the necessary asterisk tells us: such a growing commitment to act was only just crystallizing shortly before his death.

Machel's death, together with those of many of his top advisors, came when his plane, returning from a meeting in Lusaka, crashed into a hill across the border in South Africa. And it was no accident, it seems apparent, although the allegation that the South Africans had used a false signal to pull the plane off its course has been difficult to prove.[30] Nonetheless, this is the picture that emerged in the aftermath of the crash, even though the site had been meticulously scoured and apparently cleaned up – with compromising evidence removed – by South African security officials before any word of the crash was passed on to Maputo. It is also true that, after the ANC's post-apartheid ascension to power, its Truth and Reconciliation Commission undertook a "Special Investigation into the death of President Samora Machel" as part of its formal duties.[31] In the absence of definitive evidence – the apartheid apparatus having had plenty of time to destroy any such evidence prior to the South African transition – the TRC could conclude only that "the investigations conducted by the Commission raised a number of questions, including the possibility of a false beacon and the absence of a warning from the South African authorities. The matter requires further investigation by an appropriate structure." But, to my knowledge, nothing more has been heard of any such "further investigation" – in large part, no doubt, because there has remained no evidence to investigate.

Mondlane and Machel, then, as African heroes in history? No doubt the term hero is grandiose, but it is accurate enough, I would say, in the Hookian sense. And both were also killed too soon. Did they change history? Yes. Might they have continued to do so? Harder to say, but at the very least we can suggest the following: both had already bent history enough to have made a difference in defining Mozambique's postcolonial prospects, albeit not enough to ensure a progressive future for the country. But had they been allowed to live they might have accomplished more.

(iii) Of Executions and the "Quiet Assassination Epidemic" in Post-Liberation Mozambique – Simango, Cardoso and Others

Mozambique was haunted by assassinations then. But flip the coin for a moment and consider the spectacle of a strong leader and his party being driven by vanguardist self-righteousness to stumble into the dark waters of willfully executing its critics. For the troubling event here – albeit one not talked about enough in the consideration of Mozambique's history – is a bizarre set of events that should be better known. While death was being meted out to Frelimo by its enemies, murder was also a currency that the Frelimo leadership was prepared to traffic in. Fortunately, there is nothing in Mozambique's recent history on the order of Angola's "war of the generations" and of the killing grounds that its post-liberation history produced (I have provided an account of such developments in Angola in the following chapter). Nonetheless it is important to outline one dimension of Frelimo's record that, little noted, is especially worthy of attention, at least in part because it helps underscore the costs of the movement's uncritically vanguardist predilections. For it was this, Frelimo's overweening leadership style, that helped lead to its ultimate collapse – even though it is still in power – as a progressive force for change.

The execution of Uria Simango, with a number of his colleagues, and his wife as well, was carried out sometime in the first decade of Mozambique's independence by means of a wholly secretive and extra-judicial execution. This occurred a number of years after the establishment of a new Mozambican state with a fully constituted legal/judicial system, and yet it led to the executions of Simango and others linked to him on Machel's watch and at times and in places that have never been revealed, investigated, explained or vindicated.

Who was Simango to become a target for Frelimo's murderous practice? Simango had been a founding member of Frelimo and was elected within the movement to serve as vice-president to Mondlane as president. He was also a fairly conventional African nationalist, from what one can tell from the historical record. Indeed, in the sixties he was correctly seen by most supporters of broader changes in southern Africa as something of an anti-hero – a champion of an unassertive brand of nationalism that sought, as had nationalist movements further north on the continent, to bring just enough pressure on the colonial power to encourage it to promote the kind of neocolonial solution that nationalist movements could then ride to some form of power. But now – with the rise of Machel, with the need for a military response to Portugal ever more apparent, and with the emergence of a radically Marxist ideological tinge to the movement – Simango was, after some confrontation, encouraged to move on.

Simango wrote a provocative article in 1969 entitled "Gloomy Situation in Frelimo."[32] The article made an unconvincing attempt to turn Frelimo's version of events upside down, attacking other candidates for leadership roles – Mondlane, Marcelino dos Santos, Joaquim Chissano and Armando Guebuza. Even more arbitrarily, Janet Mondlane, Mondlane's white American wife, was singled out for a particular venomous and threatening tongue-lashing. This group was accused by Simango of murderous activities against both the more realistic nationalist wing of the party and against the voices (like Kavandame) of tribes in the north and center of the country. In Simango's reading, in short, the Mondlane wing was best characterized as a southern Mozambican clique set to dictate terms to the rest of the population. Simango also alleged that they were dangerous ideologically, prepared, in their aggressive leftism, to set the lower classes in Mozambique against proto-bourgeois Mozambicans who sought more open economic opportunities to ground their ascendancy. Nationalists vs. those with more radical hopes for a post-liberation world, a recurrent story in the sphere of the continent's liberation struggles. Meanwhile, Simango did move on, surfacing in Cairo and in Lusaka as a Coremo representative (but without any links to RENAMO, it bears emphasizing) and then, after the coup in Portugal, surfacing fatefully in Lourenço Marques/Maputo as leader of his new party, the National Coalition Party. Was he seeking to link up with other groups and individuals who opposed the coming of a Frelimo-sponsored one-party state to Mozambique?[33]

A one-party state is, nonetheless, what emerged, and among its first acts was to round up Simango and his group, mainly made up of defeated anti-Samora, anti-dos Santos activists from Dar es Salaam days. This group included Paulo Gumane, Adelino Gwambe, Mateus Genjere and even some more suspect types such as Lazaro Kanvandame and Joana Simeão (the former a militant tribalist from Cabo Delgado who went over to the Portuguese after his period with Frelimo in Tanzania and the latter widely suspected of having been a PIDE agent). The group was spirited away to Frelimo's Nachingwea camp in Tanzania and eventually, it appears, to a rough and remote camp in Niassa Province, where they were forced to live in isolation under extremely onerous conditions. How long they were there remains a matter of some speculation since Frelimo has been silent about what had occurred and when, although eventually all were extra-judicially executed. Some speculate that this occurred in the late 1970s, others suggest a period as late as 1983. There has never been any governmental or party attempt to launch a "truth and reconciliation" style effort to investigate and clarify this still relevant chapter of Mozambican history.[34]

An account of the Simango story – a piece of hagiography at 466 pages but one of considerable interest – was written by Barnabé Lucas Ncomo and published in Mozambique, its title *Uria Simango: Um Homem, Uma Causa* (Maputo: Edições NovaAfrica, 2003).[35] It is a volume that announces itself on its front cover as being "the history of the painful political trajectory of a missionary of nationalism whose commitment and dedication to the cause of the liberation of his people are lost to the collective memory of the recent history of his country." The book gives a detailed account from one perspective of just who Simango was and what he represented. Its publication in Mozambique and its public launch in Maputo in 2004 (with a group of several hundred people on hand) was particularly worthy of note.[36] Still, it caused little enough stir, with few tempted to raise key questions openly that the book might have been expected to prompt.

Ever intrepid, Paul Fauvet of AIM begins his account – in the aforementioned article on the book's launch[37] – by reporting that "[l]ike other prominent opponents of Frelimo, Simango was arrested by the triumphant liberation movement," then taken to the Frelimo base-camp in Nachingwea [in Tanzania] where he was forced to make a 20-page public confession on 12 May 1975, and to "request " re-education. Simango and the remainder of the PCN leadership "were never [to be] seen in public again." In fact, Simango, Gumane, Simeão, Gwambe, Mateus Gwenjere, Kavandame and others were all secretly executed at some undetermined date, with neither the place of burial nor manner of their execution ever disclosed by the authorities. Simango's wife, Celina Simango, was also separately executed sometime after 1981, and, again, no details or dates for her death are on public record. But it was also at Nachingwea in 1975 "that Samora Machel, according to the Tanzanian press of the time, gave a public promise that the prisoners would not be killed."

To repeat Fauvet's graphic phrase in the immediately preceding paragraph, Simango and company were "never to be seen in public again." But as Fauvet then proceeds to write:

> One of the major stains on Frelimo's history is that Machel's promise was broken. Simango, his wife, and the other "traitors" who had been rounded up were executed. [But] neither Frelimo, nor the government, has ever given details. The Mozambican public does not know when or where Simango was executed, and his sons have never been told where their parents were buried.[38] No explanation has ever been given for why the initial decision to keep them alive was reversed.

> Ncomo believes the executions took place in the late 1970s. But 1983 would seem a more likely date. This was the year in which Frelimo, under severe pressure from the South African apartheid regime, adopted a series of panicky and authoritarian measures, such as the extension of the death penalty to cover economic crimes, and "Operation Production", the botched and ill-conceived attempt to evacuate the unemployed from the cities. But we cannot know the date for sure until the people in the Frelimo leadership who took the decision, or who knew about it, break their silence.

As for the long absent acknowledgement of the events, the only ones ever pronounced from within Frelimo (as far as I can tell) came many years after the executions, regardless of whether the executions occurred in the late 1970s or in 1983, and then almost in passing. Thus, as Fauvet reports, "For years, Frelimo wouldn't even say that Simango and company were dead. This myth cracked in an angry debate in the Mozambican parliament, the Assembly of the Republic, in 1997, in which, responding to remarks by Renamo MPs about the fate of 'the reactionaries,' Sergio Vieira declared: 'The traitors were executed.' He gave no details, and his outburst seemed to embarrass Frelimo." And there were also the words, in 2005, of Marcelino dos Santos, the former Vice-President (an office he held both within Frelimo and in the country at the time of the executions). Thus, some 20 to 25 years after the events and speaking of them for the first time of the matter in public, he gave, in an interview with radio and TV journalist Emilio Manhique, a particularly chilling acknowledgement of them and of the official silence that continues to shroud them:

> Because one must see that at that moment, and naturally, while we ourselves felt the validity of revolutionary justice, the one built and fertilised by the armed struggle of national liberation, there existed, nonetheless, the fact that one had already formed a state, albeit one where FRELIMO was the fundamental power. So, it was this that, perhaps, led us, knowing precisely that many people would not be able to comprehend things well, to prefer to keep silent. But let me say clearly that we do not regret these acts because we acted with revolutionary violence against traitors and traitors against the Mozambican people.[39]

Dos Santos had long had the reputation of being something of a Soviet-lining hack so both his position and his phraseology need occasion no surprise. But note again the texture of the key phrases: "knowing precisely that many people would not be able to comprehend things" this led us "to prefer to keep silent" and that, nonetheless, "we do not regret these acts because we acted with revolutionary violence against traitors against the Mozambican people." This is Stalin-speak (however much Africanized) if ever there were such a thing.

As for Joaquim Chissano, he has only ever made passing and entirely perfunctory comments on these events, most openly breaking his silence – although then saying precious little even a good thirty years after the event – in 2012. Thus, in a TV interview with journalist Simeão Ponguana who inquired pointedly about the executions of Simango, Joana Simeão and the others, Chissano could only say that "I don't know what the circumstances were...I knew about their deaths from President Samora and thanks to this I can say they are dead. For President Samora at one point ran into me in the Palacio and he exclaimed, 'Chissano, they killed Simango, do you understand.' That was his tone. And then someone else came along so we closed our conversation, and *we never again discussed these matters*" (my translation, with emphasis added).[40] A strange temerity indeed on the part of Chissano, who, as Samora Machel's successor, would soon become president of the country for some twenty years (1986-2005).

Does Frelimo know something about Simango that we don't know and, if so, why won't they tell the Mozambican people what it is? Otherwise, it is all too easy to see the entire Simango tragedy as another instance of the most abusive kind of vanguardism. However lost the fate of Simango and others may be in the swirl of events that stalked Frelimo and Mozambique in its first independence years, these deaths must be rediscovered and reevaluated. Indeed, such a hearing might give more resonance and meaning to the freedoms that were promised in Chissano's apparent opening up the terrain of formal democratic contestation in the 1990s. For the fact is that popular empowerment has been very slow in coming, with, instead, the squabbling between Frelimo and Renamo over proven illegalities and other irregularities (often quite dangerous ones, especially from the Renamo camp) on both sides often reaching threatening proportions.

In this context, note Mozambique's depressing slide down the Economist Intelligence Unit's Democracy Index (2018) – where the country is "to now be classified as an authoritarian state."[41] The immediate justification for this downgrading has been "the running of the then recent municipal elections widely seen as fraudulent" – a fact, the Intelligence Unit states, that "could threaten continuing peace talks with Renamo." Yet it is the more general political atmospherics in the country in the present decade that remain most unsettling. There was, for example, crusading journalist Carlos Cardoso's "Mafia-style" murder in 2000,[42] an early example of Mozambique's recent "quiet assassination epidemic;"[43] indeed, as the authors of the ENACT Observer article so entitled write: "Assassinations in Mozambique are a worrying sign that violence is increasingly preferred to dialogue." Meanwhile, the assassination scourge has merely surged on.[44] Moreover, adds the Democracy Index, the "[recent] arrest of [journalist) Amade Abubacar in Cabo Delgado, and his ongoing illegal detention in a military barracks, the authoritarian designation seeming even more apt"...while other such cases can be seen to fully reflect the "incapacity and/or unwillingness of Mozambican justice to hold its own powerful people to account."[45]

Has this then meant some sad surrender of Frelimo's once much-trumpeted leftist version of its post-liberation project and a victory for elite-assisted recolonization? This seems to be the conclusion formed by many otherwise sympathetic observers, with such a recolonization marking a victory for global capitalism, for the greed of the Frelimo elite, and for the shadow-world of free-market fantasies. Mozambique is a country now ranked 181st out of 187 countries worldwide in the most recent UNDP Human Development Index, and this is merely one of the many disconcerting statistics that could be cited here. Meanwhile Frelimo is having to work even harder (and play even dirtier) than ever to stay in the saddle, as reflected in the recent European Union report on the October 2019 national election in Mozambique featured in Joe Hanlon's "General Elections/#81 – Mozambique Political Process Bulletin" (17 October 2019) and headlined: "EU hits [out at] "unlevel playing field" and "climate of fear" in harsh statement" on Mozambique:

> An unlevel playing field was evident throughout the campaign," said the European Union Observation Mission in an unusually harsh interim statement this afternoon. "The ruling party dominated the campaign in all provinces and benefited from the advantages of incumbency, including unjustified use of state resources, and more police escorts and media coverage than opponents." "Frelimo received the largest share of [public media] coverage, often in an uncritical tone," the EU noted. "The President of the Republic was often shown or mentioned in his official capacity, promoting projects and giving speeches." [Moreover] "Limitations on the freedom of assembly and the movement of opposition parties were often reported.

The EU mission also highlighted the general lack of trust. "A lack of public trust was observed in the impartiality of the national police forces, who were often perceived as more supportive of the ruling party and not managing properly the election related incidents and complaints...*The murder of a prominent national observer by members of the national police force had the effect of exacerbating an already existing climate of fear and self-censorship prevalent in Mozambican society.*"[46]

❀ ❀ ❀

Murder. Fear. Self-censorship In sum, crude, high-handed and unapologetic vanguardism – vanguardism as intimidation – is the Mozambican elite's preferred mode of politics and this, plus the elite's self-serving greed, make for a fateful and often fatal (as the above-noted "assassination epidemic" testifies) one-two combination that has, provided a particularly sad dénouement of the once much-celebrated Mozambican revolution. Many apologists for the striking of such a balance sheet on Frelimo in power will argue that any other outcome was virtually impossible in the real world of global capitalist ascendancy – either that or they charge that Frelimo was never really clean, clear or principled enough to carry off any bold scheme of national resistance to global realities in the prevailing southern African context in any case. Whatever the truth, the long-term outcome is not pretty, and, for the mass of the Mozambican population, certainly has not been very liberating.[47]

Chapter 5

When Freedom Died in Angola: Alves and After[1]

This chapter should be read in tandem with the chapter dealing with Angola's liberation struggle in this trilogy's third volume *Race, Class and The Thirty Years War for Southern African Liberation, 1960-1994: A History*; that chapter is entitled "Angola: The Counter-Revolution in the Counter-Revolution." In it I examine the case of the MPLA, the liberation movement that came, from 1974/5 to the present, to form the government of Angola. For there was a kind of revolution afoot in the southern African region after 1960 as a wide range of attempts had surfaced – in Angola, Mozambique, Rhodesia/Zimbabwe, South-West-Africa/Namibia and South Africa – to overthrow the strong residues there of colonialism and white minority rule. The question, however, was how radical such "revolutions" could become in terms of transformative economic policies and in the realizing of novel forms of progressive (egalitarian and democratic) social relations.

At first in Angola the promise offered by the MPLA seemed to many to be, potentially, revolutionary in these fundamental ways. For the threat of a starkly rightward turn exemplified by the other liberation movements active in Angola at the time – from the FNLA and UNITA – was strongly reinforced by those who had come to back them: Joseph Sese Seko Mobuto of Zaire; the apartheid state of South Africa; and the United States of Richard Nixon, Henry Kissinger and their ilk. All of the latter players would become forces of willed and self-conscious counter-revolution in Angola, a counter-revolution designed to roll back what was thought to be the MPLA's particularly threatening progressive claim to power. I invite the interested reader to seek out the analysis of this revolutionary appearance offered by the MPLA and its liberatory project in that related volume.

172

But what of the counter-revolution within such a broader context of counter-revolution explored my chapter, so titled, in *Race, Class and The Thirty Years War for Southern African Liberation, 1960-1994*? This I also I explore in my "thirty years war" volume too but, necessarily, in a shorter and more synthesized form. Here, however, I reproduce in full the essay that originally presented my argument on the second counter-revolution, that carried out by the MPLA and designed to scotch any and all progressive voices and progressive possibilities within its own camp and within those parts of the country that it had most effectively controlled.

Indeed, those who threatened to radicalize and democratize Angola's existing national project were killed, marginalized or rendered passive by the MPLA leadership's fostering of a pervasive climate of fear within the movement and within the country. So successful was MPLA's counter-revolution that the new elite in power could then build an authoritarian polity in Angola while also ensuring their own considerable privileges within a national economy soon to become fully subservient to the workings of the global marketplace. Moreover, this counter-revolutionary outcome has continued to define Angola's power structure right up to the present time. The counter-revolution would lock the MPLA's authoritarian regime into place and sustain Jose Eduardo dos Santos' personal dictatorship for the next 38 years.

The MPLA: Reinventing the Counter-Revolution[2]

In 1977, the MPLA would baldly present itself as being a Marxist-Leninist vanguard party within a one-party state that had no tolerance for disagreement or debate. This meant that the MPLA's drive to consolidate state power and elite privilege in its hands (with the initial approval and support of the Soviet Union and Cuba but eventually with the sanction of global capital) could occur without awakening within the upper echelons of the MPLA any very uncomfortable sense of its own betrayal of the Angolan revolution or of any need to win national support for this development by means of democratic persuasion.[3] Angola merely joined the ranks of the authoritarian and recolonized countries of southern Africa, while adding its leaders' names to the list of those many African elites throughout the continent that Fanon and Cabral had, some decades previously, deemed to have, self-interestedly, taken on the "masque of neo-colonialism."[4]

True, in the 1970s, it was not difficult to see the counter-revolutionary intentions and practices of the FNLA, UNITA and of their chief backers, South Africa and the United States. The MPLA's trajectory was a little more difficult to predict with total confidence. And yet, as suggested at the outset of this chapter, there was indeed to be a second kind of counter revolution, one brewing within the MPLA's own camp and one deadly to the promise spawned by the country's liberation as were any other threats to that to the country's articulation of its own purposes. Here, to show this, it will be necessary to draw more directly upon Portuguese-language sources since very few English-language writers have taken this second counter-revolution seriously enough.[5] Yet David Birmingham is one who, from very early on, had done just that, writing clearly (in a more recent essay) that

> The defining moment of Angola's loss of innocence came a generation ago, on 27 May 1977. When the younger folk in Luanda feel reasonably safe from the prying ears of the security services, they ask ever more insistently, "Daddy, where were you on 27 May?" In a country where most women are politically marginalized, they might even ask mother where she was hiding when the blood started flowing in the prisons. The pervasive fear of "preventive detention," which normally reduces freedom of speech to mere freedom of conversation, is based on folk memory of the extensive witch hunts that followed the 1977 attempt by young idealists, including some radical young women, to overthrow pragmatic graybeards. *That was the day when the Angola dream began to unravel.* That was when the old president's cancer began to take terminal hold. That was when scores between guerrilla factions were resolved. *That was when freedom died* (emphases added).[6]

In what follows we will take this formulation by Birmingham as a jumping-off place for a more adequate analysis of the "Alves moment" and its grim aftermath and turn to examining the period – the 1970s and after – in Angolan history with especial care. For, as suggested, it is a "moment" too little noted by historians, especially by anglophone historians. Nor is it analyzed carefully or critically by Angolans, albeit in large part because of the pervasive fear that continues to stifle open discussion of such a "dangerous" topic. And yet, as I will argue, it must be a crucial focus of our concern.

Moreover, there is, in fact, some highly relevant scholarly discussion of this "Alves moment" and its aftermath in Portuguese. Consider, for example, the writings of Carlos Pacheco and Jean-Michel Mabeko Tali in his *O MPLA Perante Si Proprio* on – in a phrase Pacheco uses several times in his *Repensar Angola* – the "chamado golpe de estado," the "so-called" coup attempt ostensibly led by Nito Alves. And there is, even more tellingly, the writing on the "purga em Angola" that followed the "golpe" (as surveyed by the Mateuses in their book entitled *Purga em Angola* and also by José Milhazes, Felicia Cabrita, Leonor Figueiredo [on Sita Alves] and Ricardo Reis' recent *Angola – O 27 de Maio*).[7] It is true that the People's Movement for the Liberation of Angola (MPLA) plays down these events, estimating the number of those killed in quelling the coup and punishing its instigators in the hundreds or, at most, the low thousands. But there has never been a proper and full-bore investigation, official or otherwise, and the more plausible figure (see below) for those killed during the coup and in the post-coup period of purge was at least 30,000 people summarily executed by the MPLA and its minions. This, it would seem, was only possible with considerable help from its Cuban allies – although like so much else in the story of "Alves and After" the evidence for this is purposely hidden or, at best, obfuscated. Moreover, as noted below, some estimates of the number of those killed run as high as 80,000. The "chamado golpe," the popular upsurge that underpinned it, and the purge became, shortly thereafter, the trigger for the MPLA to further impose its authoritarian control of Angolan society at its Congress of November 1977, and, as noted above, to formally constitute Angola as a "Marxist-Leninist" one-party state. 27 May 1977: a day when "freedom" in Angola did indeed finally die.

Of course, this process of authoritarian consolidation did not occur in a vacuum but, instead, was taking place under conditions of siege.

Both the National Front for the Liberation of Angola (FNLA) and the National Union for the Total Independence of Angola (UNITA) were far less savory claimants to power than was the MPLA, and their backing both by apartheid South Africa and by the hawkish assertions of the United States was equally cruel. No question: the MPLA stood up against the right enemies and the Cuban military presence, culminating in the historic defeat of South Africa at Cuito Cuanavale, supported the MPLA in doing so. Such a context can be fully acknowledged in this chapter, but it cannot disguise the fact that the cause of freedom in Angola was also blunted by the authoritarian actions of the MPLA and also, it would seem, by Cuba's military contingent that was then present in Angola. This pattern of repression is the principal focus of this segment of the present chapter and will serve to shape my efforts to establish enough concrete evidence to make such charges stick.

(a) Context

It is useful to begin by locating the roughly simultaneous armed struggles against Portuguese colonialism in Mozambique and (most centrally here) in Angola with some comments as to the crystallization, at the dawn of the Sixties – right across the southern African region and in the wake of both the Sharpeville massacre, and the first Angolan upsurge at the outset of the 1960s – of a gnawing resentment of the fact that the wave of decolonization to the north in Africa had come to an apparent halt at the Zambezi. It now appeared to nationalists in all five soon-to-be contested territories (Angola, Mozambique, Rhodesia/ Zimbabwe, South-West Africa/Namibia and South Africa) that they would have to have much more dramatic, even militarized, confrontations with the white-minority regimes in the region than had tended to be the case further to the north in Africa in order to realize their aspirations for decolonization. The emergence of such consciousness, and the organizational expressions it found, were to be distinctively defined by the dynamics of each particular territory. But the shared project of Africans (and their allies) throughout the region was also to find expression, not least in support from elsewhere on the continent (this constituting one of the few fronts of relatively successful pan-African assertion: e.g. PAFMECSA[8] and the Organization of African Unity's Liberation Committee), and also from even further afield (in the form of a growing global liberation support/anti-apartheid movement).

Concomitantly, the shared threat that challenge from below by their colonized populations represented brought a greater sense of common purpose to the white enclave and enabled it too to activate various sources of global support. The nature of western involvement was largely supportive of white domination; indeed, in the case of Portuguese intransigence, it was ultimately necessary for Portugal to undergo a revolution in order to resolve its colonial question. And in lusophone Africa? In Mozambique, for example, a military victory over the Portuguese was forged under the leadership of Frelimo's Eduardo Mondlane and Samora Machel and, in the first years of independence, developed into a self-consciously revolutionary project that stretched in its implications well beyond the goals of mere national independence. The subsequent realities of externally orchestrated destabilization, of quasi-civil war, of international pressures and of internal contradictions served to roll back the country's revolutionary aspirations and, with time, facilitated Mozambique's virtual recolonization by global capital. Mozambique emerged formally more democratic, but saw its original hopes for genuine national transformation compromised in social, economic and political terms.

Much the same story was true of Angola, even though it too managed to overthrow the yoke of Portuguese colonialism. The apparent stability of Portugal's domination was disrupted by outright rebellion in Angola in 1961 and then by the emergence of sporadic but ultimately successful guerrilla warfare and political mobilization. At the same time the new nationalism that underpinned this success was much less unified than in Mozambique, with three different movements (MPLA, FNLA and UNITA) vying for primacy. MPLA ultimately managed to establish a governmental project, one that proved to be vulnerable, for an extended period, to the guerrilla-based (and in part at least ethnically defined) opposition of Jonas Savimbi's UNITA and the latter's aggressive South African and American allies – this to be countered in part by the Cuban assistance that the regime was also, importantly, able to draw upon. In consequence, in the 1980s and 1990s and with MPLA's once-radical rhetoric long since rendered meaningless, Angola settled into a wasting pattern of civil war, the country's rival protagonists (MPLA and UNITA) funding themselves, into the new century, from international oil revenues on the one hand and the proceeds of illicit diamond trading on the other.[9] Then, with Savimbi's death in 2002, UNITA ceased to exist, but the thrust of history had by then produced an authoritarian "oil state" (in Tony Hodges' formulation[10]) and, for the bulk of the country's population, a socioeconomically disastrous, politically repressive and physically dangerous situation.

In short, the country, already burdened by a so-called "resource curse" (represented by the temptations for local elite and foreign interests alike that sprang from the oil reserves) saw the crystallization of an economy formidably subordinate to and dependent on global capital and, simultaneously, the consolidation of the selfish and authoritarian stranglehold upon state power held by the MPLA elite. Why did this happen? The wasting effects of the war imposed upon Angola played a role, enough of a distraction to sideline any more transformative project. But the fact remains that, within the MPLA camp and even in the territory that it most confidently controlled (Luanda and its hinterland), the MPLA elite were choosing for themselves a counter-revolutionary path for Angola within the setting of a differently premised regional counter-revolution being crafted at the same time by South Africa, the United States, Zaire and their allies inside Angola, especially UNITA. Here the crucial events were those identified as, firstly, the moment of the Nito Alves coup (which Pacheco has consistently termed in his work the *chamado golpe* [the so-called coup]) and, secondly, the horrific and scarring purge which followed.

(b) The chamado golpe and the purge: establishing a narrative

What occurred in post-liberation Angola under the MPLA was, in short, the imposition of a high-handed and profoundly undemocratic outcome to the liberation process; with virtually every detail of subsequent Angolan history documenting this. In taking this bullying path to overbearing power the MPLA elite would be checked, albeit only briefly in the mid 1970s, by the assertions of popular movements on the ground and the efforts of a new generation of active young Angolan idealists. But the MPLA chose to crush this popular and potentially revolutionary force during the second half of the 1970s, once again in the name of dealing with the "fraccionismo" that the core leadership had so often demonized in the past, as it asserted a unilateral claim to central power in Angola. Thus the Mateuses even quote Eduardo Macedo dos Santos to the effect that Agostino Neto said to him immediately after his being received by a tumultuous crowd on his arrival at Luanda airport on his return in 1974: "Eduardo, we're looking at a well-structured and formidable force here. We have to understand it...and dismantle it."[11] The provenance of this statement by Neto is, it must be said, not entirely uncontested, some doubting the accuracy of assigning to Macedo dos Santos this account of Neto's words. Nonetheless, the proof of the quotation's accuracy may well lie most convincingly in the fact that Neto and the MPLA proceeded to then do what Neto is said to have suggested should be done.

It is interesting, however, that in his important book *Repensar Angola*, Carlos Pacheco repeatedly refers to the "chamado golpe" (so-called coup) of Nito Alves, an event, variously described and interpreted, that brought things to a head on 27 May 1977.[12] Certainly, much remains unknown about this event: for example, was there indeed a coup or something more like a counter-coup (seeing the chamado golpe as a fiction the regime used in order to excuse its subsequent repression)? What was the relationship of the political factions, regional forces and generations? What was the interplay between civilian actors and military players? Such questions have never been fully unpacked or answered. One reason (besides the ongoing war) is that it has been dangerous for any researcher to attempt to open up such matters. As previously underscored, there has never been any effective inquiry into the events of the days "when freedom died," and the apparent testimony of Angolans, especially of the older generation, is that they fear state reprisal were they ever to dare, even this long after the fact, to raise their voices.

After all, one of the key figures at the top of the MPLA hierarchy at the time of the *chamado golpe* was the then foreign minister José Eduardo dos Santos who continued to reign as President of Angola, having presided in that position surrounded by almost complete state silence regarding these events for almost 40 years. Thus, no legal proceedings were ever launched against any of the presumptive *golpistas* at the time; many were allegedly murdered without due process or any further explanation. Nor has there ever been much of a public process through which to investigate or to further ventilate the nature of their crimes, or to explore in any detail the manner of their incarceration, alleged torture and deaths– this despite the creation of an official tribunal of investigation into the events in their immediate aftermath which was chaired by... José Eduardo dos Santos.[13]

It is the bloody aftermath of the coup and the grisly role of the MPLA leadership in implementing the massive purga that followed it that may tell us most about the coup and its import for Angolan society.[14] For there then occurred what can only be described as the crushing of a nascent popular movement of promise and potential creativity in the *musseques* of Luanda and elsewhere in the country; this was carried out at staggering human cost by the MPLA leadership. A grim, state-driven, massacre ensued, a holocaust as some have termed it, that witnessed the killing – outside all legal structures and processes – of some 30,000 people, this being the most plausible estimate, although some run as high as 80,000.[15] The latter were by no means all, or even mainly, "Nitistas": the terror (marked by death, widespread torture and long-term incarceration in detention camps: the Cadeia de São Paulo, the Campo de Concentração de Quibala and the Campo de Concentração de Calunda, for example) was sweeping enough to include a wide range of people of diverse political persuasion from various regions of the country.[16]

This cleanup process lasted for several years, thereby heightening the fear, paranoia and long-term trauma that it left in its wake. Some of the killing undoubtedly sprang from immediate and personal causes – spontaneous, and marked by score-settling and motives of revenge. Yet even such actions were unleashed (and emboldened) within the context of the state terror of the time. For it is difficult to ignore the likelihood that all this carnage was the product of the conscious MPLA-sponsored project that was in prominent play. Thus, people at a recent conference in Toronto were startled to hear the chaos of the time openly described by the Angola ambassador to Canada as having been cast, to a significant extent, along generational lines, with the events of 1977 best to be understood as a confrontation that pitched the MPLA's old guard against its younger militants![17]

It is also interesting to compare the numbers of fatalities in comparative terms, the death toll being many times the count of those killed by the Pinochet regime in the aftermath of its Chilean coup, for example. And, in proportion to their relative populations, on almost exactly the same level as the 500,000 killed by Suharto and company in their extermination of Communists in Indonesia in the 1960s. In fact, if the MPLA/Cuban war is considered by some to have been an unknown war, these events in Angola constitute, even more surely, an unknown massacre. For such numbers, if accurate, do not permit any other conclusion than that the MPLA waded through blood to establish its hegemony. Even the membership figures for the MPLA dipped precipitously in 1977 as, it would seem, the weeding-out continued (with membership down from 110,000 at the time of the coup to 32,000).[18] And this, what was left of the MPLA, was the party that could now move dramatically to further stiffen the terms of its rule, with its congress (as several times mentioned above) later in that year affirming its official transformation into a hardline Marxist-Leninist vanguard party.[19]

(c) The dialectic of coup and massacre in Angola

The coup and massacre followed by the stiffening by the MPLA of its rule later in 1977 shows that it was now sufficiently purged to be able to transform itself, easily and officially, into a vanguard party. This was to be the framework of its authoritarian domination for the next several decades, with many of its forbidding structures still prominent in the polity of the dramatically neoliberal Angola, and still under unending MPLA rule. One major question about the Nito Alves coup remains: to what extent was the coup the cause of the inordinate measure of sheer killing that followed? Or did the coup, now so exaggerated and demonized in its retelling, serve primarily as an excuse for MPLA leadership to rid itself of critics? It is difficult to escape the conclusion that this latter hypothesis offers the most convincing explanation.

There is another question too: how credible does Alves seem as leader of a push from below that threatened to force the MPLA leadership to be more responsive to its ostensible base among the mass of the Angolan people both in Luanda and beyond? He seems in many ways to be an unlikely candidate for such a popular-democratic role. He was an active militant on the Dembos forest front of the MPLA for some years and thus initially closer to Luanda and even to the MPLA's small spur command center in Brazzaville than to the movement's rather distant eastern front near the Zambian border, let alone to the MPLA's main leadership hubs in Dar es Salaam and Lusaka. Nonetheless, Alves would eventually become a central player within the organization. As such, he would be a key actor in helping to sideline both Daniel Chipenda's Eastern Revolt and the Brazzaville-centered Active Revolt within the MPLA at the time. Moreover, once in Luanda after the Portuguese coup, he was also to play a major role in suppressing such "ultra-leftist" groupings as the Amilcar Cabral committees and the Henda committees – to the latter of which Alves, in an earlier Maoist phase of his development, had once been close. It was after this Maoist phase that Alves was to become much more a protagonist of a Soviet line – this latter not a very convincing seedbed of democratic proclivities.

Nonetheless, the Luanda experience would seem to have been a learning experience for Alves in broader ways. With others, he was caught up, both as leader and participant, in the dramatic popular resistances in Luanda that were so important in backing down the FNLA's attempted march on the capital and shoring up the MPLA's claim to power. At the same time, he also seemed to sense that the MPLA leadership, increasingly identified in his thinking as dominated by right-wing forces and becoming a bourgeoisie-in-the-making, was not as interested as it might have been in building seriously upon popular energies. Now more than ever, both democratic empowerment from below and a new, more radical agenda of socioeconomic change were becoming his mantra and that of many of the younger cadres throughout the country. Moreover, his advocacy of such possibilities – too often caricatured on limited and doubtful evidence as being merely racist or crudely populist – was soon to cost him dearly within the MPLA. Thus, in 1976, Alves (by now the interior minister in the new MPLA government) and his close colleague, the ex-political prisoner José van Dunem, a key political commissar in the army (and husband of another left notable of the time, Sita Valles, a leading functionary in the government's Department of Mass Organization) were deposed from their leadership posts (as was Valles[20]). These events marked important lines in the factional battles. There also seems no doubt that many Angolans, particularly in parts of Luanda bulging with vast numbers of the impoverished (in Sambizanga, for example), took these expulsions as a personal setback, one feeding a further sense of a distancing from the MPLA establishment.

Such was the setting for a coup attempt. But what of the coup: *chamado* or real? One possible reading:

> What happened in Angola may well have been primarily a provocation, long and patiently planned, one designed to encourage the "nitistas" to lose their heads and come out into the streets, thereby justifying a counter-coup (by the government itself), this also carefully planned.

> Neto and his group were focused on the internal debate and knew the township-based Popular Committees were important centers of such debate amongst the people. In addition, as was natural, they were also concerned about the question of delegates to the [MPLA's Party] Congress.

> For it was necessary [they felt] to avoid the Nitistas arriving in numbers at the Congress announced for the end of 1977. And for good reason. For there was a real risk of their winning the principal leadership positions. The focus of Neto and his group was, without doubt, on power. And to retain it they would do anything.[21]

183

This seems plausible but hard evidence is not easy to come by. Nonetheless, the "chamado golpe" does seem to have been much more a popular demonstration – including even the brief takeover of the radio station in Luanda – than a serious coup attempt.

It is also true that it engaged the energies of some military personnel, especially those of such Dembos notables as the celebrated Monstro Imortel (João Jacob Caetano) and Bakalof (Eduardo Ernesto Gomes da Silva). Moreover, there were the bodies of the six senior MPLA notables found in a burnt-out ambulance in the capital during the events – an apparent "fact" that was resorted to as an explanation/excuse for the leadership's reprisals that followed. Yet the provenance of this atrocity was never investigated, so that the Mateuses, for example, can write of the incident evincing considerable scepticism about such official accounts as exist. Moreover, so brutal was the MPLA's response to the *chamado golpe* that it must be considered to have gone well beyond the limits of dealing with the ostensible "golpistas" themselves. In retrospect, the results of the entire affair (however interpreted) must have been entirely to the old guard's taste: internal opposition to the latter's authoritarian project, and to the ultimate rightward socioeconomic turn it was to oversee, had been strangled for at least a generation.

(d) The Cuban role

Cuba's role in facilitating Angola's victory, as well as the region's overall victory against racial tyranny, was formidable. From the very first days of its arrival, Cuba helped to assist the MPLA in countering the military intentions of the Joseph Mobutu-backed FNLA and, even more crucially, also assisted in countering the first invasion of Angola by the South African Africa Army (with the UNITA movement in tow and with American encouragement) in 1975. This pattern of vital assistance would continue, Cuba acting, at considerable cost to itself, both human and material, to help defend Angola against successive incursions by South Africa and the United States as well as the malign efforts of those countries' main Angolan cat's-paws, the FNLA and, especially, Jonas Savimbi and his UNITA movement. And the culmination of the Cuban involvement in Uganda? This was to come some years later (1987-8) with the battle of Cuito Cuanavale, an event that provided a particularly important reference point for any positive evaluation of Cuba's role. There seems little doubt that the inability of apartheid to impose its will on the region as signalled by the Angolan/ Cuban victory was also a key to the transfer of power, in Namibia, to SWAPO. It also helped, taken together with other developments, to mark the beginning of the end of the hegemony of the apartheid state both in the region and in South Africa.[22]

But what else was happening during Cuba's watch in Angola? For the MPLA was also advancing a less savory cause: the consolidation of an arrogant and authoritarian project for post-liberation Angola. But where was Cuba while this was going on? It was in an unenviable position, certainly, linked to a regime that was at once a murderous one but one whose overall cause it was also servicing militarily in what was undoubtedly a just war. Yet is also true that Cuba has not had so exemplary a record of democratic practice and concern as automatically to be given the benefit of the doubt in such matters, even if it undoubtedly has also lent itself unselfishly to a host of anti-imperialist causes over the years, domestically and through a wide range of exemplary social programs dedicated to the servicing of popular needs. For the chief point here is quite straightforward: Cuba was not likely to begin to lose confidence in the MPLA, as the formal holder of power in Angola, as the latter moved to act in a high-handed and militaristic manner in defence of its revolution. Nor did it do so.

In fact, Cuba had taken great pride in supporting the official MPLA even when the Soviet Union's confidence in the MPLA seemed momentarily to waver during these years. Gleijeses, for example, suggests that "the plotters...enjoyed the sympathy, if not the active support, of the Soviet embassy," and even quotes, in apparent agreement, the (wildly overstated) 1978 statement to a Senate sub-committee by then U.S. Ambassador to the UN, Andrew Young, that: "The Cubans and the Russians haven't been always united in Angola...When there was a recent coup attempt against Neto, it was pretty clear from African sources that the Russians were behind that coup [sic]." Meanwhile, Gliejeses affirms, "the Cubans sided with Neto."[23]

All of which (not least Young's claims) is not true. And yet recall Gleijeses' citing of Raul Castro's revealing reaction at the time to the events in question:

> In the 1960s, Cuba would probably have embroidered its role in the coup with snide remarks about the less than honorable role played by the Soviets. The Cuba of the 1970s was more restrained. A few days after the failed uprising, Raul Castro replied to his Soviet counterpart, who has asked for Cuban assessment of the revolt, in impeccable fashion: his letter contained no reference to Moscow's role, but detailed what the Cuban troops had done "at the request of President Neto in order to establish order."[24]

But there is also considerable additional evidence that the Cubans chose actively to assist the MPLA in consolidating its continued hegemony by force. As we have suggested above, however, this "fact" warrants careful scanning. Instead, scholars, of the left and right persuasions, have seemed merely to acknowledge the fact that Cuba played an important role both in defeating the *golpistas* in 1977 and in eliminating the dissidence these *golpistas* had come to represent over several years following the May 1977 events. And to leave it at that. But this is to trivialize both the differences of line that existed within the MPLA of the time and to miss the drama of the "purga". Even minimally, as one of my correspondents noted upon reading my first draft of this paper, it at the very least bears stating that:

> As far as the Cubans were concerned, I would think an important question is the precise extent to which they actively colluded in the police-security aftermath. I guess there is a distinction to observe between direct and indirect complicity. But there, quite simply, can't be any good rationale for hushing up such matters. It all sounds dreadful.

True enough, though further study (were it possible) into the records pertaining to the Cuban mission might still shed additional light on the details of the role Cuba played in these events.

Some may continue to argue that the Cubans were never entirely at ease as the MPLA regime ran amok in enforcing its rule; at best, they might then argue (as suggested above), that the Cubans were caught between a rock and a hard place – too committed, for many good reasons, to the MPLA regime to abandon it or indeed to criticize it too forcefully as it turned not only increasingly authoritarian but also murderous. Yet there are many others who would argue that the Cubans must have taken an active role in the chain of coup-related events that occurred, including the extensive "mopping up" activities mentioned, and, as my correspondent quoted in the previous paragraph suggests, should now be prepared to talk about this more openly than they have done.[25]

(e) Alves lives?

Meanwhile, as far as Angolan authorities are concerned, they have managed to sit on these matters for almost 40 years, despite demands by family members of the deceased for explanations and other more general requests for more transparency. But demands have not been frequent, sustained or loudly voiced. For the truth, most informed observers agree, is that the society remains traumatized by memories both of the chamado golpe and, even more, by memories of the pitiless killings which followed it. Only recently some questions in Angola have begun to be voiced courageously – on blogs and via other informal media – both about 40-year-old events and about present authoritarian practices. Outspoken criticisms do not come easily. Witness one recent headline, "Angola: Police Detain 23 at Anti-Government Protest in Luanda," this announcing an article which proceeds to report on "an attempted anti-government demonstration by the informal group of youths known as the Angolan Revolutionary Movement (ARM)." As the article then details: "A 2000-strong police contingent, including armed police with machine guns and dogs and hundreds of state security agents, prevented the demonstration from occurring." Shades of 1977; indeed, this item precisely epitomizes much about the texture of Angolan political life ever since that time.[26]

Lara Pawson, a BBC reporter and sometime contributor to the (British) *Guardian* newspaper, is another who has reported on the new Angola, writing in 2011 of an "Angola... stirred by the spirit of revolution," with her article's subtitle then suggesting that while "it may not be ready for an uprising on the scale of Tunisia or Egypt yet ...the tide is beginning to turn in Angola."[27] After demonstrations at that time, Pawson wrote that:

> in direct contradiction to article 47 of the new Angolan constitution approved in January 2010, which grants the citizens the right to demonstrate peacefully, Bento Bento [the MPLA provincial secretary in Luanda] announced: Whoever tries to demonstrate will be neutralized because Angola has laws and institutions and a good citizen understands the laws, respects the country and is a patriot. The secretary general of the party was only marginally more blunt: "Anyone who demonstrates," he said, "we're going to get you."

> This is not idle rhetoric [Pawson continues]. The MPLA has long relied on excessive brutality to quash opposition. As Sousa Jamba, a journalist and member of Angola's main opposition party, UNITA, wrote last week: "The scars of 1977, 1992, etc., have not disappeared. We have a history in which demonstrations in the street, particularly in the capital, end in tragedy."

As Pawson then reminds us, Jamba refers to 27 May 1977, and she notes that:

> the government's response [then] – supported by the Cuban army – was extreme. Violent retaliations went on for months, killing thousands – some say tens of thousands – of innocent people. Many men and women were arrested and tortured, and some were held in concentration camps for years.

And now? As Pawson quotes another Angolan journalist, Rafael Marques: "Opposition is frail but unhappiness with the MPLA is overwhelming."

More startling still is a more recent article by Pawson[28] that tells of the resistance clustering around the person of a second Nito Alves, the serendipitous resonance of his name being apparently more coincidental than not – though it occasions from Pawson the headline "Nito Alves: The Teenage Reincarnation of Resistance in Angola: The Imprisoned 17-Year-Old Activist Shares a Name With a Rebellious Political Figure from the 1970s, and the Authorities Are Unnerved."

And she continues:

> "They are afraid of the people, they are really nervous." So replied
> an Angola friend, a journalist since the 1970s, when I asked him
> why his country's police had been holding a 17-year-old boy in
> solitary confinement without visitors or access to lawyers since
> mid-September.

All this in response to his provocative T-shirt, one challenging the
President, José Eduardo dos Santos!

Indeed "...if [the present-day] Nito Alves really is an icon, it is
not only because of his initiative and courage. [It is also because]
he symbolizes the way that a growing number of young Angolans
have lost the fear that has cowed their parents for decades. Indeed
to anyone with knowledge about the country's...history, this particular young man is an uncanny echo of the past." And because the
present-day Alves "shares his name with one of Angola's most taboo,
and now dead political figures." True, "thanks in part to thousands of
Cuban soldiers, Nito Alves' challenge to power failed" and, as a consequence, "thousands...of people were killed in the score-settling and
purges that took place during the following week and months." Now
the new Nito Alves

> rightly or wrongly, views the man who led the 27 May uprising as a
> fallen hero, a symbol of popular resistance to the entrenched – and
> extremely wealthy – MPLA elite. In a note smuggled out of Alves'
> cell earlier this week, the teenager claims that because of his name
> and because he supports a local association that seeks justice for the
> victims of the 1977 purge, he has been threatened with death.

As Pawson concludes, "Despite their shared name being coincidental...the authorities appear to dislike the historical symbolism."

Similarly, Marissa Moorman – in her article "The Battle Over the
27th of May in Angola"[29] – also writes of the rebirth of the earlier
Alves' fame/notoriety as a positive dimension of the revival of progressive politics in Angola. She does so in reporting on the MPLA's
being upset that, this year (2013),

> a new social movement, the *Movimento Revolucionário*, organized
> a demonstration to remember the victims of the 27 de Maio as well

189

as Alves Kamuligue and Isaías Cassule – two activists who disappeared (and were later executed) last year after organizing veterans and presidential guards in a mass demonstration for pensions in arrears on 27 May 2012.

This year the demonstrators were merely beaten up, although one "so severely that he couldn't move," (although he was then "refused treatment at four Luanda health clinics," another "still in custody, having been beaten by order of the provincial commander of the National Police, accused of attempted homicide, and denied access to his lawyer."

As she also reminds us of the original period of "coup" and purge:

Estimates of the numbers (many of them young people) killed in Luanda and other cities in the aftermath [of the supposed coup] range from 12–80,000. Thousands were jailed and killed. The state's [then] newly formed secret information service (DISA), modeled on Salazar's PIDE, dates to these terrifying days. Many describe the settling of personal rivalries and party vendettas in the chaos. All agree it put an end to a vibrant, healthy, culture of political debate within the MPLA. Youthful engagement in politics was crushed or turned to vile ends...[In sum] *27 de Maio* serves as a powerful cautionary tale: one that parents use to keep their children from protesting or getting involved in politics at all (opposition politics, that is), warning that it will bring ruin or death.

She further notes that one opposition party, the *Bloco Democrático*, did publish several years ago an analysis "drawing a straight line from those events to the authoritarianism of the current leadership, the violence of the state and the intolerance of political debate." And since the publication of new books

in Portuguese about such events and since the Associação 27 de Maio, founded in the early 2000s, began to advocate for official recognition, historical investigation, and a truth and reconciliation commission of sorts for the 27th of May by victims, families of victims and friends of victims, things have begun to shift.

But "shift"? Perhaps, but not, it must be emphasized, very rapidly. As a result, Moorman concludes,

theories about what caused the 27 de Maio abound: a *thermidor* in the revolution, unresolved racial issues within the party, the contradictions of class, overzealous youth. One thing is clear: without an official reckoning, speculation and conspiracy theories will continue.

But are such indications of demonstrations and renewed questioning signs that genuine winds of change are in play? It must be hoped that this is so and that the struggle for a more genuine liberation in Angola continues – despite the decades of enforced silence and the present set of circumstances within a country very far from being open, democratic or in any way progressive in character.[30]

(iv) A Review of Lara Pawson's *In the Name of the People: Angola's Forgotten Massacre* (London: F.W.Hurst, 2004)

Lara Pawson has written a brilliant book, albeit one difficult to review for a scientific journal that adheres to the strict rules of argument, proof, and conclusion. For Pawson offers us a far more personal, troubled and lived pursuit of truth than we normally are graced with. But this does not make hers any less valid or instructive a contribution to our understanding of things southern African. Quite the contrary.

Pawson is seeking an extremely important if markedly elusive quarry, the truth about the *"vinte e sete de Maio"* and its grim aftermath in Angola, a key issue in that country's history (and in the history of southern Africa) and one that the world of Africanist scholarship has been much too slow to interrogate adequately. It was on that day in 1977 that there occurred the so-called coup (the *chamado golpe*) attempt against the MPLA government, one ostensibly orchestrated by recently sacked MPLA notable Nito Alves. And this in turn led to a bloody purge of thousands of militants by MPLA leadership. How many victims is a major unanswered question of Angolan historiography: I think 30,000 seems a reasonable estimate, but others have suggested as many as 90,000 may have perished. The creation of a culture of fear, as Pawson shows, marks the country to this day. Indeed, as David Birmingham, one of the few English-language historians to write of this event (as he first did in 1978), has stated that this was "the day freedom died in Angola."

These events occurred in the midst of the siege of Angola and of the MPLA government by a host of antagonists (the FNLA, Mobutu, the United States, UNITA, and South Africa) eager to overthrow its leftist, Soviet-lining, and apparently revolutionary government – even as the MPLA elite simultaneously worried about the popular demands for democracy and transformative social change within its ranks. The MPLA, in short, was withstanding, with substantial Cuban assistance and in defense of Angola's freedom, a weighty counter-revolutionary thrust even as it was orchestrating a counter-revolution of its own. And this "counterrevolution within the counterrevolution" (to turn Regis Debray's famous phrase inside out) would lead ultimately to MPLA's suppression of the Angolan left and to the crude but long-running dictatorship of the country's president José Eduardo dos Santos and his parasitic MPLA elite that we know all too well to this day.

Pawson takes us on a rich, revealing and infinitely sobering tour of this grim reality, a reality she first stumbled upon while working as a BBC correspondent at the turn of the present century. There is recent material on this subject in Portuguese but almost none, beyond Birmingham's work, in English. Here, however, Pawson allows herself to be instructed by Angolans, some now in exile, who still live in fear but who found the courage to share their perspectives on Angola's unsavory history. She also speaks with a number of senior Angolan functionaries and with British journalists like Michael Wolfers and Victoria Brittain who helped shape the misleading stories about the 27th of May and the MPLA regime that have (inexcusably) served as our common store of wisdom on Angola, both within academic circles and more broadly, for decades. Now Pawson finds the MPLA loyalists to be somewhat more cautious in their assertions, although still far from being apologetic, and, as presented in effective personal profiles, Wolfers and Brittain to be extremely edgy about their own.

As for Pawson, her book opens up far too many important questions for the present short review: Was there a coup or merely a demonstration on the day of the "*vinte e sete de Maio*"? Was what happened in any way stimulated by the MPLA in order to serve as an excuse for its deadly crackdown on the left? How many were killed in the event's aftermath (there was, in my judgment, a massacre of progressive youth, regardless of links to Alves and his Luanda-based group, throughout all parts of MPLA-controlled Angola)? What evidence do we have on the role the Cubans played in the mopping-up operations that left so many dead? Did the massacre facilitate the MPLA's hardening of the terms of its emerging dictatorship (it proclaimed itself a vanguard party later in 1977, with now only 32,000 left of its pre-coup membership of 110,000)? And why, throughout all the succeeding years, has there never been anything even remotely like an official inquiry into what occurred both at the moment of the coup and after it?

A grisly tale, but you really must read the book, for it is full of telling personal stories, shafts of insight, grim truths. One piece of Pawson's detective work comes close to saying it all, however. Moved to track down more information about the death of a young Angolan doctor in Luena in eastern Angola she finds that he was, in all probability, among a group rounded up and killed by the MPLA during the period of purge that followed the coup. She conveys this information to a friend whom she senses to have been related to the dead man. His almost immediate answer to her email reads as follows: "The doctor was my brother. His name was Elisiario dos Passos Vieira Lopes. His nickname was Passinhos. He was killed with his wife while their four children remained alone at home. I was in Portugal when the Twenty-Seventh of May occurred. My brother had nothing to do with that group."

Pawson, as befits her style and approach, more literary (allusive and suggestive) than scientific, comes to no hard and fast conclusions about the questions itemized above. But her research and careful writing allow her to evoke a convincing reality nonetheless, and a picture not at all flattering to the MPLA. Time after time the "right people" are seen to have suffered and paid an excruciating price, the "wrong people" merely to have had, at worst, a bad night's sleep or two. And then, again, there is that *cultura do medo* (culture of fear) mentioned by so many informants. In the words of one of them: "Nineteen seventy-seven. They killed thousands. People have been very afraid ever since."

And the horrors continue. As Pawson concludes her sobering epilogue, demonstrators are still badly beaten and disappear, while senior police officials and party bosses publicly proclaim that whoever tries to demonstrate will be neutralized and that anyone brave enough to protest "will get it." And yet a kind of struggle for genuine liberation – sometimes in the streets but also through blogs, messages on the internet and the like – manages to continue.

❀ ❀ ❀

Indeed, in 2017, José Eduardo dos Santos was president no more, after 38 years in office and in firm possession of unchallenged authoritarian power. As I have written of dos Santos' rule in surveying the most recent developments in the five territorial fronts of the war for southern African liberation in my book Race, Class and The Thirty Years War for Southern African Liberation, 1960-1994 – A History (Volume 3 of the present trilogy), in the latter-day Angola –, he was the

> principal architect of his country's present dark and threatening state and he had waded through rivers of blood to ensure his (and his fellow MPLA elite's) own position of power and wealth. Meanwhile, Angola also was to become the third-wealthiest country in Africa. For Angola forged its way not only through a particular bloody political swamp but also fell upon the country's fabulous deposits of oil and diamonds! In the process, and on dos Santos' watch, almost indescribable greed and graft came to characterize the workings of the Angolan state, and this, in turn, had seen the now ex-president become one of the richest men in Africa. It also has made his daughter, Isabel, by far the wealthiest of all women on the continent – her net worth amounting to at least 4 billion dollars on Forbes' latest estimate.[31] It is no accident that her father, José Eduardo, has been "accused of leading one of the most corrupt regimes in Africa [while] ignoring the economic and social needs of Angola and focusing his efforts on [both] amassing wealth for his family and on silencing his opposition." As Nsehe continues: "To his discredit, Jose Eduardo has always run his government like it's his personal, privately-owned investment holding company."

As I further summarized the Angolan case, however, things since his retirement have not quite worked out for him and his family as dos Santos he may have expected. I would refer the interested reader to my assessment of several further recent twists in the Angola story in that third volume of the present trilogy.

Chapter 6

The ZIPA Moment in Zimbabwean History: Dzino, Mugabe and Samora Machel[1]

As mentioned in the introduction to the previous chapter, the broader context for the various struggles for liberation from white settler rule is provided in *Race, Class and The Thirty Years War for Southern African Liberation, 1960-1994: A History*. The case in Zimbabwe is explored in that book. Here, however, I offer a closer look at one key moment in the history of the attempt by Zimbabweans to find the best means of resistance to white rule. Thus the present chapter focuses on the emergence of the Zimbabwean People's Army/ZIPA, as a promising progressive alternative to the two older movements, ZANU and ZAPU, that warred so strenuously between themselves even as they jockeyed for position in the transition from white minority/settler rule that they both sought in the 1960s and 1970s. It seeks, in short, to examine the crucial "ZIPA moment" within the broader Zimbabwean liberation struggle of the mid-1970s, and, in particular, on the light most recently shed upon that moment and on its long-term implications by Wilfred Mhanda's important autobiography *Dzino: Memories of a Freedom Fighter.*[2]

Mhanda's voice is certainly worth hearing, that of a man who, in the 1970s, helped to conceive and to establish the Zimbabwean People's Army/ZIPA as an organization that offered, however briefly, an effective military challenge to the Smith regime. The ZIPA initiative also held out the prospect of a genuine long-run alternative to the bleak fate that has since come to befall Zimbabwe and its people under the tyrannical rule of Robert Mugabe and of the ruling party, ZANU. We must regret its passing as a fallen player in the grim process that would come to define Zimbabwe under Mugabe's rule. But we can learn something from its story.

For it would be a great mistake to underestimate the contribution Mhanda can make to our understanding. For, in addition to being a notable guerrilla activist in Zimbabwe's freedom struggle, Mhanda also found time to study both the context within which the Zimbabwean liberation struggle had emerged and the complexity of the task that faced the African population in its mounting of an effective resistance both to imperialism (with its fast-shifting neocolonial calculations) and to white settler assertions, notably their Unilateral Declaration of Independence/UDI, which came to define much of the oppressive reality that such resistance faced.[3] "Find time" is something of a euphemism because Mhanda was able to write the second and longer analytical piece (cited in note 2) while held in jail, arbitrarily and for three gruelling years in the late 1970s, by the Mozambican government – the latter by that time acting, as we will see, in connivance with Robert Mugabe, a period that is well described in Chapter 8 of Mhanda's book under the title "Imprisonment."

We are fortunate that Mhanda survived long enough to see *Dzino* through to publication before his death in 2014. This book is one of the essential texts about Zimbabwe, telling from inside the important story of the rise and fall of the ZIPA initiative in the 1970s – the ZIPA moment – while also recording Mhanda's personal rise, fall and then impressive climb back to political and authorial visibility in Zimbabwe from the depths of his, and ZIPA's, defeat at the hands of Mugabe, Frelimo and Kissinger/Callaghan/Crosland.[4] I will recount Mhanda's story in section 2 of this essay and will then conclude, in section 3, by locating that account more firmly within the overall pattern of Zimbabwean history. First, I will begin by providing a background to Mhanda/Dzino's account and to the ZIPA moment. My initial entry-point will be to sketch my relatively peripheral, if nonetheless highly instructive, role in publicizing, in the 1970s, ZIPA's place within Rhodesia/Zimbabwe's liberation struggle. From there, I will then further elaborate the ZIPA story.

(i) Parts of the story, as told by Frelimo, Kissinger, Ranger, Moore and the present author

My marginal involvement in the history of Rhodesia/Zimbabwe's liberation struggle in the 1970s did, for a moment, have a special salience in the debate within southern African liberation support circles (particularly outside Africa) about that struggle and the merits of the claimants to a leadership role. Thus, an article I wrote in the mid-1970s in the U.S.-based magazine *Southern Africa*,[5] a magazine dedicated to support for the cause of southern African freedom movements, made waves in such circles, flagging as it did the ZIPA as a major player to be reckoned with.

Of course, I can make no claims to be a fully-fledged on-the-ground scholar of Rhodesian/Zimbabwean affairs but my liberation support activism and my teaching years in Tanzania, Mozambique and Canada had made me both a protagonist in and a student of the struggle for liberation in Rhodesia, as had my close friendship with the late Giovanni Arrighi, at one time a noted underground militant with the Zimbabwe African People's Union/ZAPU. True, I had devoted much more of my attention through the 1960s and 1970s to developments in Tanzania and Mozambique and even though I would go on to write further about Zimbabwe,[6] and also about Angola, the principal focus of my work was later to be primarily on Namibia and South Africa. Still, I was pleased to have my work on Zimbabwe taken up, in his doctoral work and well beyond, by my former student David Moore, from whom I continue to learn.[7]

Nonetheless, amongst my most important early teachers about Zimbabwe were comrades from Mozambique's Frelimo, notably the movement's and later his country's president, Samora Machel, and his colleague Jorge Rebelo, the movement's secretary for informational work who continued to play much the same role (under various titles and for many years) within the Mozambican government and within Frelimo, the ruling party, after the country obtained independence from Portugal in 1975. They had a tale to tell – and I was also to learn more on the ground about ZIPA, ZANU and the other movements in Mozambique when I visited in the late 1970s and worked there in the early 1980s. Their view: having witnessed at close hand the shortcomings of both ZAPU and ZANU (and the splits between and within them), they were emboldened by the steps being taken by other Zimbabwean cadres, like Dzino Machingura, to move beyond ZAPU and ZANU and to oversee the formation of a more effective united fighting force, which ZIPA promised to be. Indeed, Mozambique's Frelimo government, so recently having achieved liberation from Portugal, encouraged the group around ZIPA, as did President Julius Nyerere of Tanzania, in their efforts, both organizational and military, to fashion a new and more unified movement and an effective challenge to the Rhodesian state.

The broader context of these developments was important, as framed, not least, by the seizure of territorial power from the British government in Rhodesia by the white settlers, led by Ian Smith and his Rhodesian Front colleagues, under the banner of the "Unilateral Declaration of Independence/UDI." Similarly important was the craven response of Harold Wilson and the British state to the white settlers' defiance, Wilson maneuvering in the cause of Britain's racism and presumptive colonial overlordship. And there was also the mixed record of the African response, some would-be leaders cozying up to both the settlers and the British for favor, such as Bishop Muzorewa of the African National Congress/ANC.

At the same time, the leadership cadres of more militant movements (ZANU and ZAPU) were too busy fighting amongst themselves, both within their movements and with each other, and also with both the short-lived and opportunist newcomer Front for the Liberation of Zimbabwe/FROLIZI (1971-74) and, startlingly enough, with Kenneth Kaunda's Zambian government, to make any headway in bringing military pressure to bear on the illegal settler state. In this context any movement from below, uniting to focus the energies of the cadres of ZAPU and ZANU, was to be welcomed by concerned observers. And this was the promise of ZIPA, a promise that, momentarily at least, Frelimo (and, it would seem, Nyerere as well) embraced.

Indeed, as I then wrote with regard to Frelimo,

Frelimo officials with whom I talked in mid-1975 saw the [Zimbabwean] struggle at the time as more or less starting from scratch. Indeed, Mozambique stated at this juncture that it would not cut the vital Beira rail link to Rhodesia nor act to reinforce sanctions until Zimbabweans were ready to take advantage of such moves and present a real challenge to the Smith regime. Significantly, Mozambique did not act until fully nine months later [until, that is, ZIPA had begun to emerge as a real alternative initiative].[8]

Thus, as Machel argued at the time, "In Zimbabwe it will be a people's struggle and it will be protracted. It will allow Zimbabweans to transform the present nationalist struggle into a revolutionary struggle that implies profound changes in the society."[9] Moreover, it was in the same year that Dzino Machingura also surfaced prominently, writing that

After the fighters had realized the incompetence of the ANC leadership they decided to reconstitute themselves into an army that could fight for the independence of the Zimbabwe people. The combatants from both former ZANU and former ZAPU agreed to form a joint military command that would lead to armed struggle ... The joint military command was formed on the understanding that the liberation of Zimbabwe could only be realized through an arduous armed struggle; secondly, on the understanding that the traditional leadership of Zimbabwe has divided the people of Zimbabwe...

ZIPA is an army in the traditional sense of the word. But ZIPA is a unique and revolutionary army in the sense that it has a strategic role in transforming itself into a political movement. The ZIPA structure accommodates the shouldering of both the military and political tasks of the revolution. We have, within the ZIPA structure, a political department exclusively charged with the responsibility of shouldering the political tasks that are normally shouldered by a revolutionary political organization.

... We have to establish a formal political structure in order to give better direction to the armed body that is now fighting inside Zimbabwe. And moves to do this are already underway, moves to transform this organization into a revolutionary vanguard for the people's struggle.[10]

As I then concluded the section of my original article that included the above passages from Machingura:

This formulation, and others like it, from ZIPA's cadre of guerrilla leaders, represents something fresh and promising within Zimbabwean nationalism. Certainly, these are not the familiar formulations of ZANU or ZAPU.[11]

Further, it was also for these reasons that both Machel and Rebelo urged upon me, in the late 1970s, the importance of writing in support of ZIPA and of urging upon activists in North America and elsewhere the validity of their initiative, one that such activists might then be encouraged to support. The fact that ZIPA's undertakings were beginning to produce visible military results was deemed to be of considerable importance. We will see, in the next section, how Mhanda specifies this degree of success in his memoir where he presents an account and an analysis that is difficult to refute.

True, Terence Ranger sought in his writing of the time to trivialize my 1976 account, evincing hostility towards my argument, while offering, in contrast, a strong defence of the "old guard."[12] This latter cadre of leaders he identified as being comprised, beyond Mugabe, of such prominent figures amongst those who became governmental ministers in the first Zimbabwean government as Edgar Tekere (Manpower, Planning and Development), Enos Nkala (Finance), Edson Zvogbo (Local Government) and Maurice Nyagumbo (Mines), among others. And several of these men are brought to the fore (in Ranger's interviews which stand at the core of his article) as friendly witnesses in presenting the case for ZANU and its old guard that Ranger was putting forward.

My case (for the prosecution, I suppose) is, in contrast, represented as follows: "Essentially, Saul argued a case against choosing ZANU or the leadership of Mugabe."[13] This is also deemed by Ranger to have been, quite simply, wrong (his word) in several of its particulars. As for Ranger's case, as epitomized in the final sentences of his article:

Nothing in the careers and statements [of my interviewees] ...is a guarantee that Mugabe and his allies will succeed or even persist in revolutionary transformation. But I see no reason either to add a pessimism about the "old guard" to all the other pessimisms which we must necessarily have about the prospects for change in Zimbabwe. The positions they have adopted, the things they have said, done and written since 1975, persuade me that the only course for support groups at this moment is to offer whatever material and moral support is possible to Mugabe and to his ZANU "old guard."

Note carefully (it is important to do so) that it is not my intention to underestimate or to caricature the difficulties of making judgments about the complex politics that faced all of us who were active proponents of southern African liberation during that period. But the present must also be permitted to comment on the past. And the fact remains that, in light of what ZANU's old guard has permitted a ZANU government to become in the subsequent almost forty years leading to the present, it is difficult not to think that Ranger was just plain wrong – a word, as noted, that he once applied quite sharply to my own position – about Mugabe, about ZANU and about Zimbabwe's prospects under both.

It is also true, and a credit to his integrity and probity, that Ranger, once so much more favorably disposed towards a ZANU/Mugabe line in interpreting Zimbabwe's history, was ultimately to shift his position. Thus, in the introduction to his and Ngwabi Bhebe's two-volume compilation,[14] he would cite positively an important article therein by David Moore on ZIPA and its role,[15] with Moore's findings said by Ranger to constitute "a major work of rehabilitation." Moore, say Bhebe and Ranger, saw

> ... ZIPA not just as a failed attempt at unity between ZIPRA and ZANLA, not just as an obstacle to the logical development of the mainstream guerrilla armies, not merely as an ultra-left deviation, but as an immensely promising innovation. [And] the 'libels' against ZIPA he saw as prefiguring much contemporary ideological confrontation...

> [For] Moore [continue Bhebe and Ranger] also saw ZIPA as illustrating the potentials of an alternative ideology. ZIPA leaders were trying to base an effective unity which could win the guerrilla war on the foundation of a shared ideology, explicitly on "Marxist principles." This meant a determined effort, first at self-education and then at ideological diffusion through the whole army. Such ideological unity would overcome ethnic differences and the factional legacies of past infighting. It would sweep away the sort of pragmatic

reservations which had sabotaged the [1967] Mbeya Accord [between ZANU and ZAPU].[16]

Indeed, there is "no doubt" – Bhebe and Ranger continue – that Moore "reinstates ZIPA as much more than a sideshow" but rather as a movement that "dominated the fighting in eastern Zimbabwe during several months in 1976" and, in doing so, had introduced a style of military-cum-political work full of long-term promise. Thus, Bhebe and Ranger can further note that "much of our discussion in our second volume[17] about the interaction of guerrillas and rural society, hinges around the contrast between the attitudes and methods of ZIPA and the earlier, and later, ZANLA [ZANU's military wing] approaches to rural culture and religion"[18] – these latter being much more high-handed, manipulative and overbearing [than ZIPA's], as other evidence also suggests.

Moreover, the positive ZIPA style evoked here by Ranger was felt by Frelimo to parallel closely the innovative and expansive mode of grass-roots struggle that Frelimo's military and rural practice had exemplified in Mozambique during its years of armed struggle there.[19] Small wonder then that it supported ZIPA with such enthusiasm in its early days. But perhaps I should emphasize too that in my adopting Frelimo's line here I had sufficient misgivings of my own, based on contact with other militants and on other research, concerning the quality of the leaderships (and their flawed practices) of both ZANU and ZAPU, and so was quite ready, in my article, to associate myself with this attempt to rally support for ZIPA.

For ZIPA, in its brief moment of ascendancy, had managed both to advance its military struggle and to ground its activities very firmly in Zimbabwe's rural society. Still, as Bhebe and Ranger lamented of the moment: "Alas ZIPA had no time." For the old guard, they further explain, "were able to break it and imprison its leaders." It is true that they made here no parallel mention of the crucial role played by Frelimo in forcing ZIPA to wind down its struggle, not least by helping orchestrate the imprisonment of numerous ZIPA leaders. Nor do they examine the importance of Kissinger's and Crosland's shift in tactics, for it was at the 1976 Geneva conference that they first revealed a whole new level of support for Zimbabwe's old guard nationalist leadership. We will explore these shifts more carefully in sections 2 and 3 but the fact remains that history (and the tandem of Kissinger/ Crosland on the one hand and the Zimbabwean old guard on the other) were moving too quickly for ZIPA.

For, to reiterate Bhebe and Ranger's statement: "Alas, ZIPA had no time."

Thus, as I then wrote,

> a process of radicalization [in part exemplified by ZIPA] was under-
> way which began to parallel the kind of developments which had
> led to the emergence of revolutionary projects out of national-liber-
> ation struggles in Mozambique and Angola ... The result was signs
> of the emergence of a new kind of Zimbabwean leadership with a
> new sense of direction and new methods of working with the people
> inside the country. Not coincidentally, it had also become possible
> now, for the first time, to pose a serious military threat to Smith.
> Clearly, the handwriting was on the wall for "Rhodesia."

> Kissinger read [this handwriting on the wall], however. Left to run its
> course, the Zimbabwean struggle would produce not merely "inde-
> pendence," but a social revolution. Where, then, was Kissinger's
> opportunity? It lay in the fact that the process of radicalization had
> only just begun. Fortunately for the Secretary of State, there were
> still many of the old-guard leaders left over from earlier phases of
> Zimbabwean politics. Although some had suffered severe hardship –
> imprisonment and the like – they had passed the years since Smith's
> UDI in 1965 engaged primarily in making demands that Britain pull
> their chestnuts from the fire (remove Smith, impose majority rule,
> bring about change in Zimbabwe). There has also been much jock-
> eying for political advantage in a "soon-to-be-liberated" Zimbabwe.
> Such elements were much more reluctant to embrace the impera-
> tives of guerrilla struggle. [And such] men, perhaps unbeknownst
> even to themselves, were Kissinger's secret weapon.[20]

The nationalist old guard as "Kissinger's secret weapon"? With Smith now merely a pawn to be sacrificed in the interests of securing the kind of stable and moderate black regime Kissinger and Crosland had begun to feel would be the only safe outcome of the Zimbabwe imbro-glio. For, as Lionel Cliffe (writing with Katherine Levine) accurately editorialized in *ROAPE* at the time, the "grand strategy for Southern

Africa [that was now] being hatched by the U.S.A., Britain and their African allies" saw "Zimbabwe [as being] the key to their efforts to promote a neo-colonial solution for the whole area."[21]

Though tailoring a "false decolonization" to fit the situation there would not prove to be quite so straightforward an undertaking as Kissinger and Crosland may have hoped, their intention, in the run-up before Geneva, was clear; as Kissinger spelled out the ploy to the Senate Foreign Relations Committee in May 1976, "we have a stake ... in not having the whole continent become radical and [moving] in a direction that is incompatible with Western interests. That is the issue." Crosland was equally forthright. Stating, in December 1976, that "he had not abandoned the [goals] of the Geneva conference," he went on to say that

> If the British government gave up hope, there would be no doubt over who would eventually win on the battlefield. But if the issue were settled on the battlefield, it would seriously lessen the chance of bringing about a moderate African regime in Rhodesia and open the way to more radical solutions and external interventions on the part of others.

As I concluded at the time:

> Note in particular the order in which these dangers are presented. It was not the specter of Soviet aggrandizement which is first and foremost in the minds of such plotters [as Kissinger and Crosland were]. Rather it is social revolution that they fear![22]

(ii) Dzino's (and ZIPA's) story, as told by Wilfred Mhanda

In the first part of his book Wilfred Mhanda gives a very informative outline of his early personal history, and, as he does so, he also sketches the broader context of the emergence of ZIPA, founded as it was to fill a genuine vacuum in terms of African military resistance to the illegal and genuinely racist Smith regime. This vacuum no doubt reflected in part the weaknesses of the existing liberation movements (both ZAPU and ZANU), but the shifting regional context was also crucially important. For Kaunda had fecklessly stumbled into anticipating a "détente" between Black and White Africa in Rhodesia and beyond (one never actually on the cards on the white side, it should be noted) and had taken to playing fast and loose with the interests of established liberation movements, especially in Zimbabwe, in order to make the negotiation of such a 'détente' roll out more smoothly.[23] In this regard the aftermath of the assassination of Herbert Chitepo, a principled ZANU senior leader and one not seduced by the myth of prospective détente, provided Kaunda with an important opportunity to rein in the bogeyman of armed struggle.

Chitepo's assassination is one of the unsolved mysteries of the regional war for liberation.[24] It is true that historians have, by and large, come to identify the Rhodesian state apparatus as the principal mover of the assassination. Nonetheless there is some evidence that, in addition, the security apparatus of Kaunda's Zambia itself had a hand to play in all this. And it is even likely that deadly factional maneuvering against Chitepo within ZANU (with this perhaps having some intra-Shona sub-tribal resonance: Karanga vs. Manyika) was at play. Whatever the ultimate truth of this matter, however, the incident did become the perfect excuse for Kaunda to lock up Zimbabwean nationalists in Zambia in the interest, primarily (or so it would seem), of making detente-related negotiations with the "white south" less messy. The result: Josiah Tongogara and many others wound up in Zambian jails. Indeed, as Luise White further relates:

> ...Zambian police officials arrested fifty-seven ZANU members and officials, including Dare [ZANU's officially constituted war council] members Gumbo, Kangai, Mudzi, and Hamadziripi...Another 1300 ZANU cadres were detained at the camps in Zambia. [Meanwhile] a few members of the high command, notably Tongogara, Nhongo and Dick Moyo...fled the country before they could be arrested...[with] Julius Nyerere of Tanzania offering Nhongo and others sanctuary, [although] Samora Machel was less welcoming of Tongogara...[and ultimately] sent him back to Zambia [where he too was detained].[25]

But Kaunda's posture as regards some presumed "détente" was counter-intuitive to many at the time. Portugal's recent removal from the camp of white counter-revolution – thanks to the successes in the mid-1970s realized by nationalist insurrections in Mozambique and Angola – had, not surprisingly, caused the spirits and expectations of other freedom fighters throughout the region to rise. And within this latter number were those younger cadres in both the Zimbabwe People's Revolutionary Army/ZIPRA and ZANLA who, responding to the positive lessons offered by these examples, were willing, against some externally imposed forestalling of the freedom struggle in their country, to undertake any novel initiatives that could present a more effective challenge to the remaining centers of white power in the region – more effective, in the Zimbabwean case, than anything the aforementioned Zimbabwean old guard nationalist leadership had ever made happen. But the ZIPA group was also punctilious about not wishing to appear to be playing a narrowly factional role and was certainly loathe to propose any kind of takeover role within the broad camp (however stalled that camp might already be in its purposes) of the Zimbabwean liberation struggle. Thus, not only did the ZIPA initiative attempt to realize a genuine merging of both ZAPU and ZANU militants for purposes of realizing more effective military action but it also scrupulously refrained from allowing itself to be interpreted as seeking to outflank the established political structures of pre-existing organizations (ZAPU and ZANU).

We will return to the difficulties that this commitment created for the ZIPA cadres. More immediately, however, it seems clear that such influential regional actors as both Samora Machel in Mozambique and Julius Nyerere in Tanzania – two men long far more sceptical than Kaunda as to the possibility of any meaningful regional "détente" with the "white south" – liked what they saw of ZIPA; as a result, they strongly encouraged the reactivation of the military campaign against the Smith regime that it now proposed to undertake. And undertaking such a campaign is what ZIPA now did, opening up, as Mhanda details, three different operational fronts along Rhodesia's southern and eastern flanks – identified as the northeast front (beginning from mid-January 1976), the central-eastern front (beginning in March and operating from Manicaland in Mozambique) and the southeastern Rhodesian front, launched in April from the Mozambique province of Gaza.[26] Mhanda's careful analysis of ZIPA's operational successes and of the solidifying of its Mozambican base-camps (despite the brutal

August 1976 massacre inflicted, largely on families of civilians, at the Nyadzonia camp by the Rhodesian military) seems both accurate and historically extremely revealing, leading as it does to his further summary comment:

> ZIPA's successes in the field over the period January-August 1976 were plain for all to see. The Rhodesian regime has responded with futile counter-measures. By August, they had gone from collective punishment to the establishment of the "protected villages," extended call-ups, curfew, martial law and desperate measures such as the attack on the Nyadzonia refugee camp. To cap it all, Smith has moderated his views from "no majority rule in a thousand years" to "no majority in my lifetime" – a humiliating climb-down – and publicly accepted the principle of immediate majority rule unconditionally in a broadcast to the nation on 24 September [1976]. All this has occurred in less than eight months of the ZIPA-led war. What more evidence of the impact of our offensive was required? For the record, there were no RENAMO [the Mozambique National Resistance, this opposition movement to Frelimo being initially the creature of Rhodesian and South African counter-revolutionary operatives, although it also eventually proved capable of creating a popular base for itself inside Mozambique] incursions across the border from Rhodesia into Mozambique during the ZIPA period. Nor was the subject of RENAMO ever raised in our discussion with President Machel, his Minister of Defence Alberto Chipande, or the FPLM chief of staff, General Mabote.[27]

Such military success was a crucial dimension of the emerging ZIPA story, so much so that Zimbabwe came greatly to concern the likes of Kissinger and Crosland (whose shifting calculations we noted in the preceding section). True, the ZIPA attempt to secure the full commitment to a joint organizational initiative of all the ZAPU colleagues involved in its formation was (as ZAPU colleagues, briefly involved in ZIPA, drifted away[28]) never quite the success that had been hoped for – the cutting edge of the ZIPA grouping, after its initial formation, remaining for the most part former ZANU fighters and recruits. But ZIPA's dealing with the remnants of the ZANU hierarchy underscored other kinds of problems as well. True, the ZIPA team had no interest whatsoever in linking its initiatives to the flawed and discredited leadership of Ndabaningi Sithole. But such a view was common currency within ZANU in any case and the group turned instead to others of the older movement leadership (now, more often than not, by visiting them in the Zambian jails where they were being held) for advice on how to proceed. As it happened, they were encouraged by such leaders to continue with their military plans and this they did, as seen, with striking success.

But they were also encouraged by the incarcerated Dare group to regard Robert Mugabe, whom they otherwise did not know well and whom the Rhodesian government had only recently released from incarceration, as a senior man who might eventually make a particularly good alternative leader – a suggestion that they took seriously, although it would prove, in time, to have been poor advice, advice that would have especially costly implications for them. Nor was this suggestion well received by their Mozambican sponsor, Samora Machel. Indeed, Machel had profound misgivings about the thought of granting Robert Mugabe any importance whatsoever, let alone viewing him as being some kind of central player-in-the-making. Thus, Mhanda writes, when Tekere and Mugabe were released from custody by the Rhodesians they immediately decamped for Mozambique, but, in response, "Machel [merely] banished [them] to the coastal town of Quelimane which was far removed from the refugee camps and the border with Rhodesia because, in his own words, he 'did not trust Mugabe.'"[29] – apparently fearing the possible contamination of ZIPA if he (Mugabe) was left free to pursue his political predilections. And yet, still sensitive to the opinion of the senior ZANU cadres whose advice they had earlier sought out, the ZIPA group did maintain some contact with Mugabe in this period, much to Machel's displeasure.

The upshot was Machel's forthright response when – according to Mhanda's account of a crucial meeting between Frelimo and ZIPA command structures in 1976 – the ZIPA leadership group responded to Machel's questioning as to its long-term plans with regard to Zimbabwe's prospective leadership, by floating the name of Mugabe as a possible key player. In return they got an earful from Machel.

As Mhanda describes the moment in *Dzino*:

> Rex Nhongo then submitted our list, with Mugabe at the top. Machel leapt from his chair in disgust. He was clearly not happy that we had included Mugabe, let alone as the leader. He went on to tell us that he had removed Mugabe from the refugee camps for a good reason: "He loves the limelight," and is opposed to unity. We listened silently, allowing him time to cool down.

I was not surprised to learn this from reading *Dzino* for, strikingly, I had heard pretty much the same words uttered, and at much the same time, by Machel (even if they were not quite so dramatically acted out for me). Indeed, it was in that very conversation that I had with him that he urged me to help get the word out about ZIPA.

Meanwhile, the ZIPA cadres were now to learn some lessons about Mugabe for themselves – and soon realize, as Mugabe's personality and political predilections revealed themselves more clearly, that the Dare's advice with respect to Mugabe was mistaken[30] and Machel's reactions much more sound. For they began, in the course of those direct contacts they now had with Mugabe inside Mozambique, to see the error they had made, finding – as Mhanda writes of his actual interactions with Mugabe in Mozambique – that the latter's "tight responses and unyielding, nay autocratic, demeanor led me to wonder about his suitability as a leader." Indeed, after several days of exposure to his "reclusive" and "reticent" manner, most of the ZIPA leadership group had come to a similar negative opinion about Mugabe. In consequence,

> On my return to Chimoio, I raised my concerns with the other members of the Military Committee one by one. I did not discuss them with Nhongo who appeared to be very close to Mugabe. It had not taken us long to realize that we had a problem on our hands and that Machel had been right. We regretted our misplaced enthusiasm and the credibility we had given to the directive from the Dare. We decided to wait for their release and take up the matter with them, but when we did this in October, three months later, it was to no avail. We must remember that they found themselves in a Zambian jail under suspicion of having undermined Chitepo's leadership. After their release, they certainly did not want to jeopardize their

futures by challenging the leadership again. It is also possible that they underestimated Mugabe's ability to manipulate situations to his advantage.[31]

Kissinger and Crosland read Mugabe's character clearly however and used this understanding to their own advantage in their stifling of any too dangerous threat (such as that represented by ZIPA) that an "out-right victory" by leftist elements might have posed. Their ploy was the Geneva conference planned to begin on 28 October 1976. As Mhanda explains:

> Just as the ZIPA commanders were considering a qualitative escala-tion of the war to achieve strategic balance, the Rhodesians and their "allies" – the South Africans, the Americans and the British – were apprehensive about the implications of ZIPA military successes. ZIPA had effectively crushed the 1975 détente machinations that had so dubiously brought the war to a halt, and re-started the war, propelling it to levels never before experienced in Rhodesia's four-years war with the ZANLA guerrillas. Their concerns gave birth to a new initiative to stem the tide of revolution: the Geneva Confer-ence from 26 October to 14 December 1976. For them the conse-quences of an outright victory would leave South Africa exposed and threaten the West's strategic interests in the sub-continent.[32]

These new imperial tactics represented a climb-down by Kissinger from the bold assurances of the widely cited *National Security Mem-orandum #39: Southern Africa* (and of the Kissinger team's further responses to it), which he had sponsored only several years previ-ously,[33] this latter having stated that "the whites were here to stay" in southern Africa. True, this was thought by Kissinger still to be true as far as South Africa was concerned. But Smith's shaky settler-regime had now come to seem a pawn that could merely be sacrificed. True, this would simply mean continued efforts by "the West" to massage the transition to produce a firmly subordinate, if nonetheless black, regime in Zimbabwe. Thus, as Mhanda described things at this point in his book, the "product of Kissinger's diplomacy" was the afore-mentioned Anglo-American proposal of a Geneva conference "pitting the Rhodesians against the Zimbabwean nationalists, Britain's Sir Ivor Richard [as] its chair." In sum,

> The détente exercise engendered a calculated and deliberate regres-
> sion of the liberation movement that set the clock back to the era of
> 1960s' nationalism. The progressive form of the liberation move-
> ment was retained for political expediency, whilst its content was
> radically exorcised. Two years after the assumption of power by the
> traditional nationalist, the armed struggle reverted to its prior tacti-
> cal role of inducing constitutional negotiations.[34]

Thus, Geneva came to mark the beginning of the end for ZIPA – now
outflanked by both the ZANU/ZAPU old guard and the Kissinger/Cro-
sland duo – with the promise that it (ZIPA) had once briefly been seen
to hold now merely abandoned (Mhanda suggests the appropriateness
of the word "betrayed" here) by such former supporters as Samora
Machel. Of course, Frelimo's patience had begun to run out on Zimbabwe (with all its intra-nationalist machinations and complexities). As
a result, Machel did first pressure, even order, ZIPA to go to Geneva,
where, at the conference, the ZIPA team had, predictably, great difficulty making themselves heard as more than a subset of ZANU –
as Kissinger and Crosland had fully intended to be the case. For the
possibility of keeping ZAPU and ZANU within a peaceful settlement
framework was very much a part of the game being played there, especially by Kissinger, and, while it would take several more years for all
the pieces of feinting, dodging and weaving – and even the dallying
with various internal African potential claimants to power – to fall into
place, the die was now cast, with ZANU, ultimately, scoring a decisive
electoral victory.

In short, Machel and his Frelimo team felt inclined to sidestep
the morass they saw Zimbabwean politics as having become – and
they may even have come to consider ZIPA, thanks to the latter's supposed political dithering, as having become so entrapped. Not that this
would seem to be a sufficiently good reason for Machel's abandoning,
even imprisoning, the progressive ZIPA group that Frelimo had once
lionized – although one might choose to emphasize Mozambique's
economic weakness and its extreme vulnerability to imperial reprisals
(including from South Africa) as the real reasons for such wavering, or
to underscore Frelimo's discerning of the frailties of ZIPA as another
adequate explanation. Thus, even Mhanda continues his analysis by
stating that in the increasingly complex circumstances to come,

we could expect no support from Machel, who, after all, had cautioned against Mugabe's appointment. That we had now changed our minds seemed an ironic indictment of our inconsistency, and our misjudgment would come to haunt us sooner rather than later. We had taken Mugabe on board on the strength of the recommendation of the Dare leaders who knew him as we did not. All we could credit ourselves with was that smuggling Mugabe into our camps [had] enabled us to form an objective opinion of him.[35]

Thus, there is room for continuing debate on the pros and cons of – and the reasons for – Frelimo's shifting strategic choices, although I am doubtful as to whether so dramatic a shift away from ZIPA can be easily justified, not least with respect to the harsh way the new policy was implemented. It would seem that Frelimo had now come to much too short-sighted a conclusion regarding ZIPA,[36] and was increasingly content to leave it to imperialist players on the one hand and Zimbabwe's varied political claimants on the other to work things out amongst themselves. In short, Machel had apparently decided to follow Kissinger's lead in the hope that this would both remove Rhodesia/Zimbabwe from the map of regional struggle while also removing the Smith regime from its chosen role (as sponsor of RENAMO's penetration into Mozambique) as a wrecker in Mozambique. And yet the endgame in Zimbabwe was to drag on for several years, with Machel's late gamble on ZANU and on Kissinger proving – as Mhanda points out — to be too costly a game. Thus, in the years between the Geneva conference and the ultimate electoral settlement in Zimbabwe, Ken Flower and other Rhodesian military men were able to intensify RENAMO's assault upon Mozambique,[37] while also clearing the way for South Africa to take over full sponsorship of RENAMO in the longer run – this with incalculable costs to Mozambique that, ultimately, helped lead to the collapse of Frelimo's radical project and to the eclipse of many of its progressive regional credentials.

To be in Mozambique regularly during this period (as I was) was to see this big-power poison at work and to become inclined towards the same conclusions as Mhanda had been. For Machel and company the costs of not settling the Rhodesia/Zimbabwe question had seemed too great to bear, with the backing of the possibility of a long-term radicalization of a future Zimbabwe that ZIPA exemplified no longer worth the risks to Mozambique that were involved – this despite Machel's numerous earlier much more militant pronouncements. As Mhanda summarizes things:

> ZIPA's military successes had triggered the Anglo-American initiative in the first place. We, however, had lost the support of Machel who, after releasing Mugabe on our initiative and against his better judgment, was slowly persuaded to support him and renounce us.[38]

Yet, as Mhanda maintains, this decision also inflicted great and unanticipated costs upon Mozambique. For, as suggested above, it would take several years for this new game to play out. And in those years the Rhodesians, with South African help, were able to sow the RENAMO virus much more deeply into the Mozambican polity.

As for ZIPA, Machel and his "new best friend" Mugabe now agreed that it should merely be brutally wound down. As Mhanda continues his story:[39]

> My last day of freedom in Mozambique, 21 January 1977...was the beginning of three years imprisonment for no crime other than standing up for what we believed to be our duty. At the Chimoio barrack cells we met five other ZIPA officers who had been arrested in the camps by Rex Nhongo [and] two days later, we were transferred to Beira where we joined our eighteen colleagues who had been arrested after the meeting in Beira. Within a week, another group of 25 ZIPA officers were arrested in the camps by Rex Nhongo and subsequently transferred from Beira to Pemba...subsequent to the arrest of the approximately 50 ZIPA officers, about 600 fighters were arrested and kept imprisoned in the camps for about six months. Those particularly targeted were the leadership graduates at Wampoa College.

As Mhanda then proceeds:

> The removal of ZIPA paved the way for Mugabe to assert his authority over the army...Mugabe and the ZANU leaders had had no role in ZIPA's formation but were the beneficiaries of its successes. ZIPA owed Mugabe and the ZANU leadership nothing; on the contrary the latter had ZIPA to thank for their freedom. Without ZIPA, none of them would be where they were the day the ZIPA's commanders

were arrested. They were reaping what they had not sown...ZIPA had paved their way to power and all traces had to be obliterated.

In sum, Mugabe had merely

used the [Geneva] conference to his own advantage – and survival – by outmaneuvering both ZIPA and Machel. By consolidating his leadership, he paved the way to become Zimbabwe's first prime minister and executive president. Without the suppression of ZIPA, it is doubtful if he would have had such a smooth ride to the top.

As for Machel, Mhanda also correctly asserts that "Mugabe and his colleagues...could not have so effectively marginalized ZIPA without Machel's support." And yet, the fact that

...Machel was acutely aware of ZIPA's significant contribution to Zimbabwe's liberation struggle and chose to facilitate this betrayal defies logic. His folly or his treachery resulted in Mozambique being at the mercy of RENAMO and ten years of destructive civil war, which surely would not have happened had ZIPA survived... Thus, there is strong evidence that RENAMO, a credible military phenomenon...is clearly a post-ZIPA development that, in my view, Machel inflicted on his country by ill-judged decisions, political opportunism and the unlikely combined influences of Kissinger on the one hand and Mugabe on the other.[40]

Strong words, perhaps overly so, in light of the difficult situation in which Mozambique found itself in southern Africa. Nonetheless, the costs were certainly to be high, not only to the ZIPA project, but also to Mozambique and its revolution. Two birds killed with one stone then – and that a stone of Kissinger's and Mugabe's manufacture.

(iii) The lessons to be learned from ZIPA and its demise

In his preface to Mhanda's book, Moore underscores the fact that both our readings of the strength, effectiveness and merit of the political alternative ZIPA offered to mainline African nationalism (and, more specifically, to a Mugabe-headed ZANU) were and remain accurate, a case borne out by the further testimony offered by Mhanda. Indeed, as Moore writes,

[Saul had taken] a position on ZIPA painting them as the potential socialist saviours of Zimbabwe's revolution. [ZIPA's] demise was a result, Saul claimed, of [Kissinger and Crosland's] conniving to ensure that a moderate (read: capitalist) leadership would steer Zimbabwe's ship of state.

And here, Moore continues, "archival evidence has proven Saul to be closer to the historical mark than Ranger." As he then writes, 'It is hard not to believe that Robert Mugabe had [imperialist?] help in removing the ZIPA thorn from his side." Small wonder that even Ranger, in the long run, began to become persuaded of this as well, as his bowing to Moore's analysis demonstrates.[41]

And yet, at the same time, Moore is much less inclined to share my original sense that the ZIPA initiative, however important and promising politically, also bore the promise of much more radical policies in the socioeconomic sphere. As Moore suggests, "Aside from Saul's accuracy about the effect of the Cold War on ZIPA's fate, his emphasis on the 'socialist' potential of the young militants might have been overstated." But Moore is less than clear in explaining what it is that might have made Kissinger and Crosland so hostile to ZIPA if mere "democratization" and not a democratization linked to some intended left socioeconomic transformation were not part of ZIPA's perceived agenda.

Already, from Machingura's early interview of 1976, I have quoted him to the effect that "The target of the freedom fighters' bullets is the system of exploitation and the capitalist enterprises and armed personnel which serve to perpetuate it." Thus, the proposed economic plan for a postwar Zimbabwe that the U.S. government, Mhanda states, had had a hand in drawing up

... is a direct result of the intensification of the armed struggle in Zimbabwe. The United States and other imperialist powers see their interests threatened and they are determined to stamp out the revolutionary flame before it is too late. [Their] so-called economic plan aims at creating a socioeconomic climate conducive to the continued exploitation of the Zimbabwe people under 'majority' rule.

We are totally opposed to the so-called economic plan. We are not fighting for economic or political reforms. We are fighting for the total transformation of the Zimbabwean society.[42]

But this is – *pace* Moore – pretty militant stuff and certainly senior cadres of Frelimo, itself still in its socialist phase, told me that they saw ZIPA as following in their footsteps in ways that they felt both ZANU and ZAPU to be entirely unlikely to do.

To be fair, Moore does, in private correspondence with me, cite not only his numerous discussions with Mhanda, as well as several passages in the latter's book,[43] that both support his (Moore's) case but also suggest the kind of grim realism that shadowed Mhanda's most progressive hopes. Nor is it possible to determine what kind of socio-economic path ZIPA might have followed had it survived as a force capable of continuing to make history for itself. But it seems to me, the intention to go well beyond a lightly democratized capitalism was certainly present throughout. Indeed, it is here that I would most want to enter a contrary opinion to Moore's contention that "Cold War or not, socialism or capitalism, it is the democratic component of Machingura's [original] treatise, and ZIPA's history, that carries weight in Zimbabwe's contemporary struggles, and those all over the world." For Mhanda's means for fulfilling the democratic promise of the Zimbabwean liberation struggle are oft-repeated in his book; thus, on the one hand, he affirms that in 1980

> the ZANU-PF nationalists who assumed power were transformed relatively quickly into a new petty bourgeois elite in a radical departure from its originally declared goals of the national liberation struggle, which encompassed democratic convictions and socioeconomic transformation. The nationalists had become reformists and independent Zimbabwe become almost a caricature of the oppressive system that the liberation struggle had sought to transform, so marking a direct transition from colonialism to neo-colonialism.[44]

For his part, Mhanda remained as unequivocal in Dzino as in his much earlier interview (1976) as to the proper antidote to this kind of manifestation of "mere nationalism" and notional (rather than substantive) democracy. Thus, any focusing of the struggle for democratic rights at the expense of articulating socioeconomic demands would be counterproductive. In other words, all struggles for liberation and self-determination have, as their end, a better life for all, founded on socioeconomic justice and equalization of opportunity. For, sadly, even though it was only "through the democratisation and socialisation of power and government that genuine democracy and socioeconomic justice can flourish," and despite the fact that "Zimbabwe's war of liberation was waged to achieve these very principles of freedom, democracy, social justice and respect for human dignity," the hard fact is that all these values and goals "fell victim to the pursuit of power, narrow partisan interest, greed and insatiable appetite for wealth." As Mhanda continues:

> These noble ideals, for which many sacrificed their lives, have to all intents and purposes been divested of their progressive content. They survive only as a rhetorical and demagogical platform for grandstanding on national occasions, for raising the political temperature and whipping up partisan sentiments prior to elections. It was the abandonment of the norms, ethos and value system that sustained the liberation war that has yielded fertile ground for ethnicity, intolerance, partisanship, unbridled greed, corruption, lack of accountability, mismanagement, patronage and the tolerance of incompetence as a virtue that have all combined to bring this country to its knees.

Instead, writes Mhanda,

> What Zimbabwe requires is thoroughgoing social and cultural empowerment of its people, not "empowerment" founded on political patronage, corruption and ethnic considerations.

Moreover, such a perspective on long-term change along broadly Marxist lines seems to have been quite clearly raised for study and discussion at ZIPA's Wampoa College for ZIPA cadres, as founded by ZIPA's Military Directorate in 1976 – although "we were for the time being" also focusing on further military training and "on the consummation of the national democratic revolution."

Seek ye, first, the "national democratic revolution," then? It must be admitted that it is a trifle startling to find this latter phrase figuring so prominently here, for it has been a favorite of South Africa's ANC, a trope most often deployed by it as a formulation that has served to smother any too enthusiastic foreshadowing of a class struggle or of a possible socialist project. And we have seen into what unsavory capitalist backwaters such an eschewing of self-conscious radical purpose would lead a post-apartheid South Africa. Nonetheless, for his part,

Mhanda does frame a more radical perspective much more broadly and usefully, suggesting that a movement can talk about the twin goals of democracy and socialism convincingly and at the same time. Here is a clear sign, I choose to think, of his – and of the ZIPA leadership's – seriousness of progressive purpose. But in this respect as in some many others (to again echo Bhebe and Ranger) "Alas ZIPA had no time" to further demonstrate where its brand of across-the-board popular empowerment might ultimately have led.

Nonetheless, the phrases – the "political, economic, social and cultural empowerment of its people" – sounds like a good definition of a meaningful, and quite radical, democratic socialism (in the strong sense) to me. Indeed, Mhanda suggests, this could have been the brand of nationalism that carried the day in a new Zimbabwe: for "by the end of the 1960s, the nationalist movement was undergoing a paradigm shift driven by the experiences of successful struggles elsewhere and by the influence on military cadres [of what they had] gleaned through exposure to armed conflict in Rhodesia."[45] But in the long run, any such presumed shift did not long survive, as Mhanda came to know full well. For the march of history that we have sought to evoke here produced, on Mugabe's watch, only a Zimbabwe with exactly the shape and texture that Mhanda evokes clearly in the pages of *Dzino*:

> The Zimbabwean state that emerged in 1980 did not become an organ for popular rule. Rather, it continued to serve the interests of those who had succeeded the racist white minority rulers – the ZANU-PF elite. It became an organ for ZANU-PF rule; for the suppression of those perceived to be threats to their political dominance. Examples of this were the suppression of ZAPU in Matabeleland soon after independence, the on-going repression of opposition political parties and civil society activists, and the manipulation of traditional authority structures to serve ZANU-PF interests. In essence, the new state has continued to serve narrow interests, this time those of ZANU-PF, and to entrench its rule. All state institutions and organs comprising the state security apparatus, the law enforcement and criminal justice agencies, local authority structures and the public service authority were progressively transformed into instruments that serve ZANU-PF rule through staffing them with loyalists and dispensing patronage.[46]

True, as the Zimbabwean population turned against Mugabe in the elections he apparently lost in the early 2000s, he overturned the electoral results, muttering darkly of imperialist plotting against him and his regime. And he also oversaw the mounting of such populist ploys as the well-massaged mobilization of some sectors of the liberation war veteran community in his support, and land reform – a much-trumpeted supposed advancement of peasant claims to the land that had continued to be white-occupied for many years after liberation was another such ploy – though in practice a shallow achievement since political elites were most often the principal beneficiaries of the redistribution of the best land so claimed.[47] Meanwhile, beyond such populist gestures lay the hard fact that, for the Mugabe clique, the use of state terror and overt oppression proved to be an even more effective tactic for shoring up their authoritarian rule.

And yet, appallingly, this is also the Zimbabwe that SADC (the Southern African Development Community) has, by and large, embraced enthusiastically over the years, consistently white-washing Mugabe's stolen elections and his failed economy, and even recently and not long before his death, honoring the man as the SADC organization's Chair. True, SADC has long since become primarily a club of heads of state, many of whom are, like Mugabe, the virtual authoritarian leaders of the ex-liberation movements that now steer most of the independent southern African states; in short, Mugabe's recent ascension to head such a club need not startle us too much. Rather more surprising to me were the words of Jorge Rebelo, close confidant of Samora Machel during the ZIPA/ZANU moment. For, in my direct experience, Rebelo shared Machel's initial enthusiasm for ZIPA and his suspicion of Mugabe, and also encouraged me to write as positively about ZIPA as I did in the mid-1970s. Now, Rebelo sings to a very different tune: a few years ago he answered a query as to how he understands the front-line states' almost total silence about what has happened in Zimbabwe as follows:

> I personally have, like most Mozambicans who were linked to the liberation struggle, a soft spot for Mugabe because he was our comrade in arms. He actually fought for the liberation of his country and, for

many years, Zimbabwe grew and had a system that was producing development. This meant that Zimbabwe was considered the bread-basket of the region. It was a rich country...[And if things are now completely different] we [still] have this same attitude towards him.[48]

Rebelo has every right to have changed his mind about Mugabe. But it is difficult to see why he would do so in light of what has happened in Zimbabwe in the years since. Moreover, if Mugabe is indeed an "old comrade from the struggle" how much more true is that of the ZIPA comrades that Machel, and no doubt Rebelo, were nonetheless prepared to abandon so cruelly in the 1970s and who have not been mentioned since. True, Rebelo does catalogue, albeit quite sympathetically, some of the mistakes Mugabe made once in power and the often less then salutary outcomes of his policies. So why then this apparent rewriting of liberation struggle history and the celebration of a Mugabe whose arrogant dictatorship is exactly what others, like Mhanda, predicted for him long ago?[49] If Rebelo were to write his memoirs and cover such matters we might learn more about the nuances of the endgame in Zimbabwe – especially if he were to read *Dzino* and respond to it. And we might come that much closer to being able to reach a fully informed verdict on the "ZIPA moment."

And what, finally, of Wilfred Mhanda, aka Dzino? Dead now, in May 2014, but an important figure, in the larger scheme of things, up until the end. In his book, his close account of the ZIPA moment is key. But Mhanda's shedding of further light both on his own story and on the nature of Mugabe's Zimbabwe is important. For he gives both a close account of his immediate three post-ZIPA years of incarceration in Mozambique's bleak rural holding pens, and also of his release and return to Zimbabwe at the time of that country's independence where he was re-arrested and jailed for some days in "free" Zimbabwe by the new ZANU government. There followed his virtual exile from Zimbabwe (on a scholarship and working) for seven years in Germany, this stay marked by occasional harassment from both Zimbabwean diplomats there and by some German officials who had been egged on by ZANU-sourced misinformation about him. He then returned to Zimbabwe to work as a research chemist in such Zimbabwean-based firms as the Delta Corporation, Metal Box and Cairn Foods. But he was also to play a modest but important role within Zimbabwe's emergent civil society, active[50] (as recalled in a section of his book entitled "I become a civil society activist") in seeking to bring more coherence and order, through his Zimbabwe Liberators Platform, to the troubled world of the war veterans, to their legitimate demands for fair compensation and to the manipulative manner in which both government and some very bent leaders of many of their organizations sought to use and abuse them.

And then, not very long before his death, there was his completion, and his seeing through to publication, of *Dzino*, which is in so many ways the best book on the struggle to produce a genuinely free, equal and democratic Zimbabwe. It is a book that I have been able to draw on frequently here for it demonstrates clearly that for Mhanda/Machingura, as for many other Zimbabweans, the hope for an end to the Mugabe nightmare and for the building of a genuinely new and fully liberated Zimbabwe is not dead. In fact, as Dzino amply demonstrates – to reiterate a familiar line in concluding chapters in this book – the struggle to realize such goals in Zimbabwe continues.

Chapter 7

The Struggle for South Africa's Liberation: Success and Failure[1]

In 2015 I was invited to take part in one of a series of lectures/discussions held at the University of Johannesburg to celebrate the 60th anniversary of South Africa's Freedom Charter, first launched at Kliptown on 26 June 1955. As I have emphasized throughout this book, the country's liberation struggle against a particularly nasty and imposing brand of racist rule in South Africa, and the multi-faceted liberation movement that it spawned, had by 1994 produced a famous and significant victory. At the same time, I also sought to underscore the role played by capitalist actors and by ANC elites in massaging a socioeconomic outcome to this struggle that was in line with their own narrow interests. A key interpretive tool here – one already mentioned in a previous chapter – was the analysis of Steve Biko. For Biko had, in the 1970s, imagined the plausibility of such a modest outcome. But he also argued that the racist preoccupations of the then ruling group in South Africa's apartheid system would make such a result impossible for them either to imagine or to achieve. What follows expands on the premise that Biko was correct the first time, while also demonstrating how the result that Biko first hypothesized but saw as being most unlikely came to be realized.

I began my UJ presentation by noting that it was true I was from Canada and had only arrived in Africa, in Tanzania to be specific, in 1965 at the age of 27. Nonetheless, I said, it was in Africa that I grew up, at least politically: not, initially, in South Africa but in Tanzania where I taught for many years. I also had the opportunity there to work with Mozambique's Frelimo in exile in Dar es Salaam, to visit, with Frelimo soldiers, the liberated areas of a new Mozambique in Tete Province in 1972 and later to teach in a liberated Mozambique at the Universidade de Eduardo Mondlane. Of course, I had visited South

Africa throughout these years too, even once, in the 1980s, doing so illegally (having been refused a visa), and I had had several books banned by the apartheid government. In addition, I had taught more recently (at the turn of the present century) in Johannesburg at the University of the Witwatersrand. In the 1960s and the 1970s, however, my "African education" began not with the Freedom Charter but, as suggested above, with Tanzanian realities and with the writings of Frantz Fanon, Amilcar Cabral and Julius Nyerere from which I have quoted liberally above. Thus, while I was well aware of what the Freedom Charter had to say in 1955 and honored it, in Dar es Salaam we were beginning to judge movements throughout the continent not by what they said in the heat of struggle but by what they did once they were in power. And we were looking for voices – like those of Fanon, Biko and the others – within the camp of liberation that could instruct us.

(i) Beyond the Freedom Charter

How then was I to suggest that we think about the Freedom Charter on its 60th anniversary? In considering this challenge I found it helpful to harken back to an earlier occasion, one 30 years ago: the moment of the 30th anniversary of the Freedom Charter. For I had discovered a book of that time, one edited by Raymond Suttner and Jeremy Cronin, that marked that anniversary. And in the book I found a particularly suggestive text written by Steve Tshwete, a Robben Island graduate and an ANC National Executive Committee member who died in 2002. Although little noted now this important document was entitled "Understanding the Charter clause by clause" and it helped me to bridge from the moment of the Charter to the present moment (in 2015) when another possible recasting of the politics of the new South Africa does not seem beyond contemplation. Thus Tshwete, harking back to the Freedom Charter, pointedly wrote:

> This [the Freedom Charter] is a document of minimum and maximum demands – maximum for the progressive bourgeoisie ... and minimum for the working class [and the poor?]. In other words, the bourgeoisie would not strive for more than is contained in the Charter, while the working class will have sufficient cause to aspire beyond its demands.

What happens after the implementation of the people's charter – whether there is a socialist democracy or not – will certainly depend on the strength of the working class in the class alliance that we call a people's democracy.

If the working class is strong enough, then a transition to a working class democracy will be easily effected. At that point in time there will be realignment of forces. Mobilization will be on a purely class basis and the working class ideology will constitute the engine of transition.

But if, on the other hand, the working class has not been prepared for this historical role and is thus weak in the people's democracy, the bourgeoisie will turn the tables. There will be a relapse to pure capitalist relations of production. The Freedom Charter takes the working class a step nearer to its historical goal, while it does not tamper much with the bourgeois order.[2]

I also found a further quote to my purpose from no less an authority than Thabo Mbeki as cited by William Gumede in his book *Thabo Mbeki and the Battle for the Soul of the ANC*: "Thus as early as the late-1980s Mbeki could be found 'privately telling friends that he believed the ANC alliance with the Communist Party would have to be broken at some point, especially if the ANC gained power in a post-apartheid South Africa ... [T]he ANC would govern as a center-left party, keeping some remnants of trade union and SACP support, while the bulk of the alliance would form a left-wing workers' party."[3]

Is this not, in South Africa, precisely the moment, anticipated by both Tshwete and Mbeki (although they would not have phrased the point quite as I do), when the country must choose between, on the one hand, the exhausted and, for many progressive intents and purposes, failed nationalism of the ANC and, on the other, the attempt to build a vehicle for a fresh and much more radical politics that, as anticipated in our first chapter, would be a politics to be carried forward by South Africa's proletariat and precariat,[4] these two forces together crafting an effective alliance of "the working class and the poor"?

In short, I felt compelled to step outside the Freedom Charter frame of the seminar series while also taking seriously Tshwete's point that the Charter was, first and foremost, more promising in its implications for an aspirant South African bourgeoisie than it was for the country's working class and its poor. Indeed, in attempting to provide a deeper understanding of what has happened in southern Africa, I have found it far more useful to invoke the names and writings of militants from the sixties and seventies like Fanon, Cabral, Nyerere and Biko than I have to reference the Freedom Charter. For had not a capitalism-friendly ANC in the 1990s, chosen (in Fanon's words) "to settle the [decolonization] problem" around "the green baize table before any regrettable act has been performed or irreparable gesture made," the stage thus being set for global capitalism's victory and an eventual accession by the ANC to positions of formal power and privilege.[5]

We have found similarly heterodox interpretations of the content of the earlier decolonizing moment in the work of Cabral, Nyerere, and others and we will not rehearse them again here. But are not these sceptical portraits of African liberation as it occurred north of the Zambezi not also more accurate than anything to be found in the Freedom Charter with regard to what has come to pass in South and southern Africa? Indeed, one would do better to start to paint a clear picture of the liberation struggle and its outcome in South Africa not with the Freedom Charter but with something once said by a South African figure: Steve Biko, the key intellectual force behind the country's Black Consciousness Movement in the 1970s.

Thus, in an interview of the time, Biko was asked to identify "what trends or factors in it ... you feel are working towards the fulfillment of the long term ends of blacks," and he responded that the regime's deep commitment to a racial hierarchy had acted as "a great leveller" of class formation amongst the black population, dictating as it did "a sort of similarity in the community" – such that the "constant jarring effect of the [apartheid] system" produced a "common identification" on the part of the people."[6] In contrast, he suggested that in the more liberal system envisaged by the Progressive Party of the time, "you would get stratification creeping in, with your masses remaining where they are or getting poorer, and the cream of your leadership, which is invariably derived from the so-called educated people, beginning to enter bourgeois ranks, admitted into town, able to vote, developing new attitudes and new friends ... a completely different tone."

For South Africa is, he continued,

> ...one country where it would be possible to create a capitalist black society. If the whites were intelligent. If the Nationalists were intelligent. And that capitalist black society, black middle-class, would be very effective at an important stage. Primarily because a hell of a lot of blacks have got a bit of education – I'm talking comparatively speaking to the so-called rest of Africa – and a hell of a lot of them could compete favorably with whites in the fields of industry, commerce and professions. And South Africa could succeed to put across to the world a pretty convincing integrated picture with still 70 per cent of the population being underdogs.

Indeed, it was precisely because the whites were so "terribly afraid of this" that South Africa represented, to Biko, "the best economic system for revolution." For "the evils of it are so pointed and so clear, and therefore make teaching of alternative methods, more meaningful methods, more indigenous methods even, much easier under the present sort of setup."

Yet it is of crucial importance to note again here that Biko was both correct and incorrect at the same time. Apartheid did not stay in place so firmly or so long as to teach the black population that black consciousness would be, had to be, a necessary and sufficient vector of transformation in South Africa. At the same time, he was correct in seeing that the one way open to the dominant classes was that of defusing black anger and growing resistance in SA by dropping apartheid and opting for a free-standing capitalist system of color-blind class distinction. Then, and in line with Cabral's worst nightmares, they could even move to invite the ANC inside the tent of a new post-apartheid system of class power and distinction. On Biko's analysis, they simply could not follow such a course, of that he was confident. And yet, pace Biko, this is the transition that did occur. In the end there were numerous complications, especially between 1990 and 1994 – as many whites of the far right of the National Party (including even De Klerk), the Freedom Front, and the AWB remained slow to accept the dawning logic of any settlement on capital's new terms. Nonetheless, up to a point, this process did produce a successful transition beyond apartheid and a step forward: I would be the last to argue otherwise. But what occurred, simultaneously, was a recolonization of South Africa by capital, with the ANC/SACP acting as the crucial intermediaries in guaranteeing such an outcome. And it is here that the vast mass of the South African population have been the real losers.

How else to explain the feeble result that the transition away from apartheid has produced in South Africa? How else, indeed, could we interpret it? Note on this latter subject the attempted explanation of no less a militant than Ronnie Kasrils.[7] Thus Kasrils has written of the ANC and the SACP as having "chickened out," while identifying the period 1991-96, which he labels as having been the ANC's Faustian moment, a moment when "the battle for the soul of the ANC got under way and was eventually lost to corporate power." Here, he says, was the fatal turning point when we were "entrapped by the neoliberal economy – or, as some today cry out, when we 'sold our people down the river'... [whereas, in fact,] this devil's pact...has bequeathed an economy so tied to the neoliberal global formula and market fundamentalism that there is very little room to alleviate the plight of most of our people."[8]

> What I call our Faustian moment came when we took an IMF loan on the eve of our first democratic election. That loan, with strings attached that precluded a radical economic agenda, was considered a necessary evil at the time, as were concessions to keep negotiations on track and take delivery of the promised land for our people. Doubt had come to reign supreme: we believed, wrongly, there was no other option; that we had to be cautious...[In fact, however], we chickened out [emphasis added]. The ANC leadership needed to remain true to its commitment of serving the people. This would have given it the hegemony it required not only over the entrenched capitalist class but over emergent elitists, many of whom would seek wealth through black economic empowerment, corrupt practices and selling political influence.
>
> [For] the balance of power was [then] with the ANC, and conditions were favorable for more radical change at the negotiating table than we ultimately accepted. It is by no means certain that the old order, apart from isolated rightist extremists, had the will or capability to resort to the bloody repression [anticipated] by Mandela's leadership. If we had held our nerve, we could have pressed forward without making the concessions we did...

s[Instead] all means to eradicate poverty, which was Mandela and the ANC's sworn promise to "the poorest of the poor," were lost in the process. Nationalization of the mines and the heights of the economy as envisaged by the Freedom Charter was abandoned. The ANC accepted responsibility for a vast apartheid-era debt, which should have been cancelled. A wealth tax on the super-rich to fund developmental projects was set aside, and domestic and international corporations, enriched by apartheid, were excused any financial reparations. Extremely tight budgetary obligations were instituted that would tie the hands of any future governments; obligations to implement free trade policy and abolish all forms of tariff protection were accepted, in keeping with neoliberal free trade fundamentals. Big corporations were allowed to shift their main listings abroad. In [Sampie] Terreblanche's opinion, these ANC concessions constituted "treacherous decisions that [will] haunt South Africa for generations to come."[9]

The ANC lost its nerve? Merely chickened out? That's one explanation. But we have already seen (in the preface to Section III) an even more shaky explanation of the form South Africa's transition took from no less a subtle observer as Naomi Klein which I refer the reader back to here.[10] For Klein argued that the ANC had lost any accurate sense of what was going on and been short-sighted and naïve as regards the dangers inherent in the capitalist entanglements it was taking on. As she quoted one of her informants, William Gumede: "We missed it! We missed the real story ... I was focusing on politics – mass action, going to Bisho ... But that was not the real struggle – the real struggle was over economics."

At that point Klein further note both that Gumede "came to understand that it was at those 'technical' meetings that the true future of his country was being decided" and that "few understood this at the time." Really? She can still register apparent surprise that "as the new government attempted to make tangible the dreams of the Freedom Charter, it discovered that the power was elsewhere." But surely, we can ask: had Padayachee, Gumede, and even Klein not read their Fanon? For it is impossible to think that the ANC leadership, having sought assiduously to will such an outcome, such a false decolonization, from at least the mid-1980s, could have missed it – missed, that is, the main point as to what was happening to South Africa.

But, as previously pointed out, this is just not good enough to be an explanation of the ANC's actions. True, the longtime Communist Party and ANC activist (and later a minister in the Zuma government), Jeremy Cronin,[11] who, in a 2013 speech entitled "How we misread the situation in the 1990s," presents a somewhat similar argument to Klein's in explaining what he calls the errors of the 1990s. Mere naiveté is again presented as being the key, Cronin also seeing the ANC as having taken its eye off the ball – albeit for 19 years. His variant of this argument: "In particular, we vastly overestimated the patriotic credentials of South African monopoly capitalism (and its ...narrow [range] of BEE/Black Economic Empowerment hangers-on)"; these advised us "to open all doors and windows to attract inward investment flows." The result:

> [A]lmost the exact opposite has occurred. Surplus generated inside South Africa, the sweat and toil of South African workers, has flown out of the open windows and open doors. Between 20% and 25% of GDP has been disinvested out of the country since 1994. Trade liberalization in the first decade of democracy blew a cold wind through our textile and clothing sector, through our agriculture and agro-processing sector and by 2001 a million formal sector jobs had been lost.

As for the 19-year lag in the ANC's catching onto what was happening, Cronin raises the key question, asking "Why had it taken us nearly 19 years to appreciate the need for a second, radical phase of our democratic transition?" But he gives no answer to his question nor makes any attempt to explain two decades of what, on his analysis, must have been an extraordinary level of official naiveté as to the progressive propensities of South African monopoly capitalism. Why indeed? Thus, for Kasrils, the ANC/SACP lost its nerve, for Klein, the ANC was short-sighted, and for Cronin the ANC simply misread (for 19 years) the situation ... while waiting, no doubt, for the much discussed second, more revolutionary, phase of the "national democratic revolution" to kick into action.

But surely a more straightforward explanation in terms of class dynamics is the more potent one: a new class, politically victorious as centered and represented by the ANC, gained power on the back of the liberation struggle broadly defined (a struggle that took place both outside and, principally, inside the country) and used that power in both its own interest and in the interests of global capitalism. Thus, veteran ANC/SACP hand and present-day MP Ben Turok can admit that he is driven to "the irresistible conclusion ... that the ANC government has lost a great deal of its earlier focus on the fundamental transformation of the inherited social system," and to the assertion that "much depends on whether enough momentum can be built to overcome the caution that has marked the ANC government since 1994. This in turn depends on whether the determination to achieve an equitable society can be revived."[12] Cautiously phrased perhaps, but making an important point, nonetheless. Indeed, we have seen previously, another longtime ANC/ SACP loyalist, Rusty Bernstein, was prepared – in writing to me not long before his death in 2002 – to go even further, suggesting that the ANC's "drive towards power has corrupted the political equation" in various ways that he then proceeds to specify in sobering detail.[13]

Moreover, buried in Bernstein's statement is one other 64 million dollar question about the transition: why and how was the UDF persuaded merely to fold its tent and disappear? It was by no means a straightforward occurrence, even though for Jeremy Seekings, an important historian of the UDF, it's a no-brainer. Quoting Peter Mokaba, then president of the South African Youth Congress: "Now that the ANC can operate legally, the UDF is redundant." Seekings then gives this point his own gloss, suggesting that such willed demobilization of the popular factor in the political equation occurred simply because it had become "apparent that the UDF [actually] had no choice but to disband in the aftermath of the ANC's unbanning." Indeed, he calls it "a logical, unavoidable, even unremarkable event."[14] Quite the contrary, however. Instead, it stands as being, literally, a defining moment in the transition to a post-apartheid South Africa. It is unfortunate, therefore, that the politically willed decline and eventual destruction of the UDF has never really been adequately researched or analyzed. It thus remains a major lacuna in any historically rooted explanation of what has become of South Africa.

For the UDF's disbanding was certainly not unremarkable to the likes of Bernstein, for example. Nor was to a number of other close observers.[15] Thus many dissenting voices were raised at the UDF's final conference against the decision to disband, this despite the fact that this conference did ultimately vote for the dissolution. In fact, Younis notes, there was marked support – if the support of the minority – "in the meeting for the retention of the UDF as an effective organ of 'people's power.'"[16]

> Proponents of this view [Younis writes] envisaged the UDF's role as one of watching over the government, [and] remaining prepared to activate mass action if the need should arrive. Many leaders and activists emphasized that the preservation of the UDF was imperative to ensure that participatory, rather than merely representative, democracy prevailed in South Africa.[17]

Indeed, Younis evokes this period (1990-1994) quite pungently: "As news of accommodation and concessions to the previous rulers made [its] way to the streets, union and community leaders and activists called for the reactivation of mass action." Not surprising that the UDF's last conference – despite being convened to seal the fate of that organization (as a majority of delegates ultimately did, be it noted) – also saw the clear and strong voicing of the view that the UDF be retained as an effective organ of "people's power." Van Kessel[18] is another who came to record the very tangible "demobilizing effect" of the UDF's ultimate demise – while finding that the ANC did little or nothing, in the longer run, to sustain people's waning spirit of active militancy. And it was she who has quoted Alan Boesak as making a sharp distinction "between the UDF years and the early 1990s":

> He noted a widespread nostalgia for the UDF years. "That was a period of mass involvement, a period when people took a clear stand. That had a moral appeal. Now it is difficult to get used to compromises...Many people in the Western Cape now say that 'the morality in politics has gone.' The 1980s, that was 'clean politics,' morally upright, no compromises, with a clear goal."[19]

But the same could be said of the workers' movement *as well.* Webster and Adler had argued from quite early on the importance of the fact that union struggles, as part of the liberation struggle more broadly defined, had managed, in the 1960s, to escape the stranglehold of conventional South African nationalism:

> The legal proscription of the nationalist movements meant that in their formative years [the] embryonic unions were able to develop leadership, organize their constituency, and define their strategies and tactics relatively independently from the ideological orientations and models of the ANC, SACP and especially their labor arm, SACTU. The space created by virtue of [such] banning and exile meant that the new unions could develop innovative approaches to organizing that differed from the populist strategies and tactics of the nationalist-linked unions of the 1950s."[20]

And yet, despite the important role these "new unions" (and eventually COSATU) did come to play in the anti-apartheid movement, they too allowed themselves, with the fall of apartheid, to be far too easily steamrollered by the ANC/SACP juggernaut. The result: here too we were to have mass involvement and bottom-up activism trumped both by short-term popular euphoria on the one hand and by the kneejerk vanguardism of the new ANC-based political elite on the other. For vanguardism (aka residual Stalinism) cannot sit comfortably with genuine active popular democracy from below. Nor need it come as a great surprise that NUMSA and others name their recent political initiative, designed to challenge the present ruling group, the United Front and namecheck the United Democratic Front in doing so, promising that it will

> lead in the establishment of a new United Front [UF] that will coordinate struggles in the workplace and in communities, in a way similar to the UDF of the 1980s. The task of this front will be to fight for the implementation of the Freedom Charter and be an organizational weapon against neoliberal policies such as the NDP [National Development Plan].[21]

More generally, might it be just as simple as Rusty Bernstein had suggested? For what Bernstein had offered us was some pretty tough stuff – tough Fanonist stuff. Indeed, if his insights were to be taken as seriously as they must be, neither historians nor politicians can easily absolve the ANC for its key role in the defeat of the liberation struggle

– even though the collapse of the Soviet bloc, the strength of SA's pre-existent, indigenous, and primarily white capitalist class, and the power of global capitalism must also be given their proper weight within the explanatory equation. But don't forget for a moment the 1985 statement by Gavin Relly, the chairman of Anglo-American, after his meeting in Lusaka with the likes of Oliver Tambo, Thabo Mbeki, Chris Hani, Pallo Jordan, and Mac Maharaj, that "he had the impression the ANC was not 'too keen' to be seen as 'marxist' and that he felt they had a good understanding 'of the need for free enterprise.'"[22] Time was to demonstrate fully how perceptive was Relly's 1985 reading of the ANC top brass' emerging mindset even at that early date.

For the fact remains that Fanon (albeit *avant la lettre*) is closer to the mark than anyone else in helping us interpret developments in southern Africa: the national middle class-in-the-making, the nationalist elite, did indeed discover its historic mission: that of intermediary! And, in the end, as seen through its eyes its mission has had very little to do with transforming the nation; instead, it has consisted, prosaically, of being the transmission lines between the nation and a capitalism, rampant though camouflaged, which today puts on the mask of neo-colonialism...or, perhaps more accurately put, of recolonization.

❀   ❀   ❀

What next? Surely, the next question must be: what will Biko's 70 per cent – left out, left behind – do about it?[23] Will they stick, on balance – in declining numbers, with clearly diminishing enthusiasm and for want of an as yet convincing alternative – with the ANC: the party of Mandela and, ostensibly, of liberation? Or will more of them begin to drift even further to the right, to the more competent-seeming, if still starkly business-oriented, DA? Or will they increasingly be enveloped in the demobilizing folds of xenophobia, right-wing evangelical religions, and the like with incalculable continuing costs to the country?

On the other hand, many may continue to veer left. Here one can allude to the dramatic sustaining of the rebellion of the poor in South Africa; to the further radicalization of some segments of the labor movement (epitomized, notably, by the break of South Africa's largest union, NUMSA, from any affiliation with either the ANC or the SACP); to the chaos (itself perhaps promising new possibilities) that COSATU has become; to the first signs of electoral success that have greeted Julius Malema's unapologetically populist Economic Freedom Front; to the seeds of a new feminism implied in such actions as the #RhodesMustFall initiative in Cape Town in 2015; and to, amongst other tantalizing expressions of promise, the initial stirrings of the United Front, first instigated by NUMSA but with a broad appeal to other workers and to civil society activists.

It remains far too early to predict with any confidence that such initiatives will continue to flourish and even cohere into an effective and politically viable counter-hegemony to the ANC's present grip on power. And yet the game is clearly afoot as at no other time since 1994 as, slowly but surely, the struggle for a more equal and more genuinely liberated South Africa continues. But perhaps any turn left has been deflected by, in the wake of Zuma's fall, the resurgence of a naïve Ramaphosaism (Cyril Ramaphosa being Zuma's successor as President but also a chief architect of the massacre at Marikana.) Has this kind of maneuver once again forestalled a turn to the left? We can take comfort in the fact that some have turned left; that more will; that, eventually, many might. Let's see.

(ii) On disagreeing with my critics[24]

To participate on the panel at the session where my talk was presented at the University of Johannesburg in August 2015 (a talk now included as Section A of the present chapter) the organizers had invited two old stalwarts of the ANC, Albie Sachs, author, activist and, until recently, a judge on South Africa's Constitutional Court, and Ben Turok, also a South African author, activist and, since liberation, a vocal ANC MP (although recently retired from this post, and now, in 2019 at the age of 92, deceased) in parliament, to be discussants.

In Johannesburg

As it happens, I know both of them well from exile days, Ben during the period (the 1960s) when he was a Tanzanian government land surveyor[25] and I was a lecturer at the university in Dar es Salaam and Albie from the period when (during the 1980s) we were both teaching at the University of Eduardo Mondlane in Maputo, Mozambique.

Let me set the recent scene in Johannesburg. As is well known, both Albie and Ben are long-serving and loyal members of the ANC while I, for my part, was presenting a paper at UJ [the University of Johannesburg] sharply critical of what I took to be the ANC's slavish adherence to the line of global neoliberalism since the fall of apartheid; the ANC's easy countenancing of a growing economic disparity between the few rich (albeit of increasingly diverse racial backgrounds) and vast numbers of poor in SA; and the way that, as both a movement and a party, the ANC had consistently undermined any attempts at genuine, relatively autonomous, and democratic political practices from below, even before 1994 but, markedly, also after coming to power in that year.

I wasn't too surprised that both Albie and Ben were critical of my paper – although they were so in their own quite different styles. More importantly, however, both commented in ways that I felt largely dodged my main line of argument. Albie, on the one hand, politely chose to hark back to a rather romantic evocation of the ANC's role in the liberation struggle while also sticking to the rehearsing of important, albeit often quite formal, constitutional achievements, rather than exploring, as my paper invited him to do, the apparent weaknesses and elite-serving nature of the government's overall political and economic policies. I should also add here that, while he has been unable to submit a follow-up text thinking through the substance of the UJ event, I thank him for his engagement in the seminar.

Meanwhile Ben, though quick to attack me personally (and rather caustically so), also primarily harked back to the highly principled political practices of the Tambos and Kotanes during the glory days of struggle. Indeed, when I called Ben's bluff in the subsequent round of discussion on the economic dimensions of the ANC practices once in power, he seemed to agree with much of the detail of what I had said, stating that he had recently retired from his parliamentary seat (although not from his ANC membership) in protest.

Not surprisingly, a further focus of discussion rose out of another comment of mine in response to Albie and Ben's comments. I suggested that they were primarily speaking with voices from the past, looking at things going forward from the old days of apartheid and measuring achievements solely in terms of the overcoming of racial inequities. While I could not disagree that this progress was real, I suggested if they were to view earlier practices and choices in light of the way things have turned out – beginning with the vast class differences that continue to grow and the extreme poverty gap within the country – they would be forced to ask more searching questions of the past. Then, I suggested, they would find themselves forced into articulating a much less comfortable kind of analysis.

The reaction of the large (at least 300 persons) audience in attendance – mostly much younger than we three on the panel – was also revealing, and, I sensed, rather unexpected to both Albie and Ben. For, judging by the audience's response (as measured both by various comments from the floor, including two particularly strong interventions by Salim Vally and Trevor Ngwane) and their supportive applause, it seemed largely accepting of my critical analysis and somewhat intolerant – if respectful (because of their struggle credentials) – of those from my two discussants.[26]

I had caught the same whiff of general discontent when I spoke elsewhere, not only at a book fair but at both the University of the Witwatersrand and Khanya College in Johannesburg. Those of us who have counselled the need for a new/next liberation struggle in South Africa will have to keep our ears close to the ground and be prepared to renew our support for those who seek South Africa's more genuine liberation as it becomes, in due course, more possible. We will also have to keep our eyes on the activities of global corporations (including those based in Canada) that once again are profiting from and reinforcing social inequality in SA, and also those of our government which seems content to follow in former Canadian prime minister Brian Mulroney's unseemly footsteps – and, for that matter, Pierre Trudeau's earlier but equally unseemly ones.[27]

(a) Turok in print

As noted, Ben Turok has been kind enough to write a brief but more developed version of his comments printed in the issue of *Transformation* focused on the UJ workshop. I wondered which Turok was going to show up in the article: for, in addition to celebrating the ANC's passage into power, Ben had also been startlingly critical, in a recent book, of both his party and the path it had chosen to take. As I quoted in my essay that day (see, in this chapter, above), Turok felt driven to "the irresistible conclusion ... that the ANC government has lost a great deal of its earlier focus on the fundamental transformation of the inherited social system" and to the further assertion that "much depends on whether enough momentum can be built to overcome the caution that has marked the ANC government since 1994. This in turn depends on whether the determination to achieve an equitable society can be revived."[28] Unfortunately, however, there is not nearly enough of this kind of reflection in his *Transformation* note.

True, he recalls "a meeting of the ANC branch in London where we were briefed on a proposed bill of rights for the Constitutional Guideline document. The omission of socioeconomic rights was obvious – such 'a downplay of economic issues [being] in stark contradiction to the ANC's 1969 Morogoro Consultative Conference view that the broad purpose of the struggle was the complete political and economic emancipation of our people'." Even more serious, he suggests, is the fact that

> Evidence is accumulating that in the early discussions between Mbeki and people like Willie Esterhuyse, who was clearly flying kites for the ruling class, an economic transition was not on the agenda. The position seems to have persisted even at the Convention for a Democratic South Africa (Codesa) negotiating forum, where the property and sunset clauses were a guarantee against radical economic measures.

As he then asks, "So why did the ANC soft-pedal economic issues during the transition period?" A good question but his answer, although several-fold, is a limited one. First of all, he says, the "ANC in exile was far [being] from an elite." But Fanon never said the new elites of northern

Africa were an "elite" in advance of their taking formal power, just that they quickly became one as the realities of such leaders taking power... with the personal opportunities springing therefrom now laid before them and with global capital continuing to attempt to seduce them.[29]

But what of this seduction by capital that was going on simultaneously in South Africa? For there is certainly evidence of this factor during the transition period– beginning from the mid-1980s – and, even more dramatically, from 1990 and into the post-apartheid period: the new government was forced to acquiesce in the Washington consensus on macroeconomic policy when it implemented the controversial Growth, Employment and Redistribution (Gear) program in 1996. " 'Financial prudence' became the watchword of Treasury policy, and has remained so ever since," Turok suggests. But was the new ANC government simply forced to acquiesce?

For *forced* is the key word to be scrutinized here. In fact, we might more appropriately ask, is it not the case that the ANC leadership had chosen, quite enthusiastically and from fairly early on, to play the new game that was emerging on the terrain of global capital-logic? After all, Mbeki and others had been negotiating so vigorously in the last period of exile to enter upon this very terrain. In short, "Was the negotiated political transition a sellout by an intermediary elite?" (as Turok phrases the position of those with whom he disagrees). This may not be the best and most exact way to put such a question, but is it really so ungenerous (to use Turok's word) to answer such a question with a guarded yes, as Fanon and others had done with respect to other African settings? In any case, this is, at the very least, a question worth discussing, as historians of South Africa will be doing for a long time

Turok has another story to tell. Again, with respect, I must say something which applies both to this brief text but even more forcibly to his UJ intervention: that is his conclusion that I and others rely much too exclusively upon anecdotal views (albeit, insofar as such views are part of my argument, it bears noting that these are the views of such noted participant observers as Chris Hani, Jay Naidoo, Pallo Jordan, Sampie Terreblanche, Steve Biko, Rusty Bernstein and Ronnie Kasrils) that "should be located in historical fact to test their merit."

For starters this is obviously a batting order of quite considerable mere anecdotalists. Moreover, I was in Johannesburg to mark, at the South Africa Book Fair, the launch of my history of South Africa, in which there are many proofs proposed, and firm location in historical fact in this and other of my recent books. Or, I might add, if you would like further to test the argument's merit, just look around you and see.

Needless to say, there is also self-evidently something real and positive to discuss in the transition: I had acknowledged as much throughout my paper – despite the fact, a fact Ben picks up on, that my UJ paper was originally entitled "The struggle for South Africa's liberation: success or failure." I could as easily have written the title as "success and failure," of course. For I do have a sense, in light of South Africa's current situation, that we would not be wrong to see more failure than success in much that has characterized the transition from apartheid to the present. But the debate on this question must continue.

(b) Enter Freund

[The Turok article mentioned above is followed, in the issue of *Transformation* that contains the extended "John Saul in Johannesburg" feature, by an extended piece on my life and works by Bill Freund, the noted historian of Africa and South Africa who has been associated with *Transformation* since its founding a number of years ago. Freund had no role to play in the University of Johannesburg seminar and debate, so I was surprised to find him included on the journal's rota for this feature. I was all the more surprised by the querulous, even hurtful, tone of his comments. In my "rejoinder to my critics" I was instructed to respond to Freund's diatribe; hence, both Freund's essay and the paragraphs that constitute my response can still be found there for anyone who is interested. I have chosen not to include that material here, however – including, as it did, my too testy response. I proceed here instead to the several concluding paragraphs of my piece.]

❁   ❁   ❁

A dialogue of the deaf then? In part, no doubt. But a dialogue about the nature of South Africa's transition away from apartheid (and towards what: a capitalist success story? a novel sort of subordination within the global Empire of Capital? socialism? barbarism?) really must occur more fully and openly than it has so far, and it must be among an ever-widening circle of South Africans. This kind of empowerment was at work, modestly but usefully, at UJ. And it is on display in this issue of *Transformation*. Of course, Ben Turok did address, in his piece, the Achilles heel of left thinking, viz.,

> The ANC has been in power for two decades and is still the domi-
> nant force in the country. It controls parliament, the cabinet, the pub-
> lic service, the army and police, state-owned enterprises and many
> other institutions. I find Saul's formulation of a political choice
> between "a failed nationalism" and "the working class and the poor"
> unsatisfactory, but there is undoubtedly and urgent need to address
> the question of change.

As we know, however, there are other voices on the left in South Africa and they are trying to find new ways to be heard. But let's end here with Turok's last sentence, above: there is "an urgent need to address the question of change." Fair enough: in sum, the discussion, the struggle, continues.

(iii) Appendix: Nelson Mandela and South Africa's Flawed Freedom[30]

Has the time also come when it might be possible to move past the well-deserved praise-song phase of Nelson Mandela's death in order to strike a more careful balance-sheet on the meaning for present-day South Africa of his storied career?

It remains difficult to speak dispassionately on such matters. Nor can there be any debate about the quality of the man or the crucial importance of the role he played, especially in his early years of defi-ance and in his long, unbending period in prison. Then we saw his courage and his conviction that racist rule, with all its enormities, could not be allowed to stand shone forth.

And yet his latter-day role – as he moved from prison into the Presidency of an ostensibly new South Africa – was a much more debatable one. True, in his first moments of freedom in 1990, at the very moment that he emerged from captivity, he spoke of the need for multiple nationalizations and for the injection of genuine social and egalitarian purpose into public life.

Nonetheless, Mandela – never a man of the socioeconomic left – soon found his commitment to a radical socioeconomic policy shift fading fast. Moreover, in this his position was merely coming into line with that of the ANC's upper echelon as they returned from exile.

Mass popular organizations on the shop floor and in the townships had become, in the 1980s, much more central to the struggle against apartheid than any military resistance mounted from exile by the ANC. Increasingly, what was most feared by the South African business and state establishments was the possible emergence of a revolutionary force, popular and ever more deeply radicalized, that might spring from any sustained confrontation with the combined oppressions of both apartheid and of international capitalism.

Business guru Zac de Beer had once warned defenders of capital's stake in South Africa to guard against precisely this: the danger that "the baby of free enterprise" might be "thrown out with the bathwater of apartheid"! And, by the mid-1980s, the Brian Mulroneys of the world could also see that apartheid – long a profitable partner of capital, with racial oppression helping to keep labor cheap – had become dispensable. Better to move to decapitate a dangerous popular movement in order to safeguard the existing pattern of class rule and socioeconomic power.

Moreover, such arguments did find willing listeners in those ANC notables who had spent the 1980s informally negotiating with both the South African state and with capital – while promising the latter a very tame transition indeed. And by now Mandela was ready to accept a freedom that merely embraced a neoliberal version of South Africa, one in line with global capitalism's priorities.

Not surprising, then, that very little has changed in the lives of the vast mass of South Africans – a sad anticlimax to the once proud anti-apartheid struggle in South Africa. True, Mulroney had, by the end of the 1980s, hesitated – still suspicious that the freedom-fighters of the ANC, including Mandela, were mere terrorists. Nonetheless, more savvy guardians of corporate power closer to the scene had grasped the fact that only the cooptation of the ANC into a formal position of power could forestall a revolution.

And this is exactly what happened. The ANC passed into power, and, as the party of liberation, proceeded actively both to demobilize the people and to seal a deal with global capital. The predictable result: though the economic gap between black and white has shrunk somewhat (with some blacks becoming very wealthy indeed) the gap between rich and poor (still mainly black) has widened dramatically. Crime rates have risen as a reflex of the gross, class-defined imbalance in personal incomes, while among Mandela's successors – Zuma and his cronies – corruption flourishes.

More promisingly, there are also signs of more militant resistance. It is true that a genuinely effective and credible counter-hegemonic national alternative to the ANC has been slow to emerge. But the extent of social protest against the state – demonstrations, protests and other forms of social disobedience – that is evident at the local level is now higher than anywhere else in the world.

Here too may also lie the silver lining in Mandela's passing from the scene. For, after an initial and fully understandable period of general mourning, the removal from the ANC of the brilliant luster of Madiba's public image and the halo of his almost supra-historical resonance might mean a further diminishing of the once seemingly impregnable image that the ANC, at least at the national level, has managed to sustain. If so, a further beneficial levelling of the playing field of political contestation would occur and, after Mandela, the struggle for a more meaningful liberation could further intensify in South Africa.

Chapter 8

Liberation Struggle – Then, Now and Next

In the spring of 2018 I was invited to speak at Carleton University at a double workshop. The first of the two sessions focused on the contribution (and otherwise) of Canada – both of Canada's government and corporations on the one hand and of Canada's various movements in support of the region's liberation struggles on the other – to the ending of race rule in southern Africa. The second, held the next day, sought to honor Linda Freeman (the noted scholar and activist who was soon to retire from Carleton) by reflecting on the current situation in southern Africa (a central focus of her writing) with papers to anchor a proposed festschrift to mark her retirement. I had been honored with invitations to speak at both sessions of the Carleton workshop, and I was pleased that, on rereading my material, that two presentations flowed quite coherently and usefully into one another.

The present chapter was not accepted by the editors, who wanted me to focus on the recent changes of regime that were then rocking South Africa and Zimbabwe, as I then did. Nonetheless, I am pleased to be able to include this chapter here, a chapter that, as it stands, blends a consideration of the "then" and the "now" (plus a brief reflection on the possible next phase – see below) of southern African developments and of Canadian interest and involvement in them; it therefore parallels Linda's interest, both scholarly and political, in exploring both these dimensions and I also include it here as a further paper dedicated to Linda Freeman.

On Rethinking Liberation Struggle, Liberation Support and the Continuing Fight to Liberate Southern Africa

At Carleton I first argued that we can best see the work of activists for southern African liberation as having constituted, both within the region and beyond, a very mixed record indeed, one defined by both success and failure. Thus, at one level, the liberation of the various territories in the region (Angola, Mozambique, Zimbabwe, Namibia and South Africa) from the cruel structures, formalized and state sanctioned, of white-racist rule constituted a step forward. At the same time, the fact that such liberation was merely accompanied by a renewal on the socioeconomic front of the region's absolute subordination to the workings of global capital constituted a considerable qualification to the claim of having realized any striking success; so too did the over-bearing and continuing checks by post-liberation governments in the region on such genuine popular empowerment as might otherwise have been expected to surface as an essential part of some more genuine and fulsome liberation. For surely such a liberation might otherwise have been expected to facilitate the expression of a much more substantive democratic voice.

Thus, even if the income gap between black and white in southern Africa has narrowed somewhat, the income/class gap between the relatively few well-off and the vast and ever more impoverished majority of the poor, has grown precipitously throughout the now liberated region (as it has in Canada, even if it occurs here at a much higher point in the global wealth-hierarchy of nations). And, as stated, the degree of empowerment of the mass of the population in the countries of the region is also at a low ebb, caught up in the mesh of intransigent authoritarianisms (Angola, Zimbabwe) or, at best, in a kind of passive engagement with political life as spectator sport, this to be distinguished from the active popular engagement that one might have hoped for and even expected. In fact, since its presumed "liberation," southern Africa is still cast all too clearly in terms of top-down authoritarianism, deepening socioeconomic inequality and palpable popular disempowerment – a result, to repeat, that many of us would be reluctant to hail too quickly or too uncritically as truly liberating. This is true even if the removal of the obscenity of pure white-racist rule – the trademark of what were the real "shit-holes" of Africa (to borrow Donald Trump's celebrated phrase) – was realized. Of course, the dismantling of such white settler colonialism was indeed liberating – even a win – of that there can be no question. But was it enough? Scarcely.

For, to go no further afield, the swag that, among others, Canadian corporations (Barrick Gold and the rest) continue to walk away with from southern Africa is considerable. And this is only one of the reasons that those (both here and in the region) who feel most strongly about the goals of equality and democratic voice for southern Africa, should confess that much of the substance of the struggle for southern Africa had been lost and that the vast majority of people in southern Africa continue to pay a heavy price for such a defeat.

A. Then: Mulroney wins?

Let me evoke three anecdotes in order to better capture this sobering reality, one from the years of struggle, one from the years of transition to a new regional reality (the late 1980s-early 1990s), and one that reflects retrospectively on southern African outcomes. The first moment, one that helps illuminate the texture of Canadian political and corporate life that was attendant upon the southern African liberation struggle, occurred some years ago, right here at Carleton University. The occasion was a visit to the university (as reported in the *Toronto Telegram*, of 25 February 1970) by the then Prime Minister, Pierre Elliott Trudeau, to discuss Canadian foreign policy and specifically Canada's official policy towards events in southern Africa. Here at Carleton, Trudeau was challenged by a student who asked how Canada's policy of trading with South Africa could be reconciled with Canadian condemnations of apartheid; in response Trudeau replied that "I have a very poor answer to that. We are keeping on with our trade despite the fact that we condemn the policy [apartheid] in the United Nations. We are not very proud of this approach." Indeed, he went on to say, of his government's apartheid policy (or, rather, lack thereof): "It's not consistent. Either we should stop trading, or we should stop condemning." But he and his government merely continued to do both. And that pretty well sums up Canada's approach to southern Africa until the very last years of apartheid, this despite the long years many of us spent both acting in firm opposition to official and corporate Canada and in work in Canada in support of the liberation movements in southern Africa.

As I've suggested in my book *On Building a Social Movement: The North American Campaign for Southern African Liberation Revisited*,[1] our efforts – those of TCCR, TCLSAC, CIDMAA and the like – were often very imaginative, and sometimes even effective, in bringing appropriate attention to the very slimness of official Canada's role in opposing racial inequality and injustice in southern Africa. But to what end? Isn't it true that we were not so very successful in encouraging the government to reconsider the moral legitimacy of its position or in building a movement truly effective at helping force such an outcome? True, we probably did constitute a pain in the neck that Canada's political and corporate establishment couldn't quite ignore. And, taken together with (a) the dramatic actions of the impressively widespread popular movement of southern Africans on the ground (especially in South Africa) and (b), the startling (as discussed below) and discernible shift of commitment of an increasing number of global corporations to distance themselves from the writ of apartheid, this all meant that Canada, its government and its capital, would begin to shift their allegiances too.

Not too surprising, then, that many of us within the Canadian liberation support movement began to fear that we had mainly served to encourage our country and its capital to become part of the global effort to tailor southern Africa's freedom to fit capital's interests (and, in South Africa, to sanction the co-optation of the rising ANC-linked elite into the role of partner of capital and its continuing power). This is an accurate picture of the record and the fate of the Canadian-based liberation support/anti-apartheid movement: *put simply, we had won but we had also lost, and lost grievously. As had the vast mass of Africans in southern Africa.* The pertinent question then: could we/they not have accomplished much more than to become a partner in facilitating the recolonization of southern Africa by the Empire of Capital? If so, what more? And how?

Or should we simply resign ourselves to accepting that, in effect, we (the advocates in Canada and southern Africa of more sweeping and substantive change) did not win the struggle in Canada in helping to determine, on our narrow front, a more positive fate for southern Africa than would occur; instead Brian Mulroney and his cronies had won. Thus, in the late 1980s the balance of forces had changed as capital[2] began to realize that its commitment, both tacit and real, to apartheid's racism (and to the guarantee to capital of a ready supply of cheap black labor-power apartheid had long provided) carried a cost and a danger that capital could and would not now continue to pay – this despite the profits apartheid had guaranteed for it over the years. Not surprising, then, that in South Africa (as in the other territories already liberated in southern Africa) capital began to switch sides, the more astute seeking out the ANC's leadership and seducing them into a sweetheart deal – *the dropping of apartheid in favor of a continuing commitment to sustained capitalist control and the cooptation of the region's "victorious" liberation movements into capitalism's circle of power.*

Indeed, the Canadian establishment would now buy into this switch in corporate strategies in southern Africa. Thus, Australia's Malcolm Fraser went to South Africa, in 1986, with an "Eminent Person's Group" of his Commonwealth colleagues to explore the situation there on behalf of the Commonwealth. The EPG feared more violence and bloodshed and Fraser, in particular, warned that in any escalating conflict "moderation would be swept aside, The government that emerged from all of this would be extremely radical, probably Marxist, and would nationalize all western business interests." Time, in short, to drop apartheid. And Mulroney agreed. In fact, at a meeting held in Johannesburg several years ago, this was precisely the reading of Canadian policy confirmed for me by the then Canadian High Commissioner to South Africa. She had been a senior bureaucrat in External Affairs when Mulroney switched tacks and she confirmed that Mulroney had seen the sense in Fraser's warning and responded warmly to it. True, he still had Cold War-linked misgivings about the ANC, its Moscow links and terrorist proclivities, but to the goal of ingratiating himself with the Black Commonwealth Mulroney could now add the role of spearheading the forces of enlightened capitalism. This was deemed, the High Commissioner confirmed to me, the correct move to make by both the Canadian state and, ultimately, by Canadian capital.

It is no coincidence, then, that Mulroney was, in 2015, presented with the Order of the Companions of O. R. Tambo in South Africa, in the Gold category no less, this order bestowed by South African President Jacob Zuma. This is an order that formally recognizes "the contributions made by individuals who contributed to a non-racial, non-sexist, democratic and prosperous South Africa as envisaged in the country's Constitution." The awarding of it was deeply ironic in light of the way Mulroney had treated Tambo when the latter was alive; for when Tambo came to Toronto to meet with TCLSAC the next day after he had a meeting with Mulroney he was extremely offended – shaking with suppressed anger – by the patronizing way Mulroney treated, even interrogated, him as if he were a suspected Soviet-stooge-style terrorist.[2] But it's also indicative of the way Zuma's (and the ANC's) mind now worked. For Mulroney is the only Canadian so honored from the years of support struggles that occurred in Canada for the liberation of South Africa.

Did this not confirm exactly what was suggested above: that it was the likes of Mulroney who had won the struggle for southern/South African liberation? Of course, in buying capital's line, the ANC leadership (not least Zuma), those who now granted Mulroney his award, had also won, albeit as an emergent ascendant elite. And with the results that we can now see: South Africa's ever deepening inequalities and the country's lack of real development or, in class terms, real liberation either (however true it is that, in terms of racial and political liberation, something real had been won). But, to repeat, both the ANC elites and global capital could be said to have won – and very much to their advantage – the southern African liberation struggle.

And, finally, we must note the similarly ironic ending that also played out in a range of North American circles beyond those of the state and corporate worlds. In fact, for too many activists within the anti-apartheid movement the racist structures in southern Africa had all along been their target. And now, once "we" had apparently "won" such a struggle, defined in such exclusively racial terms, and even though this outcome was closely linked to a recolonization of the region by global capital, the liberation support/anti-apartheid movement in North America simply, for many, evaporated. Some did keep asking other, closely related, questions about continuing class, gender and political oppression both in southern Africa and in Canada and about what could be done on these fronts. And some also began to ask related questions about the reality of "global apartheid" and the validity of anti-apartheid parallels with respect to the Palestine/Israel contestation. In short, many did leave to engage in other equally meritorious struggles on other fronts (on the latter points, see also the final section of this chapter).

Yet it is the case that too many onetime militants who walked away from southern Africa did so a little too smugly. Thus one erstwhile comrade is quoted in my book as saying that she saw the Canadian movement's dissolution as "the only appropriate response." She argued, "for me, after '94, I said I'm done, now you need to work it out internally" – this said despite the undoubted fact that Canadian firms were amongst those hemming in the choices open to South Africans. Indeed, by the 1990s, activism in support of South Africa had become a safe cause, with, in the rueful words of another Toronto activist, "Solidarity events [going] from pickets outside the LCBOs in 1982 to business luncheons and the [awarding of honorary Canadian] citizenships [to] ANC cadres in the mid-1990s."[4]

Meanwhile, others spoke out more clearly. Thus Black-American human-rights lawyer and activist Gay McDougall argued that part of the movement's problems "was the fact that [it had] focused so intensely on race." For "Americans in general" she wrote, "believe in civil and political rights but not in economic and social rights [because] we don't believe that people should have a right to livelihood, to health, shelter, homes." The anti-apartheid movement had not dealt with the tough questions about the future, she reflected. "I don't want to be harsh here because I think we did real good with what we saw out there to do. But it was, in many ways, a shallow movement politically." Indeed, as I then have also quoted Bill Minter: "Despite the celebration of Mandela and the new South Africa" many "were well aware that the media celebration concealed stubborn realities and economic inequality still to be addressed. But neither in South Africa nor in the United States [and not, for that matter, in Canada] were there clear strategies for dealing with these issues, much less a vision for how grassroots activists might be involved," he wrote.[5]

Questions remain then: Was an untransformed, smug Canada, a Canada in which continuing inequality grows apace, capable of going any further, of doing anything more? Is it now? Or, to repeat, did Mulroney not, alongside such South African figures as Mbeki, Zuma and Ramaphosa,[6] win the struggle for southern African liberation? And could we (alongside similarly motivated comrades in southern Africa) hope to win next time? For answers to these questions – answers premised on a real, and not merely romanticized, perusal of what was accomplished last time and also on what we might truly hope to accomplish next time – are sorely needed. A day of reckoning must surely come in southern Africa, and we may again be called on for support.

B. Now: Recolonization and After

The title of the second day's workshop as at Carleton was originally entitled "A Turning Point – Hegemonies in Decline in Southern Africa." I was surprised for this title (one that was even shorn of a tentativeness in judgment that question-marks might otherwise have implied) seemed to take for granted rather more than could be readily affirmed After all, one might ask: Whose hegemony? What decline? And where and when had there been or is there likely to be (in any proximate future) such a turning point in the region? For as far as I could tell there had been no significant decline in any of the prevailing hegemonies that have come to define southern Africa since its liberation? Nor had there been any discernible turning point towards such a decline that might promise a more positive future for the region.

By the time the workshop was held its title had been changed to "Change or No Change in Southern Africa – What's Next?" This was a title that captured a more sober and inescapable understanding. It is also true that, since the original discussion that led to the framing of the workshop's first title, there had been dramatic developments: for example, a coup had, at last, removed the villainous Robert Mugabe from the presidency of Zimbabwe, while a political crisis within the

ANC, sparked by months of popular demonstrations, had brought about the resignation of Jacob Zuma, President of South Africa. Yet it soon became apparent that such novel developments were not, at Carleton, to be taken as marking, by definition, any significant turning point. The new title was now more circumspect (and more accurate) than the original.

Why so? Because the prevailing situation in southern Africa, one that offered so little prospect of liberation even prior to the recent quasi-coups in both Zimbabwe and South Africa, seemed now to offer little more in the way of any such prospect. Despite the success in ending overt institutionalized racial domination, "liberated" Southern African countries have, as suggested, merely been recolonized by global capital, with that capital's undoubted hegemony now even more firmly in place than ever (I can see no decline on that front even if the global empire's center of gravity has shifted and diversified itself, now constituting a system that I have characterized as forming a new "Empire of Capital"). In addition, that empire's hegemony is shared throughout southern Africa with, and guaranteed by (the almost wholly parasitical) national regimes, with these constituted, in every case, by the very same movements and elites that gained formal power during the transition from white rule some decades ago. And yet there is little decline in such regimes' power and primacy either – except with regard to the extent of their increased lack of credibility in moral and socioeconomic/developmental terms, and of a similar lack of credibility in their claims of having realized popular empowerment.

In short, a severe questioning of the legitimacy of such structures seems to be in order, not least because far more was hoped for, even expected from, these countries' liberation. This has been most dramatically true in Angola and Zimbabwe, where there has been tangible fear on the part of ordinary people towards the new, indigenous hegemons. And it has begun to be true in Mozambique as well. Indeed, throughout the region, the once triumphant thrust of nationalism that carried such regimes to power is now pretty much exhausted as a positive political resource. The result: the continuing hegemony of the region's range of unholy alliances between local state and global capital increasingly give off a bad odor to the populace of these countries. But does this mean that the post-liberation system of liberation-as-recolonization is declining in potency or that, with such a decline, there are much weaker prospects for the system, or even the individual regimes (however venal and corrupt they may be), to survive into the foreseeable future?

Unfortunately, the answer must be no, for the moment. There has been no significant decline in the power of the oligarchs of state and capital. There is also little evidence that global capitalism has become weaker in any way that suggests vulnerability. In sum, there is no startling turning point away from the status quo on the horizon anywhere around the globe, and certainly not in southern Africa. If in some oblique way the continuing hegemony of the southern African order, structured by liberation nationalism and by the market-driven economics of recolonization, can be said to be suffering any decline, what kind of transformative outcome (and what turning point towards it) can be seen on the horizon of any regime in the region? Are we not more likely to see instead the continuing decline of a stale regional liberation: not so much some promising turn to the left as a slump into greater political chaos, increased tyranny and/or more extreme social distemper?

But might not this very decline give further impetus to the rise of new and more promising counter-hegemonic projects with some chance of success? Unfortunately, there are not yet so many promising signs in the region as one might hope, nor is any promising turning point in the offing in the immediate future. True, there has been a significant level of turmoil in most of the states in southern Africa. For example, South Africa is – in terms of its level of incidents of resistance in both township and workplace – a consistent rival of China for top spot on the world's table of the highest rates of such unrest.[7] Moreover, this endemic "reality of resistance" seems also to have contributed to the fall of Zuma.[8] At the same time, it has yet to produce anything like a new and convincing hegemonic counter-movement of left-wing provenance. And such a discouraging outcome is less, it seems to me, due to lingering attachment to the primacy and legitimacy of the liberation movements from earlier decades of resistance than it is a reflection of the inability of any viable left to convincingly demonstrate the ideological and organizational attributes of a new and plausible hegemonic program.[9]

Here we must register the importance of the fact that capital has, at least for the moment, won the global struggle at the most fundamental level: at the cultural level. For doesn't the inability of the left to respond appear to register the simple fact that ascendant global capitalism – with its locally empowered intermediaries in so many countries of the world – has become so strong that most people, even amongst those who might feel able to take the risk of resisting, either lapse back into pursuit of their own individual advancement or else lack the confidence that there remains any viable alternative to the conditions they find themselves now strapped to? As Thatcher once famously said, "There is no such thing as society; there is only the individual and his/her family." What we are left with is the nightmare charted so clearly by Brough Macpherson, my old teacher at the University of Toronto: liberalism as mere "possessive individualism" has triumphed. And to hell with the rest of you.

And yet, as also indicated in the previous section, such a conclusion may be just too sweeping. A few months ago, for example, we celebrated in Toronto the 45th anniversary of our launch of TCLSAC. I recognized at least a hundred old comrades from those bygone days. I also spoke with many of them. Virtually every one of them had continued to do things in their lives that reflected the commitment they had exemplified in their TCLSAC days. Of course, many of them came to TCLSAC with some progressive commitment already in place and lent TCLSAC that commitment for a period, while others suggested to me that they had an opportunity to discover the meaning of political commitment with TCLSAC, a commitment to radical change that they were later able to carry over into other theatres of struggle. It seemed to me, in short, that every campaign and every struggle we engage in adds to the numbers of those Canadians who seek justice, equality and decency in our society. Nonetheless, a big issue must be faced: how easily, with so much pulling people in the other direction, can we see such efforts adding up, one hundred activists at a time, into an effective and potentially hegemonic mass movement?

Not that I would want to end this section on a depressing note – not with the startling growth in Canada of the "Black Lives Matter" and "Me Too" movements, the outpouring of rage at the Colten Boushie murder and other horrors perpetrated, both historically and presently, against Canada's indigenous people and the work of Naomi Klein and Avi Lewis and others around the "Leap Manifesto," to cite only a few pertinent examples and to go no further afield; I also take inspiration from the work of my son Nick, his group at Community Food Centers Canada/CFCC, and the many activists busy across a wide spectrum on various important socioeconomic fronts in the spheres of food, health, housing, education and the like.[10]

And what of southern Africa? After all, the big bad wolf (plenty big and plenty bad) of settler colonialism is dead. Things are certainly better than they would have been under white rule (imperial, settler and corporate) in southern Africa, – of that there can be no doubt. Throughout the region, it took guts, hard work and determination to win even as much as was won. At the same time, looking at the subsequent tangible fallout of "victory," it is difficult to perceive any very heartening record and/or residue of liberatory accomplishment. Where did all that energy go? What was there to show for it?

C. Next: Plus ça Change...

There are some limited signs that the struggle continues in the region: surely the fact these countries have faced unwinnable struggles before and fought back to win is a valuable historical memory. This is true in South Africa certainly, a country of deep inequalities (now at least as much of class as of race).[11] Many would say that there are not enough such positive signs. It is a sobering fact that, despite deep thought and sharp action, South Africa's record of continuing contestation with power (think, again, of Marikana) has yet to produce any very viable left contender for hegemony and state power. Instead, we merely get Zuma vs. Ramaphosa. Not very much, one fears.

And in Zimbabwe more people have perhaps chosen to vote with their feet (on their way to South Africa, Botswana and beyond) than have stood their ground, but who can blame them after decades bottled up in a country where Mugabe's tyranny, now ended by a coup, has been followed by the rule of a Crocodile (the chilling sobriquet of Emmerson Mnangagwa, Mugabe's successor as President). In Angola there are heartening, if still relatively mild, signs of fresh resistance – but small wonder that people in such a fear-ridden place proceed with caution, despite the fact that Eduardo dos Santos and his clan, since their eclipse, no longer ride roughshod over people there. Meanwhile, in Mozambique and Namibia most people – but, again, not all – keep their heads down.

What to say about Zuma and Mugabe, Ramaphosa and Mnangagwa? And about the near future and eventual outcome of any revolutionary struggle in the region? Perhaps such a struggle will eventually resume, even though it will take time (and things could get worse before they get better). Nonetheless, at times the only formula seems to be "The more things change, the more they stay the same."[12] For, unfortunately, turfing Mugabe and Zuma out of office has represented a mere reshuffling of the same old deck of exhausted nationalism and of corrupt political elites, with not, as yet, anything coming close to heralding a serious and meaningful regional transformation. Still, one final phrase for the wise: *On s'engage, puis on voit:* continue to engage in genuine oppositional struggle throughout the region, and we might see more clearly how well we on the left can do.[13]

An Envoi: On Writing and Acting on the Premise that the Struggle Continues

The final words of the preceding section may provide all of the envoi that is required for this volume, those words as well as the concluding envoi in another volume in this final trilogy of my writing life entitled *Race, Class and The Thirty Years War for Southern African Liberation, 1960-1994: A History.* In the latter volume I also brought my account of that struggle to an interim conclusion by discussing briefly the fates of such presidents as José Eduardo dos Santos (for 38 years the president of Angola), Robert Mugabe (for 37 years the Prime Minister/President of Zimbabwe), and Jacob Zuma, the erstwhile president of South Africa, each case offering a sorrier spectacle than the last. All have been toppled from power. Nor are their successors more promising, thrown up, as they have been, from within the same underachieving liberation movement/ruling party milieu (although the jury is still out on João Lourenço, Angola's president since dos Santos stepped down in 2017). But the situation is even more sobering elsewhere within the region under the present rule of the ZANU's "Crocodile," Emmerson Mnangagwa, and South Africa's Cyril Ramaphosa of the ANC.[1] So: five liberation movements, all still – if rather disreputably – in power decades after helping win their country's "liberation," and this within a region that has also been recolonized by global capital. What next? The struggle continues? Perhaps, but whatever else is true, the current state of "liberation" in southern Africa presents an open challenge to all who care about the region and its fate. For that reason, permit me to add a few final thoughts.

The late Neville Alexander, in "liberated" South and southern Africa's bleak times, took strength from what he considered to be a hopeful prediction (offered by Patrick Bond), one that Alexander quoted as follows:

"The dynamic of progressive change will emerge from the alienation of those who suffer most from neoliberalism, in South Africa and across the world, and from the creativity of those who demand and imagine a better world,"[2] [with Alexander then seeing much promise the fact that] the struggles of the urban poor and the rural poor are being supported, and often led, by socialist and other radical activists who often constitute a bridge [to] the immediate past and whose understanding of the international and national systems are informed by the incipient revolt of the intelligentsia and of students against the debilitating abstractions of "economics" as taught in most universities today.

Alexander concludes that "the intellectual movement back to re-establishing the link between social conditions and the production, exchange and the distribution of 'man's worldly goods' [among] young students and other activists [everywhere]...heralds the beginning of the systematic rehabilitation not only of socialism as an alternative to what exists at present but also of the indispensability of the historical materialist method of social analysis even and precisely in our post-industrial age."[3]

To which I would merely again quote Hemingway: "Isn't it pretty to think so." Because, damn it all, it is. Nor can I think of anyone who could have said such things any better than my friend Neville has here and many times elsewhere in his writings. For his refusal to follow the likes of Mandela,[4] Mbeki, Zuma and Ramaphosa into the greasy swamp of free-market fantasies" is exemplary. Social democratic/liberal and ANC claims to the contrary notwithstanding, *trickle up* (to the 1%, the 5% or the 10%), and not *trickle down* is the rule of rampant capitalism as it is experienced in the real world that it has structured. The alternative: hope – as this book's title expresses it – hope in the best Blochian/Marxist sense discussed in chapter 3 – and, more precisely, revolutionary hope. This latter would, in practice, find leaders closely linked to, and articulating/helping to focus, the democratically expressed voices of the working class and the people. And such demands so expressed would have to be articulated in such a way as to defy global-capitalist logic, while placing popular needs and demands at the core of a movement that seeks the socioeconomic and political empowerment of *everyone*. There are many southern Africans who agree with these latter formulations, as my first-hand experience of the region has taught me, although – as we have seen – such progressive southern Africans are still looking for the political means to make any such understanding more general and more decisively hegemonic.

Let me then repeat in this regard – and as also evoked in a previous chapter – the wisdom of my friend, the African economist Samir Amin, on such matters. His death,[5] as I was concluding this envoi, encouraged me to recall how long he had been advocating a more radical decolonization from capitalist control from the system's center than anything that had yet occurred in Africa; something better could only be achieved (to cite his dramatic formulation) through an actual and active *delinking* (emphasis added!) of the economies of the global South from the Empire of Capital that otherwise holds the South in its sway. For Amin, such delinking was defined as "the submission of external relations [to internal needs, demands and requirements], the opposite of the internal adjustment of the peripheries to the demands of the polarizing worldwide expansion of capital." To him this seemed "the only realistic alternative [since] reform of the [present] world system is utopian." For "history shows us that it is impossible to 'catch up' within the framework of world capitalism"; in fact, "only a very long transition" (with a self-conscious choice for delinking from the world of capitalist globalization as an essential first step) beyond the present situation of global polarization will suffice."

But Amin also knew autarky was no answer either and that it is important not to understate the challenges inherent in the simultaneity of both a top-heavy global economy on the one hand and a rising saliency of popularly empowering demands and freshly articulated South-South linkages, on the other. Thus, links such as those foreshadowed in the World Social Forum seek, multinationally, to sponsor a redefinition of the workings of the global economy; small wonder, then, that Amin would devote so much of his later years to political work within this World Social Forum network, helping to recraft from below a worldwide movement and sensibility designed, if not to overthrow capitalism, to at least begin effectively to regulate it in the interest of socially responsible and democratic purposes. To make, in short, the "globally necessary" increasingly the "globally possible"!

True, even at the level of the national economy Amin did not propose an immediate extirpation of market relations, even though he realized that any unrestrained market economy would further encourage the socioeconomic dangers attendant upon burgeoning class-differentiation. For Amin was realistic enough to see that too bold a rush to social control and collectivism might tend to overburden those charged with the management and planning of fledgling progressive states in the global South. All the more important for Amin was the creation and empowerment of national movements capable of countering the logic of capitalism's embrace, global and national. But he knew full well that this would be a tough challenge. For so strong are the global pressures against any challenge from the left that crafting the political foundations necessary to ground such a revolutionary socioeconomic push would (however "nationally necessary") not readily become the "nationally possible." Small wonder that Amin saw both global and national struggles for a radical delinking from the presumed logic of market primacy and for a drive to carry the global economy beyond capitalism as being two sides of the same coin.

❀   ❀   ❀

In sum, if the predominant importance of the kind of planning (democratically-driven and needs-focused, both globally and locally) that we have suggested is ever to be achieved, it will have to embody a practice of planning which ensures that the center of gravity of the economy remains egalitarian, collectively premised and popularly centered and controlled. Thus, the bottom line of any substantive liberation from global constraints and from antagonistic class pressures would have to be (as Amin emphasized) a staunch commitment to a transition away from market power and entrepreneurial class interest. Only this would help ensure that no bourgeoisie, either foreign or domestic, would be permitted to play a role that it could use to justify a claim on their part to be allowed to snatch inordinate wealth or superordinate power. Indeed, the fact is that only the counter-exercise of genuine popular power would be able to guarantee a radical delinking from global-capitalist imperatives that otherwise can promise the poor, both globally and locally, only ill. It is time, to repeat, to make the globally and nationally necessary both the globally and the nationally possible.

But if any such attempt to make the "necessary" the "possible" is to be on history's agenda, we must also attempt to divine what rival camps are most likely to be on either side of any such a struggle to "revive – or to suppress – a renewal of the liberation struggle in Southern Africa." One should avoid exaggeration, but it seems fair to argue that amongst those opposed to progressive change (as documented in Section III) will be the venal political leadership elites in each of the five countries that formally and successfully contested southern Africa's future under race rule in the first liberation struggle years. For all today's leaders remain linked to the exact same movements that first came to power in the independence moments of the 1970s, the 1980s and the 1990s. And they continue to live off such much earlier victories of their movements right up to the present day.

There are exceptions to this general pattern and some stalwart and principled actors amongst the bureaucratic managers of such regimes and even, occasionally, among the membership of the political elites that oversee them who try to do better. Yet many such leaders have also managed to fool themselves into accepting the trickle-down mantras that have come, too often, to rationalize their activities, their deference to corporate persuasion, and their increasing personal wealth. At the same time, the bulk of such intermediaries (to employ Fanon's decisive sobriquet) on behalf of global capitalism have been far more brazenly smart, cynical and rapacious than this.[6]

Meanwhile, the ever-incisive Dale McKinley has further specified the identity of a second camp of those who will be engaged on the "wrong" side in any second liberation struggle that may yet come to define the southern African region. True, McKinley is well aware of the unsavory nature of many of the principal actors in the camp of South [and southern] Africa's political leadership and he has written two valuable books on the subject.[7] But more recently, McKinley[8] briefly offers, as well, a strong indictment of corporate capitalism – this also being a particularly strong force in the second camp we are identifying here. For he writes that "the history of corporate capital is a history of criminality"[9] and then uses this dramatic epithet as a key guideline in the understanding contemporary South and southern Africa, stating that

> ...the very raison-d'être of corporate capital is its insatiable drive to extract surplus value and accumulate ever-increasing profit by finding new and inventive ways to further exploit and commodify both human and natural resources...Put differently, the entire architecture and edifice of corporate capital – inclusive of its more recent technological additions – foundationally requires the constant production, reproduction and eventual destruction of both people and planet. As such, criminality is and indeed must be, at the heart of its construction and lived reality.

McKinley then continues, "At the center of this journey is the ideological and financial 'capture' of the dominant political parties in power and thus also of the institutional purpose and policy direction of national states. This has been most often and effectively realized through the individual and class corruption of politicians as well as state bureaucrats and officials." Thus, in McKinley's opinion,

> in South Africa, the most telling early transitional example of the success of this criminalisation process is the fact that corporate capital literally got away without having to pay and/or answer for their active support of, and massive benefits from, an apartheid-capitalist system that was a crime against humanity. In allowing corporate capital to seamlessly transfer its criminalised frame into the "new" South Africa, [with] the ANC as ruling party, [placed] itself, the state and South African society as a whole squarely within that frame." For South Africa [as had been the parallel case throughout the region] has created in the ANC a political party in power whose leaders' class and policy interests are umbilically tied to those of corporate power.[10]

❀ ❀ ❀

"State capture," degraded and undemocratic polities, further subordination to (instead of a slow but sure "delinking" from) global capital, with all these features framed by any number of cruel variations on "corporate criminality"; we have seen ample proof of the malevolent implications of such aspects of the southern African reality above. And of course, we have seen right-wing populism/fascism loose on the global stage for the past century: Hitler, Trump and Stalin (in the latter case, a pseudo-socialist fascist dictatorship surely), with such unsavory figures paralleled in recent southern African history by the likes of Mugabe, dos Santos, and Zuma. And finally, to top it all off, there is, more recently, COVID-19! True, because of the timing of both this book's actual completion and its ultimate publication the virus' stalking of the world has been largely undiscussed here. But, in such a grim world, there is one final question: what hope can there still be for a truly liberated future? For an answer to this crucial question only one more paragraph remains – although the struggle in practice to concretize the movement, the tactics, the substance, of such an answer will be work of many coming years (and of many paragraphs of history).

In short, what of the role, the power and the significance of any oppositional "third camp" in a new struggle to actually liberate liberation by resisting recolonization by global capital and the ascendancy of the local African casts of facilitators and oppressors. This is a camp comprised of those popular forces that continue to work politically from below and that are just beginning (especially perhaps in South Africa) to find political shape, unity and counter-hegemonic purpose – as they had once done against equally great odds in becoming the foot-soldiers in the earlier confrontation with race-rule. Are we correct in thinking that their struggle – as revived and as even now undergoing some minimal degree of genuine renewal in ideology and organization – can continue? And can the masses – and those they choose to lead them – really hope to mount a new struggle as necessarily revolutionary and transformative as befits the times? There will be no glib and facile prophecies of success here. In fact, Lenin once quoted Napoleon to the effect that *"On s'engage, puis on voit.."* So – and have we any other choice? – we will just have to work (*"s'engager"*) to make sure the struggle does continue. And, if it does, then: *we will see.*[11]

By Way of an Introduction

1. *On Building a Social Movement: The North American Campaign for Southern African Liberation Revisited* (Trenton, N.J., and Halifax, Nova Scotia: Africa World Press and Fernwood Books, 2015/6).
2. *The Thirty Years War for the Liberation of Southern Africa, 1960-1990* (Cambridge: Cambridge University Press, forthcoming).
3. The book was originally envisioned by two of my long-time publishers, Kassahun Checole of Africa World Press and in New Jersey and Asad Zaidi of Three Essays Collective in Delhi, as being something of a mini-omnibus designed to collect together the most worthwhile of my writings - writings both theoretical and empirical – produced since the middle of the first decade of this century. The collections which contained such writings were *A Flawed Freedom: Rethinking Southern African Liberation* (London, Toronto and Cape Town: Pluto Books, Between the Lines, and Juta/University of Cape Town Press, 2014); *Liberation Lite: The Roots of Recolonization in Southern Africa* (Delhi and Trenton, NJ: Three Essays Collective and Africa World Press, 2011); *Decolonization and Empire: Contesting the Rhetoric and Reality of Resubordination in Southern Africa and Beyond* (Delhi, London & New York and Johannesburg: Three Essays Collective, Merlin Press, University of Witwatersrand Press, 2007) and *Development After Globalization: Theory and Practice for the Embattled South in the New Imperial Age* (Delhi, London, New York, Halifax and Durban/Pietermaritzburg: Three Essays Collective, Zed Press, Fernwood Press and University of KwaZulu-Natal Press, 2006). The original launching-pad for this series of varied essays (all of the above having been written after my near-fatal fall in 2003) was *The Next Liberation Struggle: Capitalism, Socialism and Democracy in Southern Africa* – Toronto, London, New York and Durban/Pietermaritzburg: Between The Lines, Merlin Press, Monthly Review Press & University of Kwazulu/Natal Press, 2005). Nonetheless, as I worked towards the realization of such a project I began to think of it as more appropriately forming an integral part of a "Southern African Liberation Trilogy," with its first section, entitled "In Theory," serving to constitute a presentation of the methodological underpinnings of the trilogy. Indeed, the very first chapter (below) continues to reflect something of this original "omnibus" intention, being primarily constituted of the blending of a number of my post-2000 theoretical essays into a coherent and sustained argument. On this matter the reader is also referred to footnote 4 that immediately follows.
4. The (anonymous) reviewer of my manuscript, recruited by one of the prospective publishers of the present book, had also noted in his/her review that the first theoretical chapters of this book "present, arguably, the first holistic and combined view of Saul's theoretical arsenal for the understanding of African political history which up until this book has been a bit scattered." This section, in the reviewer's opinion, thus "allows for a rare and important but...potent and directed theoretical/ideational argument for a Marxist theory framed by progressive and emancipatory morals, values and judgment, as well as an understanding and practice/use of Marxist theory in a most open, varied and non-reductionist manner." This is what I hoped would be the case for Section I and I am just immodest enough to accept the compliment graciously. I do hope, however, that others may find Section 1 to be similarly instructive and useful.
5. See also, for a more detailed account, my memoir *Revolutionary Traveller: Freeze-Frames from a Life* (Winnipeg: Arbeiter Ring Publishing, 2009).
6. See C.B Macpherson, *The Political Theory of Possessive Individualism* (Oxford: Oxford University Press, 1962).

7. On this, see again John S. Saul, *On Building a Social Movement (ibid.)*.

Chapter 1

1. Hugh Stretton's *The Political Sciences: General Principles of Selection in Social Science and History* (London: Routledge and Kegan Paul, 1961); as suggested this book has been, since I first read it in the 1960s, of immense importance to the development of the epistemology that became crucial to my work. Beyond epistemology, I should also note here the importance to me in the broader realms of political science and political philosophy of works by the above-mentioned C. B. Macpherson (notably his *Political Theory of Possessive Individualism* [Oxford: Oxford University Press, 2010 [reprint edition]) and *The Life and Times of Liberal Democracy* [Oxford: Oxford University Press, 2012 [reprint edition]) and by my friend Ralph Miliband (Parliamentary Socialism (London: Merlin Press, 2009 [new edition]), *Socialism for a Sceptical Age* [London: Polity Press, 1995] and *The State in Capitalist Society* (London: Merlin Press, 2009). Of especial importance to the development of my thinking have also been Sheldon Wolin's *Politics and Vision*, Expanded Edition (Princeton, N. J.: Princeton University Press, 2004) and *Democracy Incorporated: Managed Democracy and the Specter of Inverted Totalitarianism* (Princeton, N. J.: Princeton University Press, 2010), the paperback edition with a new preface by the author. In addition I will cite several African-based writers in a following subsection of this chapter: Frantz Fanon, Amilcar Cabral, Julius Nyerere and Steve Biko, among others.
2. Thus, in true omnibus fashion, I base my discussion – in sub-sections A, B(i) and B(ii), and C(iii) and C(iv) of this chapter – on several previous Merlin Press publications: "Identifying class, classifying difference" in Colin Leys and Leo Panitch (eds.), *The Socialist Register 2003* (London: Merlin, 2002) and 2003 "Globalization, Imperialism, Development: False Binaries and Radical Resolutions," in Colin Leys and Leo Panitch (eds.), *The Socialist Register 2004* (London: Merlin Press). These were subsequently collected in my 2006 *Development After Globalization: Theory and Practice for the Embattled South in the New Imperial Age* – Delhi, London & New York, Halifax & Durban/Pietermaritzburg: Three Essays Collective, Zed Press, Fernwood Press and University of KwaZulu-Natal Press:, this being the first of the four volumes comprise a set of closely-related works that I have cited in endnote #3 of my preceding introductory chapter.
3. E. H. Carr, *What is History?* (New York: Alfred A. Knopf. 1962) 5, 26.
4. Stretton, op.cit., 141: Stretton makes these observations in the wake of a very useful case study in his chapter 4 and entitled "For example: What caused Imperialism?" In my opinion, the book as a whole should be read by every fledgling social scientist (not to mention by some of their older peers).
5. Gavin Kitching, *Marxism and Science: Analysis of an Obsession* (University Park: Pennsylvania State University Press, 1994), 168.
6. Kitching, *ibid.*, 169-70.
7. Lucio Colletti, "Marxism: Science or Revolution" in Robin Blackburn (ed.), *Ideology in Social Science: Readings in Critical Social Theory* (Glasgow: Fontana/Collins, 1972).
8. "I would say," Colletti (ibid., 375) argues in this respect, "that there are two realities in capitalism: the reality expressed by Marx and the reality expressed by the authors he criticizes."
9. Stephen A. Resnick and Richard D. Wolff, *Knowledge and Class: A Marxian Critique of Political Economy* (Chicago: University of Chicago Press, 1987); "By entry points we mean that particular concept a theory uses to enter into its formulation, its particular construction of the entities and relations that comprise the social totality" (p. 25).

Endnotes

10. Resnick and Wolff, *ibid.*, 99.

11. Resnick and Wolff, *ibid.*, 281. That this approach can also lead to very soft definitions of capitalism and anti-capitalist struggle – see J. K. Gibson, *The End of Capitalism (As We Knew It)* (Cambridge: Blackwell, 1996) – is worth noting but Resnick and Wolff's approach remains a very strong one.

12. The quotations are from Laclau's contribution "Structure, History and the Political" in Judith Butler, Ernesto Laclau and Slavoj Žižek, *Contingency, Hegemony, Universality: Contemporary Dialogues on the Left* (London: Verso, 2000, 2013, 2016).

13. See Slavoj Žižek's essay "Holding the Place," (in Butler, *et.al., ibid.*), with the quotation used in my text drawn from p 321. As Žižek continues, "the much-praised postmodern 'proliferation of new political subjectivities,'the demise of every 'essentialist' fixation, the assertion of full contingency, [all] occur against the background of a certain silent renunciation and acceptance: the renunciation of the idea of a global change in the fundamental relations in our society (who still seriously questions capitalism, state and political democracy? [as Laclau seems to ask for]) and, consequently, the acceptance of the liberal democratic capitalist framework which remains the same, the unquestioned background, in all the dynamic proliferation of the multitude of new subjectivities. In short, Laclau's claim about my [Žižek's] anti-capitalism also holds for what he calls the 'democratic control of the economy,' and, more generally for the entire project of 'radical democracy': either it means palliative damage-control measures within the global capitalist framework, or it means absolutely nothing." So Žižek writes, scornfully yet accurately.

14. Kitching, *op.cit.*, p. 68. As Kitching further explains, "The reason is that Marx was, if nothing else, an extremely intelligent man, and economic reductionism is an extremely silly, not to say incoherent, idea in which to believe."

15. Eric Olin Wright, "Giddens' Critique of Marxism," *New Left Review*, 138 (March-April 1983), p. 24.

16. See, for example, Nicos Mouzelis ("Sociology of Development: Reflections on the Present Crisis," *Sociology*, 22, 1 [February, 1988]) who argues that "the neglect of the political... is the Achilles heel of all development theory," including Marxist theories of development, but also finds in Marxism's potential openness to embracing the tension between "systemic and agency terms" the key to its ability to overcome any collapse into economistic reductionism (pp. 39-40).

17. Karl Marx, *Capital*, vol. 3: The Process of Capitalist Production as a Whole (New York: International Publishers, 1964,), p. 790-1.

18. In *On Building a Social Movement: The North American Campaign for Southern African Liberation Revisited, op.cit.*, pp. 23-9.

19. For a careful case study of how so limited an outcome to the liberation struggle was consolidated in South Africa by capital, working in close association with the ANC, see Saul and Patrick Bond, *The Present as History – South Africa: From Mrs Ples to Marikana and Mandela* (Oxford and Johannesburg: James Currey and Jacana Press, 2014; second edition, 2016)

20. The work of Fanon and Cabral, cited from here, is discussed at greater length in my *A Flawed Freedom (op.cit.)*.

21. Frantz Fanon, *The Wretched of the Earth* (Penguin Books: Harmondsworth, 1967), p. 122.

22. Fanon, *op.cit.*, p. 55; as Fanon continues,"...they decolonize at such a rate that they [even] impose independence on Houphouet-Boigny."

23. Cabral was a principal architect in his native Guinea-Bissau of the second wave of anti-colonial liberation (sited principally in southern Africa, although the Portuguese colony of Guinea-Bissau was in West Africa); see his important book *Revolution in Guinea: An African People's Struggle* (London: Stage 1, 1967).

24. This (as well as other particularly interesting related material) is to be found in Cabral, *ibid.*, pp. 57-9.

25. John Gallagher and Ronald Robinson's "The Imperialism of Free Trade" was first published in *The Economic History Review,* 2nd series VI, 1 (1953), pp. 1-15, and also reprinted and featured prominently in John Gallagher's widely-cited *The Decline, Revival and Fall of the British Empire* (Cambridge and New York: Cambridge University Press, 1982 and 2004), to which the quotations in the next few paragraph are all referenced as to page numbers; see also Ronald Robinson, and John Gallagher (with Alice Denny), *Africa and the Victorians. The Official Mind of Imperialism* (London and Basingstoke: Macmillan, 1981).

26. As Gallagher and Robinson (ibid., p. 5-7) further elaborate this argument, "From this vantage point the many-sided expansion of British industrial society can be viewed as a whole of which both the formal and informal empires are only parts. Both of them then appear as variable political functions of the extending pattern of overseas trade, investment, migration and culture. If this is accepted, it follows that formal and informal empire are essentially interconnected and to some extent interchangeable."

27. Gallagher and Robinson, ibid., pp 4-5. Indeed, "it is only when and where informal political means failed to provide the framework of security for British enterprise...that the question of establishing formal empire arose" (p. 16). As they further argue, "It ought to be commonplace that Great Britain during the nineteenth century expanded overseas by means of informal empire as much as by acquiring dominion in the strict constitutional sense" (p. 1).

28. As if the Cold War were not itself as least as driven by commercial considerations as by any other cause.

29. W. Roger Louis and Ronald Robinson, "The United States and Liquidation of the British Empire in Tropical Africa, 1941-1951" in Prosser Gifford and W. R. Louis (eds.), *The Transfer of Power in Africa* (New Haven, CT: Yale University Press, 1982), pp. 31-55, to which the quotations in the next few paragraphs are all referenced as to page number.

30. See W. R. Louis and Ronald Robinson's 1994 essay "The Imperialism of Decolonization" in *The Journal of Imperial and Commonwealth History,* 22, 1 (1994; the article has been widely republished, notably as ch, 3 in James D. Le Sueur (ed.), *The Decolonization Reader* (New York and London: Routledge, 2003), pp. 49-79, to which version of this essay all quotations in the next few paragraphs are referenced as to page number.

31. As they continue (p. 73), "The ex-colonial powers would share the dividends and the burdens. Most of the new states would have to co-operate with one side or the other in the cold war if they were to fulfill their national aspirations, Though some might choose aid from the Soviet bloc, prospects of development [sic] depended on the superior economic capacity of the West. After 1956 the British fell in with the American design for Western alliances and free [!] institutions."

32. Unlike Fanon and Cabral, however, Robinson and Lewis are satisfied to conclude that, even if this new kind of thraldom is imperialist, it is nonetheless also developmental. They do not carefully argue this point, but merely assert the case for assuming a benign developmental imperialism. A startling claim and it comes as no surprise that the authors offer little evidence to support it, since there is little evidence to be found. Nor is it a claim that either Fanon or Cabral would ever dream of making; quite the contrary. The fact remains that, ensnared in the basement of an imperialist system now "managed" by the United States, Africa has yet to see, all these years later, much that might be construed as development by even the most enthusiastic of capitalism's cheerleaders.

33. *The Nationalist* (Dar es Salaam), issue of 5 December 1967.

34. I first developed the argument that follows, in much the same language, to anchor my reflections that lead off the issue on "The Global Anti-Apartheid Movement, 1946-1994" in *Radical History Review,* #119 (Spring 2014); my essay was entitled "The Southern African Victory: Liberation Realized or a Prelude to Recolonization?"

35. Of course, as I also noted, that century had also seen, among other things, the confirmation of the ascendancy of the economic might and seemingly boundless power of the United

Endnotes

States; the Russian Revolution and the rise and fall of the Soviet Union; the reawakening under Communist rule of China and that country's march back to global prominence; the horrors of Hitler and his Holocaust; and two world wars of stunning inhumanity waged at frightful cost.

36. But see, inter alia, Mark Crocker, *Rivers of Blood, Rivers of Gold: Europe's Conquest of Indigenous Peoples* (New York: Grove Press, 1997); Sophie Bessis, *Western Supremacy: The Triumph of an Idea* (London: Zed Books, 2003); Vijay Prashad, *The Darker Nations: A People's History of the Third World* (New York: The New Press, 2007) and Sven Lindqvist, *"Exterminate All the Brutes": One Man's Odyssey into the Heart of Darkness and the Origins of European Genocide* (New York: Thee New Press, 1996); for a pertinent regional study see Walter Rodney, *How Europe Underdeveloped Africa* (London and Dar es Salaam: Bogle l'Overture Publications and Tanzania Publishing House, 1972)

37. Thomas Benjamin (ed.), "Preface" to *The Encyclopedia of Western Colonialism Since 1450* (New York: Macmillan Reference U.S.A, 2005).

38. In W. E. B. Du Bois' introduction (entitled "The Forethought") to his The Souls of Black Folk (New York: New American Library, 1903), p. 19.

39. Prashad, *op.cit.*; his phrase "the darker nations" characterizes a "non-white world" in a much more positive, pro-active phrase than "non-white," and referring to people who are, more positively (and proudly), brown, yellow, black and other tones.

40. See Crocker, *op.cit.*, especially Part III, "The Dispossession of the Apache" and Richard Drinnon, *Facing West: The Metaphysics of Indian Hating and Empire-Building* (New York: New American Library, 1980).

41. Leo Panitch and Sam Gindin, *The Making of Global Capitalism: The Political Economy of American Empire* (London: Verso Books, 2012). But note the use of both the terms "global capitalism" and "American empire" in the book's title. Perhaps this would once have seemed a repetition of terms; increasingly, however, the presumed link between these two phrases seems to be ever more a contradiction in terms.

42. Nayan Chanda, "U.S. Sours on Globalization: Protests may have abated, but globalization has fewer supporters in the U.S. as job numbers don't add up," *Businessworld*, 25 May 2011.

43. See Giovanni Arrighi, *Adam Smith in Beijing: Lineages of the 21st Century* (London: Verso Press, 2007).

44. "Asian economies to outstrip Western nations by 2030," *Toronto Star,* 11 December 2012.

45. Dave Lindor, "U.S. Intelligence Analysts: American Power is in Terminal Decline," *Information Clearing House,* 13 December 2012.

46. See Ellen Meiksins Wood, *Empire of Capital* (London: Verso, 2003) and my *Empire and Decolonization (op.cit.)*.

47. Besides economic and political imperialisms – so complementary, as is emphasized here, within the present Empire of Capital (although not merely reducible the one to the other) – there are also distinct forms of cultural imperialism, ranging from the global tyranny of the English language to the impact of branded products ("Coca-colonization"), from the hegemony of pop culture (on film, television and the internet) to the much trumpeted triumphant common sense of the free market (despite its being a virtual recipe for persistent and deepening inequality). Such realities certainly deserve further independent elaboration and more precise social explanation.

48. For a very different prognosis as to the future of "socialism" see Rick Salutin's tart, timely and exemplary article, "What word could replace socialism? How about socialism," in *The Toronto Star,* 30 November 2018.

49. I draw here from, among other sources, the same essay from which I also drew my argument for the self-conscious deployment of a "moralizing science" to further our understanding. This essay's second section was entitled "Marxism: Anti-Reductionist and Non-Essentialist."

50. Himani Bannerji, *Thinking Through: Essays on Feminism, Marxism and Anti-Racism* (Toronto: Women's Press, 1995), pp. 30-1. In a related manner, Joan Acker seeks a "fluid

view of class as an ongoing production of gender and racially formed economic relations, rooted in family and communities as well as in the global organization of capital," thereby helping to overcome the way in which "women's movements and anticolonialism and antislavery struggles' have often been "divorced from class struggle." See her 'Rewriting Class, Race and Gender: Problems in Feminist Rethinking" in Myra Marx Ferree, Judith Lorberg and Beth B. Hass (eds.), *Revisioning Gender* (Thousand Oaks, Calif.: Sage Publishers, 1999), pp. 62-3.

51. Katha Pollitt, "Race and Gender and Class, Oh My!" in her *Subject to Debate: Sense and Dissents on Women, Politics and Culture* (New York: Random House, 2001), pp. 218-219. As she continues: "Everybody sees that now – even John Sweeney talks about gay partnership benefits as a working-class issue – except for a handful of old New Leftists, journalists and mini-pundits who practice the identity politics that dare not speak its name."

52. Lynne Segal, "Whose Left? Socialism, Feminism and the Future," *New Left Review*, 185 (January-February, 1991), pp. 87, 90. Segal critiques, in particular, those former socialist-feminists like Zillah Eisenstein who had begun to abandon the link between socialism and feminism in favor (in Segal's summary) of a feminist politics that seeks to "unite all women...in their specific identity as women."

53. Nancy Fraser, "From Redistribution to Recognition? Dilemmas of Justice in a 'Post-Socialist' Age," *New Left Review*, #212 (July-August 1995), p. 68.

54. Rosemary Hennessy and Chrys Ingraham, "Introduction: Reclaiming Anticapitalist Feminism" in their edited volume *Materialist Feminism* (New York and London: Routledge, 1997); such authors regret that crucial concepts like "social structure, production, patriarchy and class ... have been dismissed by post-modernist feminists [and by "a flourishing postmodern cultural politics"] in favor of analyses that ... focus almost exclusively on ideological, state, or cultural practices, anchor meaning in the body and its pleasures, or understand social primarily in terms of the struggle over representation" (p. 5).

55. See, for example, Carol A. Stabile, "Feminism and the Ends of Postmodernism" and Martha Gimenez, "The Oppression of Women: A Structuralist Marxist View" (p. 82), in Hennessy and Ingraham, *ibid.*

56. Hennessy and Ingraham, *op.cit.*, p. 11.

57. Rosemary Hennessy, *Profit and Pleasure: Sexual Identities in Late Capitalism* (New York and London: Routledge, 2000), p. 232.

58. Thus Bob Sutcliffe ("Development after Ecology," in V. Bhaskar and A. Glyn [eds.], *The North, the South and the Environment: Ecological Constraints and the Global Economy* [London: St. Martin's Press, 1995]) demonstrates the necessity of developing a progressive politics that is sensitive simultaneously to ecology and to the imperatives of global redistribution: "The only hope for a radical redistribution towards the future is a radical redistribution away from the rich in the present. If greater equality in the present is one of the traditional concerns of red politics, greater equality between generations is an essential characteristic of the new green politics. But not all reds are yet green; nor do all greens look as if they will become reds. The future of sustainable human development depends of a more thorough mixing of the colours" (p. 255).

59. Sabina Lovibond, "Feminism and Postmodernism," *New Left Review*, 178 (November-December 1989), p. 28. Whether, in seeking to resist both "mere" relativism on the one hand and liberal/neoliberal universalism on the other, the Enlightenment is the best point of reference for the Left may be open to question.

60. Oliver Cox, *Caste, Class and Race* (New York: Monthly Review, 1948); this is not, I would hope, to diminish the horrors (and the significance) of the Holocaust, amongst other historical horrors.

61. Mark Cocker, *Rivers of Blood, Rivers of Gold: Europe's Conquest of Indigenous Peoples* (New York: Grove Press, 1998), p. xiii. See also Sven Lindqvist, "Exterminate All the Brutes": *One Man's Odyssey into the Heart of Darkness and the Origins of European Genocide* (New York: The New Press, 1996).

Endnotes

62. Richard Drinnon, *Facing West: The Metaphysics of Indian-Hating and Empire Building* (New York: New American Library, 1980), p. xvi-xviii.

63. Frank Furedi, *The Silent War: Imperialism and the Changing Perception of Race* (New Brunswick: Rutgers University Press, 1998), p. 240.

64. Note, too, the link made by Hannah Arendt (in her *The Origins of Totalitarianism* [New York: Harcourt Brace, 1951]) between the racisms of imperial expansion and that of genocidal anti-semitism (the latter being a racism with a unique historicity) in the German case.

65. Edna Bonacich, "Class Approaches to Ethnicity and Race," in *The Insurgent Sociologist* (Special Issue on "Race and Class in Twentieth Century Capitalist Development"), 10, 2 (Fall, 1980).

66. David Morley and Kuan-Hsing Chen (eds.), Stuart Hall: *Critical Dialogues in Cultural Studies* (London and New York: Routledge, 1996), and Paul Gilroy, Lawrence Grossberg and Angela McRobbie (eds.), *Without Guarantees: In Honor of Stuart Hall* (London: Verso, 2000).

67. See my "Introduction: The Revolutionary Prospect" to John S. Saul and Stephen Gelb, *The Crisis in South Africa, Revised Edition* (New York and London: Monthly Review Press and Zed, 1986), Harold Wolpe, *Race, Class and the Apartheid State* (London: James Currey, 1988) and John S. Saul "Cry for the Beloved Country: The Post-Apartheid Denouement," *Monthly Review*, 52, 8 (January 2001)

68. John Gabriel and Gideon Ben-Tovim, "Marxism and the concept of racism," *Economy and Society*, 7, 2 (May 1978), p. 147.

69. Robert Biel, *The New Imperialism: Crisis and Contradiction in North/South Relations* (London: Zed Books, 2000), pp. 131-2.

70. Ankie Hoogvelt, *Globalization and the Postcolonial World: The New Political Economy of Development*, Second Edition (Houndmills: Palgrave, 2001), p. xiv.

71. The increasing trend towards a multi-national, multi-racial empire of global capitalism *per se* as discussed earlier in this conclusion should also reinforce the skepticism of Aijaz Ahmed and others regarding the possibility of a progressive fit for such concepts as "The Third World" and "Tri-continentalism."

72. Sutcliffe seeks, however, to incorporate these variables "in a way that allows imperialism once again to become an important theoretical concept." See his "The Place of Development in Theories of Imperialism and Globalization," in Ronaldo Munck and Denis O'Hearn (eds.), *Critical Development Theory: contributions to a new paradigm* (London and New York: Zed, 1999), p. 144.

73. Sutcliffe, *ibid.*, 150-2

74. See also on this subject Mahmoud Dhaouadi, "Capitalism, Global Humane Development and the Other Underdevelopment," in Leslie Sklair (ed.), *Capitalism and Development* (London: Routledge, 1994).

75. Paul Gilroy, *Against Race: Imagining Political Culture Beyond the Color Line* (Cambridge, Mass.: The Belknap Press of Harvard University Press, 2000), pp. 58-61.

76. Gilroy, *ibid.*, p. 334.

77. On the pitfalls of humanistic voluntarism, see Gabriel and Ben-Tovim, *op.cit.*

78. Gilroy, *op.cit.*, p. 335.

79. As cited in Liz Fawcett, *Religion, Ethnicity and Social Change* (Houndmills: MacMillan Press, 2000), 3

80. Tom Nairn, "The Modern Janus," *New Left Review*, 94 (November-December 1975), 3.

81. Michael Lowy, *Fatherland or Mother Earth? Essays on the National Question* (London: Pluto Press, 1998), pp. 2, 4.

82. Ronaldo Munck, *Marxism @ 2000: Late Marxist Perspectives* (Houndmills: MacMillan Press, 2000), esp. ch. 7, "Difficult Dialogue: Marxism and Nation," p. 133

83. Michael Lowy, *Fatherland or Mother Earth? (op.cit.).*

84. Bryan Turner, *Religion and Social Theory: A Materialist Perspective* (London: Heinemann Educational Books, 1983), p. 282

85. As Hopkins writes (in the introduction to Dwight N. Hopkins, et. al. [eds.], *Religions/Globalizations: Theories and Cases* [Durham: Duke University Press, 2001]), "For the majority of cultures around the world, religion thoroughly permeates and decisively affects the everyday rituals of survival and hope. Reflected in diverse spiritual customs, sacred symbols and indigenous worship styles, global religions are permanent constituents of human life."

86. I say this with some feeling in light of my experience living and working in Mozambique in the 1970s and 1980s when the ruling liberation movement, Frelimo, paid what seems in retrospect to have been an unnecessarily heavy price in terms of popular legitimacy for eliding a struggle against the overbearing institutional presence of the Catholic Church with an attack on religious sensibility.

87. Michael Lowy, *The War of Gods: Religion and Politics in Latin America* (London: Verso, 1996). p. 4.

88. Lowy (*ibid.*, pp. 6-10) reminds us, for example, of Marx's pithy footnote in *Capital* (volume 1, chapter 1) in which he suggests of the Middle Ages and of antiquity that "Catholicism there and politics here played the dominant role," albeit in interaction with permissive economic conditions; Lowy's discussion of Engels' approach both to Thomas Munzer's millenarianism and to English Puritanism is also instructive.

89. *Ibid.*, p. 12.

90. See also on this subject James Bentley, *Between Marx and Christ: The Dialogue in German-Speaking Europe*, 1870-1970 (London: Verso, 1982).

91. Interestingly, Mariategui evokes Sorel as the first Marxist thinker who understood the "religious, mystical and metaphysical character of socialism" (Lowy, op.cit., pp. 18); for Mariategui as postcolonial theorist see Young, *op.cit.*, ch. 15, where he is quoted as advocating that "We must give birth, through our own reality, our own language, to an Indo-American socialism."

92. Lowy, *ibid.*, pp. 5, 31.

93. Hopkins, *op.cit.* (see fn. 84), p. 2

94. Chapter 3 of Fanon's *The Wretched of the Earth* (New York: Grove Press, 1968) is, again, the crucial text here, and applies to ethnic as well as to national consciousness.

95. Munck, *op.cit.* (see fn. 81), p. 135.

96. Lowy, *Fatherland or Mother Earth, op.cit.* [see fn. 80]), p. 55

97. Munck, *op.cit.*, p. 133.

98. Ernesto Laclau, *Politics and Ideology in Marxist Theory: Capitalism, Fascism, Populism* (London: New Left Books, 1977). For my early deployment of Laclau (amongst other theoretical resources) to understand the weight and substance of ethnicity in Africa see "The Dialectic of Tribe and Class," ch 14 in my *State and Revolution in Eastern Africa* (New York and London: Monthly Review and Heinemann, 1979).

99. The dangers to democratic values and practices that the adoption of a hard version of secularism represents is argued, albeit somewhat idiosyncratically and not entirely convincingly, in William Connelly, *Why I am not a Secularist* (Minneapolis: University of Minnesota Press, 1999).

100. Enrique Dusserl, "The Sociohistorical Meaning of Liberation Theology," in Hopkins, *et al.* (*op.cit.*), p. 41.

101. Radhika Coomaraswamy, "In Defense of Humanistic Way of Knowing: A Reply to Qadri Ismail," *Pravada* (n.d.), pp. 29-3

102. Karen Armstrong, *The Battle for God* (New York: Ballantine Books, 2001), p. 367, although Armstrong's studies convince her that under some circumstances "many of the ideals of modern Europe would be congenial to Muslims" (p. 59).

103. Mark Jurgensmeyer, "The Global Rise of Religious Nationalism," in Hopkins, *et al.* (*op.cit.*), p. 66.

104. Benjamin Barber, *Jihad vs McWorld* (New York and Toronto: Random House, 1995), p. 222 and *passim*.

Endnotes

105. This has not been the practice of most socialist modernizers of the past; twenty-first-century socialists have much to learn from the mistakes of their predecessors in this respect. Moreover, many complexities still have to be confronted, for example indigenous modernizers seeking to introduce liberatory themes of women's emancipation will have their work cut out for them in many cultural contexts, however deftly they proceed.

106. The failure of the Left or its defeat? Something of both no doubt – although, as Panitch reminds us ("The Meaning of 11 September for the Left," *Studies in Political Economy*, 67 [Spring 2002], p. 47), "Whatever responsibility the Left must take for this defeat, there can be no doubt about the major role played by American imperium's world-wide suppression of progressive forces" – adding that "one aspect of this was its cynical sponsoring of reactionary religious fundamentalism as a tool against the secular left in that part of the world on which it has now made war."

107. Arrighi, *op.cit.*, p. 40.

108. Ralph Miliband, *Socialism for a Sceptical Age* (London: Verso, 1995), p. 192; see also, on this subject, Manuel Castells, *The Power of Identity* (Malden and Oxford: Blackwell, 1997), esp. ch. 1, "Communal Heavens: Identity and Meaning in the Network Society" and ch. 2, "The Other Face of the Earth: Social Movements against the New Global Order."

109. Thus Wole Soyinka, noting the dictatorial turn taken by once promising nationalisms in Africa, suggests that the populace's retreat to narrower "cultural identities ... is entirely logical." See his *The Open Sore of a Continent: A Personal Narrative of the Nigerian Crisis* (New York and Oxford: Oxford University Press, 1996), p. 139.

110. Graham Saul, "Environmentalists, What are we fighting for?' (Toronto: Metcalf Foundation, 2018).

111. Saul, *ibid.*, p. 8, where it leads off a section entitled "The Stakes Could Not Be Higher."

112. Colin Leys and Leo Panitch, *Coming to Terms with Nature/Socialist Register 2007* (London: Merlin Press, 2006).

113. Leys and Panitch, "Preface" to their book (*ibid.*), pp. ix-xv.

114. Michael Lowy, "Eco-Socialism and Democratic Planning" in Leys and Panitch, *op.cit.* (pp. 295-309).

115. Smith is quoted by Lowy (*ibid.*, p. 294) from his "The Engine of Eco Collapse" (*Nature and Socialism*, 16, 4, 2005).

116. Lowy, *ibid.*, p. 294.

117. Lowy, *ibid.*, pp. 306-7.

118. Jacklyn Cock quoted Leys and Panitch in her paper "Connecting Nature, Power and Justice" presented to the SASO conference at the University of Stellenbosch in July 2008 but I have taken the bulk of my quotations here from her paper "Moving Towards an Alternative Eco-Socialist Order in South Africa" which is in an online symposium entitled "A New Counter-Hegemonic Politics in South Africa: What Now? What Next?" that I edited for joint release by both *Africafiles* and the *Review of African Political Economy* blog in 2015.

119. Karl Marx and Friedrich Engels, "Manifesto of the Communist Party" in Robert C. Tucker (ed.), *The Marx-Engels Reader*, Second Edition (New York: W. W. Norton, 1978), pp. 474, 476, 482. At the same time, they write (p. 481) that "the organization of the proletarians into a class, and consequently into a political party, is continually being upset by competition between the workers themselves" – adding, however, that "it [the proletariat] rises again, stronger, firmer, mightier."

120. The following section draws on my "What Working-Class?: Non-Transformative Global Capitalism and the African Case," a paper originally prepared for a workshop organized by David Harvey at CUNY in New York, May 2011, and, as revised, then included in Baris Karagaac (ed.), *Accumulations, Crises, Struggles: Capital and Labor in Contemporary Capitalism* (Zurich and Berlin: LIT VERLAG, 2013) and then included as "The New Terms of Resistance: Proletariat, Precariat and the Present African Prospect," in my *A Flawed Freedom* (op.cit.)

121. This Wikipedia entry draws heavily on Judy Fudge and Rosemary Owens (eds.), *Precarious Work, Women and the New Economy: The Challenge to Legal Norms* (Toronto: Hart, 2006), especially their introduction, and also on Leah Vosko's chapter in the same book, "Gender, Precarious Work and the International Labor Code: The Ghost in the ILO Closet."

122. Marx and Engels, *ibid.*, p. 482.

123. Karl Marx, *The 18th Brumaire of Louis Bonaparte* (New York: International Publishers, 1963), p. 75.

124. Karl Marx, *Class Struggles in France* (New York: International Publishers, 1964), p. 50; as he continues, "at the youthful age at which the Provisional Government recruited them [they were] thoroughly malleable, capable of the most heroic deeds and the most exalted sacrifices, as [they were] of the basest banditry and the dirtiest corruption."

125. Self-evidently, this reference to the stratification within the proletariat/precariat mass does not refer to the more obvious kind of class differentiation in African settings, that between the upper and most favored echelons of Africa's hierarchy (the most affluent of owners, politicians and state functionaries, and enterprise managers and their attendant retinues) and those below them on the social ladder; such class differentiations are generally clear enough.

126. In Arrighi and Saul (*op.cit.*).

127. See my "The 'Labor Aristocracy' Thesis Reconsidered" in Richard Sandbrook and Robin Cohen (eds.) *The Development of an African Working Class* (Toronto and London: University, 1975) and, with the same title but in a somewhat modified version, as chapter 12 in *The State and Revolution in Eastern Africa* (London and New York: Heinemann and Monthly Review Press, 1975).

128. Eddie Webster, personal communication. I have also cited this suggestive communication in my concluding chapter in Saul and Bond, *op.cit.*

129. See Jonathan Barker, *Street-Level Politics* (Toronto: Between the Lines, 1999).

130. Dangerous? Even as I originally completed this piece I learned, via the internet, of a new book by Guy Standing set to appear, entitled *The Precariat: The New Dangerous Class* – thus underscoring in one title both concepts I deploy here: "the precariat" and "the dangerous class." I later discovered that Standing and I are working along quite different lines since, beyond the title, the flyer I received announcing the book's launch summarized its content as follows: "The Precariat is a new class, comprising the growing number of people facing lives of insecurity, doing work without a past or future. Their lack of belonging and identity means inadequate access to social and economic rights. Why is this new class growing, what political dangers does it represent and how might these be addressed?" I was rather surprised to hear only dangers being mentioned in this announcement, and also in Standing's book when I subsequently read it. As explained here, I take the concept "precariat" to have a rather different meaning and the reality on the ground (in South Africa, for example) to be much more promising than Standing's usage of the concept sought to imply.

131. George Packer, "The Megacity," *The New Yorker* (Nov. 13, 2006).

132. Bill Freund, *The African Worker* (Cambridge and New York: Cambridge University Press, 1988).

133. Freund, *ibid.*

134. Peter Gutkind, *The poor in urban Africa: a prologue to modernization, conflict and the unfinished revolution* (Montreal: McGill University Center for Developing Areas Studies, 1968).

135. Ken Post and Phil Wright, *Socialism and Underdevelopment* (London and New York: Routledge, 1989), pp. 151-2.

136. Jonathan Barker, *op.cit.*, p. 13.

137. Jonathan Barker, "Debating Globalization: Critique of Colin Leys," *Southern Africa Report (SAR)*, 12, 4 (September, 1997).

Endnotes

138. Barker is sceptical about the priority (or even wisdom) of seeking to discover some counter-hegemony to encompass and generalize the diversity of such important and legitimate claims. On this aspect of the question he is effectively answered, in my opinion, in *Southern Africa Report,* by Colin Leys, "Colin Leys Replies," *SAR,* 12, 4 (September 1997) and Veronica Schild, "Their Hegemony or Ours," *SAR,* 3, 4 (August 1998).
139. Ralph Miliband, *Socialism in a Sceptical Age* (London: Verso, 1995), p. 192.
140. *Ibid.,* pp. 194-5.
141. There is also another issue. For, in their broad margins, the descriptive categories "proletariat" and "precariat" are ideal types, those so defined slipping in and out of many such categorizations (proletariat, precariat, religious zealot, ethno-nationalist protagonist, gender activist, environmentalist) depending on conditions and realities both objective and subjective. The similarity at their base of prominent populisms of both the right and the left (the constituencies of Trump on the right and Sanders on the left in the United States, for example) can be disconcerting. Some categories are more flexible than others: a member of the proletariat can act primarily as a citizen in a demonstration against some activity of the state (in South Africa, for example), whereas a precarian cannot so easily act as a member of the proletariat. Nonetheless, political unity between members of each of those categories is always, on many important fronts, quite possible.
142. The documentation on this subject is substantial but for a useful overview of COSATU and the organized working class as it emerged into the post-apartheid milieu and into a "neoliberalizing world" see Eddie Webster and Glenn Adler, "Exodus Without a Map: The Labor Movement in a Liberalizing South Africa" in Bjorn Beckman and Lloyd Sachikonye (eds.) *Labor Regimes and Liberalization: The Restructuring of State-Society Relations in Africa* (Harare: University of Zimbabwe Press, 2001). See also, for an analysis of more recent developments, Roger Southall and Eddie Webster, "Unions and parties in South Africa: COSATU and the ANC in the Wake of Polokwane" in Bjorn Beckman, Sakhela Buhlungu and Lloyd Sachikonye (eds.), *Trade Unions and Party Politics: Labor Movements in Africa* (Cape Town: HSRC Press, 2010). See also, inter alia, Carolyn Bassett and Marlea Clarke, "South African trade unions and globalization: going for the 'high-road,' getting stuck on the 'low-road'," *World Organization, Labor and Globalization,* v. 2, #1 (Spring 2008) and Sakhela Buhlungu, *A Paradox of Victory: COSATU and the Democratic Transformation in South Africa* (Scottsville, S.A: University of KwaZulu-Natal Press, 2010).
143. See Rusty Bernstein's revealing 2002 letter to the author, later published as "'The turning point...': Letter from Rusty Bernstein to John S. Saul" in *Transformation,* #64 (2007); this letter is quoted at length in chapter 8.
144. On the virtues of a new "small-a" alliance between organized labor and civil society, one that could displace the presently existing "large-A" Alliance from political centrality in South Africa, see John S. Saul, *Revolutionary Traveller (op.cit.),* pp. 292-6 and Patrick Bond, "South African splinters" *(op.cit.).* See also Peter Alexander, "Rebellion of the poor: South Africa's service delivery protests – a preliminary analysis," *Review of African Political Economy,* v. 37, # 123 (March 2010).
145. Gillian Hart, "Provocations of Neoliberalism: Contesting the nation and liberation after apartheid" in Brij Maharaj, Ashwin Desai and Patrick Bond (eds.), *Zuma's Own Goal: Losing South Africa's 'War on Poverty'* (Trenton, N.J.: African World Press, 2011), p. 82.
146. Hart, *ibid.,* p. 83. Bond's characteristic mode of argument is epitomized by Hart, *ibid.,* p. 96.
147. Hart, *ibid.,* p. 96.
148. This is not a phrase that Hart uses.
149. See John S. Saul, "Race, Class, Gender and Voice" *(op.cit.).*
150. The complexities of township life, the realities of the struggle for equity there, and the simultaneous danger of slippage to less than savory outcomes have been well documented in recent literature. But see, in addition to Peter Alexander (as cited in footnote 26), the running compilations of township unrest being assembled by John Devenish at the

University of KwaZulu/Natal. See too such fine "township insider" accounts as that by Jacob Dlamini and entitled *Native Nostalgia* (Aukland Park, S.A.: Jacana, 2009), a book at once (and brilliantly so) sociological and autobiographical.

151. This section draws on the essay (# 1) "Race, Class, Gender and Voice: Four Terrains of Liberation," in *Studies in Political Economy* and later included in my *Liberation Lite* (op.cit.).

152. See my chapter, entitled "Africa," in Ghita Ionescu and Ernest Gellner (eds), *Populism: its meanings and national characteristics* (London: Weidenfeld and Nicholson, 1969).

153. See Arrighi and Saul, *Essays on the Political Economy of Africa* (New York: Monthly Review Press, 1973) and Saul, *The State and Revolution in Eastern Africa* (New York and London: Monthly Review Press and Monthly Review Press, 1979)

154. Here I draw on my essay "Is Socialism Still an Alternative, " this being Essay 5 in my *Liberation Lite* (op.cit.).

155. Private correspondence (from a sender to be unnamed)

156. Leo Panitch, "Reflections on Strategy for Labor" in Leo Panitch and Colin Leys (eds.), *Working Class, Global Realities/Socialist Register 2001* (London: Merlin Press, 2000), p. 367.

157. Material in this paragraph is drawn from my book *Development after Globalization* (op.cit.), especially ch. 3, "Identifying Class, Classifying Difference," where this overall argument is spelled out at much greater length.

158. I have cited Amin's concept of delinking in preparing the essay "The Empire of Capital, Recolonization and Resistance: Rethinking the Political Economy of Development in the global South" for its inclusion in my *Revolutionary Traveller* (op.cit.), pp. 354-367, and I have here only mildly recrafted that argument for present purposes.

159. I first cited Thomas' formulation in the book I edited, *Mozambique, A Difficult Road: The Transition to Socialism in Mozambique* (New York: Monthly Review Press, 1985) and evoked it to complement Amin's concept of "delinking" in the essay cited above (in *Revolutionary Traveller, ibid.*).

160. My principal writings on this theme are to be found in my *Recolonization and Resistance* (op.cit.), especially ch. 4, "South Africa: Between 'Barbarism' and 'Structural Reform' and ch. 5, "Structural Reform: A Model for the Revolutionary Transformation of South Africa" and they form the basis for the present argument.

161. See, as quoted several times in these paragraphs, Andre Gorz, *Socialism and Revolution* (New Haven: Anchor, 1973).

162. See Alex Callinicos, "Reform and Revolution in South Africa: A Reply to John Saul," in *New Left Review*, #195 (September-October 1992), as well as my reply, in the same issue, under the title "John Saul replies" (upon which I draw here).

163. As argued above, democratic means will be necessary not only to facilitate negotiation between diverse players within and without the socialist camp, but also to hold leaders (important in their leadership function perhaps but too often would-be vanguardists, with whatever benign excuses they may make) to the humane purposes which they ostensibly seek to advance. Genuine democracy in the realm of political power is every bit as important as socialist structures in the productive realm (although these latter, as explicit in any meaningful definition of socialism, can and should be democratic as well).

164. Gorz (op.cit.) keeps returning to this crucial point as well, noting that "the bourgeoisie will never relinquish power without as struggle and without being compelled to do so by revolutionary action on the part of the masses." What is at stake, ultimately, is a trial of strength,and those popular forces whose cumulative empowerment is so central to the project of structural reform will ignore this at their peril. This is one of the grim realities (the other side is trying too!) that has helped to distort revolutionary movements throughout history; even a movement thast is firmly democratic and more open to the full range of possibilities that structural reform promises will be challenged in this way.

165. Boris Kagarlitsky, *The Dialectic of Change* (London: Verso, 1998).

166. Adam Przeworski, *Democracy and the Market* (Cambridge: Cambridge University Press, 1991), p. 122.

167. The positions of Kolko and Gray are discussed in the first section of the essay (ch. 5 in my *Liberation Lite [op.cit.]*, at pp. 78-83) from which the section reprinted in the present book here has been extracted.

168. These quotes from Merrington are from his excellent article "Theory and Practice in Gramsci's Marxism," *The Socialist Register 1968* (London: Merlin Press, 1968).

169. Merrington, *ibid.,* 151; at stake for Merrington (and Gramsci) here was the necessarily "radical redefinition of the essential problem, the nature of power in...society: underlining the active work of politicization and mobilization of the masses [and] restoring the possibility of revolutionary initiative by conscious political agency based on the ideological and political unity between 'intellectuals' and 'the masses' making up the revolutionary bloc." As Merrington continues, "The problem is to elaborate the specific character of a 'collective will' which will make possible the passage from a sectoral, corporate and hence subaltern role of purely negative opposition to a hegemonic role of conscious action towards the revolutionary goals: not, that is, seeking a partial readjustment within the system but 'posing the question of the state in its entirety.' For this to be possible, the partial determined character of opposition must become a universally-oriented challenge over the whole range of social relations."

170. See Ernst Bloch, *The Principle of Hope,* in three volumes (Cambridge, Mass: MIT Press, 1986); Bloch, *On Karl Marx* (New York: Herder and Herder, 1971); Bloch, *Man on His Own* (New York: Seabury Press, 1970 and Bloch, *Spirit of Utopia* (Stanford, CA: Stanford University Press, 2000). As the American trade magazine *Library Journal* wrote at the time of the initial publication of one of his books: "Bloch offers a basis for renewal that is evident in youth culture, radical Christianity and the New Left Revolution."

171. See, *inter alia,* Jamie Owen Daniel and Tom Moylan (eds.), *Not Yet: Reconsidering Ernst Bloch* (London: Verso. 1997) and Peter Thompson and Slavoj Žižek (eds.), *The Privatization of Hope: Ernst Bloch and the Future of Utopia* (Durham and London: Duke University Press, 2013).

Chapter 2

1. In *Journal of Contemporary African Studies,* volume 24, #3 (July 2014) and volume 34, #2 (April 2016).

2. But see my *Revolutionary Traveller: Freeze Frames from a Life* (Winnipeg: Arbeiter Ring, 2009) for a more extended autobiographical account; there is also, on the region itself, my *The Thirty Years War for Southern African Liberation: 1960-1994* (Cambridge: Cambridge University Press, forthcoming) and, on the southern African struggle as undertaken in Canada and the wider world, my *On Building a Social Movement: The North American Campaign for Southern African Liberation Revisited* (Trenton, N.J. and Halifax, N.S.,: Africa World Press and Fernwood Books, 2017).

3. *On Building a Social Movement (ibid.).*

Preface to Section III

1. On the "Empire of Capital" see Saul, *Decolonisation and Empire: Contesting the Rhetoric and Reality of Resubordination in Southern Africa and Beyond* (Delhi, London and Johannesburg: Three Essays Collective, Merlin Press, Wits University Press, 2008).

2. Saul, "Race, Class, Gender and Voice: Four Terrains of Liberation," *Review of African Political Economy,* 37, 123 (2010), 61-69. See also Saul, "The Strange Death of Liberated Southern Africa," Transformation, 64 (2007), 1-26.

3. Frantz Fanon, *The Wretched of the Earth* (Harmondsworth: Penguin Books, 1967), 122.

4. On the shifting nature of South African-domiciled capital's contingent links with racial supremacy, shifts that would ultimately redefine such capital's attitudes towards the prospect of black majority rule, see Saul, "On Taming a Revolution: The ANC and the Bleak Denouement to the Anti-Apartheid struggle," *The Socialist Register 2013* (London: Merlin Press, 2012).

5. On this subject see the articles that appear in the special themed section on "Southern Africa: The Liberation Struggle Continues," in *Review of African Political Economy/ ROAPE*, 38, 127 (2011), 77-134.

6. Colin Leys and John S. Saul, "Lubango and After: 'Forgotten History' as Politics in Contemporary Namibia," *Journal of Southern African Studies*, 29, 2 (2003), 300-25.

7. Ibbo Mandaza, *Zimbabwe: The Political Economy of Transition*, 1980-1986 (Dakar: CODERIA, 1986).

8. *Ibid*, p. 51; on the more recent period, Richard Saunders, "Zimbabwe: liberation nationalism – old and born again," *ROAPE*, 38, 127 (2011), 123-34.

9. *Ibid*.

10. On the growing neo-imperial role being played by South Africa with regard to Zimbabwe and the entire southern African region see, especially, D. Miller, O. Oloyede and R. Saunders, "South African Corporations and Post-Apartheid Expansion in Africa: Creating a New Regional space"; Richard Saunders, "Crisis, Capital, Compromise: mining and empowerment in Zimbabwe"; and William Martin, "South Africa's Subimperial Futures: Washington Consensus, Bandung Consensus, or Peoples' Consensus?' all in Miller *et al, South Africa in Africa* (*op.cit.* – see afternote 4).

11. Norrie McQueen, *The Decolonisation of Portuguese Africa* (London: Longman, 1997), 236-37.

12. Saul, "Mozambique: not then but now," in ROAPE, 38, 127 (2011), 93-101.

13. See the opening paragraphs of this chapter.

14. See, *inter alia,* Sampie Terreblanche, *A History of Inequality in South Africa*, 1652-2002 (Scottsville: University of Natal Press, 2002); Jeremy Seekings and Nicoli Nattrass, *Class, Race and Inequality in South Africa* (New Haven: Yale University Press, 2005); M. MacDonald, *Why Race Matters in South Africa* (Cambridge, Mass: Harvard University Press, 2006); H. Bhorat and R. Kanbur, eds., *Poverty and Policy in Post-apartheid South Africa* (Cape Town: HSRC Press, 2006); Shireen Hassim, *Women's Organisations and Democracy in South Africa: Contesting Authority* (Madison: University of Wisconsin Press, 2006).

15. In writing this section I draw on my essay "On taming a revolution: the South African case" in Leo Panitch, Greg Albo and Vivek Chibber (eds.), *The Socialist Register 2013* (London: The Merlin Press, 2013).

16. Recall Mandela hailing the free market as a "magic elixir" in his speech to the joint session of the Houses of Congress in Washington in 1994.

17. Indeed, some of these persons would also be involved in the breakaway Congress of the People (COPE) movement that, in the wake of Mbeki's overthrow and in (false) anticipation of Zuma's radicalization of the ANC project, launched itself in 2008 and contested the 2009 election, unsuccessfully, as a possible right-wing alternative to the ANC.

18. But see, in contrast, Alan Hirsch's smug *Season of Hope: Economic Reform under Mandela and Mbeki* (Scottsville: University of Natal Press, 2005), especially 3-4. It would be difficult to find a more revealing statement of the rose-tinted consensus that premised economic thinking in the Mandela and Mbeki years than is to be found in this book.

19. "Cosatu: rich list shows South Africa inequality," redistributed by Africafiles at infoserv@ africafiles.org, 6 September 2011. See also Patrick Bond, "South African splinters: from 'elite transition' to 'small-a alliances'," *ROAPE*, 38, 127 (2011), 113-22.

20. See Pippa Green, *Choice, Not Fate: The Life and Times of Trevor Manuel* (Rosebank: Penguin Books, 2008). The book is an example of hagiography (with regard both to Manuel and to the ANC at its most conservative) but the lead title is also a shorthand

Endnotes

advertisement for the way in which the ANC would apparently like to present itself to right-thinking readers.

21. The quotations and citations in the paragraphs that follow are from Naomi Klein's book *The Shock Doctrine: The Rise of Disaster Capitalism* (Toronto: Alfred A Knopf Canada, 2007) and from its chapter 10, "Democracy Born in Chains: South Africa's Constricted Freedom."

22. On this issue, too, see John S. Saul, "On taming a revolution" (*ibid.*).

23. I draw here on my article "The Transition in South Africa: Choice, fate ... or recolonization?," *Critical Arts* (Durban), 26, 4, 2012). And I quote Rusty Bernstein from a letter he wrote to me not long before his death, a letter which is published as "'The turning point, etc...': Letter from Rusty Bernstein to J. Saul," *Transformation*, 64 (2007), 140-44.

24. Ben Turok, *From the Freedom Charter to Polokwane: The Evolution of the ANC's Economic Policy* (Cape Town: New Agenda, 2008), p. 174 et *passim*. Both Turok's work and that of Mark Gevisser (*A Legacy of Liberation: Thabo Mbeki and the Future of the South African Dream* [New York: Palgrave Macmillan, 2009], on the subject of the Mbeki years and their aftermath) are discussed at greater length in my "The Transition in South Africa," as cited in the previous afternote. See also William Gumede, *Thabo Mbeki and the battle for the soul of the ANC* (London: Zed books, 2007) and Daryl Glaser (ed.), *Mbeki and After: Reflections on the Legacy of Thabo Mbeki* (Johannesburg: Wits University Press, 2010).

25. Moeletsi Mbeki, "Wealth creation: Only a matter of time before the hand grenade explodes," *Business Day,* 10 February 2011.

26. Peter Alexander, "Rebellion of the Poor: South Africa's service delivery protests – a preliminary analysis," *ROAPE,* 37, 123 (2010), 25-40.

27. "The rise of Julius Malema: The black man who is rude about whites is doing rather well," *The Economist,* 30 June 2011.

28. Zwelinzima Vavi, "Keynote address to the Civil Society Conference," 27 October 2010, available at: http://www.cosatu.org.za/show.php?id=4170

29. "Zwelinzima Vavi's keynote address to the SACBC Justice and Peace AGM" (Cosatu Press release 26 February 2011).

30. Saul, "Starting from scratch: a debate," chapter 10 of *The Next Liberation Struggle: Capitalism, Socialism and Democracy in Southern Africa* (Toronto, Scottsville, New York and London: Between the Lines, University of KwaZulu-Natal Press, Monthly Review Press and Merlin Press, 2005).

31. Democratic Left Front, *1st Democratic Left Conference Report* (Killarney, South Africa, 2011).

32. Mazibuko Jara and Vishwas Satgar, "New times require new democratic left," *Mail & Guardian Online,* 7 February 2011, available at: http://mg.co.za/article/2011-02-07-new-times-require-democratic-left/

33. "Forging a New Movement: NUMSA and the Shift in SA Politics," online at polity.org.za as Polity: The South African Civil Society Information Service (January 19, 2014); see also EddieWebster, The 'Numsa Moment' in a New Counter-Hegemonic Politics in South Africa: What Now? What Next?" (2015) at ROAPE Online, 2015, at ROAPE@outlet.com.

34. Geoffrey York, "ANC's Radical Voices Growing Louder: Proposed Agenda Includes Black Economic Ownership, Farm Expropriation, Nationalization and Tighter Controls on the Courts," *The Globe and Mail* (Toronto), 8 June 2012.

35. For an evaluation, at the time, of alternative voices in South Africa that may yet be heard from more forcefully, see John S. Saul, "Liberating Liberation: The Struggle against Recolonisation in South Africa," chapter 6 of John. S. Saul and Patrick Bond, South Africa: The Present as History (Oxford: James Currey, 2014).

36. See Saul, "Race, Class, Gender and Voice," ibid.

Chapter 3

1. Here I build upon my experience of both living in and visiting Tanzania and Mozambique over decades, having first written about them both in the 1960s and 1970s. Nonetheless, the present chapter is based in large part on an essay published in a South African symposium entitled *Marxisms in the 21st Century: Crisis, Critique and Struggle*, edited by Michelle Williams and Vishwas Satgar for Wits University Press (Johannesburg, 2013). The present chapter was to have synthesized (as it did in its original published form) these two national experiences, although Mozambique is now considered separately in Chapter 4 of the present volume. They were then to have been viewed in light of recent ANC moves to demonize their efforts to realize, for the first time, socialist transformation within the region, the better to rationalize the ANC's lack of transformative practices (as briefly reviewed in this chapter but examined in more detail in chapter 7). There is little of progressive import that can be learned from the challenges that these two countries have faced if both their successes and their failures are not more sensitively assessed than the ANC has done.
2. For the making of a key distinction between the historically necessary and the historically possible see Roger Murray, "Second Thoughts on Ghana," *New Left Review*, 42 (March-April 1967), 25-39.
3. See David Harvey's interview with Arrighi, "The Winding Paths of Capital" in *New Left Review*, 56 (March-April 2009). For a more skeptical view of my friend Arrighi's account of his views in the 1960s (reflecting my rather different memories of the time and of our discussions), see my "Arrighi and Africa: Farewell Thoughts," being chapter 3 in my *Liberation Lite* (Delhi and Trenton, N. J.: Three Essays Collective, 2010/11), 53-4.
4. Thabo Mbeki, "The Fanon Thesis: A Rejoinder," *Canadian Journal of African Studies*, 18, 3 (1984), 609-612.
5. See Mbeki's interview in the ANC journal *Mayibuye* (March 1991), p. 2; and also as quoted by Pippa Green in her article "The outsider who has measured vision against reality" in *Business Report* (16 February 2006). See as well John S. Saul, "The Strange Death of Liberated Southern Africa," being chapter 5 of my *Decolonization and Empire: Contesting the Rhetoric and Reality of Resubordination in South Africa and Beyond* (Johannesburg: University of Witwatersrand Press, 2008) where I have also cited some of the quotations presented here and provided a more extended version of a related argument.
6. In 1994 Nelson Mandela hailed the free market as a "magic elixir" in a speech to the joint session of the Houses of Congress in Washington. His strident statement in favor of the GEAR strategy to have it replace the mildly more radical RDP, was, as per its august invocation from on-high, non-negotiable.
7. Thabo Mbeki, "The Fanon thesis..." *(op.cit.)*, 612.
8. William Gumede, *Thabo Mbeki and the Battle for the Soul of the ANC* (Cape Town: Zebra Press, 2005), 38.
9. Marc Gevisser, *Thabo Mbeki: The Dream Deferred* (Johannesburg: Jonathan Ball, 2007), as quoted in Ben Turok, *From the Freedom Charter to Polokwane: The Evolution of the ANC's Economic Policy* (Cape Town: New Agenda, 2008) pp. 57-8. Gevisser also reports that Mbeki's first instructions to Trevor Manuel, upon the latter's taking over as Finance Minister in 1996, was for a policy that "called precisely for the kind of fiscal discipline and investment-friendly tax incentives that the international financial institutions loved and that Manuel already believed in." See, in addition, Mark Gevisser, *A Legacy of Liberation: Thabo Mbeki and the Future of the South African Dream* (New York: Palgrave-Macmillan, 2009).
10. Turok, *ibid.*, 174.
11. As Turok (*ibid.*, p. 263) continues this thought, "much depends on whether enough momentum can be built to overcome the caution that has marked the ANC government since 1994. This depends on whether the determination to achieve an equitable society can be revived" (264-5).

Endnotes

12. On "recolonization" see my *Decolonization and Empire (op.cit.)*, especially ch. 2, "Recolonization and the New Empire of Capital," 47-80.

13. For my more detailed retrospective reflections on the Tanzanian case see, *inter alia*, my "Tanzania Fifty Years On (1961-2011): Rethinking Ujamaa, Nyerere and Socialism in Africa" in *Review of African Political Economy*, #131 (March 2012); "Julius Nyerere's Tanzania: Learning from Tanzania," chapter 7 of my *The Next Liberation Struggle: Capitalism, Socialism and Democracy in Southern Africa* (Toronto, Scottsville, S.A., New York and London: Between the Lines, University of KwaZulu-Natal Press, Monthly Review Press, and Merlin Press, 2005), and as well as Lionel Cliffe and John S. Saul, eds., *Socialism in Tanzania*, volume I, *"Politics"* and volume 2, *"Policies"* (Nairobi: East African Publishing House, 1972 and 1973); I have drawn directly on these materials in this section.

14. Julius K. Nyerere, "Economic Nationalism," being chapter 29 in his *Freedom and Socialism* (Nairobi and London: Oxford University Press, 1968), 264-5.

15. *Mwongozo wa Tanu 1971* (Dar es Salaam: Tanu, 1971).

16. Walter Rodney, "Class Contradictions in Tanzania" (1975), available at https://www.marxists.org/subject/africa/rodney-walter/works/classcontradictions.htm.

17. Samir Amin, *Delinking: Towards a Polycentric World* (London: Zed Books, 1985); Clive P. Thomas, *Dependence and Transformation: The Economic of the Transition to Socialism*. New York: Monthly Review Press, 1974); William L. Luttrell, *Post-Capitalist Industrialization: Planning Economic Independence in Tanzania* (New York: Praeger, 1986).

18. Luttrell, *ibid*.

19. On the workers see, inter alia, Pascal Mihyo, "The Struggle for Workers Control in Tanzania" in *MajiMaji* (Dar es Salaam, 1974) and, in edited form, in *Review of African Political Economy*, #4 and Henry Mapolu (ed.), *Workers and Management* (Dar es Salaam: Tanzania Publishing House, 1976); on peasants see Leander Schneider (2003), "Developmentalism and its failings: why rural development went wrong in 1960s and 1970s Tanzania," Ph.D dissertation, Columbia University, 2003, and Schneider, Leander Schneider (2004), "Freedom and Unfreedom in Rural Development: The Theory and Practice of Julius Nyerere's Rural Socialism," in *Canadian Journal of African Studies*, 38, 2 (2004); on women see Ruth Meena (2003), "A Conversation with Bibi Titi: A Political Veteran" in Marjorie Mbilinyi, Mary Rusimbi, Chachage S. L. Chachage, and Demere Kiyunga (ed.), *Activist Voices: Feminist Struggles for an Alternative World* (Dar es Salaam: Tanzania Gender Networking Programme, 2003), p. 152l and, on the students at the university, John S. Saul, *Revolutionary Traveller: Freeze-Frames from a Life*, (Winnipeg: Arbeiter Ring, 2009), ch. 1, "The 1960s – Tanzania," Michelle Bourbonniere, "Debating Socialism on the Hill: The University of Dar es Salaam. 1961-71," M.A. dissertation, Dalhousie University, August 2007, and Karim Hirji, *Cheche: Reminiscences of a Radical Magazine* (Dar es Salaam: Mkuki na Nyota Publishers, 2011).

20. Leander Schneider, "Colonial Legacies and Postcolonial Authoritarianism in Tanzania: Connects and Disconnects," *African Studies Review*, 49, 1 (April 2006).

21. Schneider, *ibid*.

22. On the cases mentioned here – the repression of both workers and students (particularly university students) – see the relevant materials cited in footnote 19.

23. Ruth Meena, *op.cit.*, p. 152. The interview with Bibi Titi, on which this article focuses was carried out by Ms. Meena in 1988.

24. The new "Growth, Employment and Redistribution" strategy announced in June 1996 as displacing the Reconstruction and Development Programme/RDP of 1994.

25. Michelle Williams, *The Roots of Participatory Democracy: Democratic Communists in South Africa and Kerala, India* (New York and London: Palgrave MacMillan, 2008), 91.

26. "Rusty Bernstein: A Letter," as quoted above and as reproduced as an Appendix in John S. Saul, *Liberation Lite: The Roots of Recolonization in Southern Africa* (Delhi and Trenton, NJ: Three Essays Collective and Africa World Press, 2010), 104-111.

27. Peter Alexander, "Rebellion of the poor: South Africa's service delivery protests – a preliminary analysis," *Review of African Political Economy*, # 123 (March 2010).

28. Moeletsi Mbeki, "Wealth creation: Only a matter of time before the hand grenade explodes," *Business Day* (10 February 2011).

29. "Zwelinzima Vavi's keynote address to the SACBC Justice and Peace AGM," Cosatu Press Release (Feb. 26, 2011).

30. Frantz Fanon, *The Wretched of the Earth* (Harmondsworth: Penguin Books, 1967), 253, 255.

31. Fanon, *ibid.,* p 253.

Chapter 4

1. My thanks for their help in my preparation of this chapter to Clare Smedley and Peter Lawrence of *The Review of African Political Economy* and to Paul Fauvet.

2. See Stendhal, *The Charterhouse of Parma* (New York: The Modern Library 1995), p.395, translation by Richard Howard; as Stendhal continues, "We are about the speak of ugly matters, which for more than one reason we should rather suppress, but which we are forced to discuss by events which fall within our province."

3. See on this my article on Mozambique entitled "Mozambique: Not Then But Now," *Review of African Political Economy*, v. 38, #127 (March, 2011), the section on Mozambique in an essay published in a South African symposium entitled *Marxisms in the 21st Century: Crisis, Critique and Struggle* as edited by Michelle Williams and Vishwas Satgar for Wits University Press (Johannesburg, 2013), and also the entries on Mozambique that appear in my *Race, Class and The Thirty Years War for Southern African Liberation, 1960-1994: A History* (Cambridge: Cambridge University Press, forthcoming).

4. Norrie McQueen, *The Decolonization of Portuguese Africa: Metropolitan Revolution & the Dissolution of Empire* (Harlow: Longman, 1997), pp. 236-7.

5. Alice Dinerman, *Revolution, Counter-Revolution and Revisionism in Post-Colonial Africa: The Case of Mozambique* (Milton Park and New York: Routledge, 2006), 19-20.

6. Gretchen Bauer and Scott D. Taylor. *Politics in Southern Africa: State and Society in Transition* (Boulder: Lynne Reiner, 2005), pp. 134-5.

7. The politics of the extra-judicial execution of opponents once a post-liberation state and legal system is in place demands reflection, whether or not one is opposed (as I am) to capital punishment. Moreover, it is self-evident that the killing of the enemy is a inevitable part of warfare, even in just wars like the southern African liberation struggles. It is also regrettable that, in such cases, the necessity to kill can also have a coarsening effect on combatants' moral predilections and values.

8. Nor is this only true of the Mozambican historiography. As regards South Africa, for example, the decision by the UDF to vote itself out of existence in 1991 rather than continue as a powerful social-political watchdog that could keep a critical eye on the ANC has always been a startling one – one that I have noted elsewhere (see my chapter 2, "The Transition: The Players Assemble, 1970-1990," in particular at pp. 90-1 and 96) in John S. Saul and Patrick Bond, *South Africa, The Present As History: From Mrs Ples to Mandela and Marikana* (Johannesburg and Woodbridge, U.K.: James Currey and Jacana, 2014). In trying to find out why this happened I have heard numerous allusions to the role played by ANC violence (including even killing) against vocal dissenters within the UDF, and also clear signs of fear about pursuing the topic any further.

9. Other variations of this theme are explored in my discussion of Ernst Bloch's politics of hope in chapter 1, Section C of this book.

10. As the Wikipedia entry on Ben Barka records, "Many theories attempting to explain what happened to him were put forward over the years, but it was not until 2018 that details of his disappearance were established by Israeli journalist Ronen Bergman in his book *Rise and Kill First: The Secret History of Israel's Targeted Assassinations* [New York: Random House,

Endnotes

2018]. Based on research and interviews either Israeli intelligence operatives involved in planning the kidnapping of Ben Barka, Bergman concluded that he was murdered by Moroccan agents and French police, who ended up disposing of his body."

11. Lumumba's demise was marked in the *Guardian* newspaper 50 years later (17 January 2011) by an article by George Nzongola-Ntalaja entitled "Patrice Lumumba: the most important assassination of the 20th century: The U.S.-sponsored plot to kill Patrice Lumumba, the hero of Congolese independence, took place 50 years ago today." It was described as being "the culmination of two interrelated assassination plots by the American and Belgian governments, which used Congolese accomplices and a Belgian execution squad to carry out the deed." The article then seconds Belgian author Ludo De Witte in calling it "the most important assassination of the twentieth century." See also Victoria Brittain, "Political assassination as a strategy against liberation movements" (Victoria Brittain [/taxonomy/term/4437] 19 October 2006), an article posted at Pambazuka News).

12. Louise White, *The Assassination of Herbert Chitepo: Texts and Politics in Zimbabwe* (Bloomington: Indiana University Press, 2003).

13. Nathan Shamuyarira, *Crisis in Rhodesia* (Nairobi: East African Publishing House, 1967), pp. 75-6.

14. Thomas Carlyle, *On Heroes, Hero Worship and the Heroic in History* (Lincoln, Nebraska: University of Nebraska Press, 1966); V. G. Plekhanov, *The Role of the Individual in History* (New York: International Publishers, 1940); Sidney Hook, *The Hero in History: A Study in Limitation and Possibility* (New York: The Humanities Press, 1943) and Leonid Grinin, "The Role of the Individual in History: A Reconsideration" in *Social Evolution & History,* 9, 2 (September 2010).

15. I learn directly from Rhys Williams, however, that he is still working to produce a final text of the talk he gave in Australia – a testimony, no doubt, to the sheer complexity of the task of pinning down answers to the kinds of questions he has chosen to raise. See also, for a guarded scholarly advocacy of a revival of the history of great men, Margaret MacMillan's *History's People* (London: Profile Books, 2017).

16. See the section on Ernst Bloch and Hope as cited in fn. #8.

17. Hook had begun his intellectual life as a convinced Marxist and only slipped away from that position when he witnessed the deadening distortions that the Soviet Union under Stalin would inflict upon Marxist theory and also the full impact of the resultant anti-democratic and self-righteous (vanguardist?) thrust such a sub-Marxist creed now came to thrive upon. Not that this gave him any excuse for the excesses of his eventual rabidly right-wing post-Marxist position, a position that found him joining the ranks of the Encounter magazine apparatus, this journal being a key CIA-sponsored Cold War ideological weapon of the capitalist right. An unsettling trajectory.

18. Grinin, *op.cit.*

19. Hook sets up a careful discussion of "'If' in History" in that chapter by setting off from the question: "Under what circumstances can a scientifically credible rather than an imaginatively credible answer be given to questions of this sort?" (p. 120). He seeks to provide an answer in the pages that follow.

20. *Eduardo Mondlane*, author not identified, in the "Panaf Great Lives" series (London: Panaf, 1972)

21. See Herb Shore's exemplary biographical sketch, "Resistance and Revolution in the Life of Eduardo Mondlane," published as one of the two introductory essays to a second edition (the first edition was published by Penguin Books in 1969) of Mondlane's *The Struggle for Mozambique* (London: Zed Books, 1983); I was honored to be asked to write a new foreword to the second edition.

22. See George Roberts, "The assassination of Eduardo Mondlane: FRELIMO, Tanzania, and the politics of exile in Dar es Salaam," *Cold War History, 2017* (vol 17, #1, pp. 1-19).

23. Shore, *op.cit.*, p. xxvii.

24. Personal communication.

25. I transcribed and translated this passage from a tape then in the possession of the late Aquino de Bragança. I am grateful to Aquino for the subsequent opportunity to quote from it several times in later years. In it Mondlane also stressed the importance of learning from the "concrete experience, including the errors of the socialist countries which since 1917 have worked and lived the socialist experience."

26. See my "Foreword" cited above, p. xi.

27. As a friend wrote in reaction to a similar section in a earlier draft: "What would have happened to Mondlane's 'democratic sensibility' had he lived? In the absence of a democratic culture among the people don't you think the iron law of oligarchy could be relied upon to operate – the result being overdetermined?" A good question.

28. See Barry Munslow (ed.), *Samora Machel: An African Revolutionary* (London: Zed Books, 1985); Iain Christie, *Machel of Mozambique* (Bedfors, U.K.: Panaf Books, 1989); and, especially, Sarah LeFanu, *S is for Samora: A Lexical Biography of Samora Machel and the Mozambican Dream* (London: Hurst and Co., 2012).

29. Simango is an anti-hero in the history of Mozambique's freedom struggle but one whose ultimate fall, long incarceration and eventual execution (horrific and bloody as these were) nonetheless provides an instructive clue as to the texture of the new Mozambique, as we will see in this essay's final section.

30. See LeFanu's entries on Mbuzini (site, inside South Africa, of the fatal crash of the airplane carrying Samora Machel and his colleagues from Lusaka to Maputo on the fateful night of Machel's death), on Tupolev (the brand of aircraft being flown on that night), on Aircraft and on Difficulties in Sarah LeFanu (*op.cit.*); see also her entries on Samora, Simango and much else in that book.

31. "Special investigation into the death of President Samora Machel" in *Truth and Reconciliation Commission of South Africa Report*, vol 2 (Cape Town: Juta, 1998), pp. 494-502. As evidence of the continuing interest in this story see "The Day Botha Killed Samora Machel of Mozambique," *Zimbabwe Herald*, 18 October 2010 (http://panafricannews.blogspot.com/2010/10/day-botha-killed-samora-machel-of.html); Paula Akukizibwe, "Who killed Mozambique's Samora Machel," This is Africa, March 2014 (https://thisisafrica.me/politics-and-society/who-killed-mozambiques-samora-machel/); Tetenda Gwaambuka, "Who Killed Samora Machel, *The African Exponent*, 8 July 2016 (https://www.africanexponent.com/post/7516-who-killed-samora-machel); and "The mysterious death of Samora Machel," *Le monde diplomatique*, November, 2017 (https://mondediplo.com/2017/11/12machel);

32. Uria Simango, "Gloomy situation in Frelimo" (widely circulated at the time in Dar es Salaam, which is where I obtained the copy I still have).

33. Fauvet suggested something more (in his article "Biography of Uriah Simango launched," first published at the site Mozambique Tera Queimada by the Agência de Informação de Moçambique news service on 28 July 2004 (https://mozambicanos.blogspot.com/2012/08/biography-of-uria.simango-launched.html); there he writes that "When extremist Portuguese settlers staged an abortive coup in September, and seized control of Radio Clube de Mocambique (the forerunner of Radio Mozambique), Simango appeared at the radio station, apparently giving his backing to the coup." If true, this would have stamped him as a dangerous enemy, but, as we shall see, Frelimo has never said this.

34. Another of my correspondents agrees that Frelimo's handling of the Simango case is indeed ugly but further states that "far more ugly [is the fact that] Frelimo leaders succumbed, as did leaders of every stripe all over the world, to neoliberalism, [finding]"

ways to advance their own careers as 'patriotic entrepreneurs' [by] teaming up with foreign investors." Which is the uglier I leave to the reader to decide. As for me, on many occasions I have noted Frelimo leaders' opportunistic choosing of the neoliberal path; unfortunately, the political brutality described in this chapter has earned rather less attention.

35. Barnabé Lucas Ncomo, Uria Simango: *Um Homem, Uma Causa* (Maputo: Edições NovaAfrica, 2003).

36. As Fauvet writes of the Barnabé launch, "many of the faces in the audience were young, quite probably students, and their presence surely indicates a thirst for knowledge about recent Mozambican history and that is certainly a positive phenomenon. [But] they will not be satisfied by the dismissive approach to Ncomo's book taken by leading Frelimo intellectual Sergio Vieira. Having obtained a pre-launch copy, Vieira savaged the book in his weekly column in the Sunday paper "Domingo." Vieira's comments may well be substantially correct – but his polemic did not convince anyone who did not already support Frelimo."

37. Paul Fauvet, *ibid.*

38. At least one of those sons has carved out a prominent political career. Citing Wikipedia: "Daviz Mbepo Simango (born 7 February 1964) is a Mozambican politician who has been mayor of Beira since 2003. He is also the President of the Democratic Movement of Mozambique (MDM). He is the son of Uria Timtoteo Simango the first Vice-President of Frelimo and Celina Tapua Simango. He joined the opposition RENAMO in 1997 and became Mayor of Beira in 2003 as its candidate. On 6 March 2009, he founded a new party, the MDM." Moreover, as one of my Mozambican contacts informs me, with his old schoolmate and friend Filipe Nyusi now the country's president, Renamo, "in a fit of paranoia, is currently accusing Simango's party, the MDM, of working with Frelimo to destroy Renamo." Daviz Simango died on February 22, 2021.

39. This is dos Santos speaking in an interview with Radio and TV journalist Emilio Manhique in 2005, justifying the executions of an earlier time as well as the sepulchral silence that has surrounded their occurrence ever since.

40. This exchange – described by one observer as "a rather miserable and evasive interview" – with Chissano constituted a 2012 TV interview with journalist Simeão Ponguana; I have this reference from my friend Paul Fauvet.

41. "Mozambique falls on democracy index, get classified as 'authoritarian'" according to the Economist Intelligence Unit's Democracy Index – 2018, as reported by the Club of Mozambique (https://clubofmozambique.com/news/mozambique-falls-on-democracy-index-gets-classified-as-authoritarian/). This is not to suggest that either the Economist Intelligence Unit or the Club of Mozambique can be taken as infallible assessors of different countries' degrees of democracy, merely that these are the kind of sources and the kind of information that we should take note of.

42. "Mozambique falls on democracy index, get classified as 'authoritarian,'" *(op.cit.).*

43. For details see the Wikipedia article on Carlos Cardoso who was shot down in what was described as a Mafia-style assassination; Nyimpine Chissano, the son of Mozambique's then President, Joaquim Chissano, was charged with "joint moral authorship" of Cardoso's murder. He is said to have paid for it. Apparently he died before he could be brought to trial but also see his entry on Wikipedia.

44. Rupert Horsley and Simone Haysom, "Mafia-style crimes – Mozambique's quiet assassination epidemic," *Enact Observer*, 30 April 2018 (at https://enactafrica.org/enact-observer/mozambiques-quiet-assassination-epidemic).

45. See "Mafia-style crimes," *ibid;* the authors have an extended and detailed list of 19 (16 killed and three attempted) assassinations under the sub-head "Assassinations and Attempted Assassinations in Mozambique, October 2014 to March 2018" and appended to their article; this is required (and sobering) reading for any student of developments in southern Africa). Other sections are headed "Assassination is a tool that allows for the manipulation of individuals, institutions and society at large" and "There is a growing awareness of the inextricable mix of corruption, politics and violence in Mozambique."

46. See Joe Hanlon's "General Elections/#81 – Mozambique Political Process Bulletin," October 17, 2019 and headlined: "EU hits 'unlevel playing field' and 'climate of fear' in harsh statement" at https://cipeleicoes.org/eng/2019/11/05/eu-hits-unlevel-playing-field-and-climate-of-fear-in-harsh-statement/.

47. Saul, "Mozambique – not then but now" *(op.cit.)* and, more generally, "Race, Class, Gender and Voice: Four Terrains of Liberation," being ch. 1 in my *Liberation Lite: The Roots of Recolonization in Southern Africa* (Delhi and Trenton, NJ: Three Essays Collective and Africa World Press, 2011).

Chapter 5

1. This chapter complements the one on Angola's liberation struggle against the Portuguese colonial state that appears, entitled "Angola: The Counter-Revolution within the Counter-Revolution," as chapter 7 in my *Race, Class and The Thirty Years War for Southern African Liberation, 1960-1994 – A History*. The present essay provides a fuller analysis of the so-called Nito Alves coup in 1978 and its aftermath (including the massacre of thousands of Angolans by the MPLA government and their Cuban allies), that appears there and was first published in this longer form as "'When freedom died' in Angola: Alves and after" in the *Review of African Political Economy*, 42, #142 (December 2014). I also add, as an appendix, a review of Lara Pawson's *In the Name of the People: Angola's Forgotten Massacre*, an intriguing book-length account of related themes from recent Angolan history. I also give a brief account of the stepping down from office – after 38 brutal years in power as Angola's president – of the country's longtime autocrat José Eduardo dos Santos in ch. 9 in my *Race, Class and The Thirty Years War* (as cited above).

2. This section both draws upon and synthesizes passages of my longer "Briefings" article, entitled "'When Freedom Died' in Angola: Alves and After" in the *Review of African Political Economy*, 41, 142 (2014) to which the reader is also referred.

3. See, on this subject, Tony Hodges' two related volumes: *Angola from Afro-Stalinism to Petro-Diamond Capitalism* (Indiana University Press and James Currey, 2001) and *Angola: Anatomy of an Oil State* (Indiana University Press and James Currey, 2004).

4. See on this my *A Flawed Freedom: Rethinking Southern African Liberation* (Delhi, London, Cape Town and Toronto: Three Essays Collective, Pluto Press, Juta/University of Cape Town Press, and Between-the-Lines, 2014), especially ch. 6, "Conclusion: The Struggle Really Does Continue in Southern Africa" in which both Fanon and Cabral serve as my principal points of reference for evaluating outcomes in southern Africa.

5. See David Birmingham's essay "The Twenty Seventh of May," first published close to the time (in *African Affairs*) in 1979 but later available under the same title as chapter 13 of his *Portugal and Africa* (Athens, Ohio: Ohio University Press, 1999).

6. This quotation is taken from a second essay developed by Birmingham in 2003 after a trip to Angola that year, one that appeared later as ch. 11, "A Journey Through Angola," in his *Empire in Africa: Angola and its Neighbors* (Athens, Ohio: Ohio University Press, 2006). Little of significance has been written in English (or, until this century, even in Portuguese), about this 1977 coup and its grim aftermath; see, however, Lara Pawson's *In the Name of the People: Angola's Forgotten Massacre (op.cit.)* and my own "'When freedom died in Angola': Alves and after" in *Review of African Political Economy*, 41 (2014). This text is also reproduced as the following section of this chapter.

7. See Jean-Michel Mabeko Tali, *O MPLA Perante Si Proprio,* (Luanda: Colleção Ensaio, 2001), especially his ch. 14, "A crise 'nitista' (1976–1977): suas origens, desenface e repercussões na gestão do estado, da sociedade e do MPLA" and, notably, section 5 of that chapter, "O malagro do golpe de estado e a viragem repressiva do regime angolano"; Carlos Pacheco, *Repensar Angola* (Lisboa: Vega 2000); Dalila Cabrita Mateus and Alvaro Mateus, *Purga em Angola: O 27 de Maio de 1977*, 5th ed. (Alfragide, Portugal: Texto

Endnotes

Editores, 2010); José Milhazes, *"Golpe Nito Alves" e Outros Momenta da História de Angola Vistos do Kremlin* (Lisboa: Altheia Editores, 2011); Felicia Cabrita, *Massacres em África* (Lisboa: A esfero dos livros, 2008) and especially ch. X, "A Revolução Perdida de Sita Valles." America Cardoso Botelho, 2008. *Holocausto em Angola* (Lisboa: Vega, 2008); and Leonor Figueiredo on Sita Alves in her *Sita Valles: Revolucionária, Communista até à Morte* (Lisboa: Alethea Editores, 2010). In addition, just as I was finishing this manuscript I received from the author an impressive new book on related themes by José Reis and entitled *Angola – O 27 de Maio: Memorias de um sobrevivente* [translation: Memories of a Survivor]: Lisboa: Vega, 2017); although a onetime MPLA militant (now living in exile from his homeland) Reis adopts a similarly critical perspective on the MPLA, on the historical role of Agostino Neto, and on the Dos Santos government to that shared by most of the writers listed here.

8. PAFMECSA connotes the Pan-African Freedom Movement of Eastern, Central and Southern Africa; for an account written for the Institute of Race Relations see Richard Cox, *Pan-Africanism in Practice: PAFMECSA 1958-1964* (London: Oxford University Press, 1964).

9. On this changing reality see Tony Hodges' two books noted in end-note 3 above.

10. Hodges (2004), *ibid.*

11. Mateus and Mateus, *op.cit.*, pp. 58–59. The Portuguese original reads: "Eduardo, estamos perante uma força estruturada e considerável. Temos de a conhecer e de a desmantelar."

12. Pacheco, *op cit.*

13. Interestingly, however, one of the military judges (João Neves, sent as part of a national team to investigate the linked events in the east of Angola) concluded of the national picture that "Foi um verdadeiro genocídio. Em Angola devem ter morrido umas 30,000 pessoas," in Mateus and Mateus, *op.cit.*, 156.

14. The coup was a topic much debated at the time in progressive Africanist circles, including in the pages of the *Review of African Political Economy/ROAPE* (of which I was then a contributing editor). For example, a much more negative view of the nature of the Alves challenge to MPLA rule is to be found in Paul Fauvet's several contributions to *ROAPE* in that period (see Fauvet "Angola: The Rise and Fall of Nito Alves." *Review of African Political Economy/ROAPE* 4 (9), 1977 and Fauvet "In Defence of the MPLA and the Angolan Revolution." *ROAPE 6* (15-16) (1979). Fauvet's analysis is dependent on the accounts in MPLA-aligned newspapers of the time; moreover, Fauvet, like Basil Davidson, who also wrote in *ROAPE* in support of his (and the official MPLA) position ("Comments on Southall and Gabriel," *ROAPE*, 6 (15–16), 1979 152–153), says next to nothing about the purge and the massacres clearly associated with it. Other *ROAPE* articles with rather different slants included Tony Southall (Tony Southall, 1979. "Review of Claude Gabriel's Angola: le tournant Africain?" *ROAPE*, 6 (14), 107–110, and then there are also both Gabriel's article "In Defence of the Angolan Masses," *ROAPE*, 7 (19), 1980, 69–74 and, by W.G. Clarence-Smith, "Further Considerations on the MPLA and Angola." *Review of African Political Economy* 7 (19), 1980, 74–76.

15. Botelho, *op.cit.* See also Cabrita, *op.cit.*, *Massacres em Africa*, especially ch. X, "A Revolução Perdida de Sita Valles," and, also, crucially, Mateus and Mateus, *op.cit.* The latter, in subscribing, after a great deal of impressive research, to the figure of 30,000, further note (151–152) that: "We have heard a 'responsavel' of DISA [Departamento da Informação e Segurança de Angola] speak of 15,000 dead. Amnesty International did a count and estimated 20 to 40 thousand dead. Adolfo Maria, an 'Active Revolt' militant, and José Neves, a military judge, both speak of 30,000 dead. The publication *Folha* speaks of 60,000. And the self-styled 27th of May Foundation ['Fundação 27 de Maio'] estimated as many as 80,000" (my translation).

16. This is a crucial point: the sheer number and political diversity of those killed by the regime suggest that far more was at stake then merely "dealing with" Alves and his immediate comrades. Alves' career was an uneven one and warrants further careful study (if such research should ever prove possible to carry out). But it is even more important to emphasize that it was, precisely, a whole new generation of regime-defined potential troublemakers who were thus being removed from the political game by the MPLA.

17. At a conference on "Africa's Unknown War: Apartheid Terror, Cuba and Southern African Liberation," held at the University of Toronto, 27-28 September 2013.

18. Mateus and Mateus, *op.cit.*, 150–151.

19. Tali, *op.cit.*

20. See Figueiredo, *op.cit.*

21. Mateus and Mateus, *op.cit.*, 176 (my translation). The original text, in Portuguese, reads: "O que se passou em Angola terá sido uma provocação, longa e pacientemente planeada, de modo a levar a nitistas a perderem a cabeça e saíram a rua, justificando assim um contra-golpe, também minuciosamente preparado. Agostinho Neto e os seus estavam preocupados com o debate interno, pois as Comissões Populares de Bairro eram grandes centros de debate com a população. E, como seria natural, também estavam preocupados com o problema dos delegados ao Congresso. Havia que evitar os nitistas chegassem ao Congresso, anunciado para finais de 1977. Com efeito. Existia o sério risco de conquistarem os principais lugares de direção. A preocupação de Neto e dos seus era, pois, o poder. E pelo poder fariam tudo."

22. Piero Gleijeses, *Visions of Freedom: Havana, Washington, Pretoria, and the Struggle for Southern Africa, 1976–1991* (Chapel Hill and London: University of North Carolina Press, 2013), 372.

23. Piero Gliejeses, *Conflicting Missions: Havana, Washington and Africa, 1959–1976* (Chapel Hill and London: The University of North Carolina Press. 2002), 372.

24. Gleijeses (2002), *ibid.*

25. See Mateus and Mateus, *op.cit.*, 100-104.

26. See MakaAngola (Rafael Marques de Morais – Founder and Director), "Angola: Police Detain 23 at Anti-government Protest in Luanda," 23 September 2013, Luanda (Accessed 1 October 2013. www.africafiles.org/angola.asp [MakaAngola 2013]).

27. Lara Pawson, "Angola is Stirred by the Spirit of Revolution," *The Guardian*, 8 March 2011.

28. Lara Pawson, "Nito Alves: The Teenage Reincarnation of Resistance in Angola: The Imprisoned 17-Year-Old Activist Shares a Name with a Rebellious Political Figure from the 1970s, and the Authorities are Unnerved," *The Guardian*, 3 October 2013.

29. Marissa Moorman, "The battle over the 27th of May in Angola," online at *Africa is a Country*, 13 June 2013.

30. See also Louise Redvers' "Dos Santos Feels Heat over 'Murder': The Disappearance of Two Activists is a Serious Challenge to Angola's Leader before he Retires," *The Mail and Guardian*, 22 November 2013. Indeed the struggle for a more genuine liberation in Angola does continue – despite the decades of enforced silence and a present set of circumstances within that country that are very far from open, democratic or, indeed, in any way progressive in character. As Redvers herself reports, "A leaked report claiming two long-missing activists were tortured and murdered by government agents has sent shock waves through Angola and sparked plans for a nationwide street protest. The episode has turned the spotlight on President José Eduardo dos Santos, who has been working hard to polish his legacy as he appears to be preparing the ground to step down after 34 years in power. Former soldiers Antonio Alves Kamulingue and Isaías Sebastião Cassule went missing in May last year after they were involved in organising a street protest in Luanda for war veterans complaining about unpaid military pensions. From the outset it was believed they had been detained by agents of the State Intelligence and Security Service of Angola (Sinse), the powerful agency notorious for operating an underground network of informants reporting to the presidency. Amid appeals from international groups

including Human Rights Watch, Amnesty International, the International Commission of Jurists and the United Nations Human Rights Commissioner, Navi Pillay, who visited Luanda in April this year, the Angolan authorities for strongly denied any involvement in the pair's disappearance and pledged to investigate. Now 18 months later, an extremely detailed, confidential Sinse report describing how the pair were tortured in police cells and murdered has been leaked to Angolan website Club-K. Reacting to the report, the office of the attorney general made the extraordinary admission that, "given the evidence collected, it became practically proven who the two missing citizens were and that they might have been murdered" (see also *Human Rights Watch* 2013, where the headline announces "Angolan Intelligence Service Implicated in Killing of Protest Organizers'). As for Nito Alves, a court order of 8 November 2013 ordered his release, with what longer-term implications for him we will have to see." Finally, for a last word here on José Eduardo dos Santos see the end of this chapter.

31. Kerry Dolan, "Daddy's Girl: How an African "Princess" Banked $3 Billion in a Country Living On $2 a Day," formerly to be found online in *Forbes* (14 August 2013) and entitled http://www.forbes.com/ sites/kerrydolan/2013/08/14/how-isabel-dos-santos-took-the-short-route-to-become- africas-richest-woman. As Mfonobong Neshe adds, in his "The Five Worst Leaders in Africa," Forbes (9 February2012): "His daughter, Isabel dos Santos, has amassed one of the Angola's largest personal fortunes by using proceeds from her father's alleged corruption to acquire substantial stakes in companies like Zon Multimedia, a Portuguese media conglomerate and in Portuguese banks Banco Espírito Santo and Banco Portugués de Investimento among others" – formerly to be found at https://www.forbes. com/sites/mfonobomngnsehe/2012/02/09/the-five worst-leaders-in-africa/.

Chapter 6

1. This chapter draws on my earlier research and a reading of Wilfred Mhanga's important memoir *Dzino: Memoirs of a Freedom Fighter* (Harare: Weaver Press, 2011). The present chapter was first published as a contribution to a special issue of the *Review of African Political Economy/ROAPE* #S1, 2016) prepared as a tribute to my old friend and colleague the late Lionel Cliffe (see footnote 2). It considers the attempt in the 1970 to craft ZIPA as an effective fighting force and also, quite possibly, as a progressive political alternative to both ZAPU and ZANU. In the event, the shift by Mozambique's Frelimo movement and its leader, Samora Machel, away from their initial enthusiastic support for ZIPA and towards an embrace of Kissinger and Crosland's preferred candidate, Robert Mugabe, was a fateful one and of crippling import, to date, in defining the sobering outcome that continues to characterize Zimbabwe. This essay underscores the importance of the brief life but historically noteworthy emergence of the Zimbabwe People's Army (ZIPA) within the struggle for Zimbabwean liberation in the 1970s. ZIPA was a movement that offered both a serious military challenge to Smith's UDI regime but also the long-term possibility of a more meaningful liberation than anything achieved since by ZANU's old guard"\ as orchestrated by Robert Mugabe. The roles played by Mugabe, Machel, Kaunda and Kissinger, Callaghan and Crosland in ensuring ZIPA's defeat are all emphasized, with a key source for this chapter's reinterrogation of ZIPA's role being the autobiography by Wilfred Mhanda, aka Dzino Machinguru.

2. *Dzino (ibid.).*

3. Two items from Mhanda's days of prominence within the ranks of Zimbabwe's liberation struggle are essential here: the first an important interview with him (as "Dzino Machingura") conducted by the Mozambican Information Agency, 22 September 1976, first published in English in the *Daily News* (Dar es Salaam) then as a booklet from the Liberation Support Movement entitled *Zimbabwe's People's Army* (Richmond, BC: LSM Press, 1976); in this text Mhanda is identified as the Deputy Political Commissar of ZIPA,

one of the important senior roles he played during ZIPA's all-too-brief existence. (This text is also reproduced as an appendix to Dzino 2011, 264–278.) A second piece, dated 1978 and written under different circumstances (as explained in my text), is an extended analysis of Rhodesia/Zimbabwe's history, from the initial conquest by Britain and also tracing efforts by Africans to establish effective resistance. This latter, written by Mhanda while incarcerated in Mozambique and now available only in xeroxed form (and in the present author's possession) was entitled "A Treatise on Zimbabwe's National Liberation Struggle: Some Theoretical Problems."

4. Mhanda, *op.cit.* Henry Kissinger was at that time the U.S. Secretary of State and James Callaghan the UK's Foreign Secretary. Callaghan and was succeeded, after becoming Prime Minister in 1976, by Anthony Crosland.

5. John S. Saul, "Transforming the Struggle in Zimbabwe," *Southern Africa* (February 1977) and also published as chapter 5 of Saul, *The State and Revolution in Eastern Africa* (New York: Monthly Review Press, 1979).

6. See John S. Saul, "Zimbabwe: The Next Round," In *The Socialist Register 1980*, edited by Ralph Miliband and John Savile (London: Merlin Press, 1980), and also published as chapter 5 of *Saul, Socialist Ideology and the Struggle for Southern Africa* (Trenton, NJ: Africa World Press, 1980); and Saul and Richard Saunders, "Mugabe, Gramsci and Zimbabwe at Twenty-Five," *International Journal* (Toronto, Fall issue, 2005) – also published as chapter 6 in *Saul, The Next Liberation Struggle: Capitalism, Socialism and Democracy in Southern Africa* (New York and Toronto: Monthly Review Press and Between the Lines, 2005).

7. David Moore, "The Contradictory Construction of Hegemony in Zimbabwe: Politics, Ideology and Class in the Formation of a New African State," Doctoral dissertation, York University, 1990; Moore "Introduction" to Mhanda, op.cit.; Moore, "Two perspectives on Zimbabwe's National Democratic Revolution: Thabo Mbeki and Wilfred Mhanda," *Journal of Contemporary African Studies* 30 (1), 2012, 119–38; and Moore, "The Zimbabwean People's Army moment in Zimbabwean History, 1975–1977: Mugabe's Rise and Democracy's Demise," *Journal of Contemporary African Studies* 32 (3), 2014, 302–318.

8. Saul, *op.cit.* (1977), 115-116.

9. Interview with Samora Machel, in *The Observer* (London), 28 March 1976.

10. This quoted passage appears in Saul, *op.cit.* (1977), p. 117, where it is in turn quoted from Machinguru (1976), op.cit.

11. Saul, *ibid.*, 118.

12. Terence Ranger, "The Changing of the Old Guard: Robert Mugabe and the Revival of ZANU," *Journal of Southern African Studies*, 7, 2 (1980).

13. This and the following quotation in this paragraph are to be found in Ranger, *ibid.*, at pages 72 and 90.

14. See N. Bhebe and Terence Ranger, eds., *Soldiers in Zimbabwe's liberation war* (London: James Currey Ltd and University of Zimbabwe Publications, 1995a) and Bhebe and Ranger, eds., *Society in Zimbabwe's liberation war* (London: James Currey Ltd. and University of Zimbabwe Publications, 1995b).

15. David Moore, "The Zimbabwe People's Army: Strategic Innovation or More of the Same?" in Ranger and Bhebe, 1995a.

16. Bhebe, and Ranger, in their introduction to *Soldiers in Zimbabwe's Liberation War (ibid. [1995a])*, 17-18.

17. See Bhebe and Ranger, *op.cit.* [1995b].

18. These latter quotations are from Bhebe and Ranger's introduction to their co-edited book (*ibid.* [1995a], 17–18). Again, while they correctly praise Moore's work on this subject Ranger was never to say another word with respect to my earlier and similarly argued writing on ZIPA that, as noted above, he had once attacked so baldly (Ranger [1980] *op.cit.*).

Endnotes

19. I had witnessed Frelimo's mode of rural struggle so I was therefore inclined to take its favorable view of ZIPA's promise seriously. As for Frelimo, this historical moment also took a marked toll on the moral compass of that movement's leadership as it felt moved in this process to redefine its approach to Zimbabwe, a fact to which we will return.

20. Saul, *op.cit.* (1977), 108-109. This citation prompts a more personal note here. The link is made to some of the writings of the time (in *ROAPE* #86, 1976) by one my oldest and dearest friends and former colleague at the University of Dar es Salaam, the late Lionel Cliffe, in particular regarding his experience while incarcerated in one of Kaunda's Zambian jails. In fact, this article on ZIPA was first published in *ROAPE* S1 (2016) in a special issue as a tribute to his memory. During our many years together in Tanzania in the 1960s and early 1970s we were close colleagues in our joint teaching, in our co-authorship and co-editing, and in our activism in support of progressive developments in East Africa. When Lionel left Tanzania he went on to a life of many accomplishments, including a spell at the University of Zambia where he became, as I did myself on different but related fronts, an active protagonist of southern African liberation. Indeed, it was as a short-term "guest" (as part of a general crackdown at the University of Zambia against those critical of President Kenneth Kaunda's policies) in one of Kaunda's Zambian prisons that Lionel talked with some of the "50-odd" Zimbabwean prisoners who had been "detained [there] since the murder" of Herbert Chitepo. Lionel wrote little about this experience though he did make a potent comment in *ROAPE* on how testimony to the International Commission of Inquiry into Chitepo's assassination had been obtained: "I know the answer to that," Cliffe wrote, "I have seen the scars!" In addition, among the fruits of this close-up exposure to the Zimbabwean struggle were several articles by Lionel in *ROAPE* at the time: an editorial on the novel neo-colonial moves in the region by Kissinger and Crosland/Callaghan (Lionel Cliffe and Katherine Levine, "Editorial," *Review of African Political Economy/ROAPE* (May-August 1976), 1-3), and a note on some of the circumstances surrounding Chitepo's assassination (Lionel Cliffe, "Some Questions about the Chitepo Report and the Zimbabwe Movement," *ROAPE*, 8 (May-August 1976): 78-80. These articles provide important background. More generally, there was, from this jail experience, an even further deepening of Lionel's commitment to the struggle for genuine liberation in Zimbabwe, southern Africa and elsewhere.

21. Lionel Cliffe and Katherine Levine, *op cit.* [1976]; Cliffe and Levine (1976) focus briefly but pointedly on imperial machinations in the plotting of a possible endgame in Rhodesia/ Zimbabwe, while Cliffe also wrote a briefing on the Chitepo Report (op.cit.); both remain worth reading.

22. This passage from my text as well as the quotes from both Kissinger and Crosland are to be found in Saul, *op.cit.* (1977), 110.

23. One reviewer for *ROAPE* of an earlier draft of this essay felt I was being too censorious towards Kaunda, suggesting that KK had all along favored Nkomo and ZAPU, while finding the ZANU gang particularly unattractive – like many other Zambians of the time growing sick and tired of their infighting. Even more importantly, the reviewer sees Kaunda primarily as working effectively to turn détente back upon its instigator, Vorster, and to finesse the latter into dropping Smith and settling the Zimbabwean situation. This view sees Kaunda further calculating that he and others would then find the breathing room to figure out how to face up to South Africa more effectively. I am not convinced that any such a favorable reading of Kaunda's détenteist fetish of the time is accurate; nonetheless we can see that we are entering into the deep waters of regional complexity (also important for situating the shifting positions of Samora Machel) but for which there is not the space here to explore further (see, however, Saul, *The Thirty Years War for Southern African Liberation: A History*, forthcoming).

24. Luise White, *The assassination of Herbert Chitepo: texts and politics in Zimbabwe* (Bloomington: Indiana University Press, 2003).

25. White, *ibid.*, and also Carol B. Thompson, *Challenge to Imperialism: Frontline states and the liberation of Zimbabwe* (Harare: Zimbabwe Publishing House, 1985).

26. Mhanda, *op.cit.*, 100 et *passim.*

27. Mhanda, *ibid.*, 142.

28. According to ZAPU head of intelligence Dumiso Dabengwa (interview with David Moore, 19 February 2016), ZAPU withdrew from ZIPA in the middle of 1976 because it did not want to participate in a process in which Machel was encouraging the ZIPA leadership to take over Zimbabwe militarily in order to rule "as we [Frelimo] have done in Mozambique." As Dabengwa put the point, "We wanted to have elections after we won the war, not military rule." In Dabengwa's (admittedly partisan) opinion the splitting of the military unity of ZIPA between cadres of diverse organizational backgrounds (coming as they had from both ZIPRA and ZANLA) also contributed to lessening Machel's enthusiasm for ZIPA, and helps to explain his yielding to Mugabe's adept handling of the Geneva conference. To be sure, as Dabengwa continues, Frelimo would later regret its decision as it took longer than expected for the pro-ZIPA cadres in the camps to be pacified after the ZIPA leaders were imprisoned.

29. Mhanda, in this paragraph, is quoted from his *Dzino, op.cit.*, at pages 135 and 111.

30. Dare was identified above as being ZANU's officially constituted war council.

31. Strikingly Mhanda, *ibid.*, also suggests that in the course of such "dithering" – reflecting, in my judgement, primarily the difficult challenges inherent in intelligently evaluating, on the complicated and divided terrain of Zimbabwean liberation politics that confronted ZIPA, the tough choices that were on offer – ZIPA may also have lost some of the credibility that it had previously had with the Mozambican government (a point to which I will return).

32. Mhanda, *ibid.*, 183.

33. See Barry Cohen and Mohamed El-Khawas (eds), *The Kissinger Study of Southern Africa* (London: Spokesman Books, 1975)

34. Mhanda, *ibid.*, 142.

35. Mhanda, *ibid.*, 138.

36. The choice against ZIPA that Mozambique now felt inclined to make was startling, especially when contrasted to the support given, in the wake of Eduardo Mondlane's assassination by the Portuguese, to Machel and his left Frelimo faction by Nyerere – this in defiance of the claims to the leadership made by Frelimo's more opportunist and anti-left "black-nationalist" claimant to the succession, Uria Simango. Moreover, Nyerere had to face down some pretty strong players (Sijaona, Maswanya and Bhoke Munanka, all supporters of Simango) within TANU circles to succeed in doing so.

37. Alex Vines, *RENAMO: Terrorism in Mozambique* (London: James Currey, 1991).

38. Mhanda, *op.cit.*, 145.

39. The quotes in this paragraph are drawn from Mhanda's *Dzino (ibid.),* from pages 175 and 178.

40. Mhanda, *ibid.*, 176-7.

41. See Moore's short but fascinating (if debatable) "Introduction" to *Dzino f*rom which the quotations of this and the following paragraphs included in my text are drawn (from pages xv and xvi specifically).

42. Machinguru (1976), *op.cit.*

43. Mhanda, *op.cit.* 69–70 and 77.

44. The quotes from Mhanda in this and the following paragraph are from *Dzino (ibid.)* at pages 210-211, 255 (twice), 241 and 127ff.

45. Mhanda *(ibid.),* 240.

46. Mhanda *(ibid.),* 253–254.

47. Debate continues among commentators on Zimbabwe, both within and outside the country, as to the fallout of such reform. Although I have yet to see evidence of the case for a positive (for the Zimbabwean peasantry, that is) reading of Zimbabwean initiatives in this sphere this is not the place to pursue the matter. Few, even amongst those who are

most enthusiastic about the positive decolonizing logic of land reform and about (some of) its results, are not inclined to concede to Mugabe anything but the basest and most self-serving motives in framing this issue in such an opportunist and right-wing-populist manner in the first place – the better to cover his authoritarian tracks and his shabby post-electoral tricks.

48. Jorge Rebelo, "Jorge Rebelo: As falas da velha raposa," Interview by E Salema and P. Rollette of Jorge Rebelo, Savana (Maputo), 4 July 2008.

49. In the criticism of Rebelo's original interview by Bosse Hammarstrom ("Bosse Hammarstrom's Views on Rebelo's Interview in Savana this Week," e-copy as forwarded to me by Fernando Lima of Savana, 2008). Hammarstrom suggests that "[t]he most troublesome part of the interview, however, is where Rebelo turns out not to be able to see the viciousness of the repressive system Mugabe is managing. 'He is our brother in arms.' That seems to excuse anything. Rebelo even thinks it would be possible to make Mugabe come to his senses and make him realise that what he is doing is wrong because the people suffers ...Then he goes on to say that Tsvangirai does not have a program [as to] how to make the country go forward! As if Mugabe had such a plan."

50. Mhanda, *ibid.*, 217-232.

Chapter 7

1. As indicated at the outset of this chapter, I draw here on the paper originally presented to a seminar in 2015 at the University of Johannesburg, one subsequently published in a somewhat different form in *Transformation*, #89 (2015)in a extended section of that journal entitled "John Saul in Johannesburg," 28-86).

2. Steve Tshwete, "Understanding the Charter clause by clause," in R Suttner and J Cronin (eds) *Thirty Years of the Freedom Charter,* (Johannesburg: Ravan Press, 1985), 213,

3. William Gumede, *Thabo Mbeki and the Battle for the Soul of the ANC* (Cape Town: Zebra Press, 2005), 38.

4. See chapter 1 for a careful definition and discussion of "the precariat." There I speak not only of the importance of the proletariat, but also of the existence of a people, poor people, marginalized in both urban and rural settings, but who are as capable of socioeconomic upsurge as those engaged in socioeconomic confrontation at the workplace. These latter can perhaps be called an underclass (or even, in a far more metaphorical and much less scientific way, seen as members of the working class). I choose, as previously argued, to see them instead as comprising a precariat, and I am confident that a politics that seeks to engage in broad-based mobilization of *both* proletariat and precariat could indeed, if mounted deftly, have cumulative and positive revolutionary potential.

5. As noted previously, the *locus classicus* from these and other of Fanon's most penetrating insights is his *The Wretched of the Earth* (Harmondsworth: Penguin Books, 1967).

6. See, again, Steve Biko in a 1972 "Interview with G. Gerhart, 24 October," www.aluka.org (accessed 30 September 2013), from which the passages quoted in these three paragraphs of my text are taken.

7. Ronnie Kasrils was a senior Umkhonto was Sizwe commander during the ANC/SACP's armed struggle period and a key activist in the development of an ANC underground inside South Africa; he was also the first deputy minister of Defence and later (amongst other such positions) Minister of Intelligence Services in several post-apartheid ANC governments.

8. The quotes in this paragraph, as well as those that immediately follow, are drawn from Ronnie Kasrils, "How the ANC's Faustian pact sold out South Africa's poorest: In the early 1990s, we in the leadership of the ANC made a serious error. Our people are still paying the price," *The Guardian* (London), 2 November 2012.

9.. As Kasrils writes in a more extended version of this text (one that served as the basis of the *Guardian* article) that is the introduction to a fourth edition of his noteworthy autobiography *Armed and Dangerous: My undercover struggle against apartheid* (Johannesburg: Jacana, 2013 [4th edition]). Nonetheless, in *The Guardian*, he summarizes: "Inexcusably, we had lost faith in the ability of our own revolutionary masses to overcome all obstacles. Whatever the threats to isolate a radicalising South Africa, the world could not have done without our vast reserves of minerals. To lose our nerve was not necessary or inevitable. The ANC leadership needed to remain determined, united and free of corruption – and, above all, to hold on to its revolutionary will... To break apartheid rule through negotiation, rather than a bloody civil war, seemed then an option too good to be ignored." But what implications did this "success" have for socioeconomic liberation? This is the question Kasrils now felt he must ask and, admirably, he continues to do so.

10. Naomi Klein, *The Shock Doctrine: the rise of disaster capitalism*, (Toronto: Alfred A Knopf. 2007), ch. 10, "Democracy Born in Chains: South Africa's Constricted Freedom", 233-261: Padyachee's startling comments are cited and interpreted by Klein on pages 240-243. But ANC leaders "simply...were outmanoeuvred on a series of issues that seemed less than crucial at the time – but turned out to hold South Africa's lasting liberation in the balance." Really? As noted earlier, this argued a degree of naiveté on the part of such leaders that is difficult to give credence to. Similarly for Gumede whose equally inexplicable "naiveté" is also recorded by Klein on pages 245-7. As for Klein who had "wanted to understand how, after such a epic struggle for freedom, any of this could have been allowed to happen" never goes too much further in her chapter than this to explain how this was "allowed to happen." Mere naiveté? Not a chance.

11. Jeremy Cronin, "How we misread the situation in the 1990s," speech to the 12th National Congress of SACTWU as issued by the SACP, 22 August 2013).

12. Ben Turok, *From the Freedom Charter to Polokwane: the evolution of ANC economic policy* (Cape Town: New Agenda, 2008).

13. See, again, Rusty Bernstein as quoted in chapter 1 in this book and in his letter to me as published in his "The turning point..." in *Transformation*, 64 (2007).

14. Jeremy Seekings, *The UDF: A History of the United Democratic Front in South Africa, 1980-1991* (Cape Town: David Philip, 2000), p. 260.

15. No more was it an adequate answer to writers like Elke Zoern (see her *The Politics of Necessity: community organizing and democracy in South Africa* (Madison WI: University of Wisconsin Press, 2011). For Seekings, the voter's box, and the much more demobilized world of the newly created South African National Civic Organization/SANCO and its wards amongst the "civics" were an entirely acceptable substitute for the UDF. Not so for Zoern who effectively underscored in her book the inadequacy of such alternatives as sites of critical democratic practice. As we now know, sadly and in the absence of any more positively empowering vision, mass action could now sometimes run all too easily to political passivity or to such perverted popular purposes as evidenced in South Africa's xenophobic riots of 2008.

16. Mona Younis, *Liberation and Democratization: the South African and Palestinian national movements,* (Minneapolis: University of Minnesota Press, 2000), 91.

17. Younis, *ibid.*, 91.

18. Ineke van Kessel, (2000) *"Beyond our wildest dreams": the United Democratic Front and the transformation of South Africa* (Charlottesville: The University Press of Virginia, 2000) and van Kessel, "Trajectories after liberation in South Africa: mission accomplished or vision betrayed?" at Zuid-Afrika & Leiden website (University of Leiden, 2011). She quotes Boesak at page 290 of *"Beyond our wildest dreams."*

19. Younis, *op.cit.*, 91; indeed, as I ended my account of the UDF's fate, "a majority did in fact, and at the ANC's urging, vote to disband the UDF – but the loss of progressive purpose that this deed represented was a very damaging one"; see John S. Saul and Patrick Bond, *South Africa – The Present as History: From Mrs. Plea to Mandela and*

Marikana (Woodbridge, U. K. and Johannesburg: James Currey and Jacana, 2014). The last few paragraphs on the UDF here are adapted from this prior text, especially pages 87-94. I also quote there from Michele Williams' valuable *The Roots of Participatory Democracy: Democratic Communists in South Africa and Kerala, India* (New York and London: Palgrave MacMillan, 2008), p. 91, in which she deftly contrasts the practices of the Communist party in Kerala (which premised its activities on "counter-hegemonic generative politics" and "a reliance on participatory organizing") and those of South African Communist Party (and, by extension, the ANC). In South Africa any sustained popular takeover of the process of transformation was never really on offer, the SACP/ANC merely opting for, in her terms, "a hegemonic generative politics" and a reliance on mere "mass mobilizing" – designed primarily to, in effect, draw a crowd to popularly hail its ascendancy. There could be very little place for a proactive UDF-like organization within such a scenario.

20. Eddie Webster and Glenn Adler, "Exodus Without a Map: The Labor Movement in a Liberalizing South Africa" in Bjorn Beckman and Lloyd Sachikonye (eds.) *Labor Regimes and Liberalization: The Restructuring of State-Society Relations in Africa* (Harare: University of Zimbabwe Press, 2001), 70. I have also cited this quote in my chapter 2 (at page 90) of Saul and Bond, ibid., in which chapter there is also a more extensive analysis of the role of the trade union movement in South Africa's national liberation struggle. As I comment there: "It is also important to again emphasize the new perspective that characterized many of these novel worker assertions and shop-floor struggles in Durban and beyond. To begin with, the new organizations being formed out of such industrial contestations sought tactically – and so as to escape excessive negative scrutiny by the apartheid state – to avoid any overly compromising links to the ANC/SACP/SACTU exile group. As well, many within the 'new trade union movement' were suspicious of such formations-in-exile as SACTU, the SACP and even the ANC, as I heard for myself from trade union organizers in SA in the 1970s – fearful, from the vantage point of their concern, to safeguard worker interests and voice, of the ANC/SACP/SACTU's vanguardist preoccupations and also of this latter triumvirate's possible embrace of a negative, all-too Soviet/Stalinist modelled attitude towards true worker-centered empowerment from below."

21. National Union of Metalworkers (NUMSA), "NUMSA Special National Congress, Declaration" at http://www.numsa.org.za/wpcontent/uploads/2013/12/SNC-Declaration-final-copy.pdf.

22. Gavin Relly, as quoted in Dale McKinley, *The ANC and the Liberation Movement* (London: Pluto Press, 1997), 84-85. See also, from about the same time (1986), the advice in his "No More Talk. Time to Act" in *The Times* (London, 30 June 1986) from Malcolm Fraser (formerly the deeply conservative prime minister of Australia) to the Commonwealth leaders. This after Fraser had served as a member of the Commonwealth's Eminent Persons Group sent to investigate the situation in South Africa. Fraser's advice: a collective turn by all Commonwealth states against apartheid *per se* and the striking of a deal "with African nationalist demands since in any escalating conflict moderation would be swept aside [and] the government that emerged from all of this would be extremely radical, probably Marxist, and would nationalize all western business interests."

23. Someone from the floor at my meeting at UJ suggested that the correct percentage breakdown would be 80 per cent-20 per cent, however.

24. This, my reply to my critics, was also featured in the issue of *Transformation* referred to above.

25. Thus Ben Turok writes in his memoir *Nothing But the Truth: behind the ANC's struggle politics* [Jeppestown: Jonathan Ball, 2003]), of his Dar days that there "the university had attracted some of the best Africanist scholars on the continent and there was a group of radicals who were extremely active intellectually. There were endless seminars, conferences and meetings. John Saul and Giovanni Arrighi were among our best friends

and both were leaders in the radical intellectual life at the university."

26. It is not difficult, in retrospect, to see here in embryo the kind of student cadre that stoked the dramatic student demonstrations and strikes that rocked South African universities – and the country's elite – in the latter part of 2015. Indeed, while we "whiteys" on the panel were invited to set the seminar's agenda, the lively discussion from the floor that ensued was driven by the sharp questions and comments of such a cadre of student proto-militants.

27. See, on this subject, my aforementioned *On Building a Social Movement: the North American Campaign for southern African Liberation Revisited (op.cit.)*. As I have underscored in the postscript to Part 3 of this book, that despite his record, Brian Mulroney was recently awarded the Order of the Companions of O.R. Tambo, an award that acknowledges foreign leaders and citizens for friendship shown to South Africa. Mulroney is the first Canadian to have been so honored This was given to Mulroney for what the present South African government calls an "exceptional contribution to the liberation movement of South Africa"! A more startling sign of the South African government's opportunist reading of the history of its own country's "liberation by recolonization" would be difficult to find.

28. Ben Turok (2008), *op.cit.,* pp. 263-5.

29. Turok, *ibid.*

30. This obituary to Nelson Mandela was first published in the *Toronto Star* to mark Madiba's passing and, later, as an Appendix in my *A Flawed Freedom (op.cit.).*

Chapter 8

1. Saul, *On Building a Social Movement: The North American Campaign for Southern African Liberation Revisited* (Trenton, N.J., and Halifax, Nova Scotia: Africa World Press and Fernwood Books, 2017). See also Linda Freeman's magnum opus *The Ambiguous Champion: Canada and South Africa in the Trudeau and Mulroney years* (Toronto: University of Toronto Press, 1997) and my critical review of it: "A Class Act: Canada's Anti-Apartheid Record," as first published in *Southern African Report*, 14, 2 (March 1999), and as then included, as an appendix, in my book, *The Next Liberation Struggle: Capitalism, Socialism and Democracy in Southern Africa* (Toronto, Scottsville, S.A., New York and London: Between the Lines, University of KwaZulu-Natal Press, Monthly Review Press, and The Merlin Press, 2005).

2. I have attempted to unpack this signifier "capital" in chapter 1 , Section 1, "In Theory" and more specifically, its sub-section entitled "Entry-point 2: "The Empire of Capital and Recolonization." For something I term "capital" does play, as a collective entity, a crucial role (albeit a shifting and contradictory one). Ascendant into the twentieth century as a determining force underlying European colonial control (in Africa and elsewhere), after World War II the centrality of such empires was displaced by the strength of American multinational capital and its orchestration of a world of false decolonization and neo-colonialism. American global hegemony has in turn begun, more recently, to be displaced by a more complex mix of competing capitals of European, North American (the U.S. government has embarked on various military-linked schemes to draw African states into its orbit, for example), Chinese, Indian, Korean, Brazilian, and other provenances, often with backing from their states of origin, and not least by a newly ascendant financial capital. Nonetheless, and fundamentally, the competition amongst these latter capitals is also disciplined by the shared purpose of global capitalist control, such capitals adding up into a far from benign but collectively quite efficacious Empire of Capital. And it is this empire that has superseded both the European colonial empires and the world of American neo-colonialism as a new empire that is recolonizing the world in the interests of capital (global yet diverse). Call this merely the deepening and diversifying of neo-colonialism if

you will; I use the term "recolonization" to characterize something new.

3. "Tambo, not Rambo: The ANC's President in Toronto," *Southern Africa Report* (October, 1987).
4. As quoted in Christopher Webb, "Hidden Histories and Political Legacies of the Canadian Anti-apartheid Movement," *Canadian Dimension* (April 2014).
5. See William Minter, "An Unfinished Victory" in William Minter, Gail Hovey and Charles Cobb, Jr. (eds.), *No Easy Victories: African liberation and African Activists over a Half Century, 1950-2000* (Trenton: Africa World Press, 2008). He also quotes Gay McDougall there.
6. On the South African side of this equation see John S. Saul and Patrick Bond, *South Africa – The Present as History: From Mrs Ples to Mandela & Marikana* (Johannesburg and Woodbridge, UK: Jacana and James Currey, 2014 & 2016).
7. Peter Alexander, 'Rebellion of the poor: South Africa's service delivery protests – a preliminary analysis,' *Review of African Political Economy*, 37, 123, 2010 and his "SA Protest Rates Increasingly Competitive with World Leader China," 23 March 2012, available at www.amandlapublishers.org.za, accessed 8 October 2013.
8. As recounted in Adrian Basson and Pieter Du Toit, *Enemy of the People: How Jacob Zuma stole South Africa and how the people fought back* (Johannesburg and Cape Town: Jonathan Ball, 2017).
9. Not a problem exclusive to southern Africa.
10. See Nick Saul and Andrea Curtis, *The Stop: How the Fight for Good Food Transformed a Community and Inspired a Movement* (Toronto: Random House, 2013) and Nick Saul, "Reimagining Your Organization" in Alan Broadbent and Ratna Omidvar (eds.), *Five Good Ideas: Practical Strategies and Non-Profit Success* (Toronto: Coach House Books, 2011).
11. Recall the reference to Alexander's findings in footnote 7, especially the report entitled "SA Protest Rates Increasingly Competitive with World Leader China."
12. Or, perhaps (as is the recent article in iHARARE [30 November 2017] it would be equally well titled as "Mnangwana Cabinet – Old wine in new bottles."
13. While I make general comments on these happenings – the passing from the ranks of dos Santos, Zuma and Mugabe – I have included more detailed comments on their implications (on a country-by-country basis) in the final chapter of *Race, Class and The Thirty Years War for Southern African Liberation, 1960-1994: A History*.

Envoi

1. For more on this subject see the concluding chapter of my *Race, Class and The Thirty Years War for Southern African Liberation, 1960-1994 – A History*.
2. Patrick Bond, *Against Global Apartheid: South Africa meets the World Bank, the IMF and International Finance (op.cit.)* p. 282 – as also quoted in the Preface to Section III.
3 Neville Alexander, *An Ordinary Country: Issues in the Transition from Apartheid to Democracy in South Africa* (Pietermaritzburg: University of Natal Press, 2002), pp. 172-3.
4. I do not lightly criticize Nelson Mandela but his career after his 1990 release from prison and his ultimate ascension to the post of South Africa's first black president constituted a disappointing anti-climax both to the his noble record of resistance to apartheid and to his remarkable and unbending courage as a political prisoner – and a prominent moral force a for change – for almost thirty years; I refer the reader to my memorial piece on Mandela, written at the time of his death, which is included as sub-section (iii) in chapter 7: "Nelson Mandela and South Africa's Flawed Freedom."
5. See "A Rebel in the Marxist Citadel: Tributes to Samir Amin," *ROAPE* On-Line, 21 August 2018), including my "On Samir Amin...and the Importance of 'Delinking.'"

6. These, alongside those of their fellow freedom fighters who are now engaged in self-enrichment with the private sector. Here, Cyril Ramaphosa's career (from trade union leader and nationalist political activist to private sector notoriety as both magnate and hammer of the workers at Marikana) was, before his more recent return to politics as now South Africa's president, a clear case in point.

7. On these matters, see McKinley's *The ANC and the Liberation Struggle: A Critical Political Biography* (1997) and, most recently, his *South Africa's Corporatised Liberation: A Critical Analysis of the ANC in Power* (2017), both cited in a footnote to ch.5 (footnote #2).

8. Dale McKinley, "Corporate criminality: Contest and consequence," *The Daily Maverick* (30 August 2018)

9. Note that McKinley uses the concept of criminality at least as much as a moral entry-point as a jurisprudential one (recall ch. 2, section A); its use is a signal that a moralizing science is at work here). McKinley is correct and and his characterization of corporate criminality, even if used primarily as a metaphor, accurate: global capital ha s found itself able to use its inordinate power to do environmental and human damage while also making inordinate profits for itself. Corporate criminality will remain primarily a moral criterion (an effective and politically powerful one) as long as there are no states or international legal bodies to make practices of multinational corporations formally illegal and judicially actionable.

10. All quotations here are from the article cited in footnote 8. McKinley emphasizes the corporate capital side of the criminality coin in South Africa, an emphasis that "gives us a much fuller and more truthful picture than that painted by the widely accepted but hugely convenient and one-sided 'explanations/analyses' that it is the state/public sector which is mostly to 'blame' for criminality and corruption." Of course "the criminality of both corporate capital and the state/public sector are most often [seen to be]mutually linked and beneficial" a point of view that also "exposes the shallowness of the well-worn argument trotted out by corporate capital that if only the state/public sector were "fixed,' then everything would be hunky-dory." For such "fixing" inevitably "translates into having a political party in power whose leaders' class and policy interests are umbilically tied to those of corporate capital." Indeed, "the hypocrisy of corporate capital's "moral" and political/social outrage" towards the state is here quite staggering, and this because "many of the most corrupt relationships and criminal practices in post-apartheid South Africa, particularly those that have been sustained over a lengthy period and which have involved the largest amounts of money, have involved corporate capital."

11. It was only as I concluded this manuscript that the grim seriousness of COVID-19 began to become apparent, a truly global pandemic – like the pandemic of free-market/global capitalism-think whose considerable power to reshape "liberation" to suit its own purposes I have grappled with in this book – of, quite possibly, unimagined proportions that I cannot even begin to speculate upon here.

INDEX

Index

Index

Index

Index

Index

white power, 15–16, 78, 90, 100, 106, 177, 206
white rule, 12, 87–88, 115, 132, 172, 195, 244, 251, 254
white settlers, 115, 117, 196, 198, 244
Williams, Michelle, 144, 146
Williams, Rhys, 153
Wilson, Harold, 198
Wilson, Hube, 2
Wolff, Richard, xiv, 9; *Knowledge and Class*, 5–6
Wolin, Sheldon, 264n1
women: in Africa, 53; emancipation of, 271n105; in Mozambique, 159–60; oppression of, 29; in South Africa, 69; in Tanzania, 142; violence against, 93, 126
"workerism," 62
working class, 5, 50, 57–58, 62, 71–73, 94, 105; ambiguities of, 51–56; praxis of, 71; protests by, 56; responses of to capital, 34; self-consciousness of, 71
workplace confrontation, 55–56, 60, 63, 116
World Bank, 23, 26, 73, 112
World Social Forum, 75, 258
World Summit on Social Development, 93
World Summit on Sustainable Development, 129
World Trade Organization (WTO), 26, 27
Wright, Erik Olin, 10
Wright, Phil, 59, 72, 95, 105

xenophobia, 37, 53, 64, 93, 126, 233

Young, Andrew, 185–86
Younis, Mona, 231
Yugoslavia: ethnic cleansing in, 38

Zaidi, Asad, xviii, 263n3
Zaire, 172, 178
Zambia, 117, 182, 198, 205, 208
Zimbabwe, xi, xv, xvii, 89, 98–99, 118–19, 133, 152, 172, 176, 195–221, 244, 250–51, 254–55, 256; Front for the Liberation of Zimbabwe (FROLIZI), 198; land reform in, 119; liberation struggle in, 195–97, 206, 214, 216, 220; Movement for Democratic Change (MDC), 99, 119; structural adjustment in, 119; Unilateral Declaration of Independence (UDI), 196, 198; white settlers in, 198; Zimbabwe African National Liberation Army (ZANLA), 202, 206; Zimbabwe African National Union (ZANU), 98–99, 118, 195, 197–202, 205–8, 211, 213–14, 216, 218–20, 256, 287n1; Zimbabwe African People's Union (ZAPU), 195, 197–200, 204, 206–7, 211, 216, 287n1; Zimbabwean People's Army (ZIPA), 195–221; Zimbabwe People's Revolutionary Army (ZIPRA), 206
Žižek, Slavoj, 7
Zoern, Elke, 292n15
Zuma, Jacob, 126, 146, 234, 242, 248, 250–51, 252, 254–55, 256–57, 262
Zvogbo, Edson, 200

www.ingramcontent.com/pod-product-compliance
Lightning Source LLC
Chambersburg PA
CBHW071731270326
41928CB00013B/2630